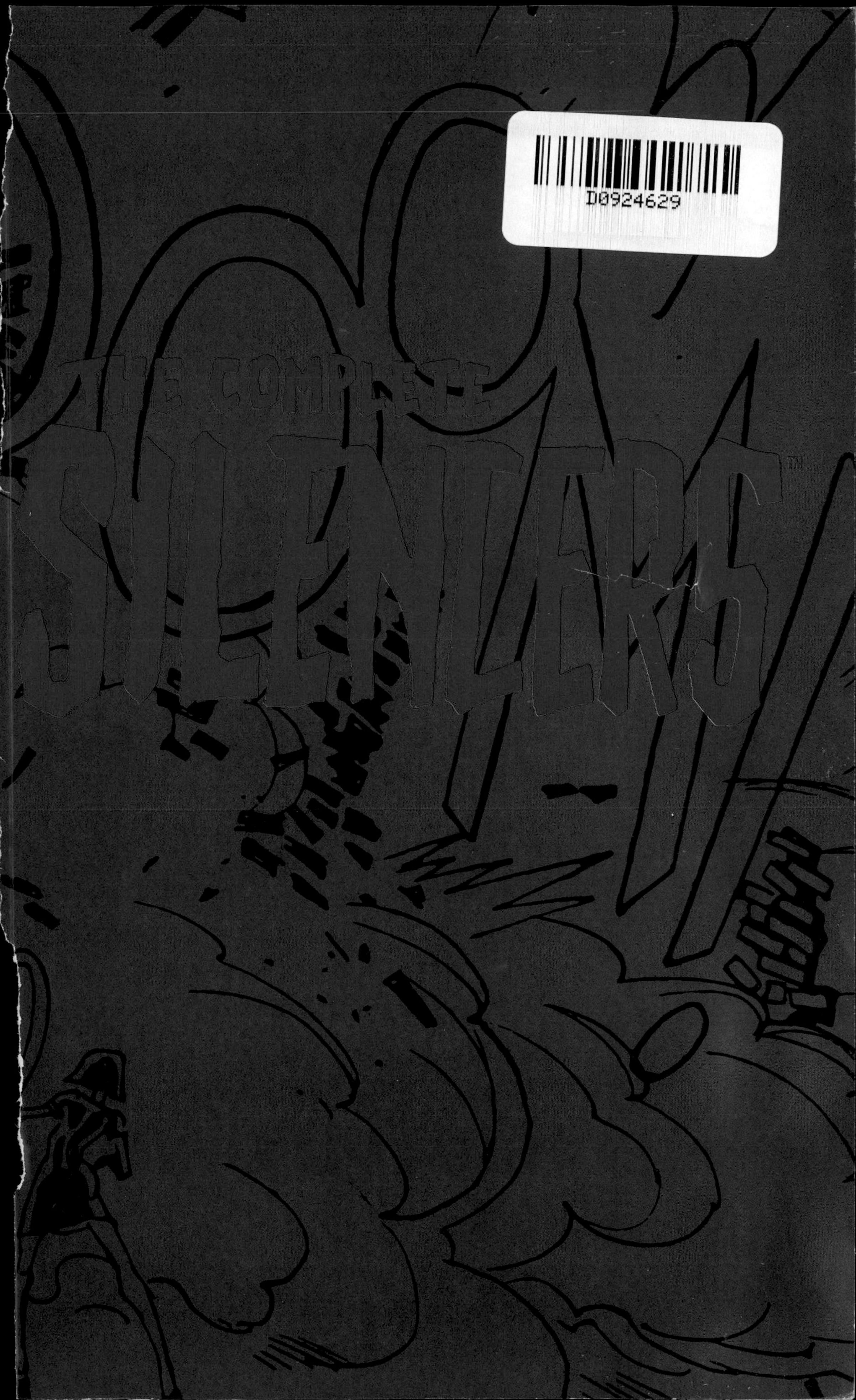
THE COMPLETE
SILENCERS™

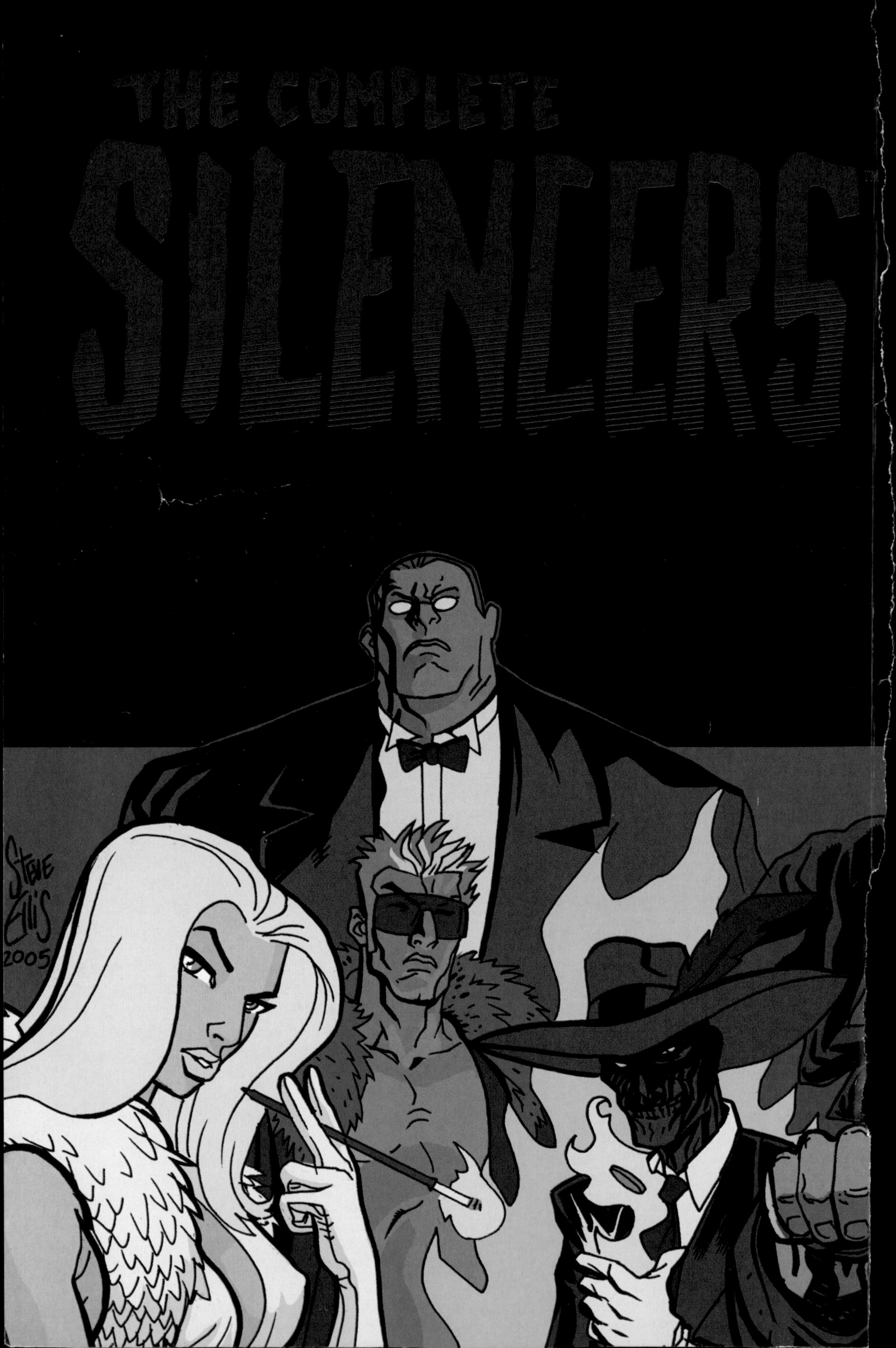
THE COMPLETE
SILENCERS
Steve Ellis 2005

STORY AND LETTERING BY

FRED VAN LENTE

ART BY

STEVE ELLIS

COLORS BY

DAE LIM YOO ("BITTER FRUIT," "TÊTE-À-TÊTE," AND "SPAZ")

DAE LIM YOO AND KURT MARQUART ("SPREE")

STEVE ELLIS ("POWERED AND DANGEROUS")

COVER AND CHAPTER BREAK ART BY

STEVE ELLIS

PRESIDENT AND PUBLISHER	MIKE RICHARDSON
EDITOR	JIM GIBBONS
DIGITAL PRODUCTION	ALLYSON HALLER
COLLECTION DESIGNER	BRENNAN THOME

Published by Dark Horse Books
A division of Dark Horse Comics, Inc.

10956 SE Main Street
Milwaukie, OR 97222

First edition: September 2014
ISBN 978-1-61655-540-5

10 9 8 7 6 5 4 3 2 1
Printed in China

International Licensing: (503) 905-2377
Comic Shop Locator Service: (888) 266-4226

THE COMPLETE SILENCERS

NEIL HANKERSON Executive Vice President | TOM WEDDLE Chief Financial Officer | RANDY STRADLEY Vice President of Publishing | MICHAEL MARTENS Vice President of Book Trade Sales | ANITA NELSON Vice President of Business Affairs | SCOTT ALLIE Editor in Chief | MATT PARKINSON Vice President of Marketing | DAVID SCROGGY Vice President of Product Development | DALE LaFOUNTAIN Vice President of Information Technology DARLENE VOGEL Senior Director of Print, Design, and Production | KEN LIZZI General Counsel | DAVEY ESTRADA Editorial Director | CHRIS WARNER Senior Books Editor | DIANA SCHUTZ Executive Editor | CARY GRAZZINI Director of Print and Development | LIA RIBACCHI Art Director CARA NIECE Director of Scheduling | TIM WIESCH Director of International Licensing | MARK BERNARDI Director of Digital Publishing

This volume collects **The Silencers: Black Kiss,** *originally published by Moonstone Books, and* **The Silencers: Powered and Dangerous,** *originally published by Image Comics.*

BITTER FRUIT PART 1

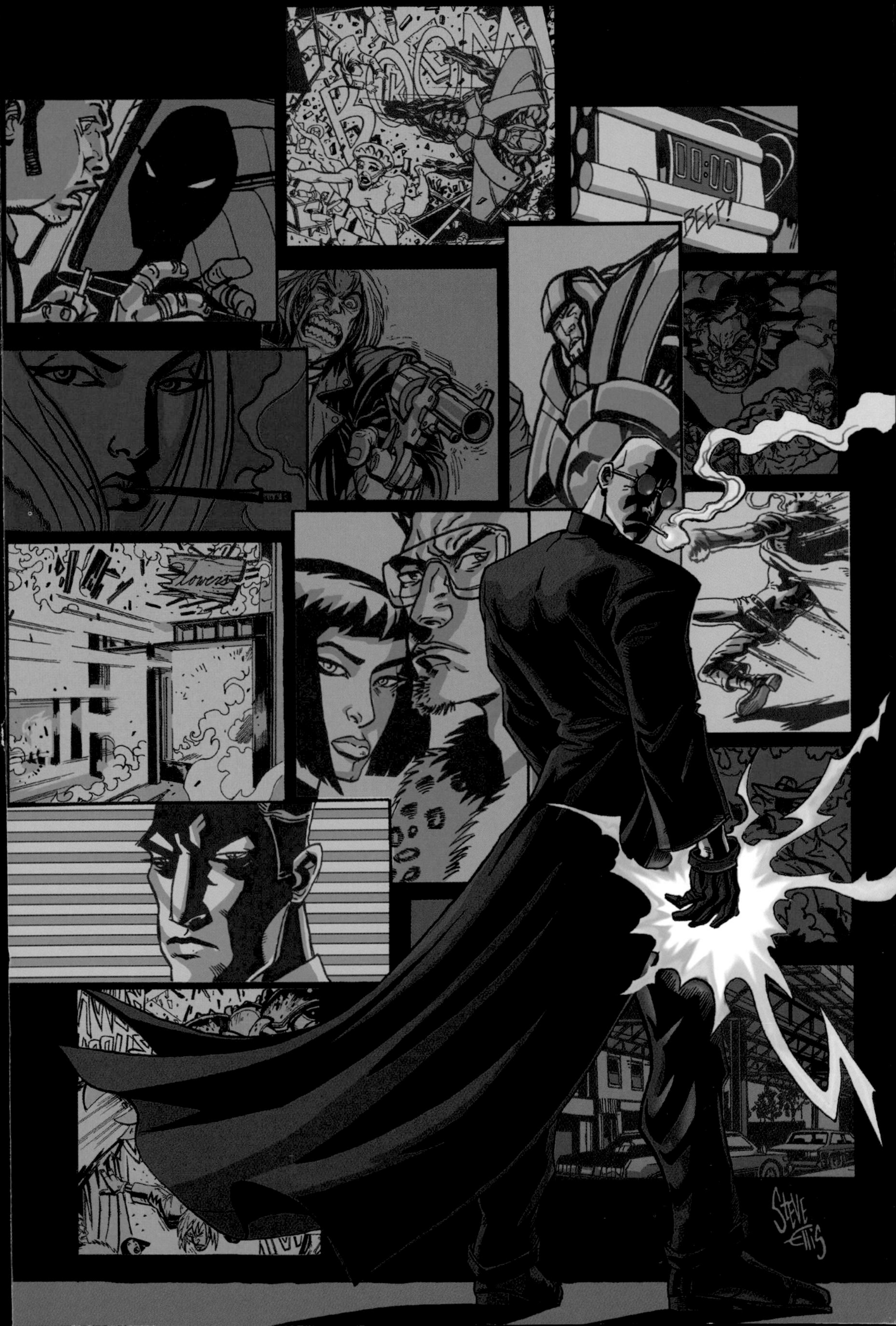

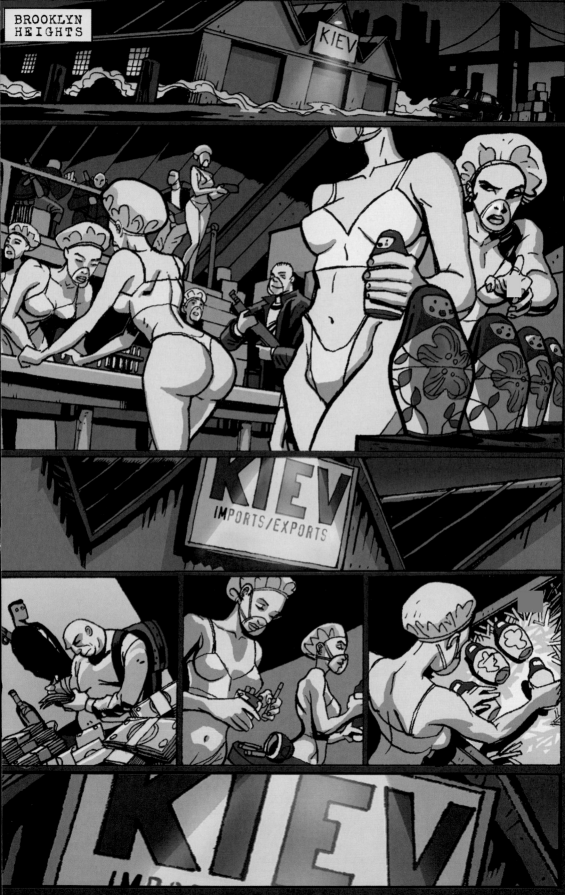

BROOKLYN
HEIGHTS

KIEV

KIEV
IMPORTS/EXPORTS

KIEV

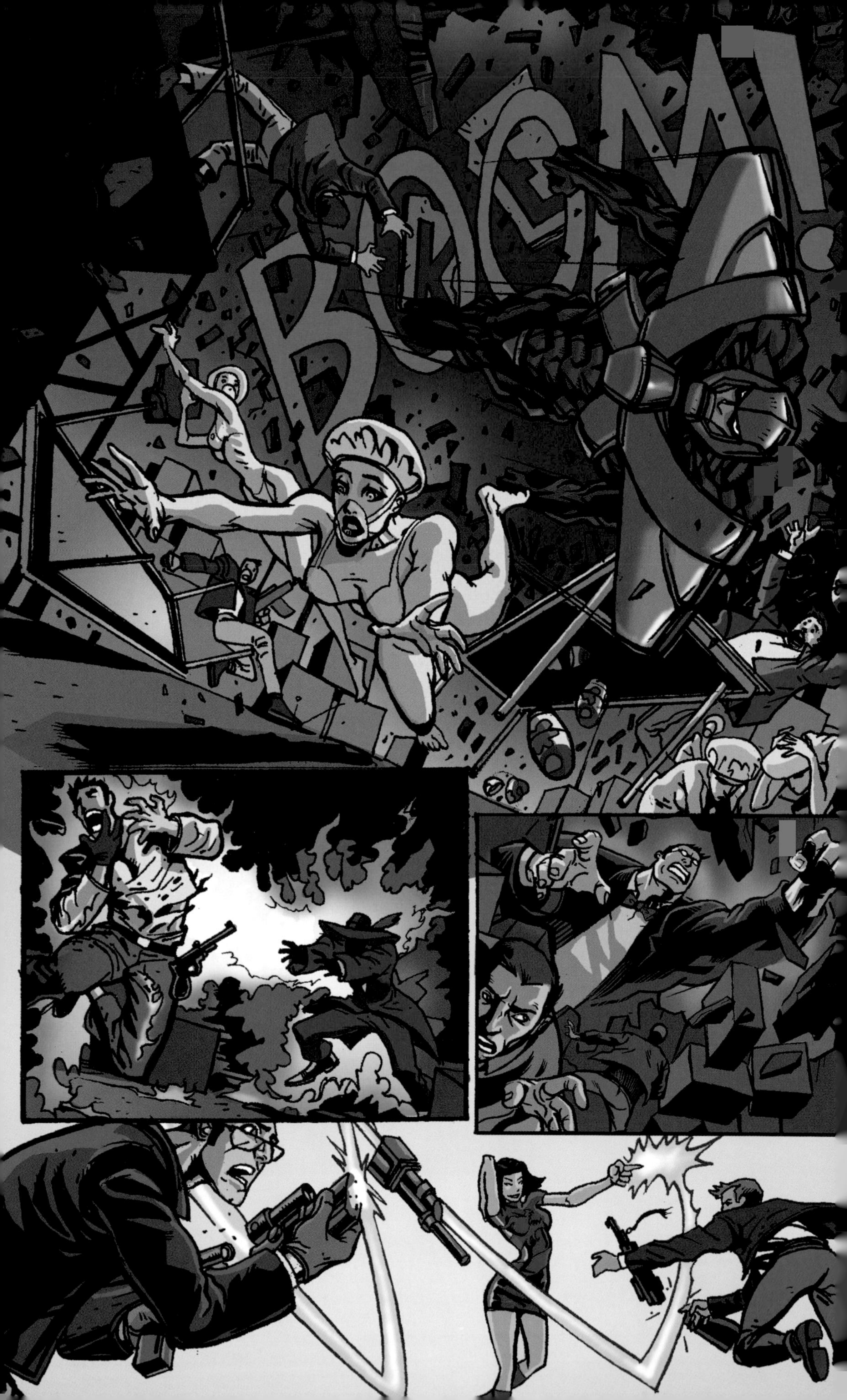
BOOM!

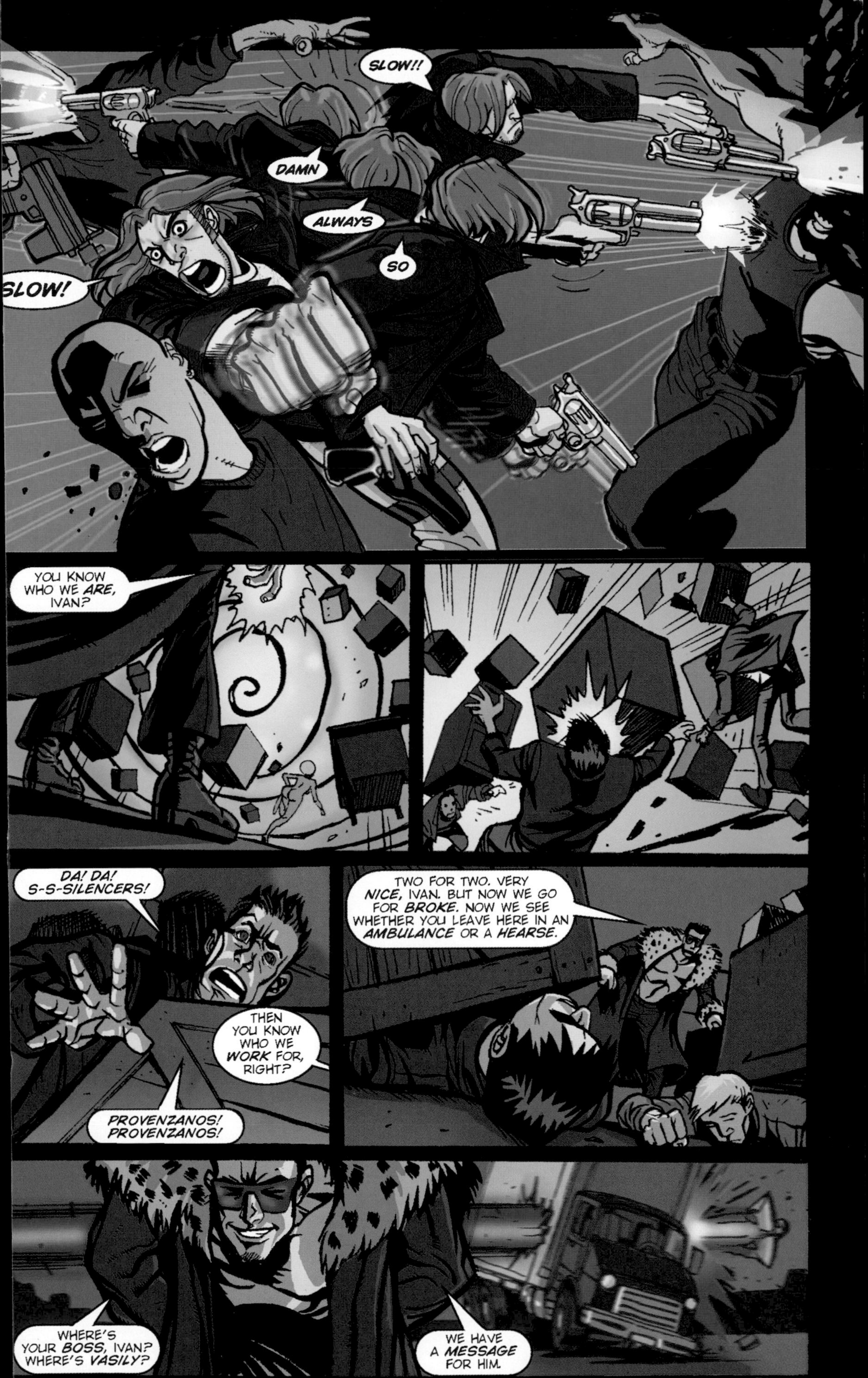
SLOW!!
DAMN
ALWAYS
SO
SLOW!
YOU KNOW WHO WE ARE, IVAN?
DA! DA! S-S-SILENCERS!
THEN YOU KNOW WHO WE WORK FOR, RIGHT?
PROVENZANOS! PROVENZANOS!
TWO FOR TWO. VERY NICE, IVAN. BUT NOW WE GO FOR BROKE. NOW WE SEE WHETHER YOU LEAVE HERE IN AN AMBULANCE OR A HEARSE.
WHERE'S YOUR BOSS, IVAN? WHERE'S VASILY?
WE HAVE A MESSAGE FOR HIM.

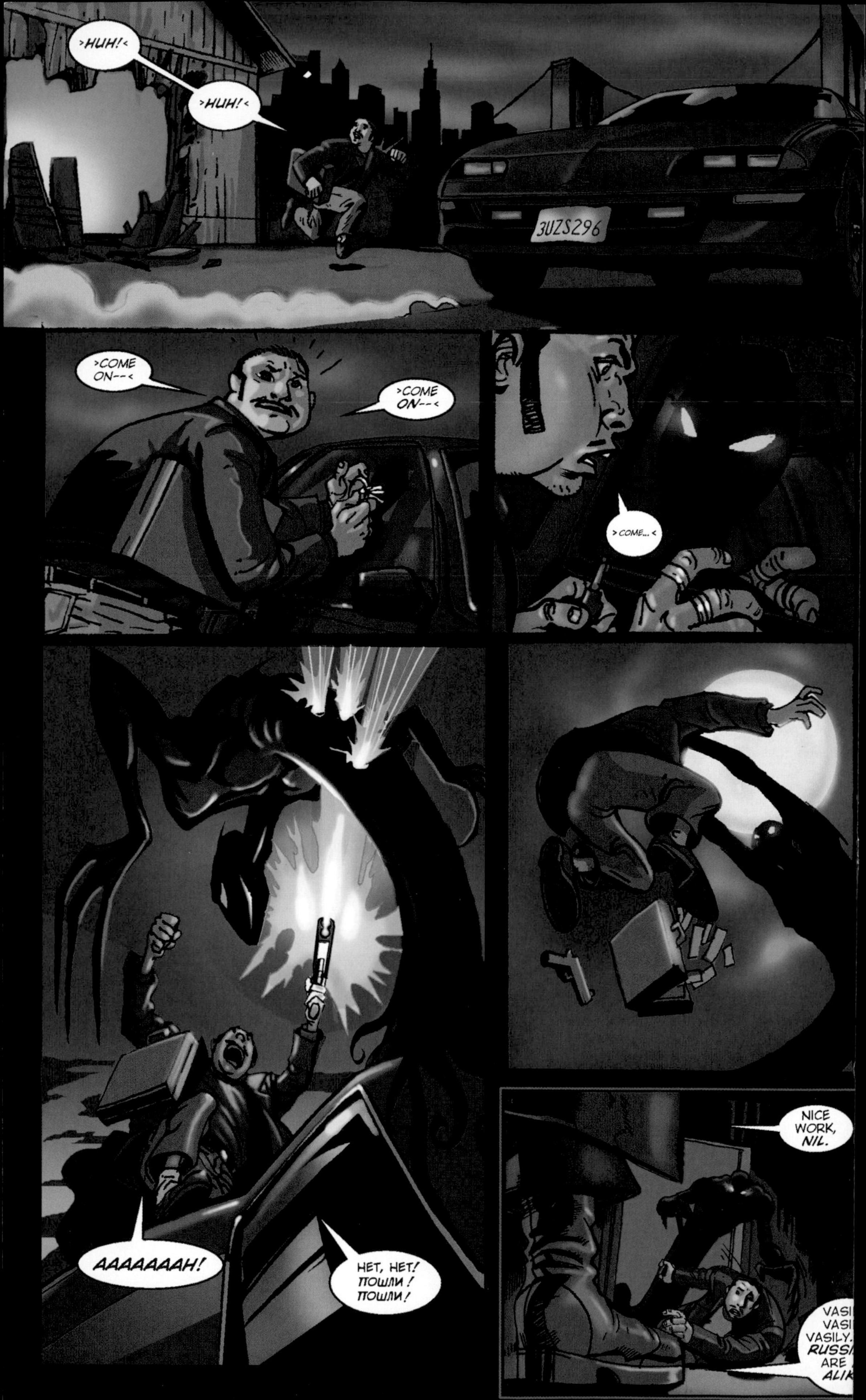
>HUH!<
>HUH!<
>COME ON--<
>COME ON--<
>COME...<
AAAAAAAH!
НЕТ, НЕТ! ПОШЛИ! ПОШЛИ!
NICE WORK, NIL.
VASI VASI VASILY. RUSSI ARE ALIK

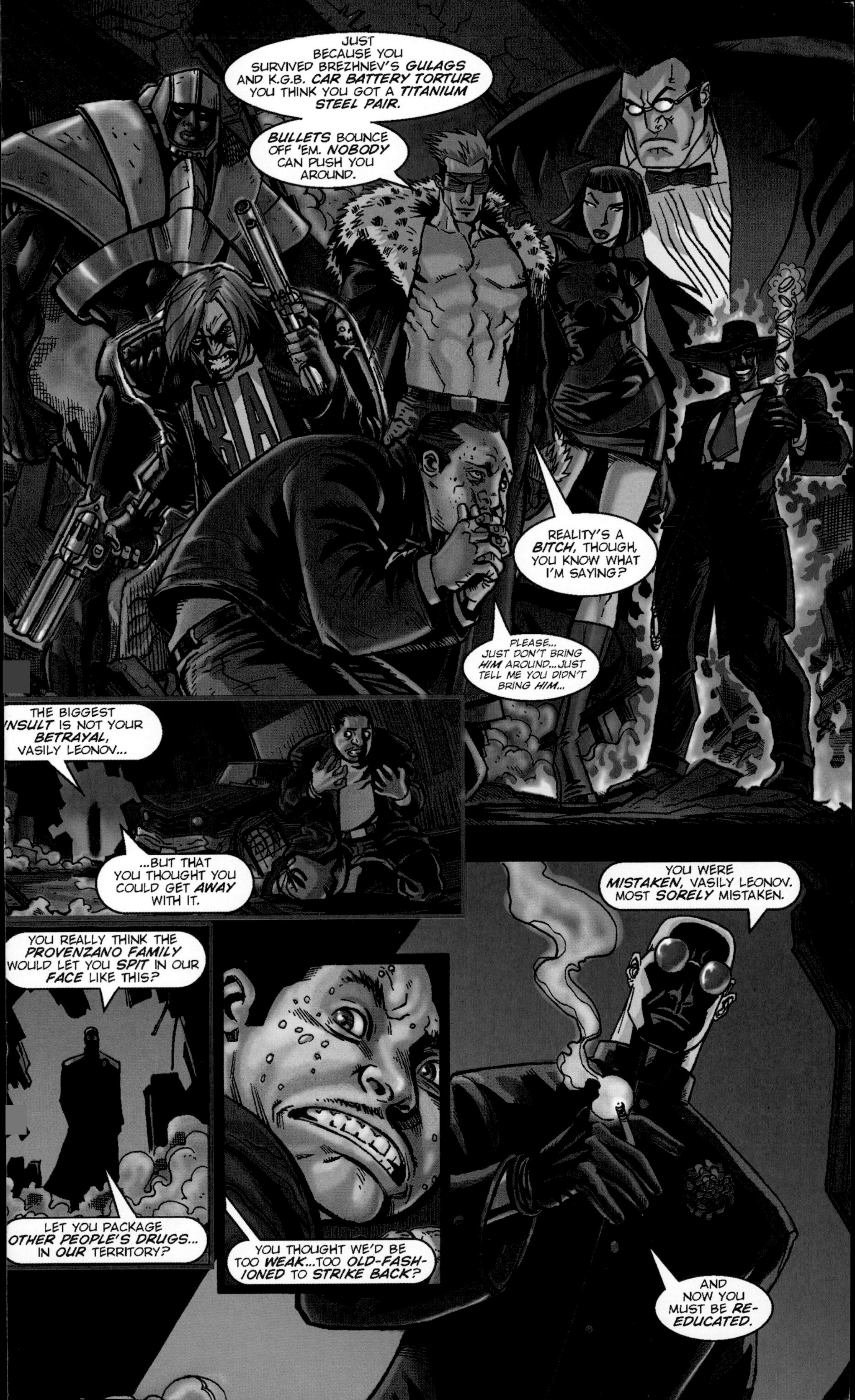
JUST BECAUSE YOU SURVIVED BREZHNEV'S GULAGS AND K.G.B. CAR BATTERY TORTURE YOU THINK YOU GOT A TITANIUM STEEL PAIR.
BULLETS BOUNCE OFF 'EM. NOBODY CAN PUSH YOU AROUND.
REALITY'S A BITCH, THOUGH, YOU KNOW WHAT I'M SAYING?
PLEASE... JUST DON'T BRING HIM AROUND... JUST TELL ME YOU DIDN'T BRING HIM...
THE BIGGEST INSULT IS NOT YOUR BETRAYAL, VASILY LEONOV...
...BUT THAT YOU THOUGHT YOU COULD GET AWAY WITH IT.
YOU WERE MISTAKEN, VASILY LEONOV. MOST SORELY MISTAKEN.
YOU REALLY THINK THE PROVENZANO FAMILY WOULD LET YOU SPIT IN OUR FACE LIKE THIS?
LET YOU PACKAGE OTHER PEOPLE'S DRUGS... IN OUR TERRITORY?
YOU THOUGHT WE'D BE TOO WEAK...TOO OLD-FASHIONED TO STRIKE BACK?
AND NOW YOU MUST BE RE-EDUCATED.

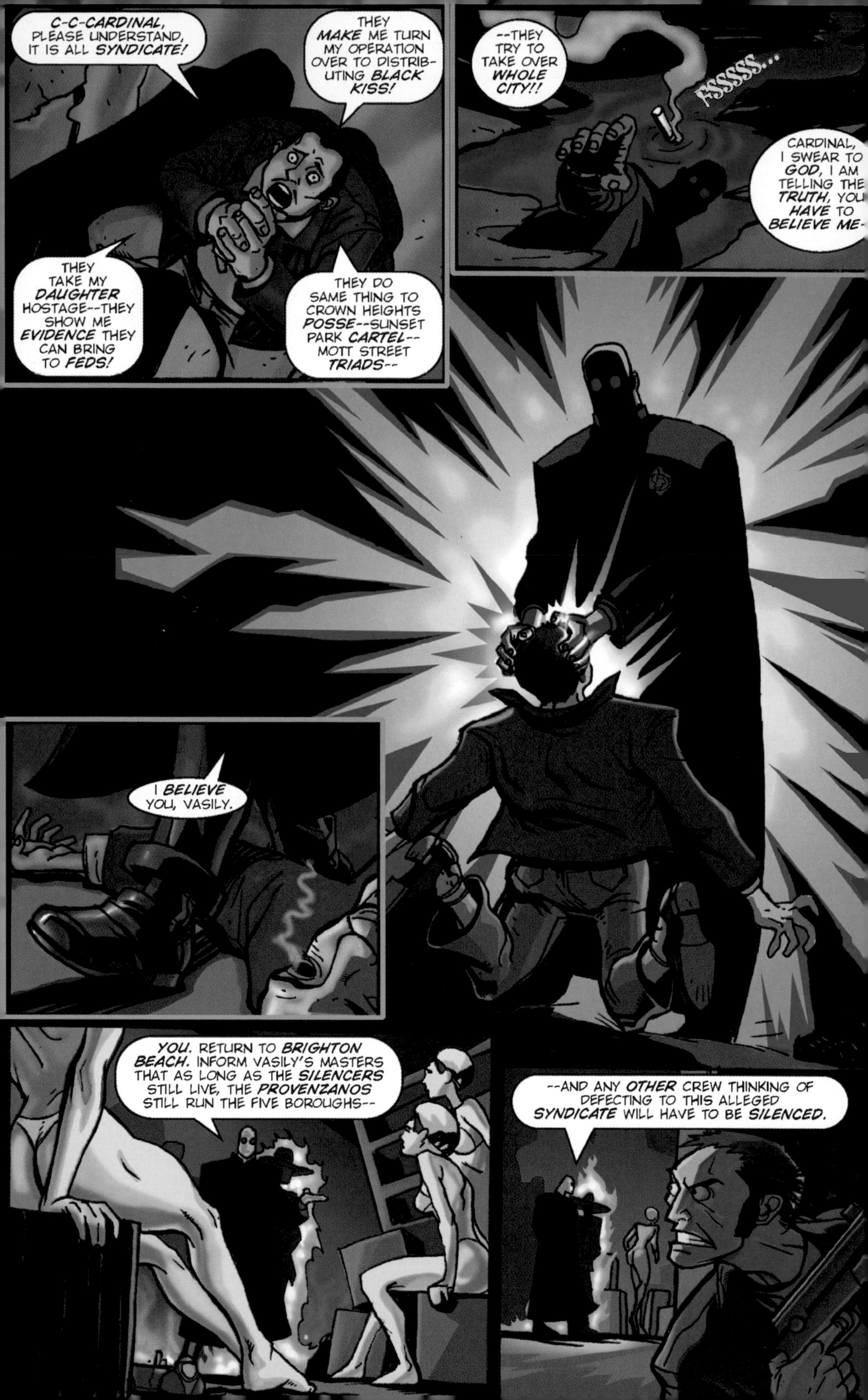
C-C-CARDINAL, PLEASE UNDERSTAND, IT IS ALL SYNDICATE!
THEY MAKE ME TURN MY OPERATION OVER TO DISTRIBUTING BLACK KISS!
THEY TAKE MY DAUGHTER HOSTAGE--THEY SHOW ME EVIDENCE THEY CAN BRING TO FEDS!
THEY DO SAME THING TO CROWN HEIGHTS POSSE--SUNSET PARK CARTEL--MOTT STREET TRIADS--
--THEY TRY TO TAKE OVER WHOLE CITY!!
FSSSSS...
CARDINAL, I SWEAR TO GOD, I AM TELLING THE TRUTH, YOU HAVE TO BELIEVE ME-
I BELIEVE YOU, VASILY.
YOU. RETURN TO BRIGHTON BEACH. INFORM VASILY'S MASTERS THAT AS LONG AS THE SILENCERS STILL LIVE, THE PROVENZANOS STILL RUN THE FIVE BOROUGHS--
--AND ANY OTHER CREW THINKING OF DEFECTING TO THIS ALLEGED SYNDICATE WILL HAVE TO BE SILENCED.

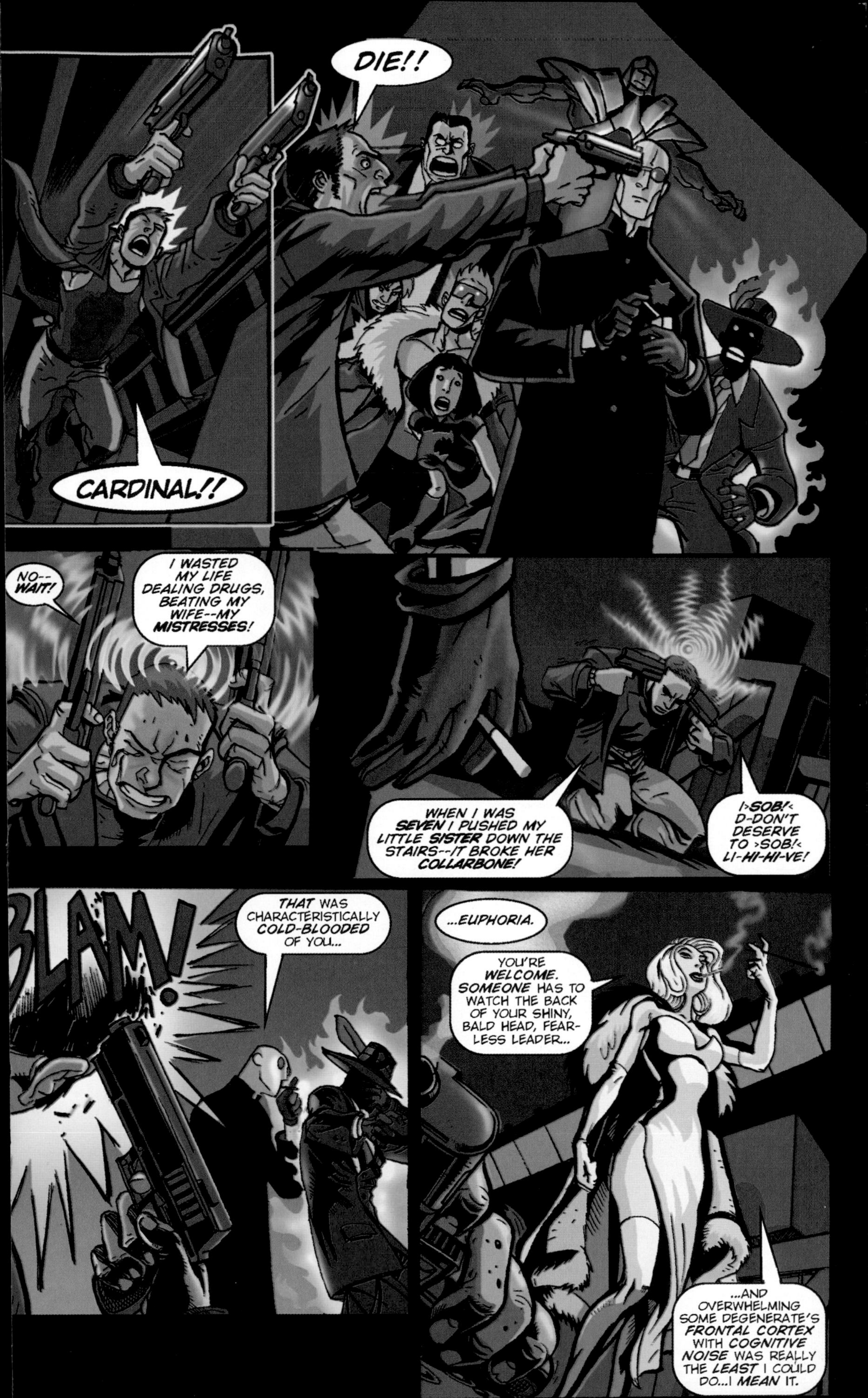
CARDINAL!!
DIE!!
NO--WAIT!
I WASTED MY LIFE DEALING DRUGS, BEATING MY WIFE--MY MISTRESSES!
WHEN I WAS SEVEN I PUSHED MY LITTLE SISTER DOWN THE STAIRS--IT BROKE HER COLLARBONE!
I >SOB!< D-DON'T DESERVE TO >SOB!< LI-HI-HI-VE!
BLAM!
THAT WAS CHARACTERISTICALLY COLD-BLOODED OF YOU...
...EUPHORIA.
YOU'RE WELCOME. SOMEONE HAS TO WATCH THE BACK OF YOUR SHINY, BALD HEAD, FEAR-LESS LEADER...
...AND OVERWHELMING SOME DEGENERATE'S FRONTAL CORTEX WITH COGNITIVE NOISE WAS REALLY THE LEAST I COULD DO...I MEAN IT.

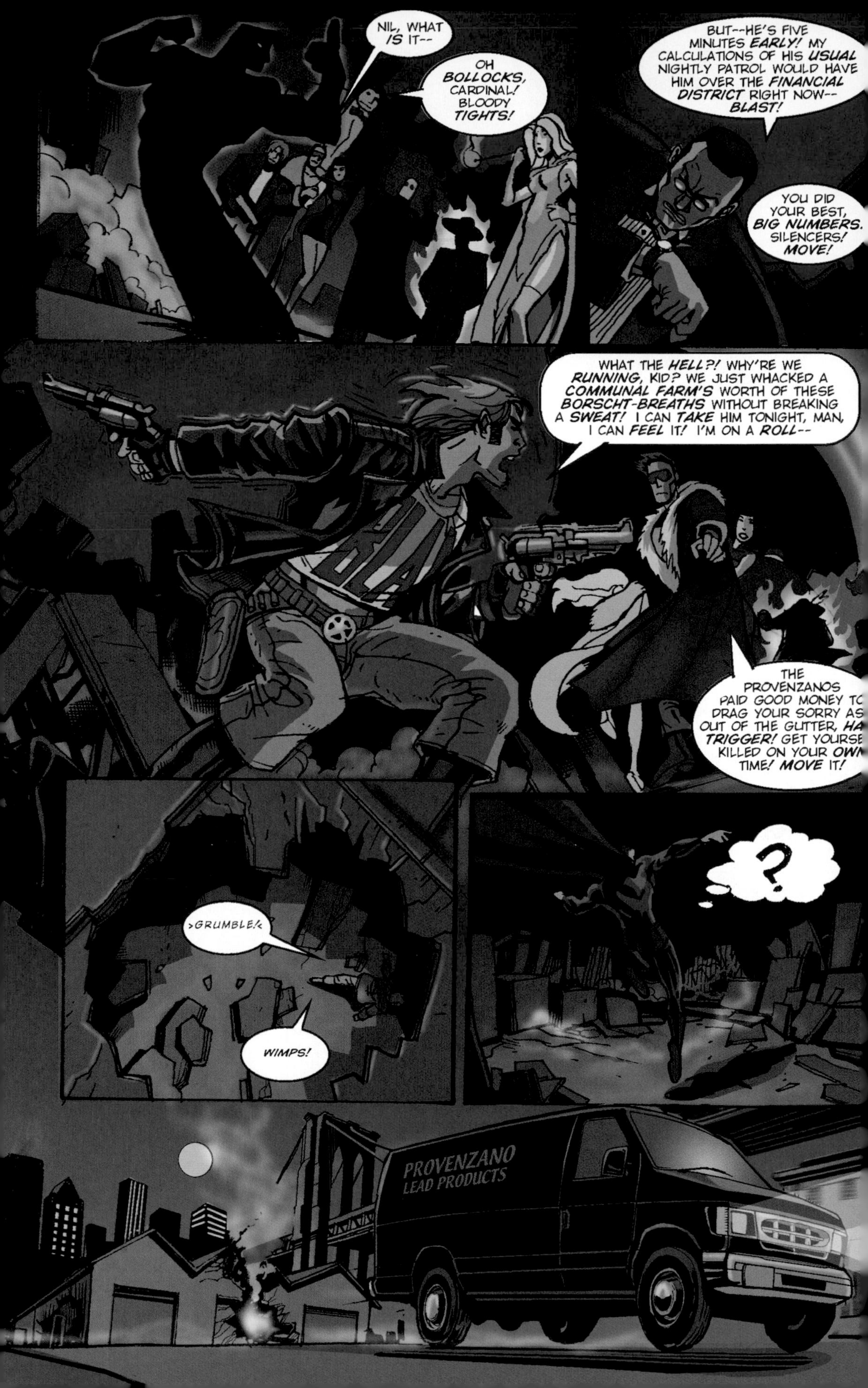
NIL, WHAT *IS* IT--
OH *BOLLOCKS*, CARDINAL! BLOODY *TIGHTS!*
BUT--HE'S FIVE MINUTES *EARLY!* MY CALCULATIONS OF HIS *USUAL* NIGHTLY PATROL WOULD HAVE HIM OVER THE *FINANCIAL DISTRICT* RIGHT NOW-- *BLAST!*
YOU DID YOUR BEST, *BIG NUMBERS.* SILENCERS! *MOVE!*
WHAT THE *HELL?!* WHY'RE WE *RUNNING*, KID? WE JUST WHACKED A *COMMUNAL FARM'S* WORTH OF THESE *BORSCHT-BREATHS* WITHOUT BREAKING A *SWEAT!* I CAN *TAKE* HIM TONIGHT, MAN, I CAN *FEEL* IT! I'M ON A *ROLL*--
THE PROVENZANOS PAID GOOD MONEY TO DRAG YOUR SORRY AS OUT OF THE GUTTER, *HA TRIGGER!* GET YOURSE KILLED ON YOUR *OWN* TIME! *MOVE* IT!
>GRUMBLE!<
WIMPS!
?
PROVENZANO
LEAD PRODUCTS

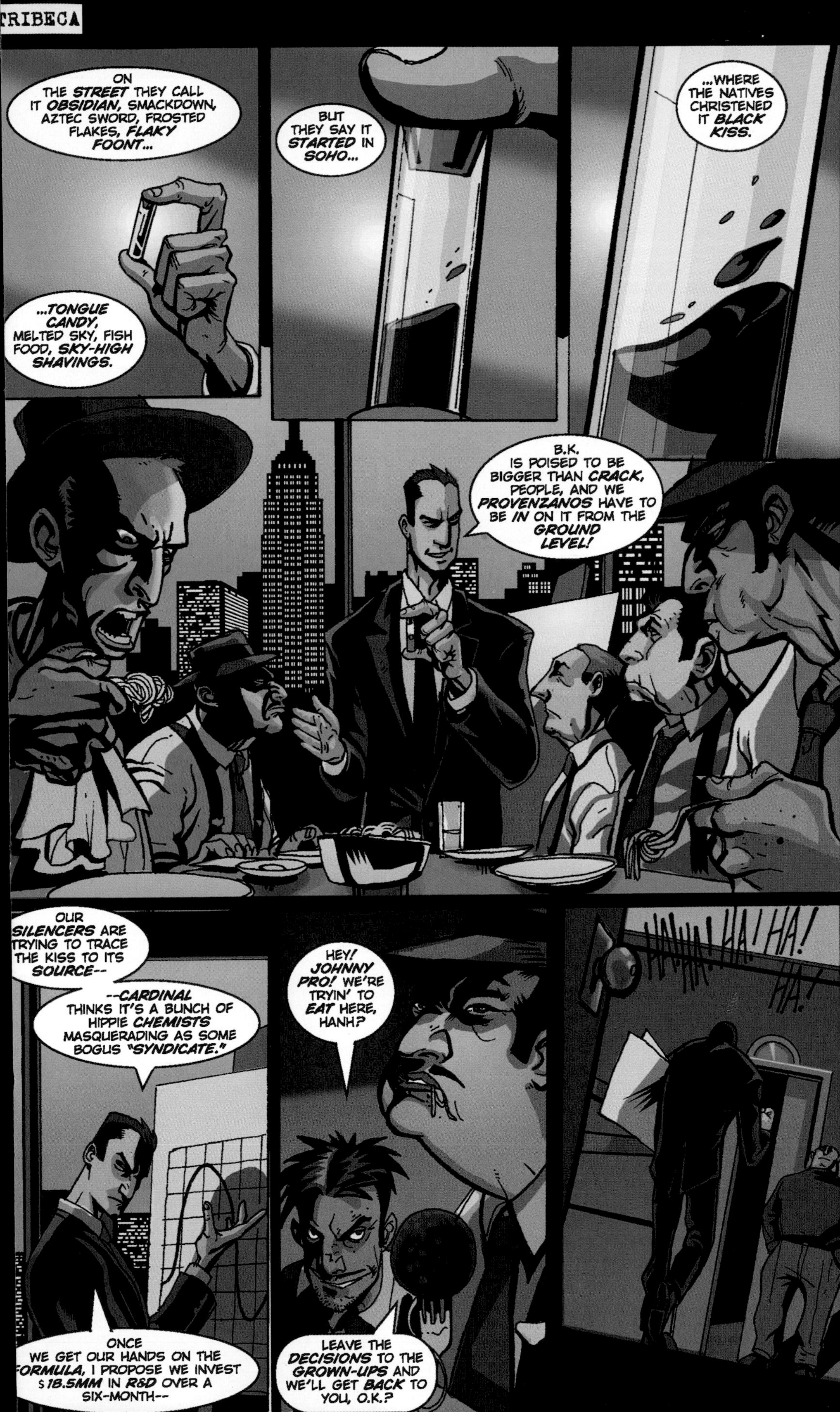
TRIBECA
ON THE STREET THEY CALL IT OBSIDIAN, SMACKDOWN, AZTEC SWORD, FROSTED FLAKES, FLAKY FOONT...
...TONGUE CANDY, MELTED SKY, FISH FOOD, SKY-HIGH SHAVINGS.
BUT THEY SAY IT STARTED IN SOHO...
...WHERE THE NATIVES CHRISTENED IT BLACK KISS.
B.K. IS POISED TO BE BIGGER THAN CRACK, PEOPLE, AND WE PROVENZANOS HAVE TO BE IN ON IT FROM THE GROUND LEVEL!
OUR SILENCERS ARE TRYING TO TRACE THE KISS TO ITS SOURCE--
--CARDINAL THINKS IT'S A BUNCH OF HIPPIE CHEMISTS MASQUERADING AS SOME BOGUS "SYNDICATE."
ONCE WE GET OUR HANDS ON THE FORMULA, I PROPOSE WE INVEST $18.5MM IN R&D OVER A SIX-MONTH--
HEY! JOHNNY PRO! WE'RE TRYIN' TO EAT HERE, HANH?
LEAVE THE DECISIONS TO THE GROWN-UPS AND WE'LL GET BACK TO YOU, O.K.?
HAHAHA! HA! HA! HA! HA!

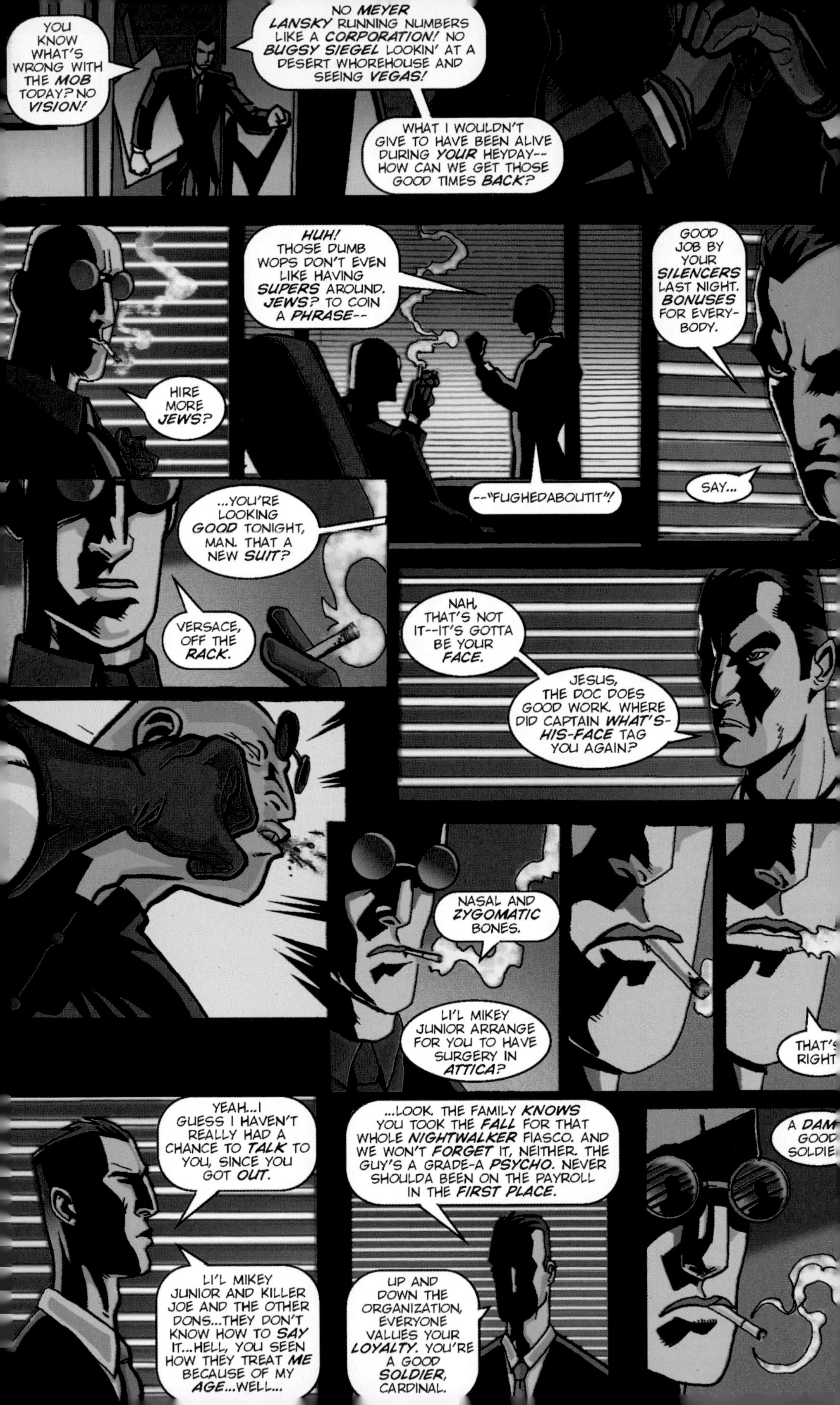

YOU KNOW WHAT'S WRONG WITH THE MOB TODAY? NO VISION!
NO MEYER LANSKY RUNNING NUMBERS LIKE A CORPORATION! NO BUGSY SIEGEL LOOKIN' AT A DESERT WHOREHOUSE AND SEEING VEGAS!
WHAT I WOULDN'T GIVE TO HAVE BEEN ALIVE DURING YOUR HEYDAY-- HOW CAN WE GET THOSE GOOD TIMES BACK?
HIRE MORE JEWS?
HUH! THOSE DUMB WOPS DON'T EVEN LIKE HAVING SUPERS AROUND. JEWS? TO COIN A PHRASE--
--"FUGHEDABOUTIT"!
GOOD JOB BY YOUR SILENCERS LAST NIGHT. BONUSES FOR EVERY-BODY.
SAY...
...YOU'RE LOOKING GOOD TONIGHT, MAN. THAT A NEW SUIT?
VERSACE, OFF THE RACK.
NAH, THAT'S NOT IT--IT'S GOTTA BE YOUR FACE.
JESUS, THE DOC DOES GOOD WORK. WHERE DID CAPTAIN WHAT'S-HIS-FACE TAG YOU AGAIN?
NASAL AND ZYGOMATIC BONES.
LI'L MIKEY JUNIOR ARRANGE FOR YOU TO HAVE SURGERY IN ATTICA?
THAT'S RIGHT
YEAH...I GUESS I HAVEN'T REALLY HAD A CHANCE TO TALK TO YOU, SINCE YOU GOT OUT.
LI'L MIKEY JUNIOR AND KILLER JOE AND THE OTHER DONS...THEY DON'T KNOW HOW TO SAY IT...HELL, YOU SEEN HOW THEY TREAT ME BECAUSE OF MY AGE...WELL...
...LOOK. THE FAMILY KNOWS YOU TOOK THE FALL FOR THAT WHOLE NIGHTWALKER FIASCO. AND WE WON'T FORGET IT, NEITHER. THE GUY'S A GRADE-A PSYCHO. NEVER SHOULDA BEEN ON THE PAYROLL IN THE FIRST PLACE.
UP AND DOWN THE ORGANIZATION, EVERYONE VALUES YOUR LOYALTY. YOU'RE A GOOD SOLDIER, CARDINAL.
A DAM GOOD SOLDIE

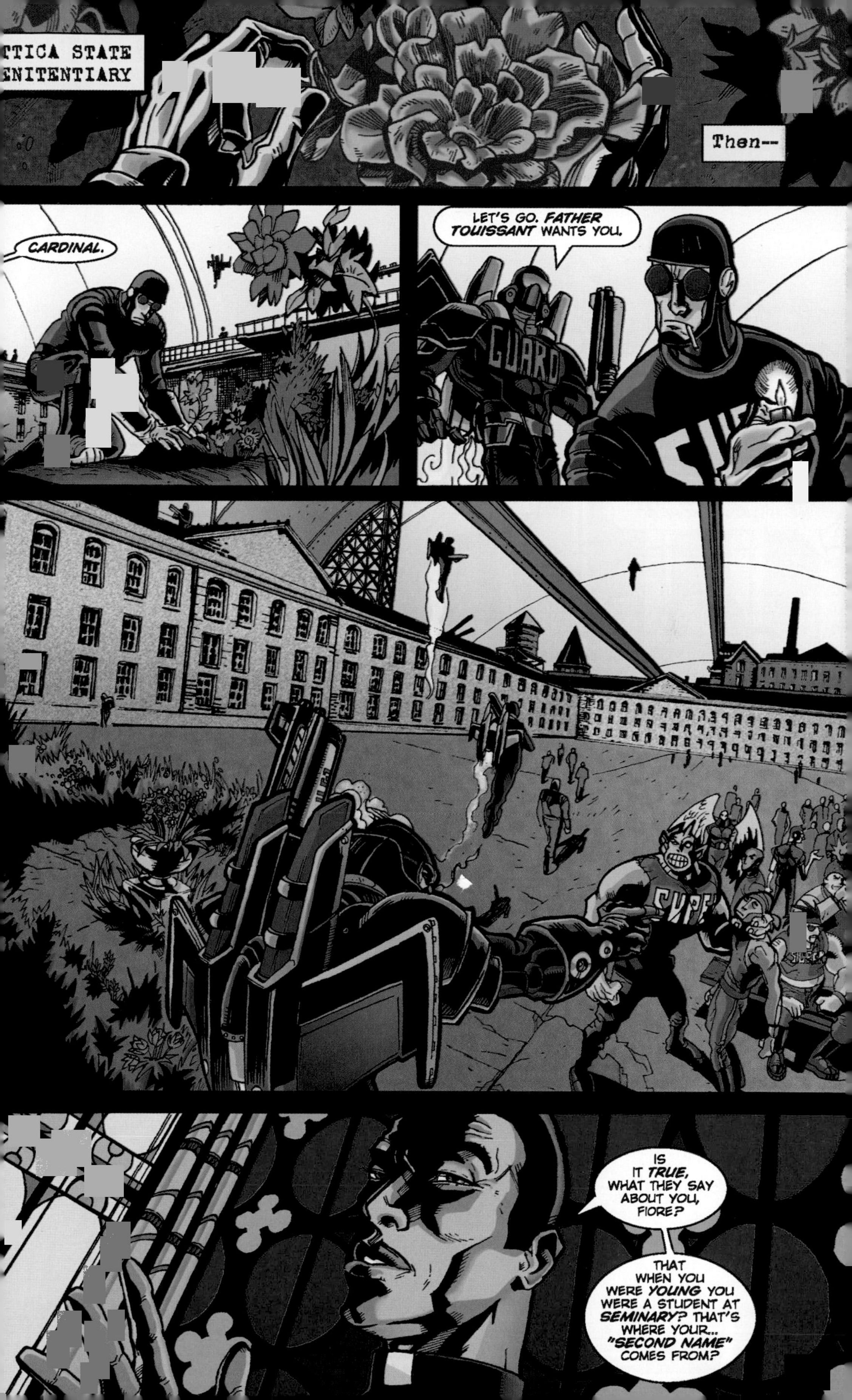
TTICA STATE
ENITENTIARY
Then--
CARDINAL.
LET'S GO. FATHER TOUISSANT WANTS YOU.
IS IT TRUE, WHAT THEY SAY ABOUT YOU, FIORE?
THAT WHEN YOU WERE YOUNG YOU WERE A STUDENT AT SEMINARY? THAT'S WHERE YOUR... "SECOND NAME" COMES FROM?

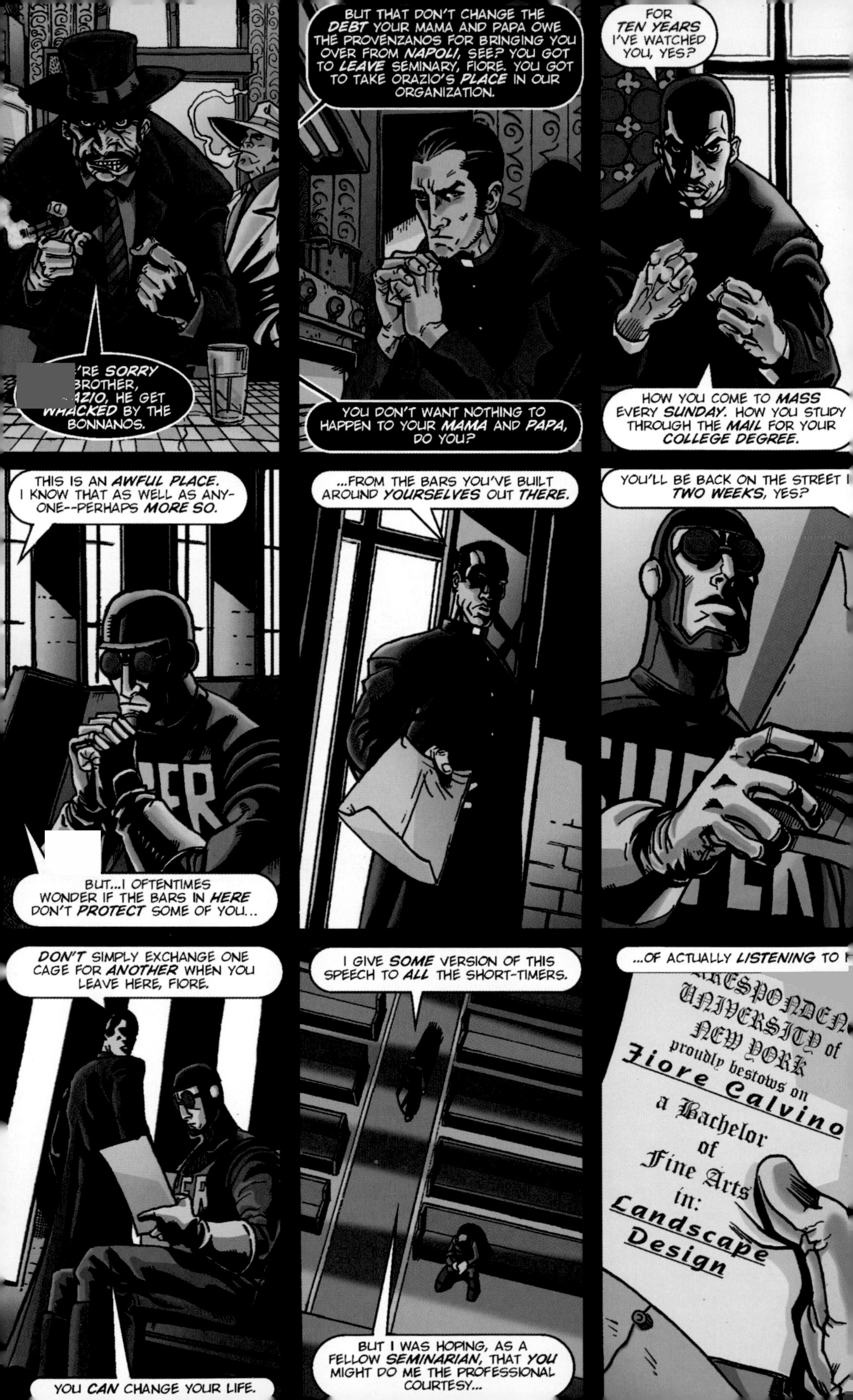

'RE SORRY BROTHER, AZIO, HE GET WHACKED BY THE BONNANOS.
BUT THAT DON'T CHANGE THE DEBT YOUR MAMA AND PAPA OWE THE PROVENZANOS FOR BRINGING YOU OVER FROM NAPOLI, SEE? YOU GOT TO LEAVE SEMINARY, FIORE. YOU GOT TO TAKE ORAZIO'S PLACE IN OUR ORGANIZATION.
YOU DON'T WANT NOTHING TO HAPPEN TO YOUR MAMA AND PAPA, DO YOU?
FOR TEN YEARS I'VE WATCHED YOU, YES?
HOW YOU COME TO MASS EVERY SUNDAY. HOW YOU STUDY THROUGH THE MAIL FOR YOUR COLLEGE DEGREE.
THIS IS AN AWFUL PLACE. I KNOW THAT AS WELL AS ANY-ONE--PERHAPS MORE SO.
BUT...I OFTENTIMES WONDER IF THE BARS IN HERE DON'T PROTECT SOME OF YOU...
...FROM THE BARS YOU'VE BUILT AROUND YOURSELVES OUT THERE.
YOU'LL BE BACK ON THE STREET I
TWO WEEKS, YES?
DON'T SIMPLY EXCHANGE ONE CAGE FOR ANOTHER WHEN YOU LEAVE HERE, FIORE.
YOU CAN CHANGE YOUR LIFE.
I GIVE SOME VERSION OF THIS SPEECH TO ALL THE SHORT-TIMERS.
BUT I WAS HOPING, AS A FELLOW SEMINARIAN, THAT YOU MIGHT DO ME THE PROFESSIONAL COURTESY...
...OF ACTUALLY LISTENING TO
UNIVERSITY of NEW YORK
proudly bestows on
Fiore Calvino
a Bachelor of Fine Arts in:
Landscape Design

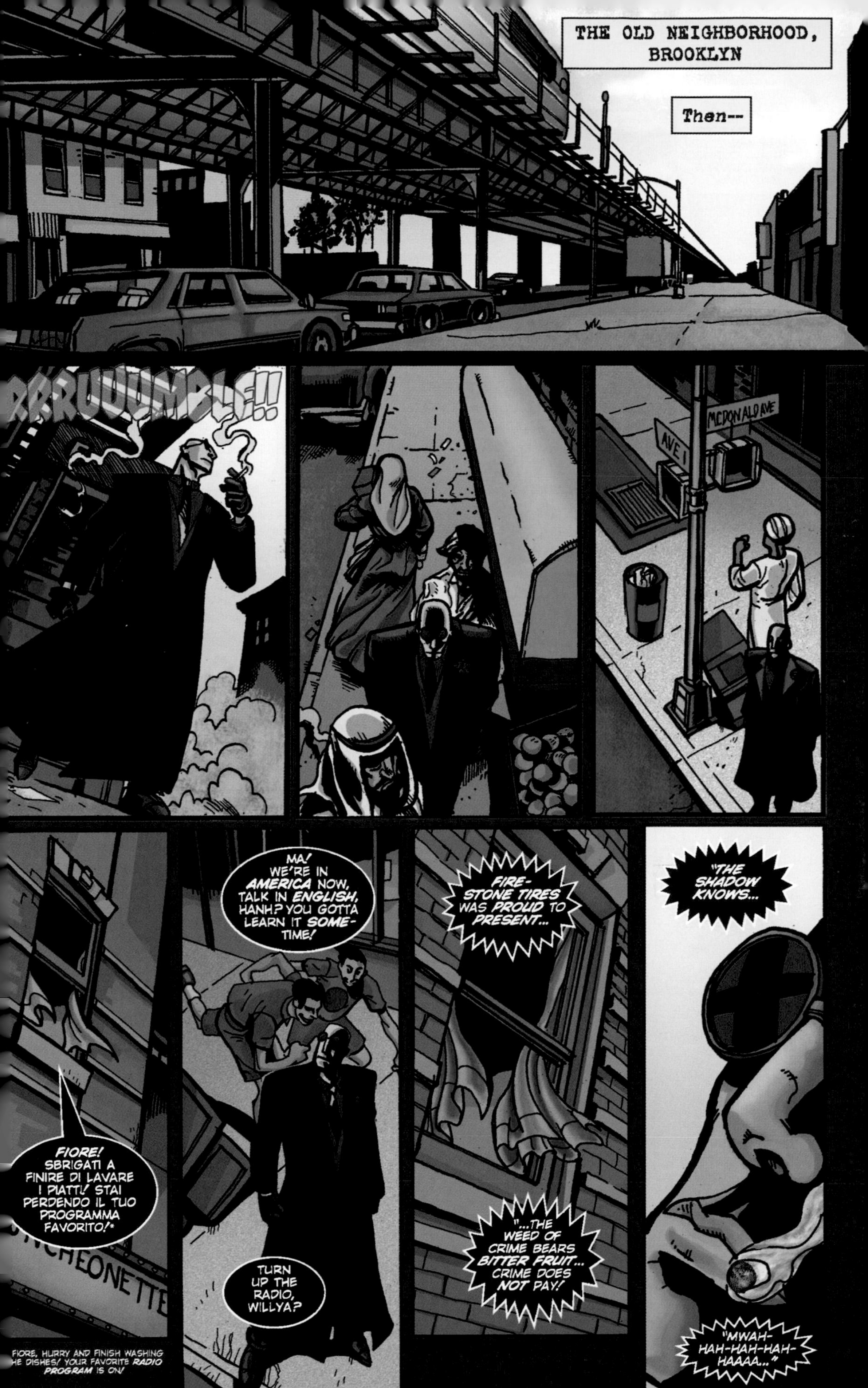
THE OLD NEIGHBORHOOD, BROOKLYN
Then--
RRRUUUMBLE!!
MCDONALD AVE
AVE I
FIORE! SBRIGATI A FINIRE DI LAVARE I PIATTI! STAI PERDENDO IL TUO PROGRAMMA FAVORITO!*
UNCHEONETTE
MA! WE'RE IN AMERICA NOW, TALK IN ENGLISH, HANH? YOU GOTTA LEARN IT SOMETIME!
TURN UP THE RADIO, WILLYA?
FIRESTONE TIRES WAS PROUD TO PRESENT...
"...THE WEED OF CRIME BEARS BITTER FRUIT... CRIME DOES NOT PAY!
"THE SHADOW KNOWS...
"MWAH-HAH-HAH-HAH-HAAAA..."
*FIORE, HURRY AND FINISH WASHING THE DISHES! YOUR FAVORITE RADIO PROGRAM IS ON!

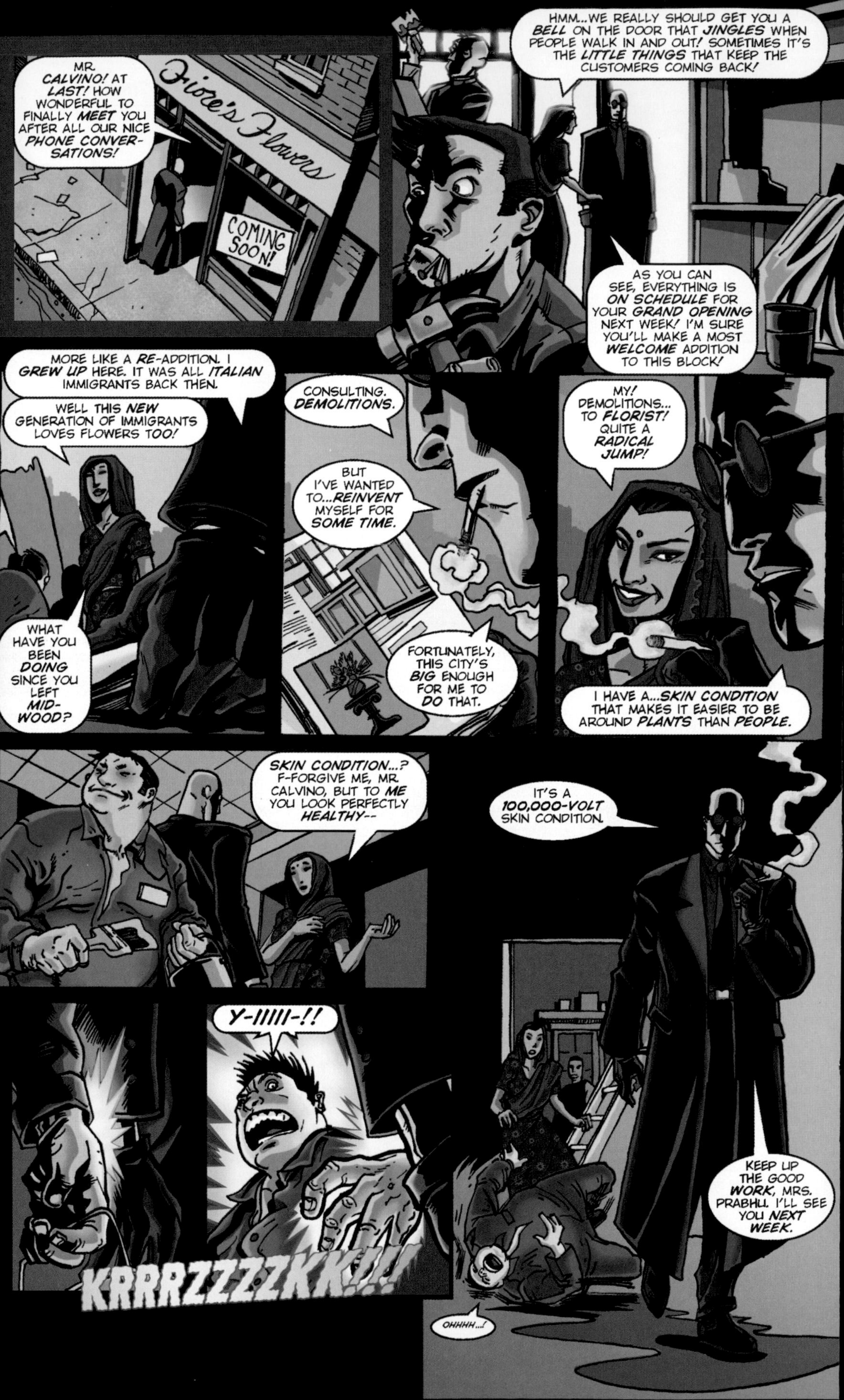

MR. CALVINO! AT LAST! HOW WONDERFUL TO FINALLY MEET YOU AFTER ALL OUR NICE PHONE CONVERSATIONS!
Fiore's Flowers
COMING SOON!
HMM...WE REALLY SHOULD GET YOU A BELL ON THE DOOR THAT JINGLES WHEN PEOPLE WALK IN AND OUT! SOMETIMES IT'S THE LITTLE THINGS THAT KEEP THE CUSTOMERS COMING BACK!
AS YOU CAN SEE, EVERYTHING IS ON SCHEDULE FOR YOUR GRAND OPENING NEXT WEEK! I'M SURE YOU'LL MAKE A MOST WELCOME ADDITION TO THIS BLOCK!
MORE LIKE A RE-ADDITION. I GREW UP HERE. IT WAS ALL ITALIAN IMMIGRANTS BACK THEN.
WELL THIS NEW GENERATION OF IMMIGRANTS LOVES FLOWERS TOO!
WHAT HAVE YOU BEEN DOING SINCE YOU LEFT MID-WOOD?
CONSULTING. DEMOLITIONS.
BUT I'VE WANTED TO...REINVENT MYSELF FOR SOME TIME.
FORTUNATELY, THIS CITY'S BIG ENOUGH FOR ME TO DO THAT.
MY! DEMOLITIONS... TO FLORIST! QUITE A RADICAL JUMP!
I HAVE A...SKIN CONDITION THAT MAKES IT EASIER TO BE AROUND PLANTS THAN PEOPLE.
SKIN CONDITION...? F-FORGIVE ME, MR. CALVINO, BUT TO ME YOU LOOK PERFECTLY HEALTHY--
IT'S A 100,000-VOLT SKIN CONDITION.
Y-IIIII-!!
KRRRZZZZKK!!!
KEEP UP THE GOOD WORK, MRS. PRABHU. I'LL SEE YOU NEXT WEEK.
OHHHH...!

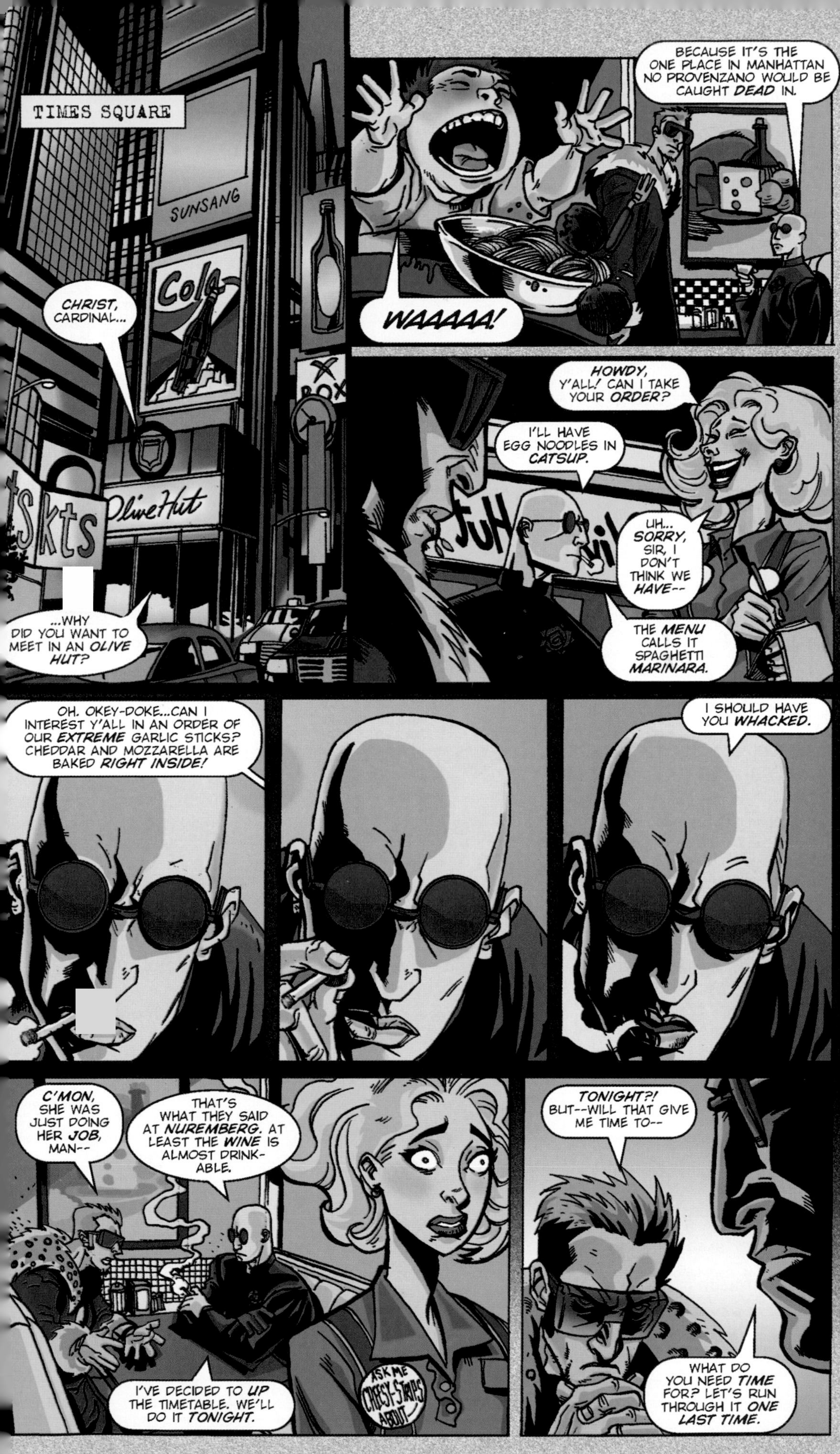
TIMES SQUARE
SUNSANG
Cola
OliveHut
CHRIST, CARDINAL...
...WHY DID YOU WANT TO MEET IN AN OLIVE HUT?
BECAUSE IT'S THE ONE PLACE IN MANHATTAN NO PROVENZANO WOULD BE CAUGHT DEAD IN.
WAAAAA!
HOWDY, Y'ALL! CAN I TAKE YOUR ORDER?
I'LL HAVE EGG NOODLES IN CATSUP.
UH... SORRY, SIR, I DON'T THINK WE HAVE--
THE MENU CALLS IT SPAGHETTI MARINARA.
OH. OKEY-DOKE...CAN I INTEREST Y'ALL IN AN ORDER OF OUR EXTREME GARLIC STICKS? CHEDDAR AND MOZZARELLA ARE BAKED RIGHT INSIDE!
I SHOULD HAVE YOU WHACKED.
C'MON, SHE WAS JUST DOING HER JOB, MAN--
THAT'S WHAT THEY SAID AT NUREMBERG. AT LEAST THE WINE IS ALMOST DRINKABLE.
I'VE DECIDED TO UP THE TIMETABLE. WE'LL DO IT TONIGHT.
ASK ME
ABOUT
TONIGHT?! BUT--WILL THAT GIVE ME TIME TO--
WHAT DO YOU NEED TIME FOR? LET'S RUN THROUGH IT ONE LAST TIME.

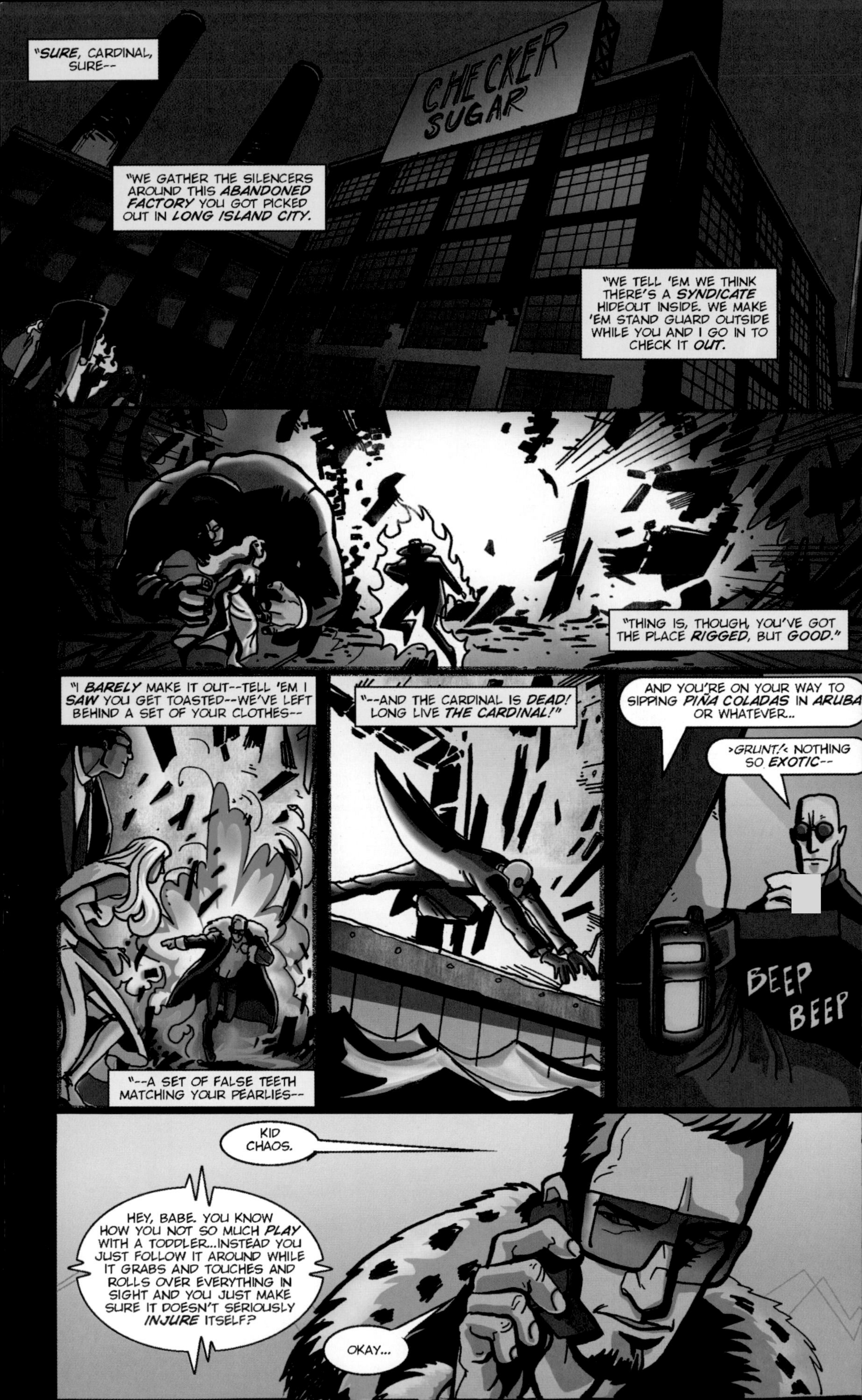
"SURE, CARDINAL, SURE--
CHECKER SUGAR
"WE GATHER THE SILENCERS AROUND THIS ABANDONED FACTORY YOU GOT PICKED OUT IN LONG ISLAND CITY.
"WE TELL 'EM WE THINK THERE'S A SYNDICATE HIDEOUT INSIDE. WE MAKE 'EM STAND GUARD OUTSIDE WHILE YOU AND I GO IN TO CHECK IT OUT.
"THING IS, THOUGH, YOU'VE GOT THE PLACE RIGGED, BUT GOOD."
"I BARELY MAKE IT OUT--TELL 'EM I SAW YOU GET TOASTED--WE'VE LEFT BEHIND A SET OF YOUR CLOTHES--
"--A SET OF FALSE TEETH MATCHING YOUR PEARLIES--
"--AND THE CARDINAL IS DEAD! LONG LIVE THE CARDINAL!"
AND YOU'RE ON YOUR WAY TO SIPPING PIÑA COLADAS IN ARUBA OR WHATEVER...
>GRUNT!< NOTHING SO EXOTIC--
BEEP BEEP
KID CHAOS.
HEY, BABE. YOU KNOW HOW YOU NOT SO MUCH PLAY WITH A TODDLER...INSTEAD YOU JUST FOLLOW IT AROUND WHILE IT GRABS AND TOUCHES AND ROLLS OVER EVERYTHING IN SIGHT AND YOU JUST MAKE SURE IT DOESN'T SERIOUSLY INJURE ITSELF?
OKAY...

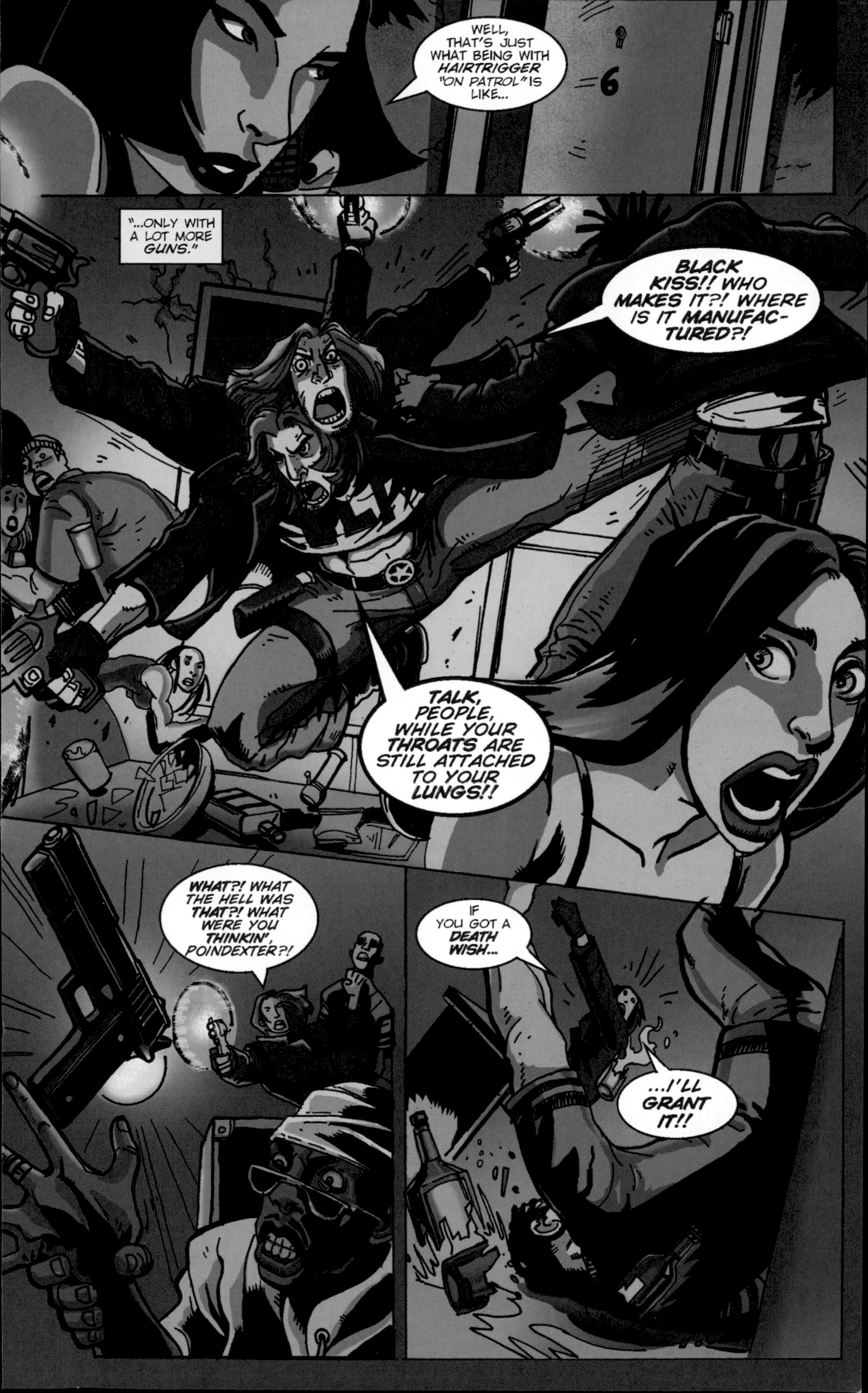
WELL, THAT'S JUST WHAT BEING WITH HAIRTRIGGER "ON PATROL" IS LIKE...
6
"...ONLY WITH A LOT MORE GUNS."
BLACK KISS!! WHO MAKES IT?! WHERE IS IT MANUFAC-TURED?!
TALK, PEOPLE, WHILE YOUR THROATS ARE STILL ATTACHED TO YOUR LUNGS!!
WHAT?! WHAT THE HELL WAS THAT?! WHAT WERE YOU THINKIN', POINDEXTER?!
IF YOU GOT A DEATH WISH...
...I'LL GRANT IT!!

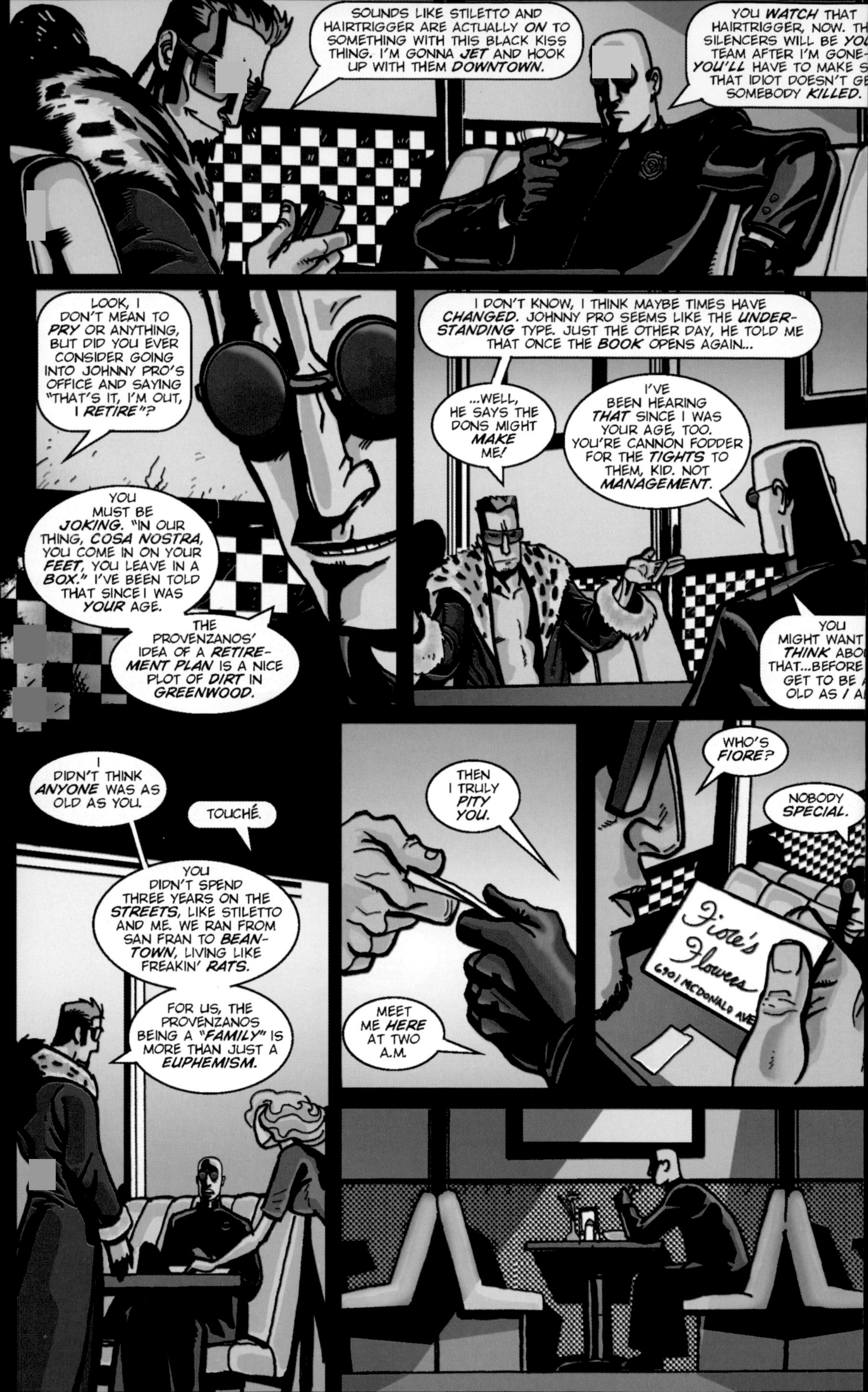
SOUNDS LIKE STILETTO AND HAIRTRIGGER ARE ACTUALLY ON TO SOMETHING WITH THIS BLACK KISS THING. I'M GONNA JET AND HOOK UP WITH THEM DOWNTOWN.
YOU WATCH THAT HAIRTRIGGER, NOW. TH SILENCERS WILL BE YOU TEAM AFTER I'M GONE- YOU'LL HAVE TO MAKE S THAT IDIOT DOESN'T GE SOMEBODY KILLED.
LOOK, I DON'T MEAN TO PRY OR ANYTHING, BUT DID YOU EVER CONSIDER GOING INTO JOHNNY PRO'S OFFICE AND SAYING "THAT'S IT, I'M OUT, I RETIRE"?
YOU MUST BE JOKING. "IN OUR THING, COSA NOSTRA, YOU COME IN ON YOUR FEET, YOU LEAVE IN A BOX." I'VE BEEN TOLD THAT SINCE I WAS YOUR AGE.
THE PROVENZANOS' IDEA OF A RETIREMENT PLAN IS A NICE PLOT OF DIRT IN GREENWOOD.
I DON'T KNOW, I THINK MAYBE TIMES HAVE CHANGED. JOHNNY PRO SEEMS LIKE THE UNDERSTANDING TYPE. JUST THE OTHER DAY, HE TOLD ME THAT ONCE THE BOOK OPENS AGAIN...
...WELL, HE SAYS THE DONS MIGHT MAKE ME!
I'VE BEEN HEARING THAT SINCE I WAS YOUR AGE, TOO. YOU'RE CANNON FODDER FOR THE TIGHTS TO THEM, KID. NOT MANAGEMENT.
YOU MIGHT WANT THINK ABO THAT...BEFORE GET TO BE OLD AS I A
I DIDN'T THINK ANYONE WAS AS OLD AS YOU.
TOUCHÉ.
YOU DIDN'T SPEND THREE YEARS ON THE STREETS, LIKE STILETTO AND ME. WE RAN FROM SAN FRAN TO BEANTOWN, LIVING LIKE FREAKIN' RATS.
FOR US, THE PROVENZANOS BEING A "FAMILY" IS MORE THAN JUST A EUPHEMISM.
THEN I TRULY PITY YOU.
MEET ME HERE AT TWO A.M.
WHO'S FIORE?
NOBODY SPECIAL.
Fiore's Flowers
6901 MCDONALD AVE

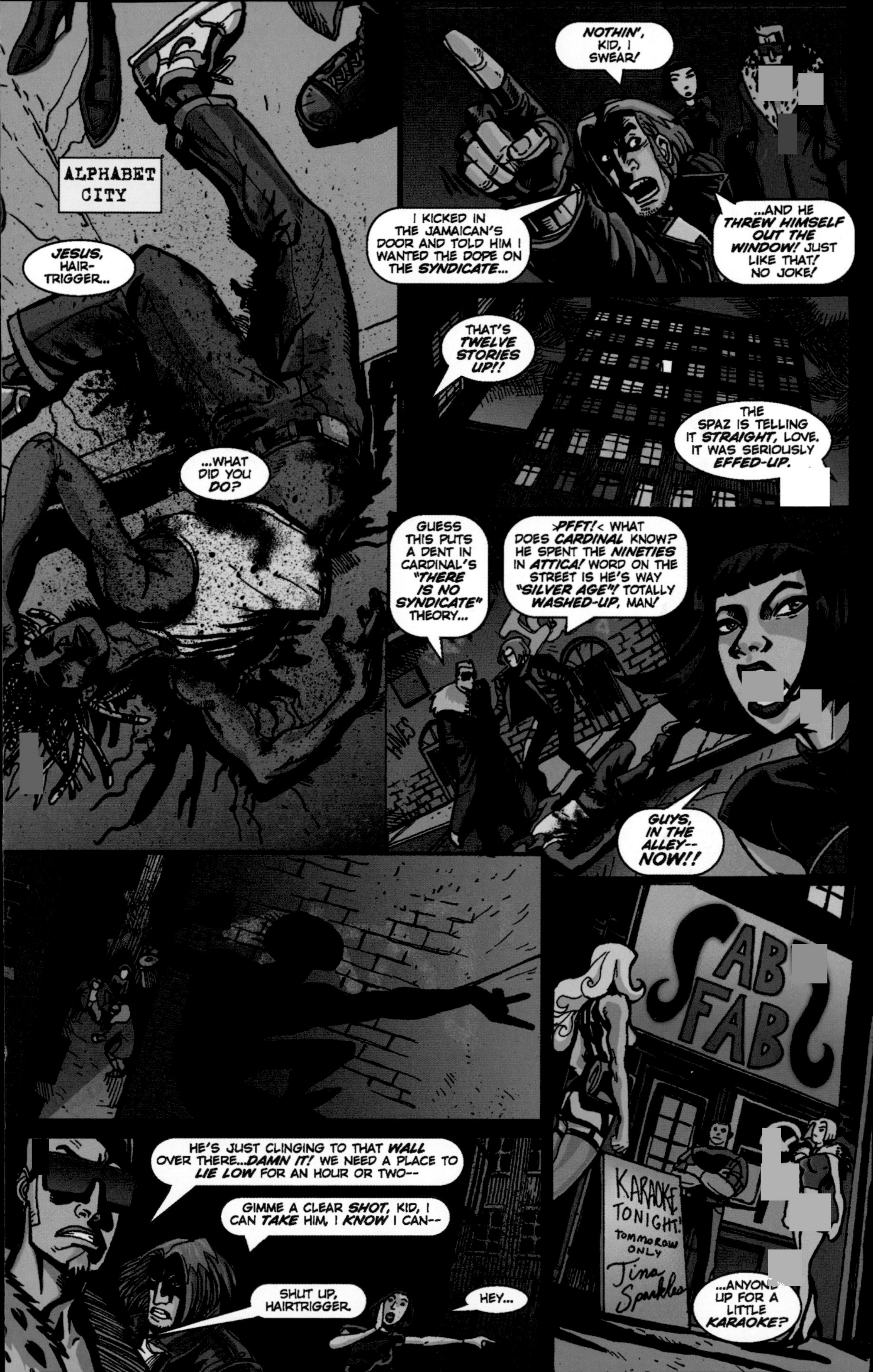
ALPHABET CITY
JESUS, HAIR-TRIGGER...
...WHAT DID YOU DO?
NOTHIN', KID, I SWEAR!
I KICKED IN THE JAMAICAN'S DOOR AND TOLD HIM I WANTED THE DOPE ON THE SYNDICATE...
...AND HE THREW HIMSELF OUT THE WINDOW! JUST LIKE THAT! NO JOKE!
THAT'S TWELVE STORIES UP!!
THE SPAZ IS TELLING IT STRAIGHT, LOVE. IT WAS SERIOUSLY EFFED-UP.
GUESS THIS PUTS A DENT IN CARDINAL'S "THERE IS NO SYNDICATE" THEORY...
>PFFT!< WHAT DOES CARDINAL KNOW? HE SPENT THE NINETIES IN ATTICA! WORD ON THE STREET IS HE'S WAY "SILVER AGE"! TOTALLY WASHED-UP, MAN!
GUYS, IN THE ALLEY--NOW!!
HE'S JUST CLINGING TO THAT WALL OVER THERE...DAMN IT! WE NEED A PLACE TO LIE LOW FOR AN HOUR OR TWO--
GIMME A CLEAR SHOT, KID, I CAN TAKE HIM, I KNOW I CAN--
SHUT UP, HAIRTRIGGER.
HEY...
AB FAB
KARAOKE TONIGHT! TOMMOROW ONLY Tina Sparkles
...ANYONE UP FOR A LITTLE KARAOKE?

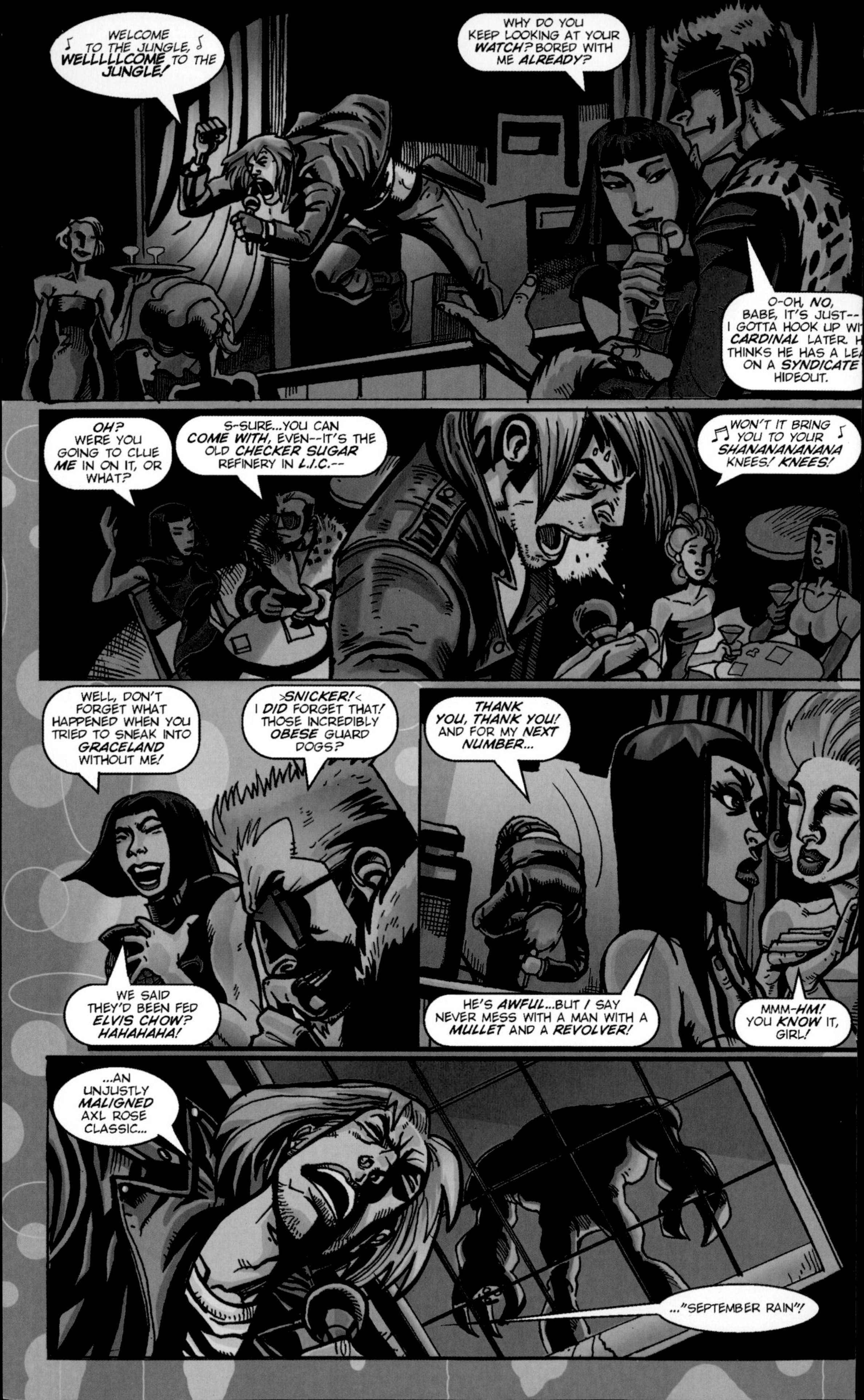
♪ WELCOME TO THE JUNGLE, ♪ WELLLLLCOME TO THE JUNGLE!
WHY DO YOU KEEP LOOKING AT YOUR WATCH? BORED WITH ME ALREADY?
O-OH, NO, BABE, IT'S JUST-- I GOTTA HOOK UP WIT CARDINAL LATER. H THINKS HE HAS A LEA ON A SYNDICATE HIDEOUT.
OH? WERE YOU GOING TO CLUE ME IN ON IT, OR WHAT?
S-SURE...YOU CAN COME WITH, EVEN--IT'S THE OLD CHECKER SUGAR REFINERY IN L.I.C.--
♫ WON'T IT BRING YOU TO YOUR ♪ SHANANANANANANA KNEES! KNEES!
WELL, DON'T FORGET WHAT HAPPENED WHEN YOU TRIED TO SNEAK INTO GRACELAND WITHOUT ME!
>SNICKER!< I DID FORGET THAT! THOSE INCREDIBLY OBESE GUARD DOGS?
WE SAID THEY'D BEEN FED ELVIS CHOW? HAHAHAHA!
THANK YOU, THANK YOU! AND FOR MY NEXT NUMBER...
HE'S AWFUL...BUT I SAY NEVER MESS WITH A MAN WITH A MULLET AND A REVOLVER!
MMM-HM! YOU KNOW IT, GIRL!
...AN UNJUSTLY MALIGNED AXL ROSE CLASSIC...
..."SEPTEMBER RAIN"!

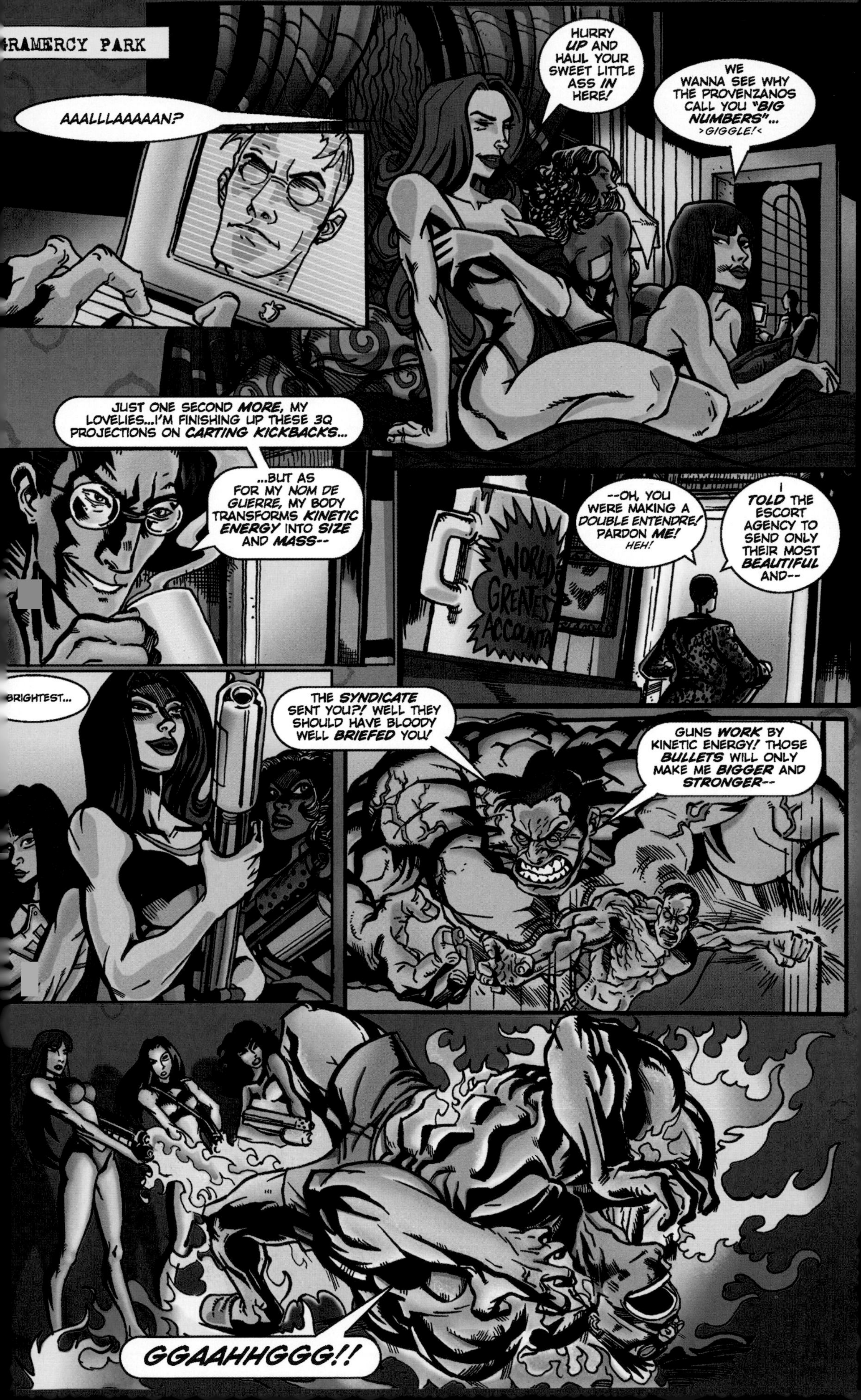
GRAMERCY PARK
AAALLLAAAAAN?
HURRY UP AND HAUL YOUR SWEET LITTLE ASS IN HERE!
WE WANNA SEE WHY THE PROVENZANOS CALL YOU "BIG NUMBERS"... >GIGGLE!<
JUST ONE SECOND MORE, MY LOVELIES...I'M FINISHING UP THESE 3Q PROJECTIONS ON CARTING KICKBACKS...
...BUT AS FOR MY NOM DE GUERRE, MY BODY TRANSFORMS KINETIC ENERGY INTO SIZE AND MASS--
WORLD'S GREATEST ACCOUNTA
--OH, YOU WERE MAKING A DOUBLE ENTENDRE! PARDON ME! HEH!
I TOLD THE ESCORT AGENCY TO SEND ONLY THEIR MOST BEAUTIFUL AND--
BRIGHTEST...
THE SYNDICATE SENT YOU?! WELL THEY SHOULD HAVE BLOODY WELL BRIEFED YOU!
GUNS WORK BY KINETIC ENERGY! THOSE BULLETS WILL ONLY MAKE ME BIGGER AND STRONGER--
GGAAHHGGG!!

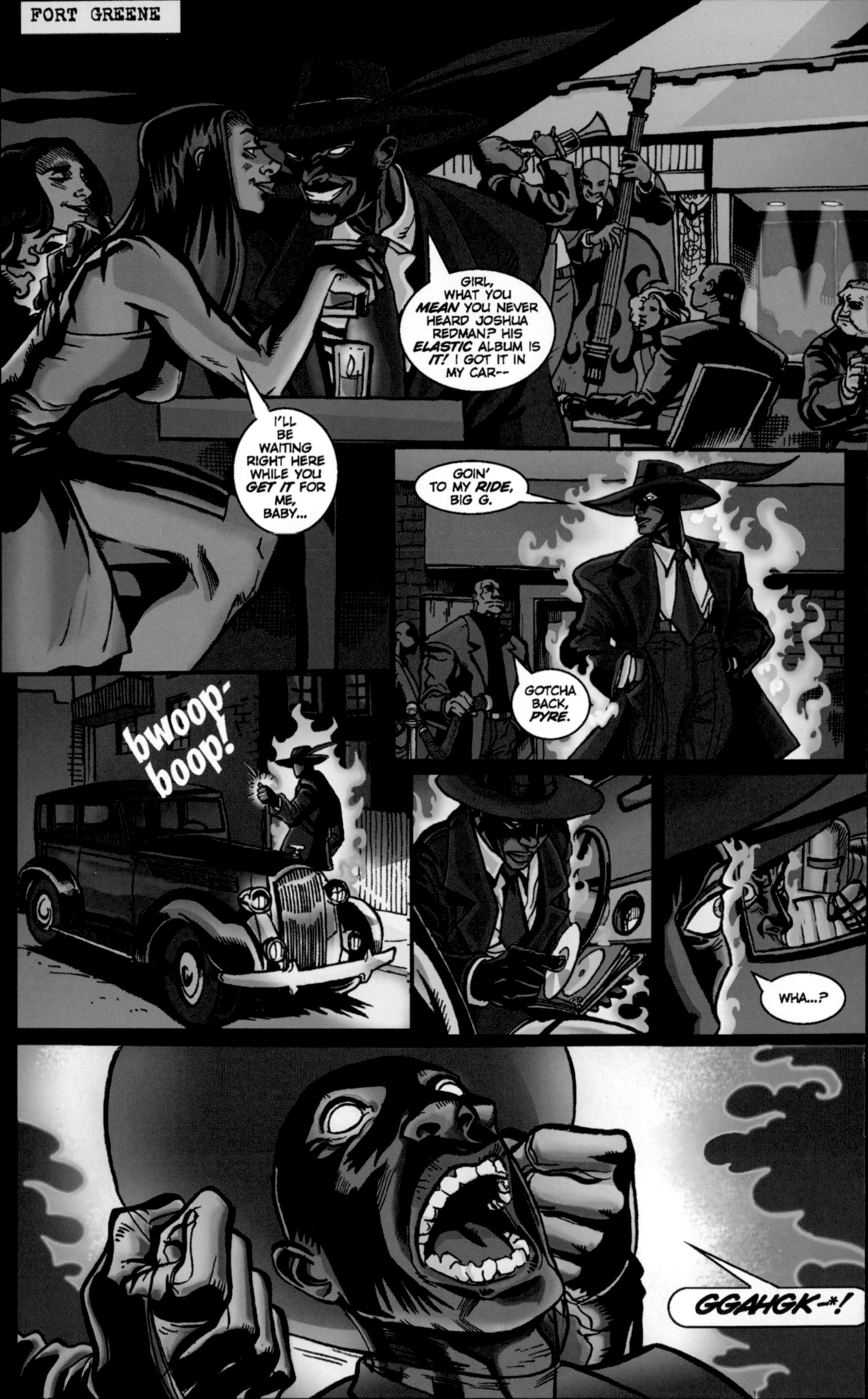
FORT GREENE
GIRL, WHAT YOU MEAN YOU NEVER HEARD JOSHUA REDMAN? HIS ELASTIC ALBUM IS IT! I GOT IT IN MY CAR--
I'LL BE WAITING RIGHT HERE WHILE YOU GET IT FOR ME, BABY...
GOIN' TO MY RIDE, BIG G.
GOTCHA BACK, PYRE.
bwoop-boop!
WHA...?
GGAHGK-*!

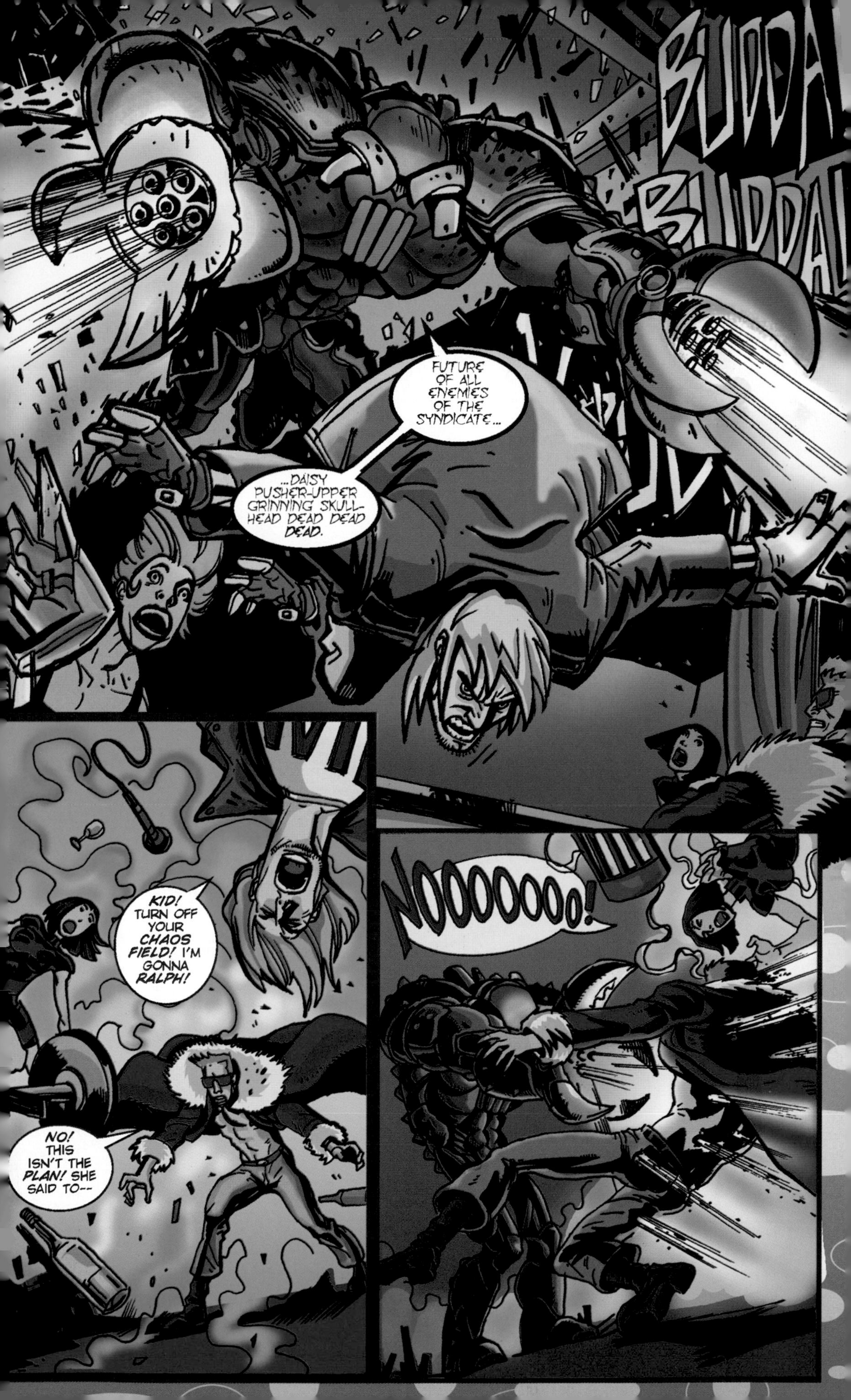

BUDDA
BUDDA
FUTURE OF ALL ENEMIES OF THE SYNDICATE...
...DAISY PUSHER-UPPER GRINNING SKULL-HEAD DEAD DEAD DEAD.
KID! TURN OFF YOUR CHAOS FIELD! I'M GONNA RALPH!
NO! THIS ISN'T THE PLAN! SHE SAID TO--
NOOOOOOO!

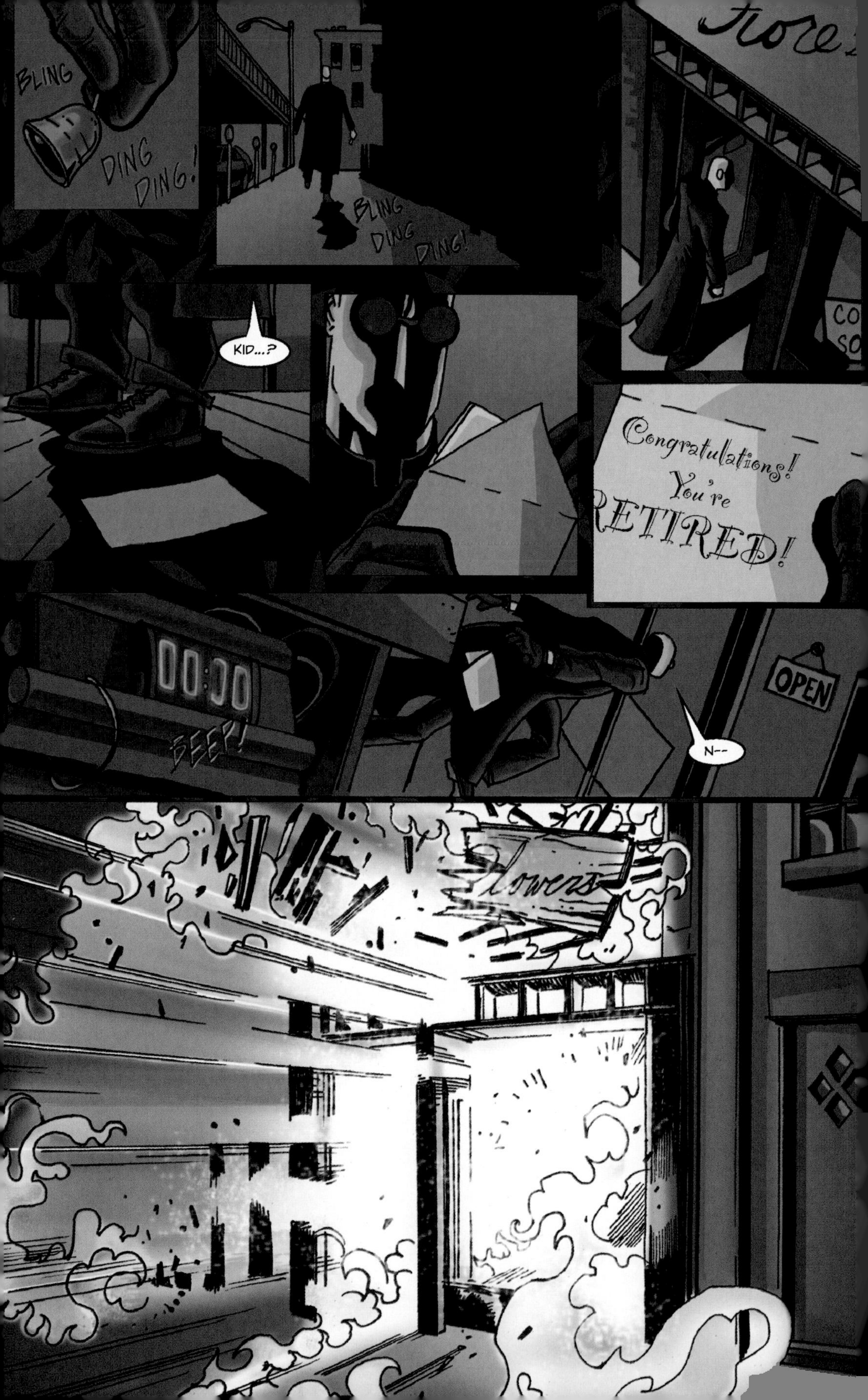
BLING
DING DING!
BLING DING DING!
KID...?
Congratulations! You're RETIRED!
BEEP!
OPEN
N--
Flowers

BITTER FRUIT PART 2

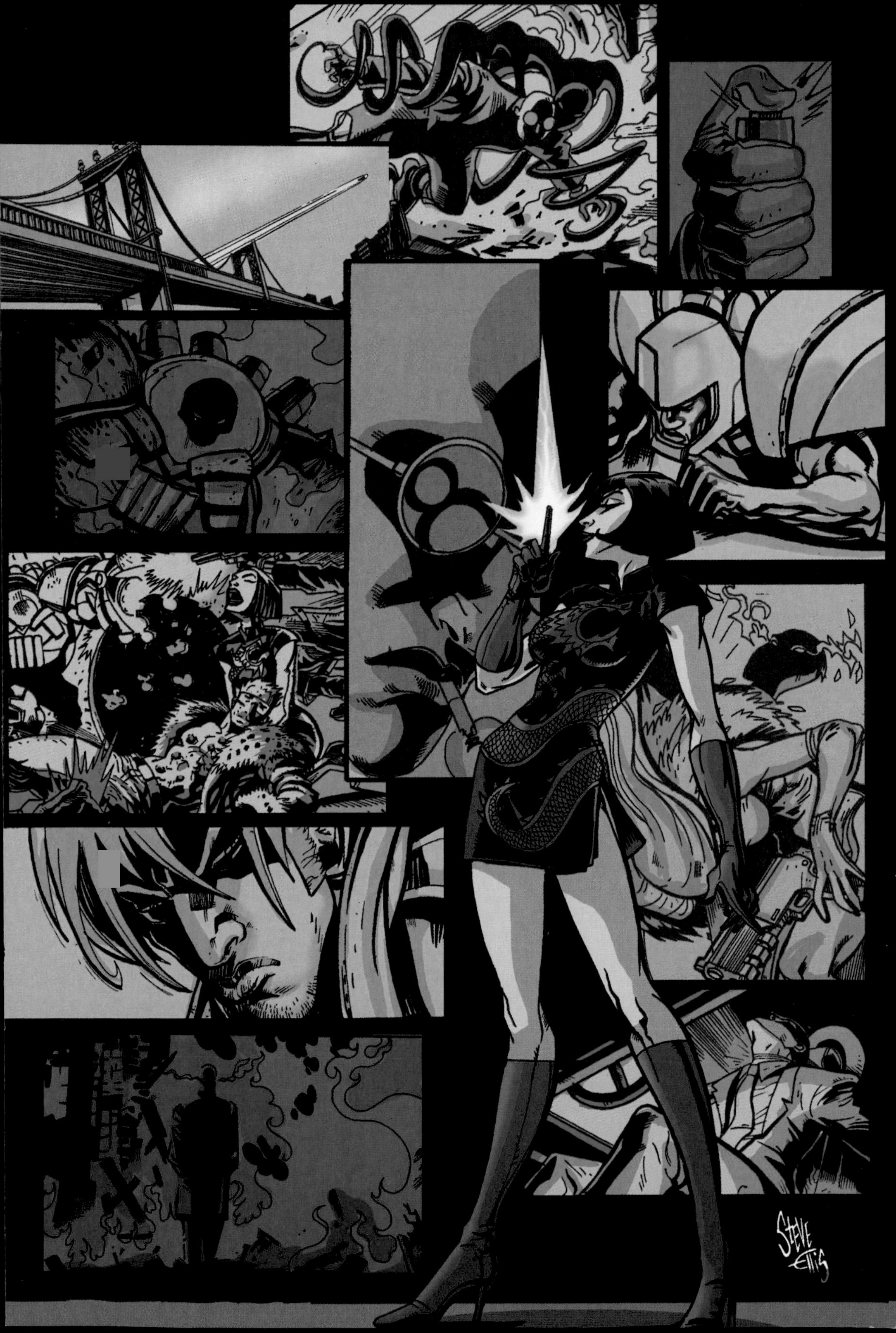
STEVE
ELLIS

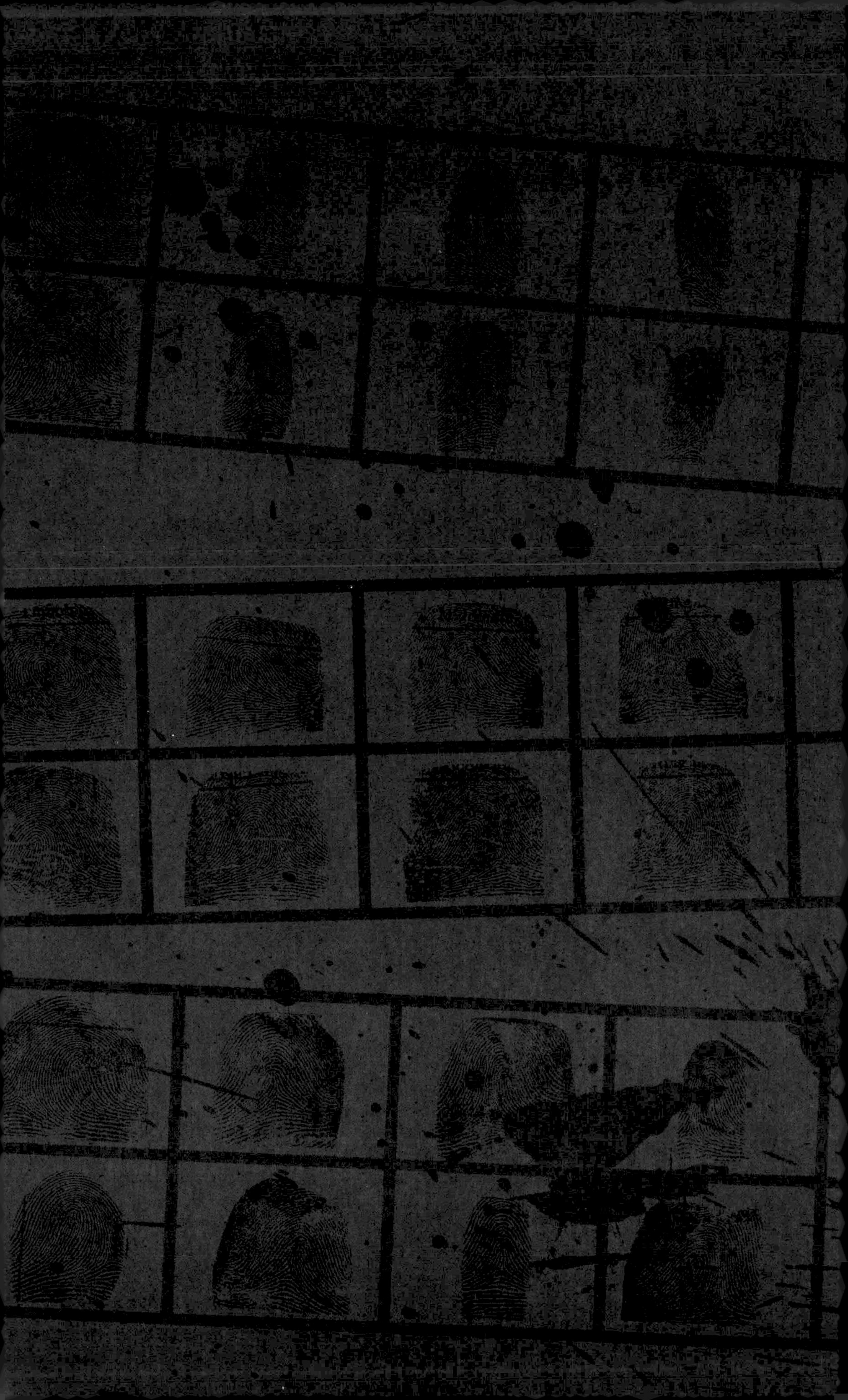

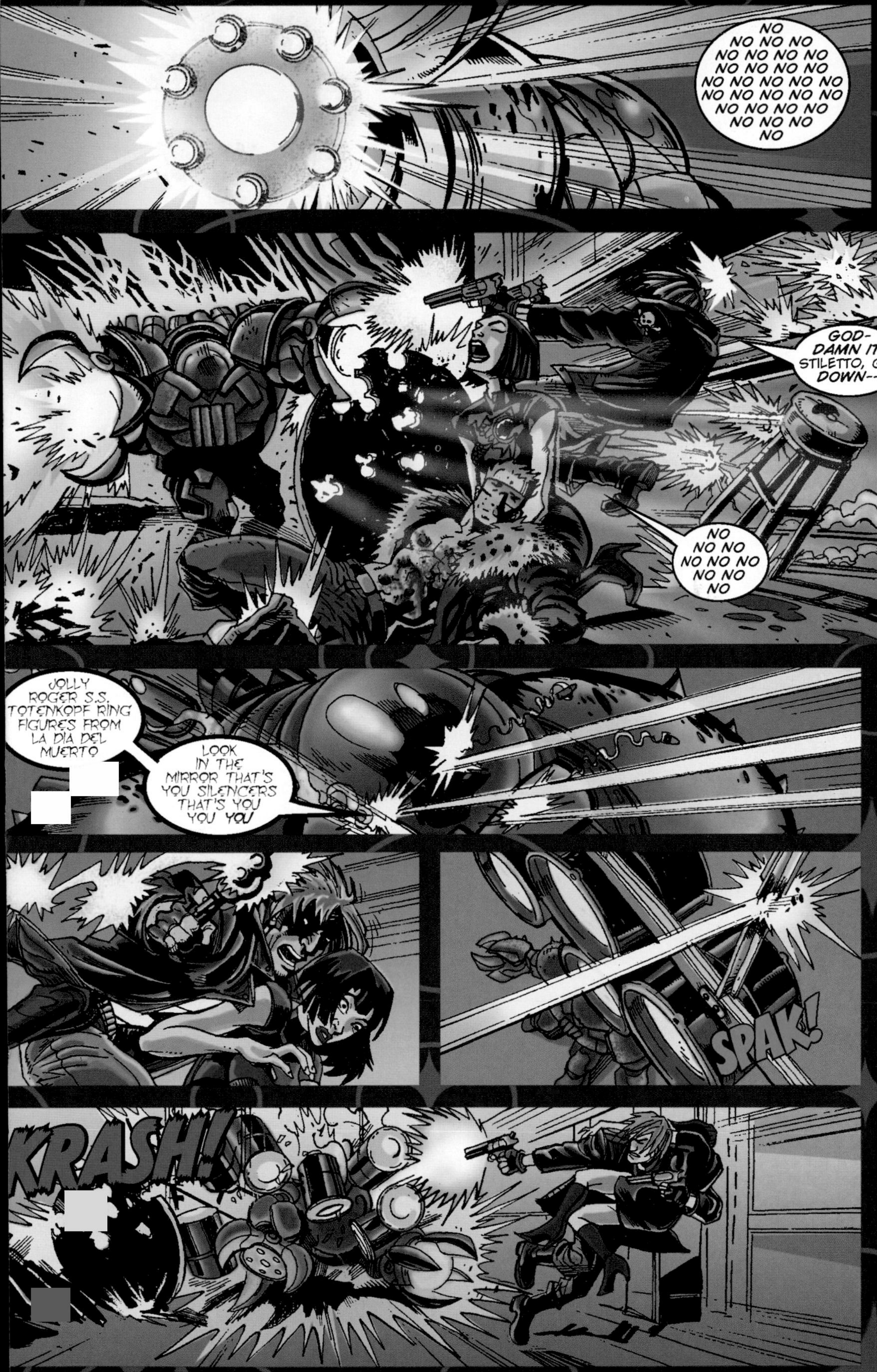
NO
NO NO NO
NO NO NO NO
NO NO NO NO
NO NO NO NO NO
NO NO NO NO NO
NO NO NO NO
NO NO NO
NO
GOD-DAMN IT, STILETTO, GET DOWN--
NO
NO NO
NO NO NO
NO NO
NO
JOLLY ROGER S.S. TOTENKOPF RING FIGURES FROM LA DIA DEL MUERTO
LOOK IN THE MIRROR THAT'S YOU SILENCERS THAT'S YOU YOU YOU
SPAK!
KRASH!

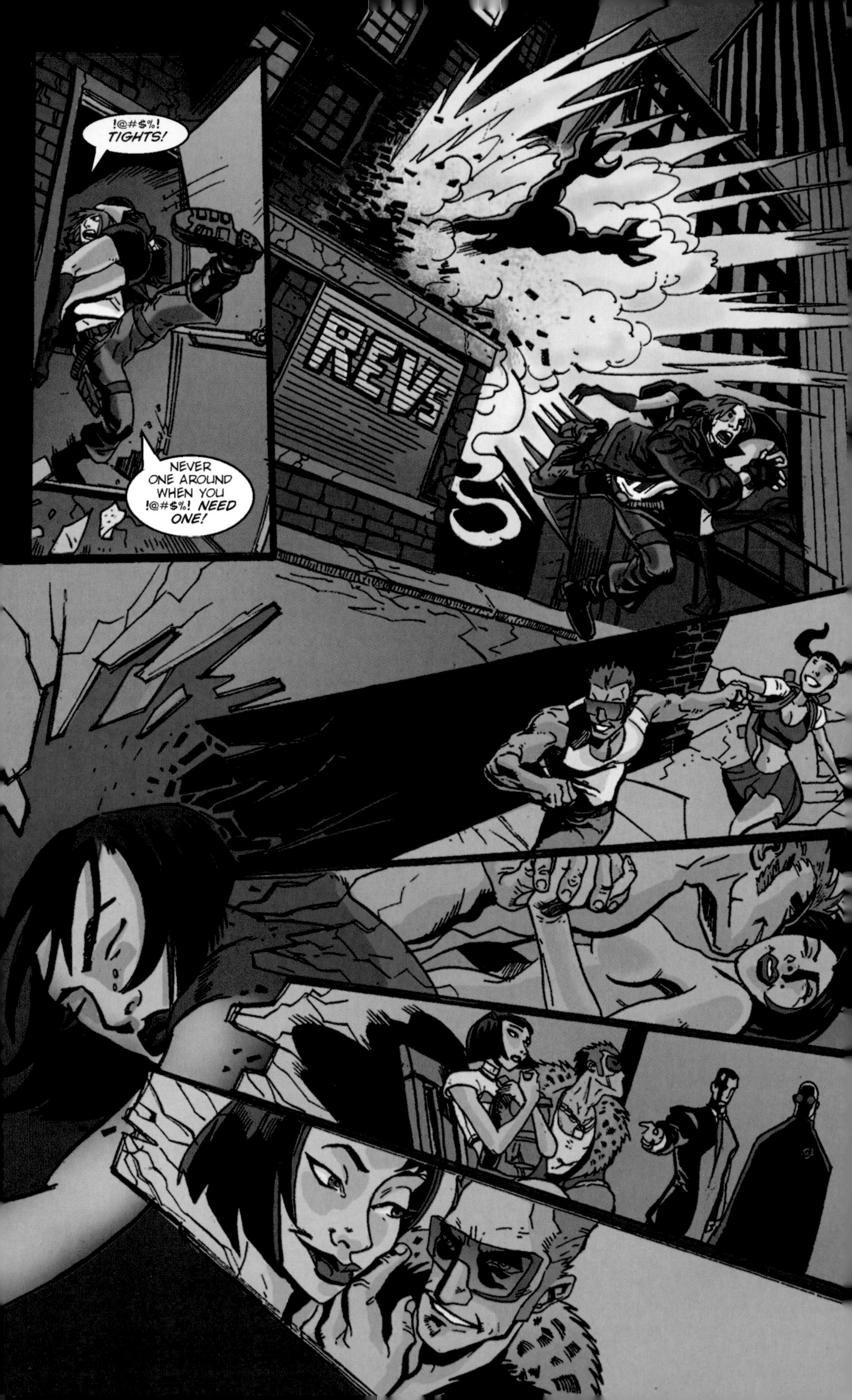
!@#$%! TIGHTS!
NEVER ONE AROUND WHEN YOU !@#$%! NEED ONE!
REV'S

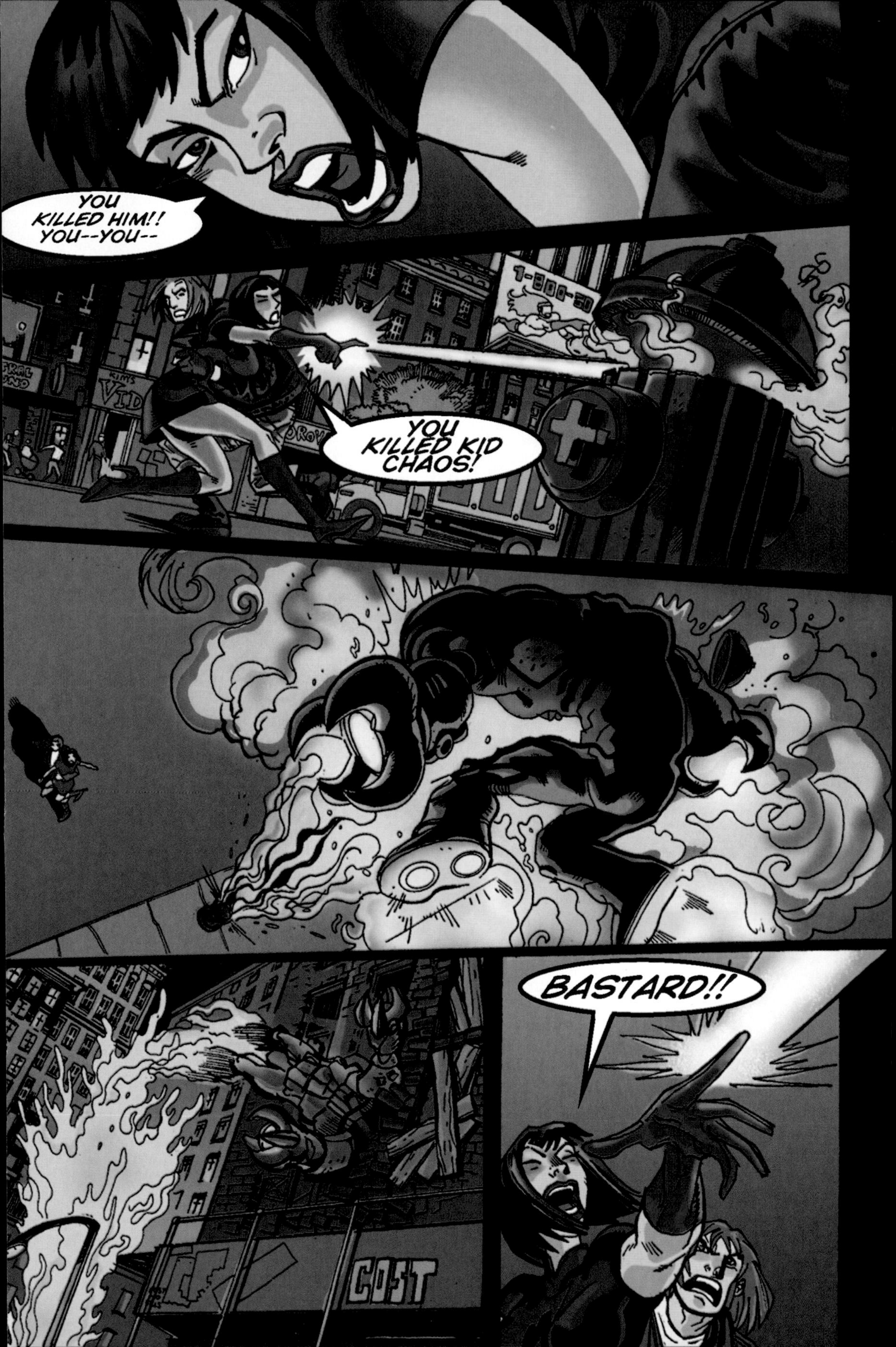
YOU KILLED HIM!! YOU--YOU--
YOU KILLED KID CHAOS!
1-800-
VID
COST
BASTARD!!

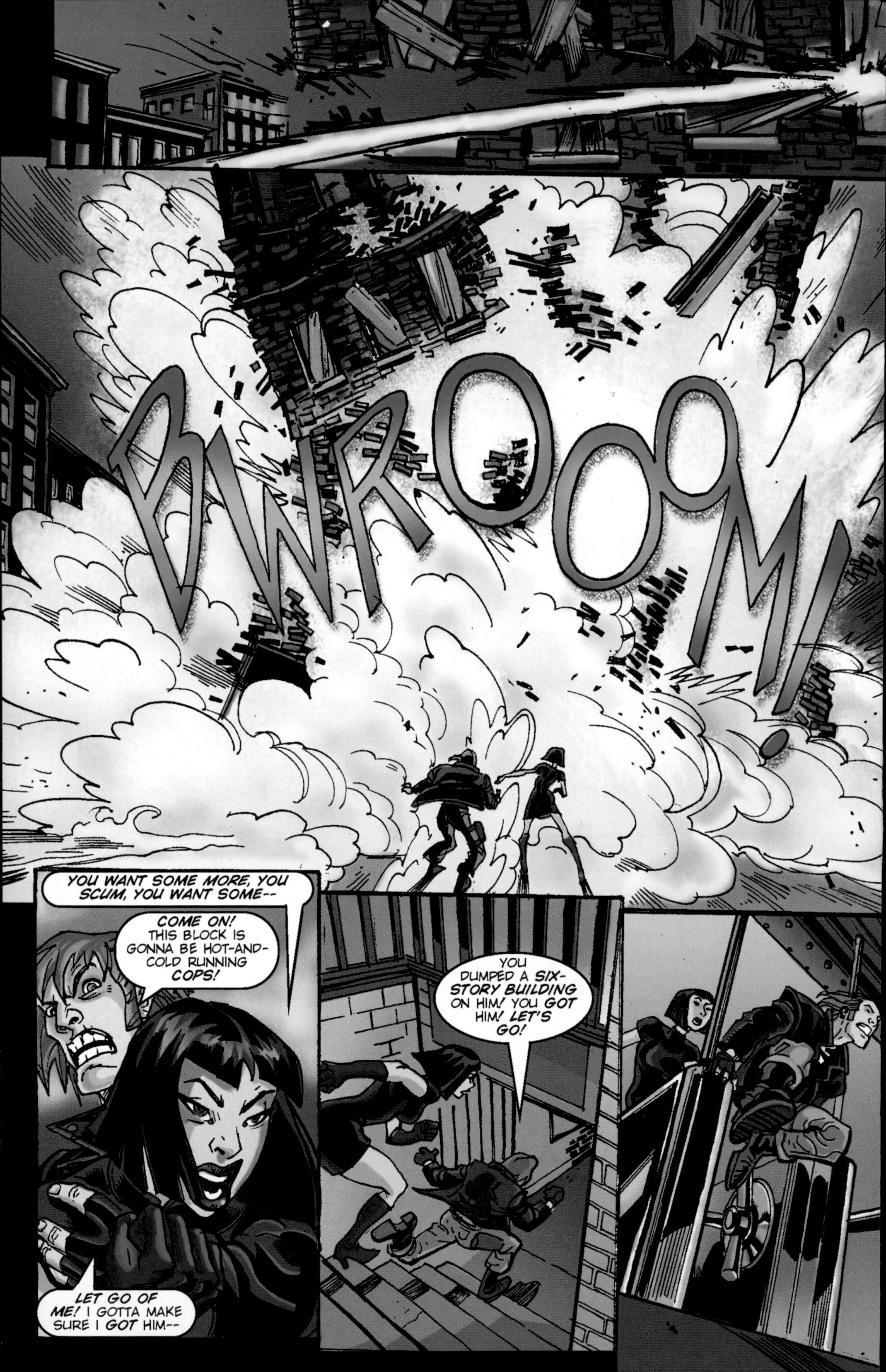
BWROOOM!
YOU WANT SOME MORE, YOU SCUM, YOU WANT SOME--
COME ON! THIS BLOCK IS GONNA BE HOT-AND-COLD RUNNING COPS!
LET GO OF ME! I GOTTA MAKE SURE I GOT HIM--
YOU DUMPED A SIX-STORY BUILDING ON HIM! YOU GOT HIM! LET'S GO!

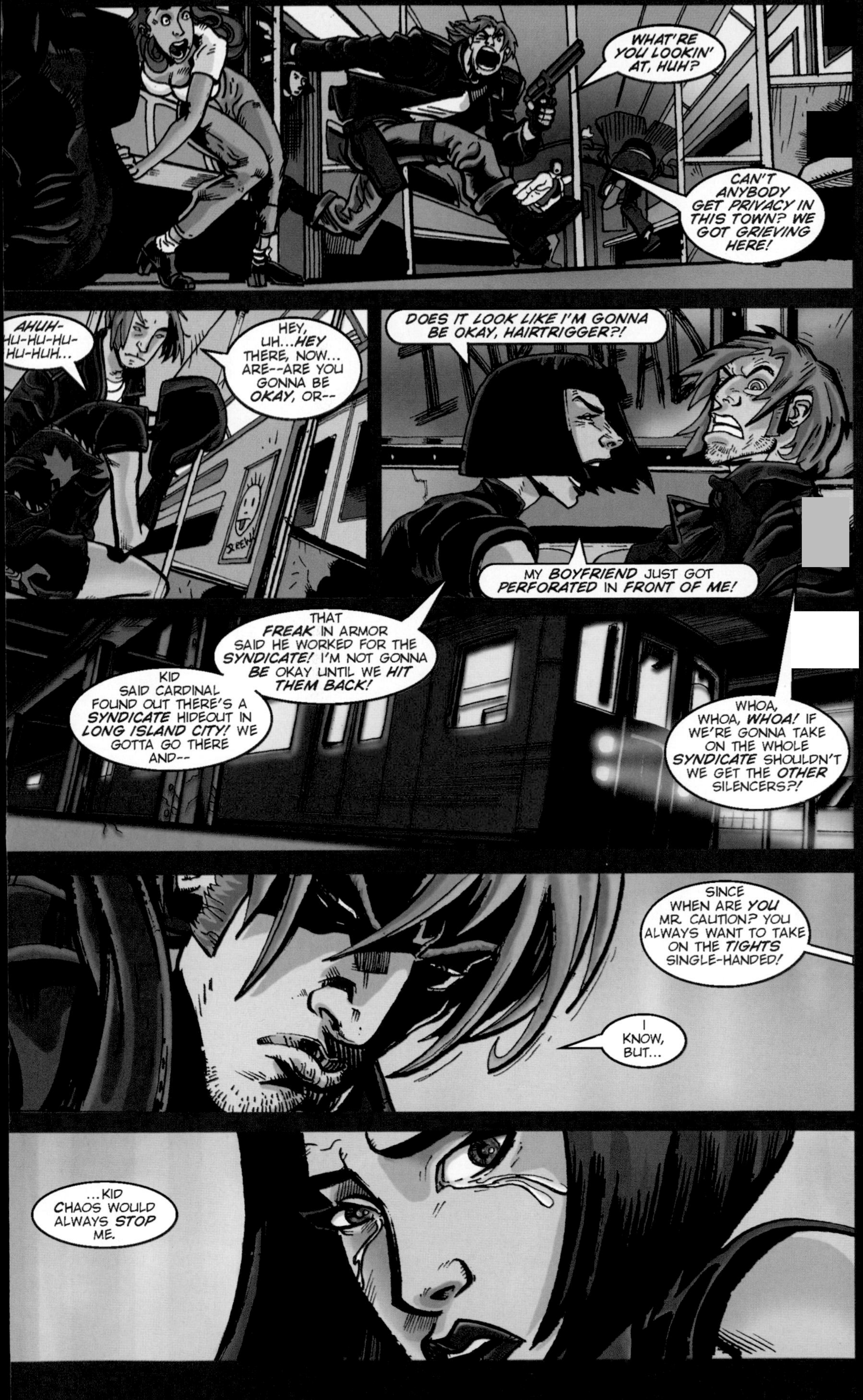
WHAT'RE YOU LOOKIN' AT, HUH?
CAN'T ANYBODY GET PRIVACY IN THIS TOWN? WE GOT GRIEVING HERE!
AHUH-HU-HU-HU-HU-HUH...
HEY, UH...HEY THERE, NOW... ARE--ARE YOU GONNA BE OKAY, OR--
DOES IT LOOK LIKE I'M GONNA BE OKAY, HAIRTRIGGER?!
MY BOYFRIEND JUST GOT PERFORATED IN FRONT OF ME!
THAT FREAK IN ARMOR SAID HE WORKED FOR THE SYNDICATE! I'M NOT GONNA BE OKAY UNTIL WE HIT THEM BACK!
KID SAID CARDINAL FOUND OUT THERE'S A SYNDICATE HIDEOUT IN LONG ISLAND CITY! WE GOTTA GO THERE AND--
WHOA, WHOA, WHOA! IF WE'RE GONNA TAKE ON THE WHOLE SYNDICATE SHOULDN'T WE GET THE OTHER SILENCERS?!
SINCE WHEN ARE YOU MR. CAUTION? YOU ALWAYS WANT TO TAKE ON THE TIGHTS SINGLE-HANDED!
I KNOW, BUT...
...KID CHAOS WOULD ALWAYS STOP ME.

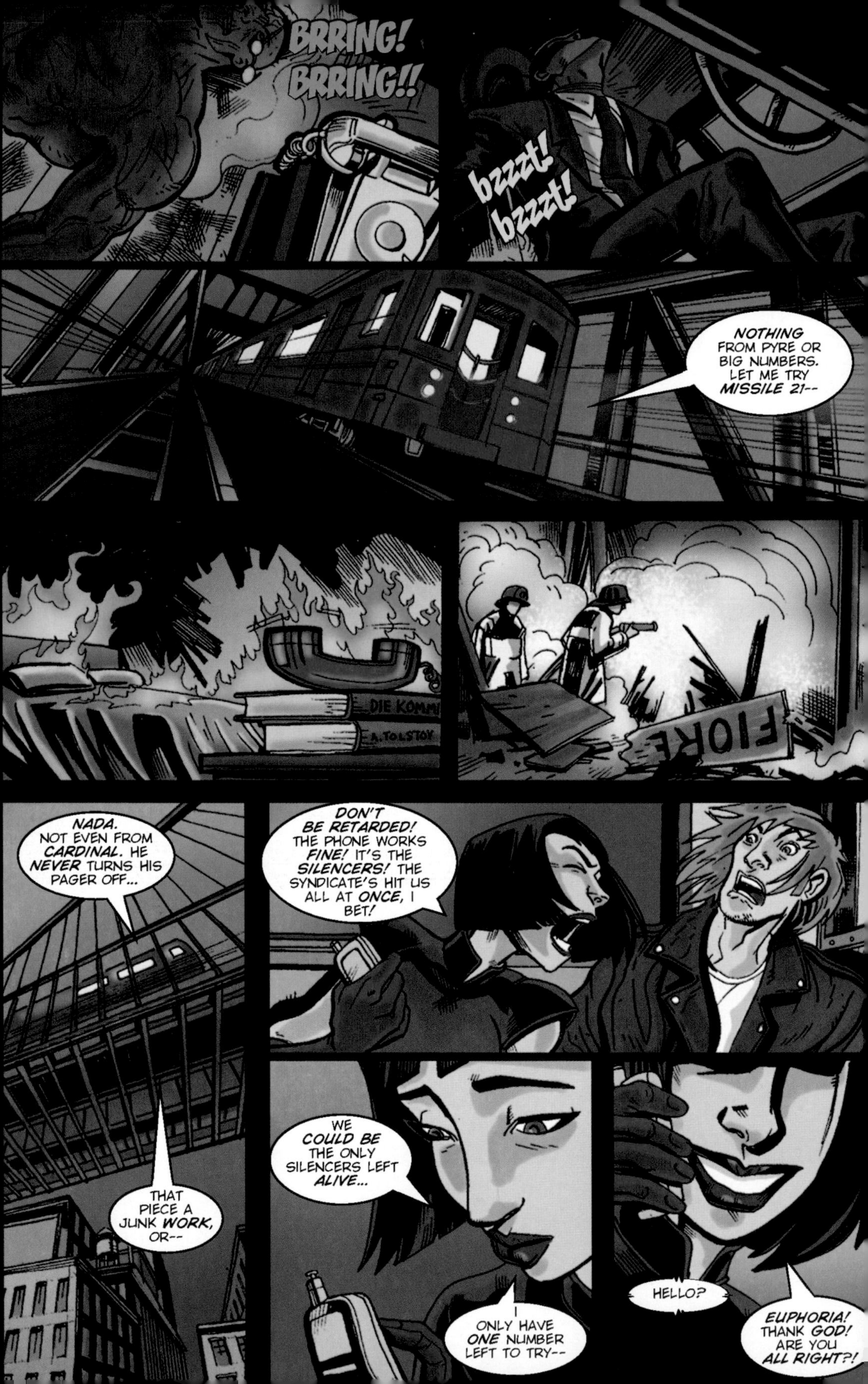
BRRING!
BRRING!!
bzzzt!
bzzzt!
NOTHING FROM PYRE OR BIG NUMBERS. LET ME TRY MISSILE 21--
DIE KOMM
A. TOLSTOY
FIORE
NADA. NOT EVEN FROM CARDINAL. HE NEVER TURNS HIS PAGER OFF...
THAT PIECE A JUNK WORK, OR--
DON'T BE RETARDED! THE PHONE WORKS FINE! IT'S THE SILENCERS! THE SYNDICATE'S HIT US ALL AT ONCE, I BET!
WE COULD BE THE ONLY SILENCERS LEFT ALIVE...
I ONLY HAVE ONE NUMBER LEFT TO TRY--
HELLO?
EUPHORIA! THANK GOD! ARE YOU ALL RIGHT?!

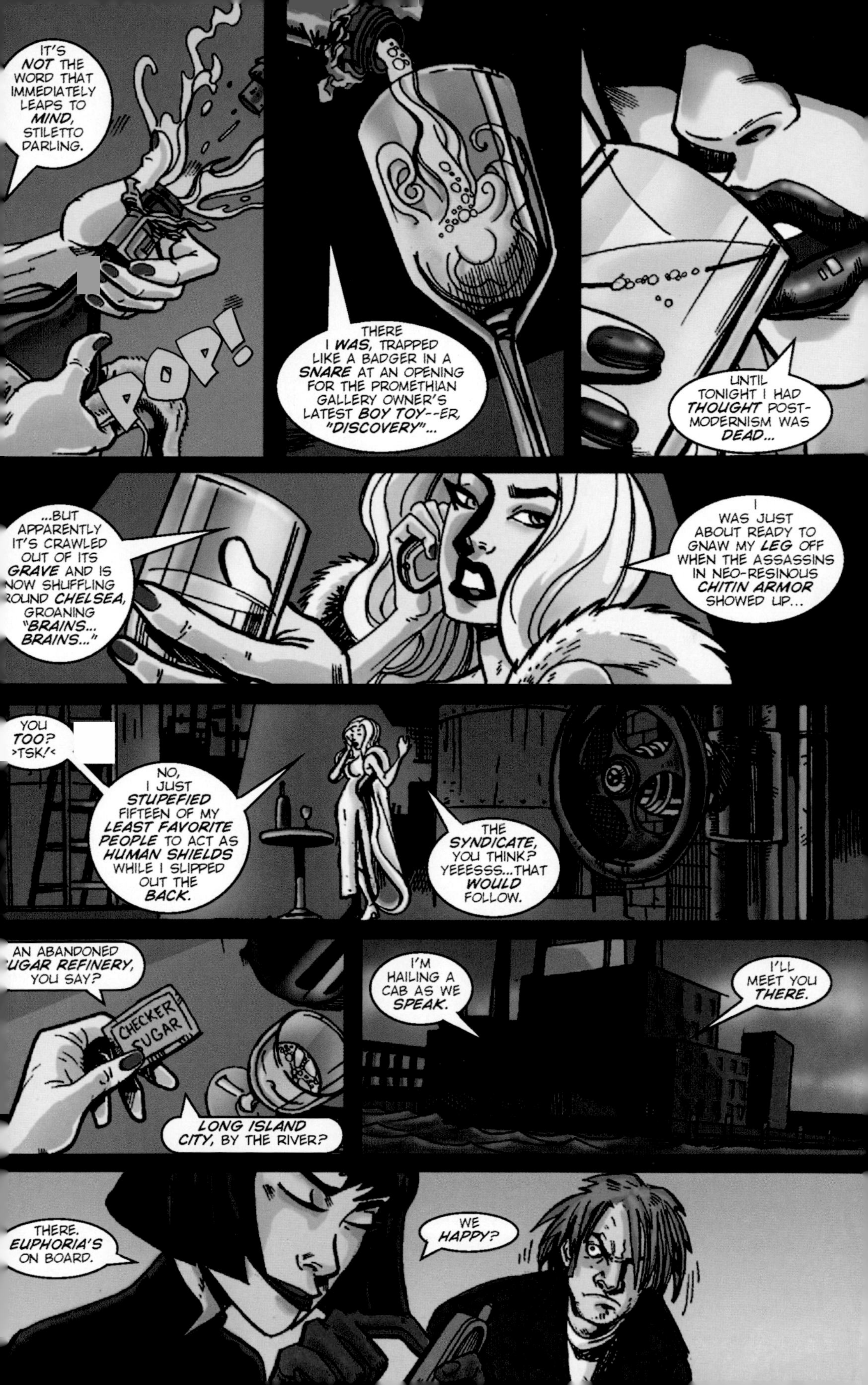

IT'S NOT THE WORD THAT IMMEDIATELY LEAPS TO MIND, STILETTO DARLING.
POP!
THERE I WAS, TRAPPED LIKE A BADGER IN A SNARE AT AN OPENING FOR THE PROMETHIAN GALLERY OWNER'S LATEST BOY TOY--ER, "DISCOVERY"...
UNTIL TONIGHT I HAD THOUGHT POST-MODERNISM WAS DEAD...
...BUT APPARENTLY IT'S CRAWLED OUT OF ITS GRAVE AND IS NOW SHUFFLING ROUND CHELSEA, GROANING "BRAINS... BRAINS..."
I WAS JUST ABOUT READY TO GNAW MY LEG OFF WHEN THE ASSASSINS IN NEO-RESINOUS CHITIN ARMOR SHOWED UP...
YOU TOO? >TSK!<
NO, I JUST STUPEFIED FIFTEEN OF MY LEAST FAVORITE PEOPLE TO ACT AS HUMAN SHIELDS WHILE I SLIPPED OUT THE BACK.
THE SYNDICATE, YOU THINK? YEEESSS...THAT WOULD FOLLOW.
AN ABANDONED SUGAR REFINERY, YOU SAY?
CHECKER SUGAR
LONG ISLAND CITY, BY THE RIVER?
I'M HAILING A CAB AS WE SPEAK.
I'LL MEET YOU THERE.
THERE. EUPHORIA'S ON BOARD.
WE HAPPY?

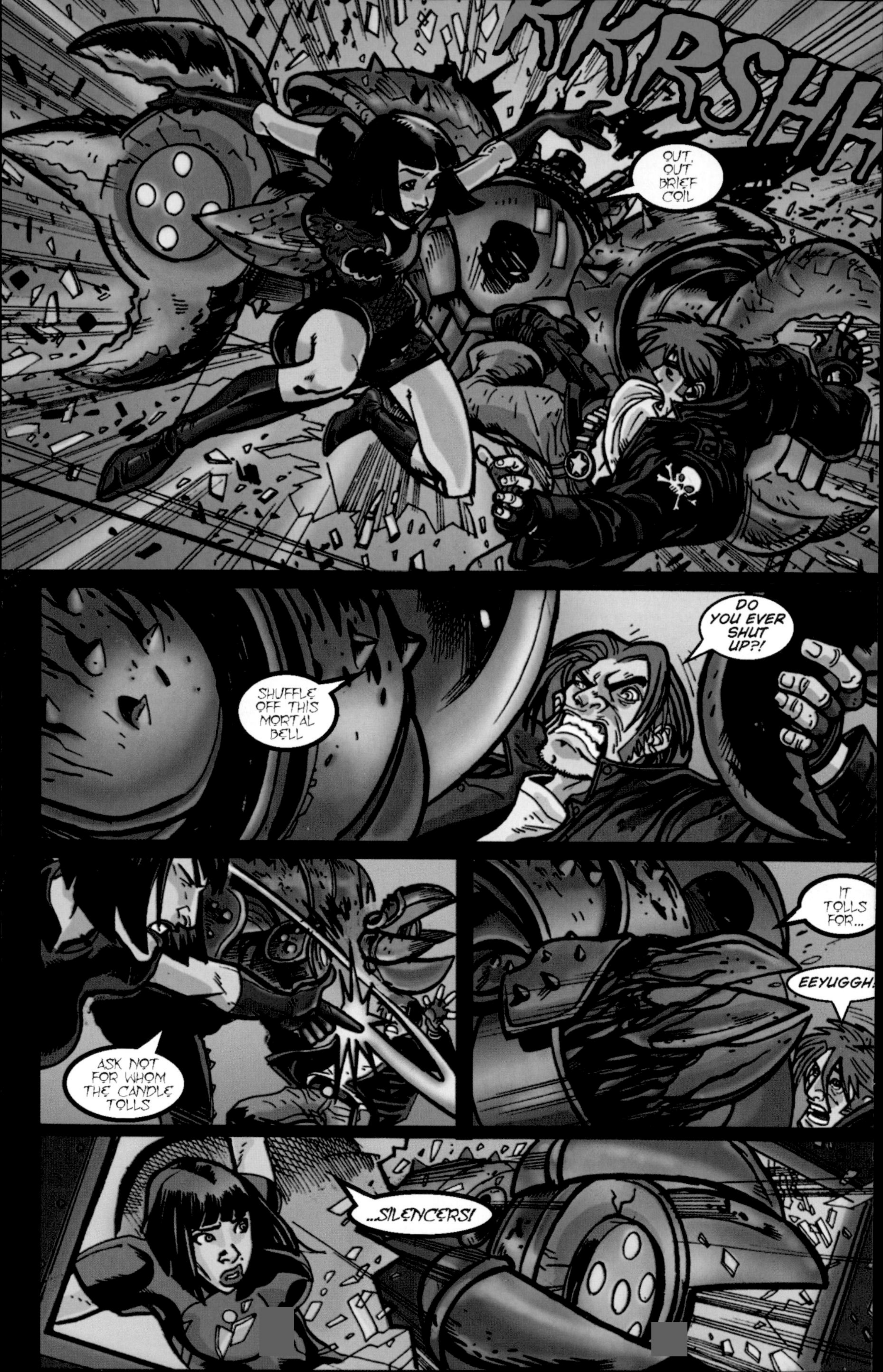
KRRSHH
OUT, OUT BRIEF COIL
SHUFFLE OFF THIS MORTAL BELL
DO YOU EVER SHUT UP?!
ASK NOT FOR WHOM THE CANDLE TOLLS
IT TOLLS FOR...
EEYUGGH!
...SILENCERS!

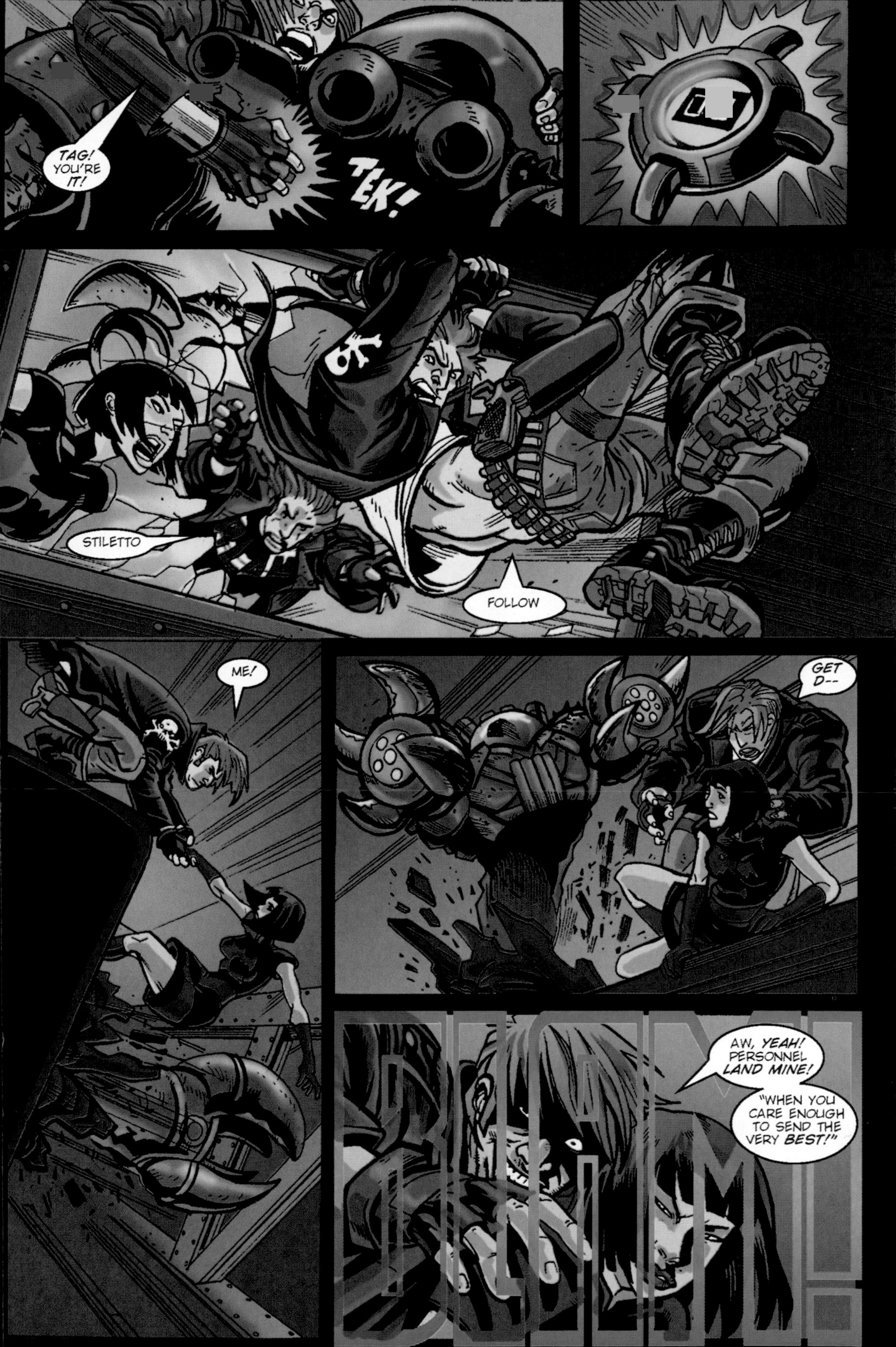
TAG! YOU'RE IT!
TEK!
STILETTO
FOLLOW
ME!
GET D--
AW, YEAH! PERSONNEL LAND MINE!
"WHEN YOU CARE ENOUGH TO SEND THE VERY BEST!"

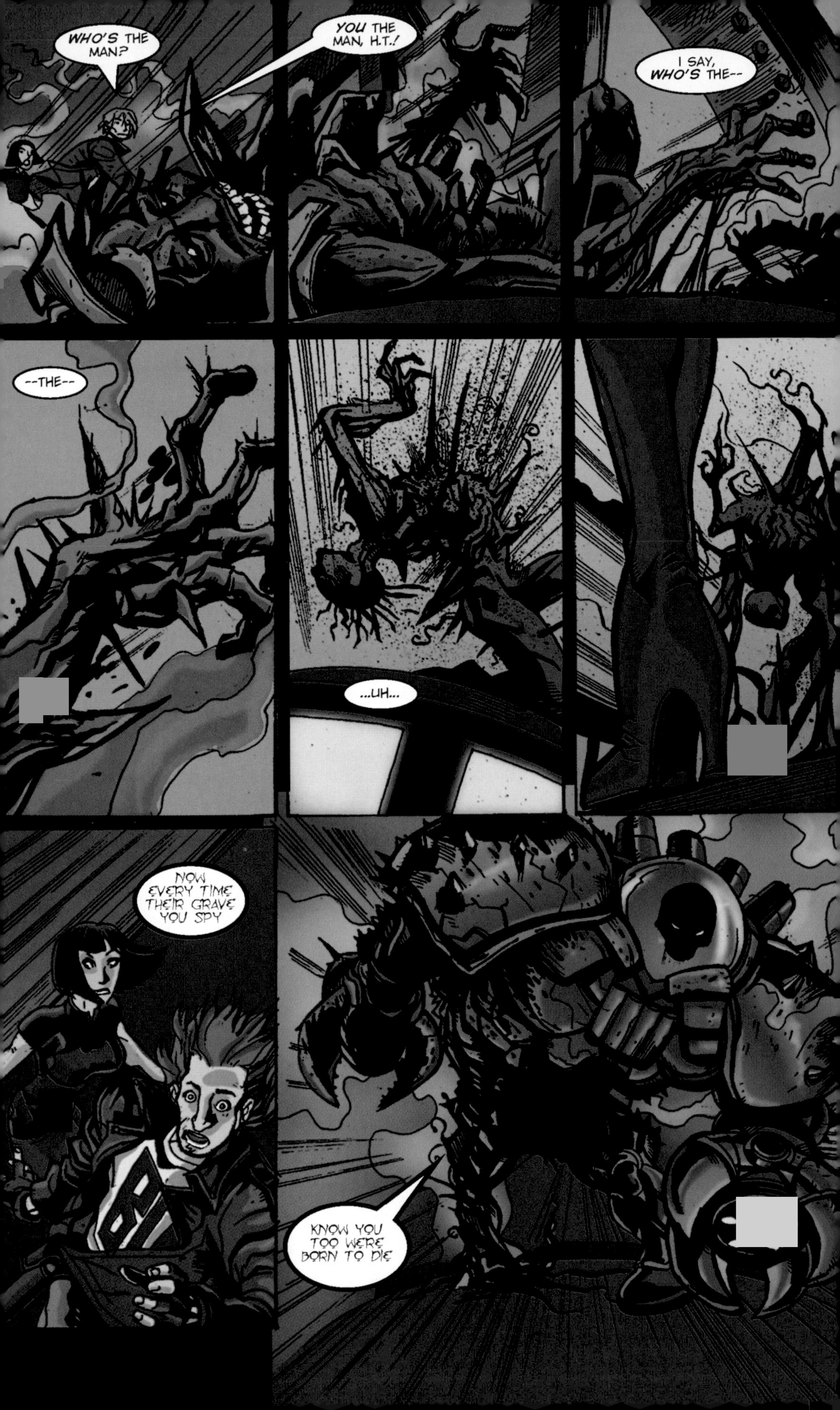
WHO'S THE MAN?
YOU THE MAN, H.T.!
I SAY, WHO'S THE--
--THE--
...UH...
NOW EVERY TIME THEIR GRAVE YOU SPY
KNOW YOU TOO WERE BORN TO DIE

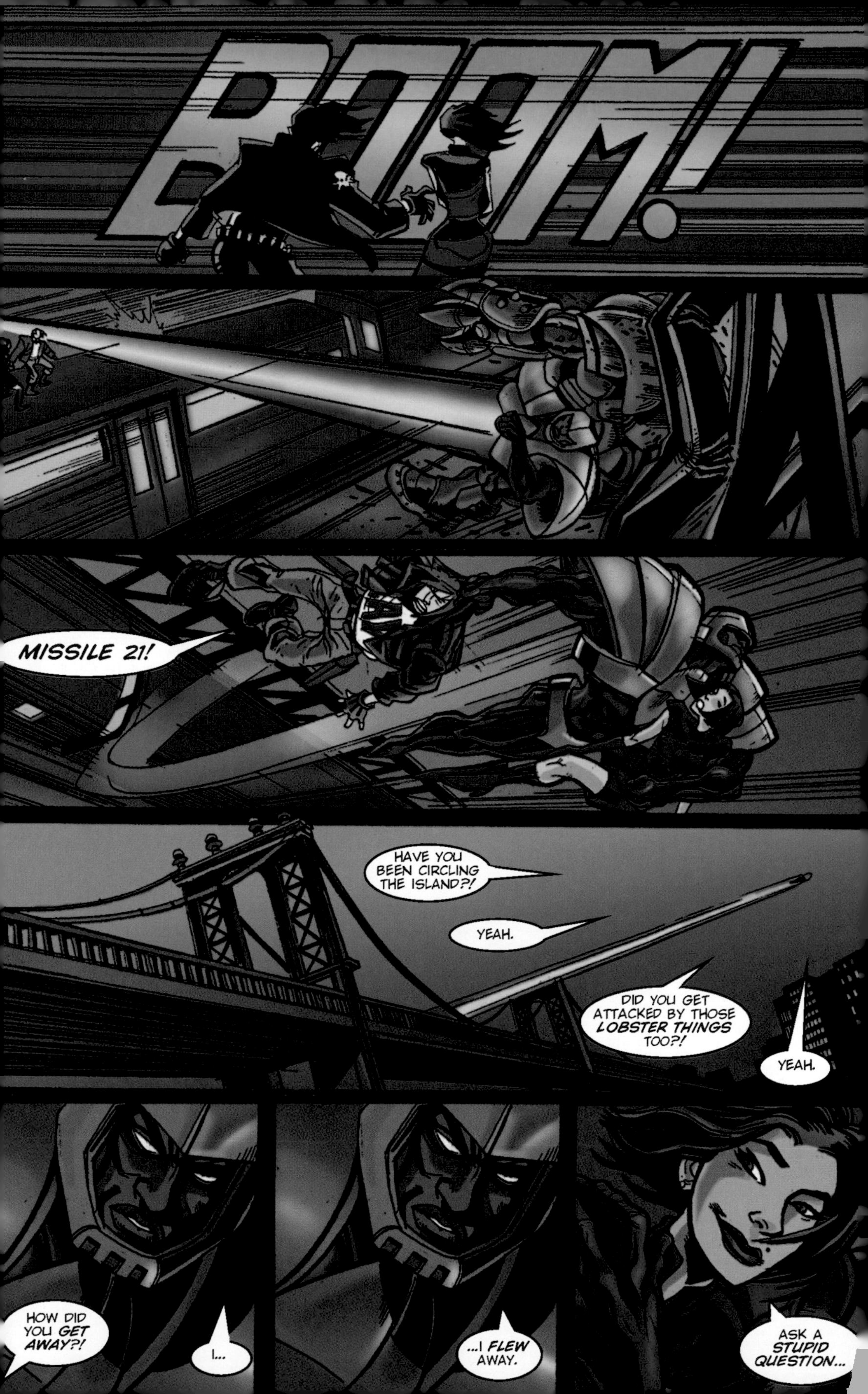
BOOM!
MISSILE 21!
HAVE YOU BEEN CIRCLING THE ISLAND?!
YEAH.
DID YOU GET ATTACKED BY THOSE LOBSTER THINGS TOO?!
YEAH.
HOW DID YOU GET AWAY?!
I...
...I FLEW AWAY.
ASK A STUPID QUESTION...

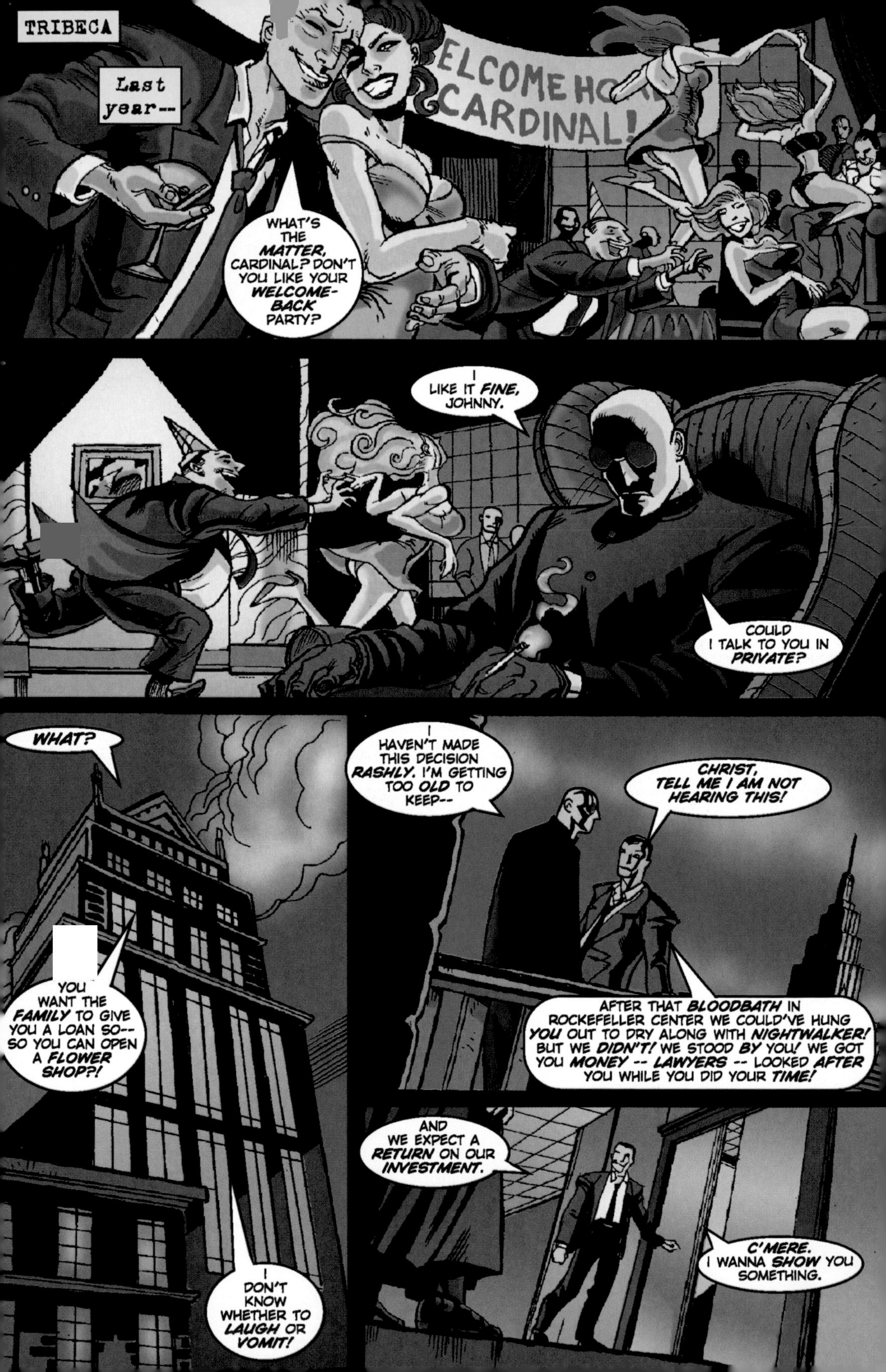

TRIBECA
Last year--
WELCOME HO[ME] CARDINAL!
WHAT'S THE MATTER, CARDINAL? DON'T YOU LIKE YOUR WELCOME-BACK PARTY?
I LIKE IT FINE, JOHNNY.
COULD I TALK TO YOU IN PRIVATE?
WHAT?
YOU WANT THE FAMILY TO GIVE YOU A LOAN SO-- SO YOU CAN OPEN A FLOWER SHOP?!
I DON'T KNOW WHETHER TO LAUGH OR VOMIT!
I HAVEN'T MADE THIS DECISION RASHLY. I'M GETTING TOO OLD TO KEEP--
CHRIST, TELL ME I AM NOT HEARING THIS!
AFTER THAT BLOODBATH IN ROCKEFELLER CENTER WE COULD'VE HUNG YOU OUT TO DRY ALONG WITH NIGHTWALKER! BUT WE DIDN'T! WE STOOD BY YOU! WE GOT YOU MONEY -- LAWYERS -- LOOKED AFTER YOU WHILE YOU DID YOUR TIME!
AND WE EXPECT A RETURN ON OUR INVESTMENT.
C'MERE. I WANNA SHOW YOU SOMETHING.

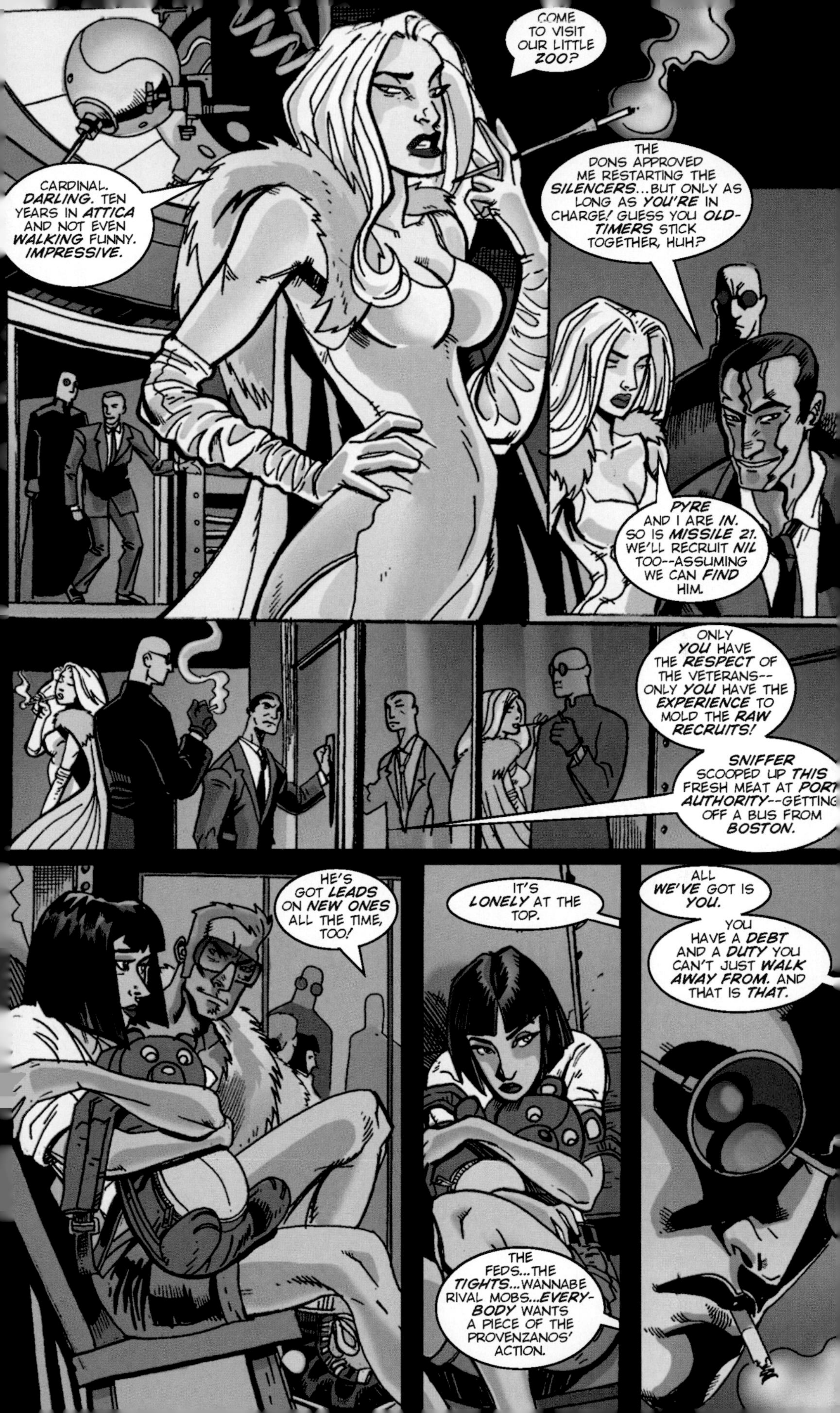

COME TO VISIT OUR LITTLE ZOO?
CARDINAL. DARLING. TEN YEARS IN ATTICA AND NOT EVEN WALKING FUNNY. IMPRESSIVE.
THE DONS APPROVED ME RESTARTING THE SILENCERS...BUT ONLY AS LONG AS YOU'RE IN CHARGE! GUESS YOU OLD-TIMERS STICK TOGETHER, HUH?
PYRE AND I ARE IN. SO IS MISSILE 21. WE'LL RECRUIT NIL TOO--ASSUMING WE CAN FIND HIM.
ONLY YOU HAVE THE RESPECT OF THE VETERANS--ONLY YOU HAVE THE EXPERIENCE TO MOLD THE RAW RECRUITS!
SNIFFER SCOOPED UP THIS FRESH MEAT AT PORT AUTHORITY--GETTING OFF A BUS FROM BOSTON.
HE'S GOT LEADS ON NEW ONES ALL THE TIME, TOO!
IT'S LONELY AT THE TOP.
THE FEDS...THE TIGHTS...WANNABE RIVAL MOBS...EVERY-BODY WANTS A PIECE OF THE PROVENZANOS' ACTION.
ALL WE'VE GOT IS YOU.
YOU HAVE A DEBT AND A DUTY YOU CAN'T JUST WALK AWAY FROM. AND THAT IS THAT.

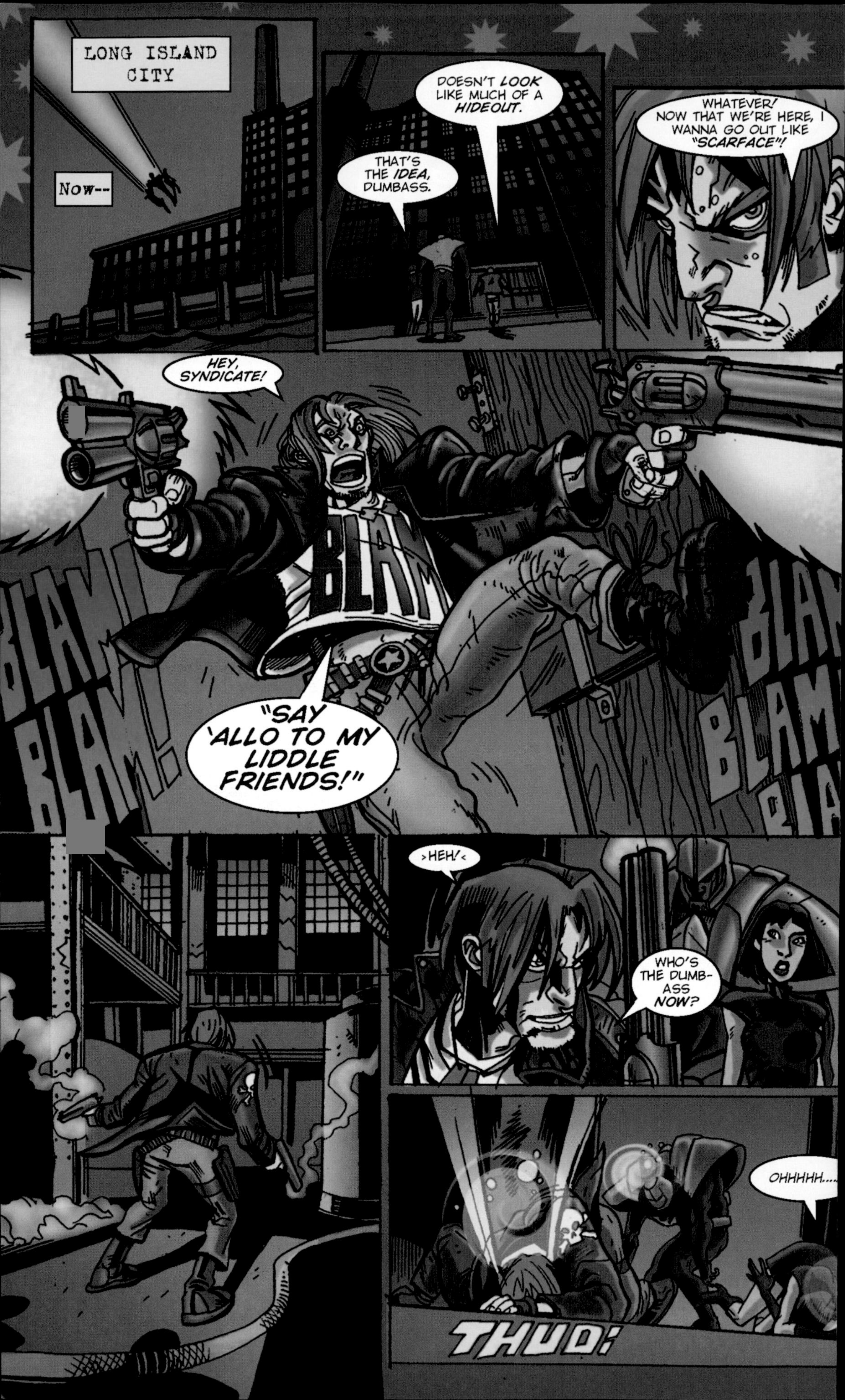

LONG ISLAND CITY
Now--
DOESN'T LOOK LIKE MUCH OF A HIDEOUT.
THAT'S THE IDEA, DUMBASS.
WHATEVER! NOW THAT WE'RE HERE, I WANNA GO OUT LIKE "SCARFACE"!
HEY, SYNDICATE!
"SAY 'ALLO TO MY LIDDLE FRIENDS!"
BLAM! BLAM!
BLAM BLAM
>HEH!<
WHO'S THE DUMB-ASS NOW?
OHHHHH....
THUD!

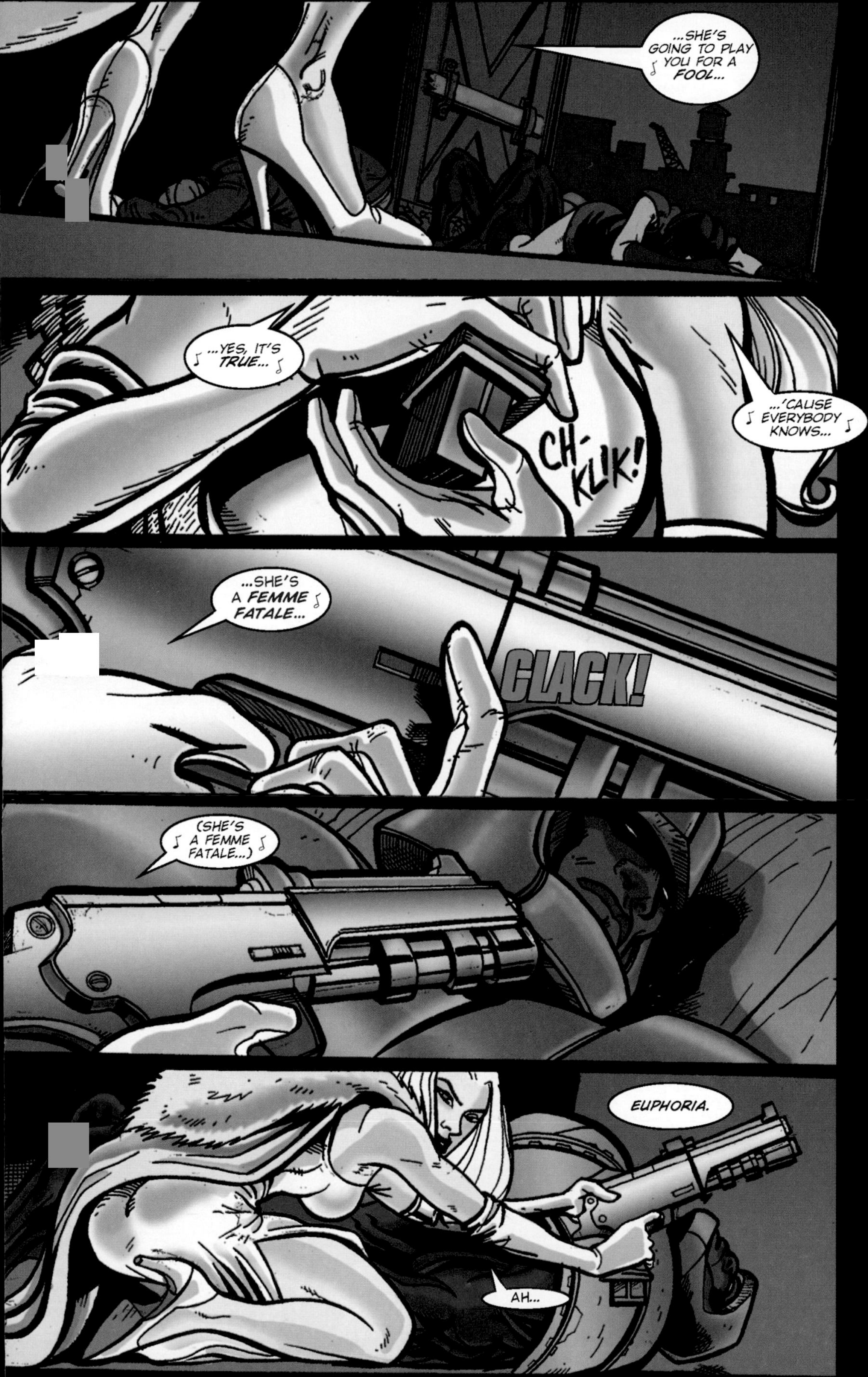
...SHE'S GOING TO PLAY YOU FOR A FOOL...
...YES, IT'S TRUE...
CH-KLIK!
...'CAUSE EVERYBODY KNOWS...
...SHE'S A FEMME FATALE...
CLACK!
(SHE'S A FEMME FATALE...)
EUPHORIA.
AH...

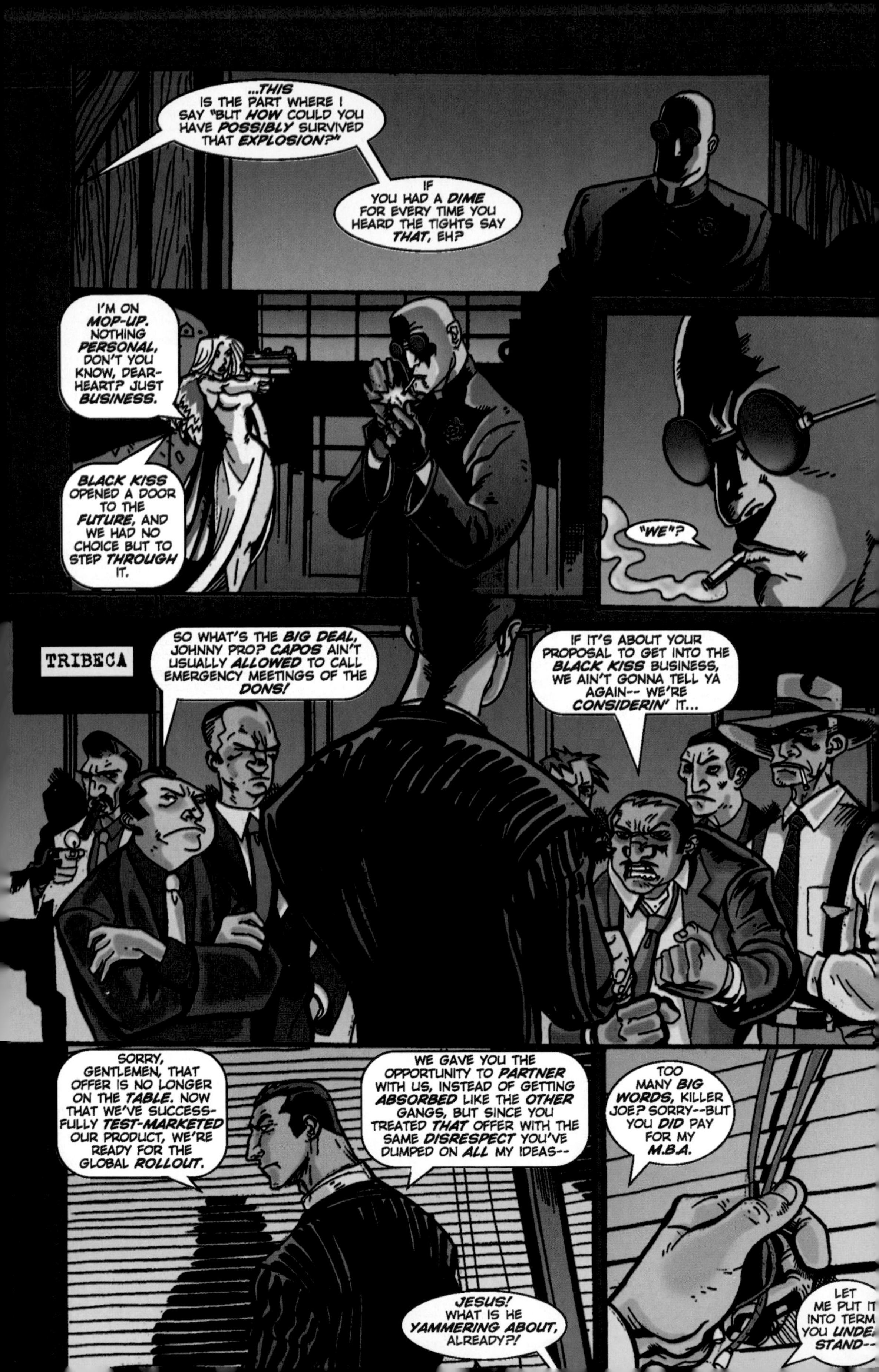

...THIS IS THE PART WHERE I SAY "BUT HOW COULD YOU HAVE POSSIBLY SURVIVED THAT EXPLOSION?"
IF YOU HAD A DIME FOR EVERY TIME YOU HEARD THE TIGHTS SAY THAT, EH?
I'M ON MOP-UP. NOTHING PERSONAL, DON'T YOU KNOW, DEAR-HEART? JUST BUSINESS.
BLACK KISS OPENED A DOOR TO THE FUTURE, AND WE HAD NO CHOICE BUT TO STEP THROUGH IT.
"WE"?
TRIBECA
SO WHAT'S THE BIG DEAL, JOHNNY PRO? CAPOS AIN'T USUALLY ALLOWED TO CALL EMERGENCY MEETINGS OF THE DONS!
IF IT'S ABOUT YOUR PROPOSAL TO GET INTO THE BLACK KISS BUSINESS, WE AIN'T GONNA TELL YA AGAIN-- WE'RE CONSIDERIN' IT...
SORRY, GENTLEMEN, THAT OFFER IS NO LONGER ON THE TABLE. NOW THAT WE'VE SUCCESS-FULLY TEST-MARKETED OUR PRODUCT, WE'RE READY FOR THE GLOBAL ROLLOUT.
WE GAVE YOU THE OPPORTUNITY TO PARTNER WITH US, INSTEAD OF GETTING ABSORBED LIKE THE OTHER GANGS, BUT SINCE YOU TREATED THAT OFFER WITH THE SAME DISRESPECT YOU'VE DUMPED ON ALL MY IDEAS--
JESUS! WHAT IS HE YAMMERING ABOUT, ALREADY?!
TOO MANY BIG WORDS, KILLER JOE? SORRY--BUT YOU DID PAY FOR MY M.B.A.
LET ME PUT IT INTO TERM YOU UNDE STAND--

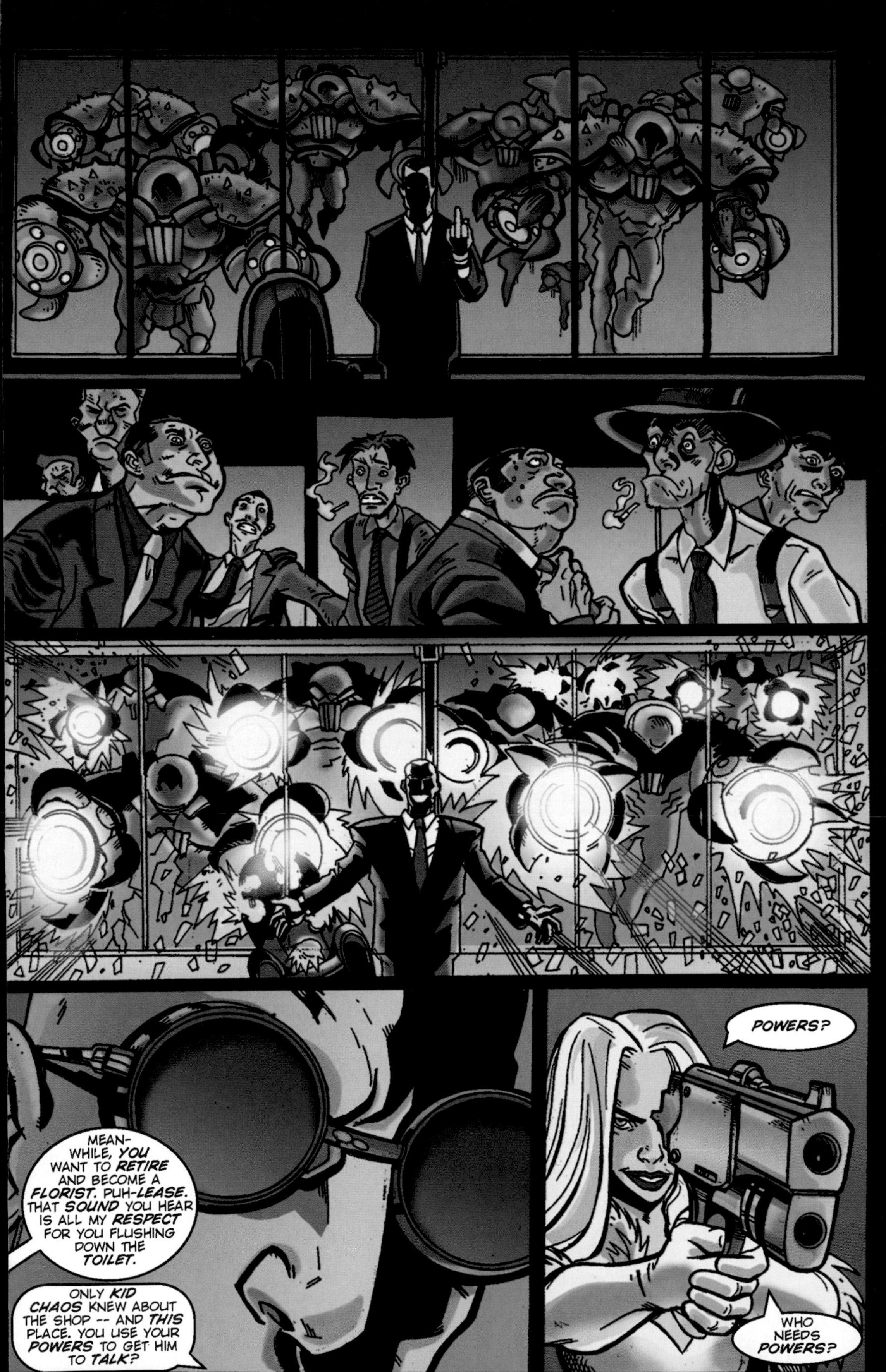
MEAN-WHILE, YOU WANT TO RETIRE AND BECOME A FLORIST. PUH-LEASE. THAT SOUND YOU HEAR IS ALL MY RESPECT FOR YOU FLUSHING DOWN THE TOILET.
ONLY KID CHAOS KNEW ABOUT THE SHOP -- AND THIS PLACE. YOU USE YOUR POWERS TO GET HIM TO TALK?
POWERS?
WHO NEEDS POWERS?

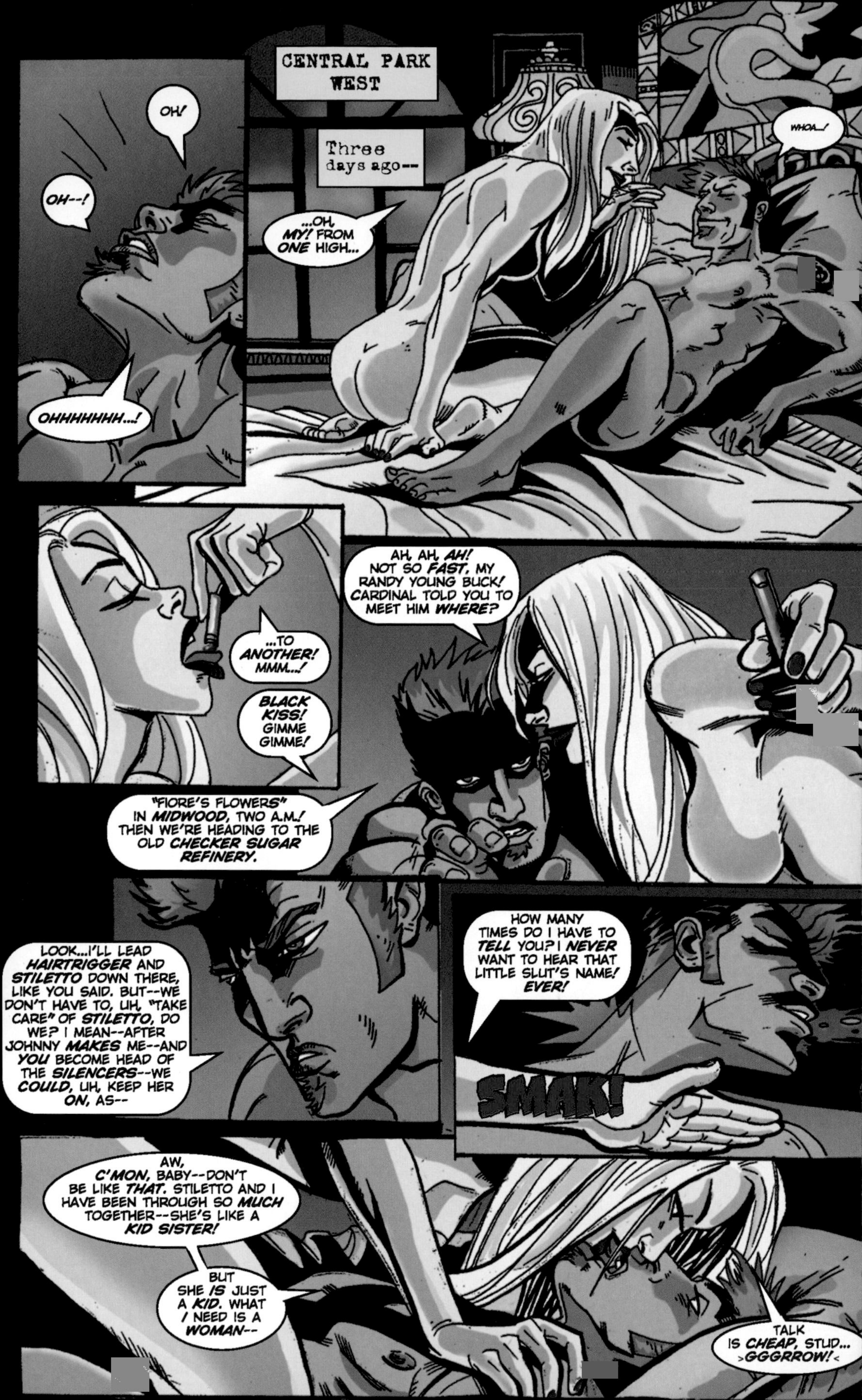

CENTRAL PARK WEST
Three days ago--
OH--!
OH!
OHHHHHHH...!
...OH, MY! FROM ONE HIGH...
WHOA...!
...TO ANOTHER! MMM...!
BLACK KISS! GIMME GIMME!
AH, AH, AH! NOT SO FAST, MY RANDY YOUNG BUCK! CARDINAL TOLD YOU TO MEET HIM WHERE?
"FIORE'S FLOWERS" IN MIDWOOD, TWO A.M.! THEN WE'RE HEADING TO THE OLD CHECKER SUGAR REFINERY.
LOOK...I'LL LEAD HAIRTRIGGER AND STILETTO DOWN THERE, LIKE YOU SAID. BUT--WE DON'T HAVE TO, UH, "TAKE CARE" OF STILETTO, DO WE? I MEAN--AFTER JOHNNY MAKES ME--AND YOU BECOME HEAD OF THE SILENCERS--WE COULD, UH, KEEP HER ON, AS--
HOW MANY TIMES DO I HAVE TO TELL YOU? I NEVER WANT TO HEAR THAT LITTLE SLUT'S NAME! EVER!
SMAK!
AW, C'MON, BABY--DON'T BE LIKE THAT. STILETTO AND I HAVE BEEN THROUGH SO MUCH TOGETHER--SHE'S LIKE A KID SISTER!
BUT SHE IS JUST A KID. WHAT I NEED IS A WOMAN--
TALK IS CHEAP, STUD... >GGGRROW!<

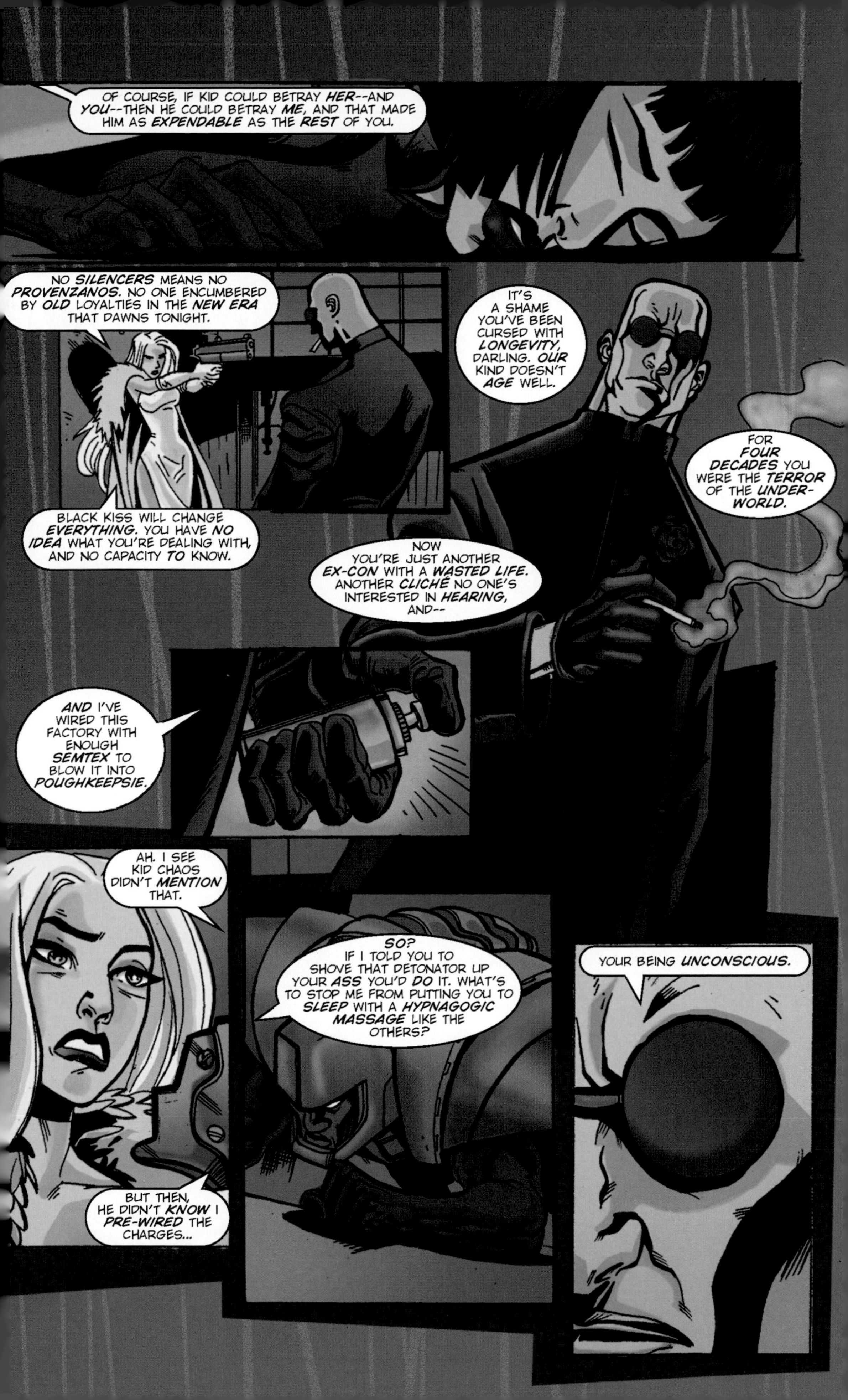
OF COURSE, IF KID COULD BETRAY HER--AND YOU--THEN HE COULD BETRAY ME, AND THAT MADE HIM AS EXPENDABLE AS THE REST OF YOU.
NO SILENCERS MEANS NO PROVENZANOS. NO ONE ENCUMBERED BY OLD LOYALTIES IN THE NEW ERA THAT DAWNS TONIGHT.
BLACK KISS WILL CHANGE EVERYTHING. YOU HAVE NO IDEA WHAT YOU'RE DEALING WITH, AND NO CAPACITY TO KNOW.
IT'S A SHAME YOU'VE BEEN CURSED WITH LONGEVITY, DARLING. OUR KIND DOESN'T AGE WELL.
FOR FOUR DECADES YOU WERE THE TERROR OF THE UNDER-WORLD.
NOW YOU'RE JUST ANOTHER EX-CON WITH A WASTED LIFE. ANOTHER CLICHÉ NO ONE'S INTERESTED IN HEARING, AND--
AND I'VE WIRED THIS FACTORY WITH ENOUGH SEMTEX TO BLOW IT INTO POUGHKEEPSIE.
AH. I SEE KID CHAOS DIDN'T MENTION THAT.
BUT THEN, HE DIDN'T KNOW I PRE-WIRED THE CHARGES...
SO? IF I TOLD YOU TO SHOVE THAT DETONATOR UP YOUR ASS YOU'D DO IT. WHAT'S TO STOP ME FROM PUTTING YOU TO SLEEP WITH A HYPNAGOGIC MASSAGE LIKE THE OTHERS?
YOUR BEING UNCONSCIOUS.

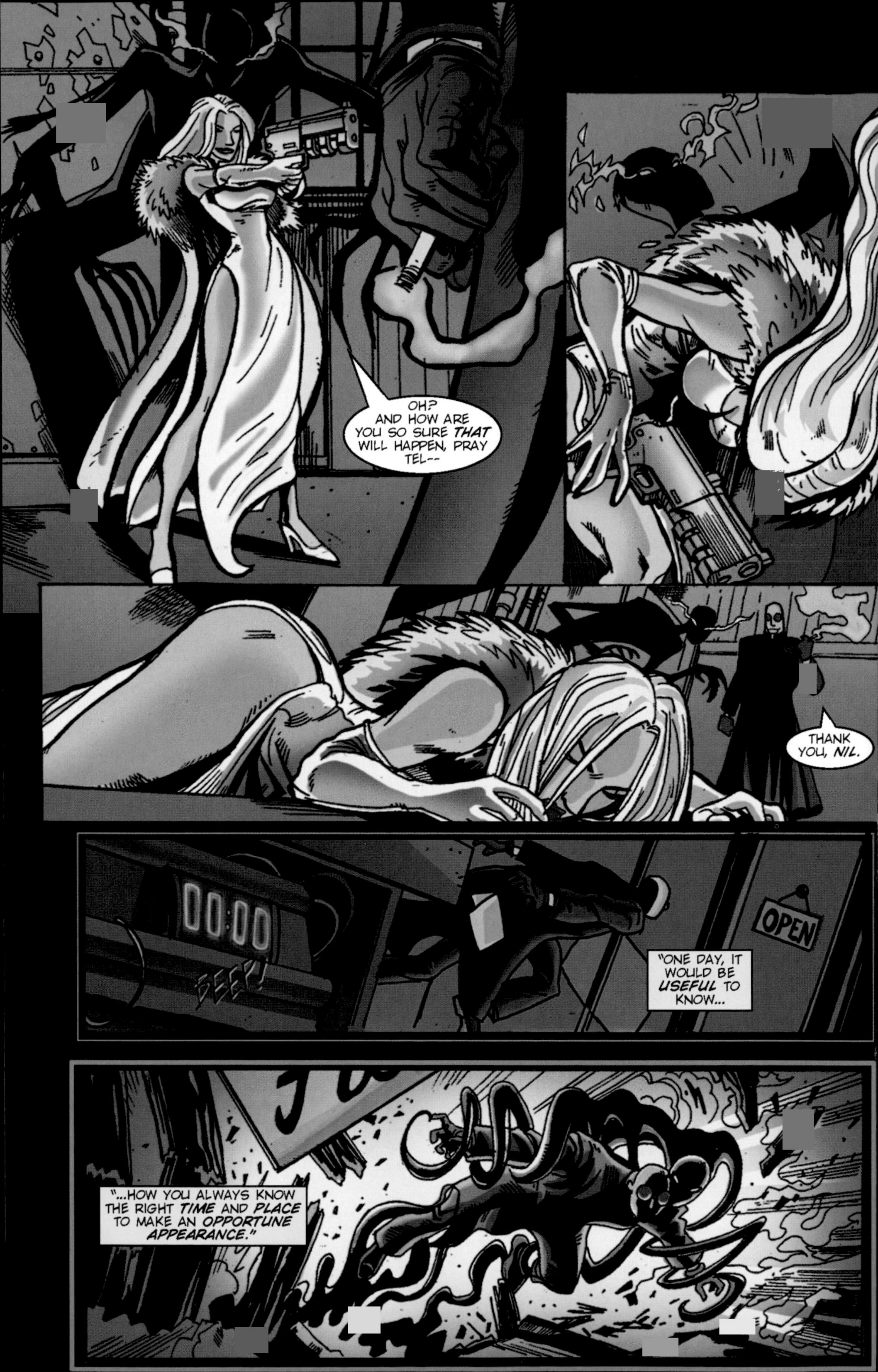
OH? AND HOW ARE YOU SO SURE *THAT* WILL HAPPEN, PRAY TEL--
THANK YOU, *NIL*.
BEEP!
OPEN
"ONE DAY, IT WOULD BE *USEFUL* TO KNOW...
"...HOW YOU ALWAYS KNOW THE RIGHT *TIME* AND *PLACE* TO MAKE AN *OPPORTUNE APPEARANCE*."

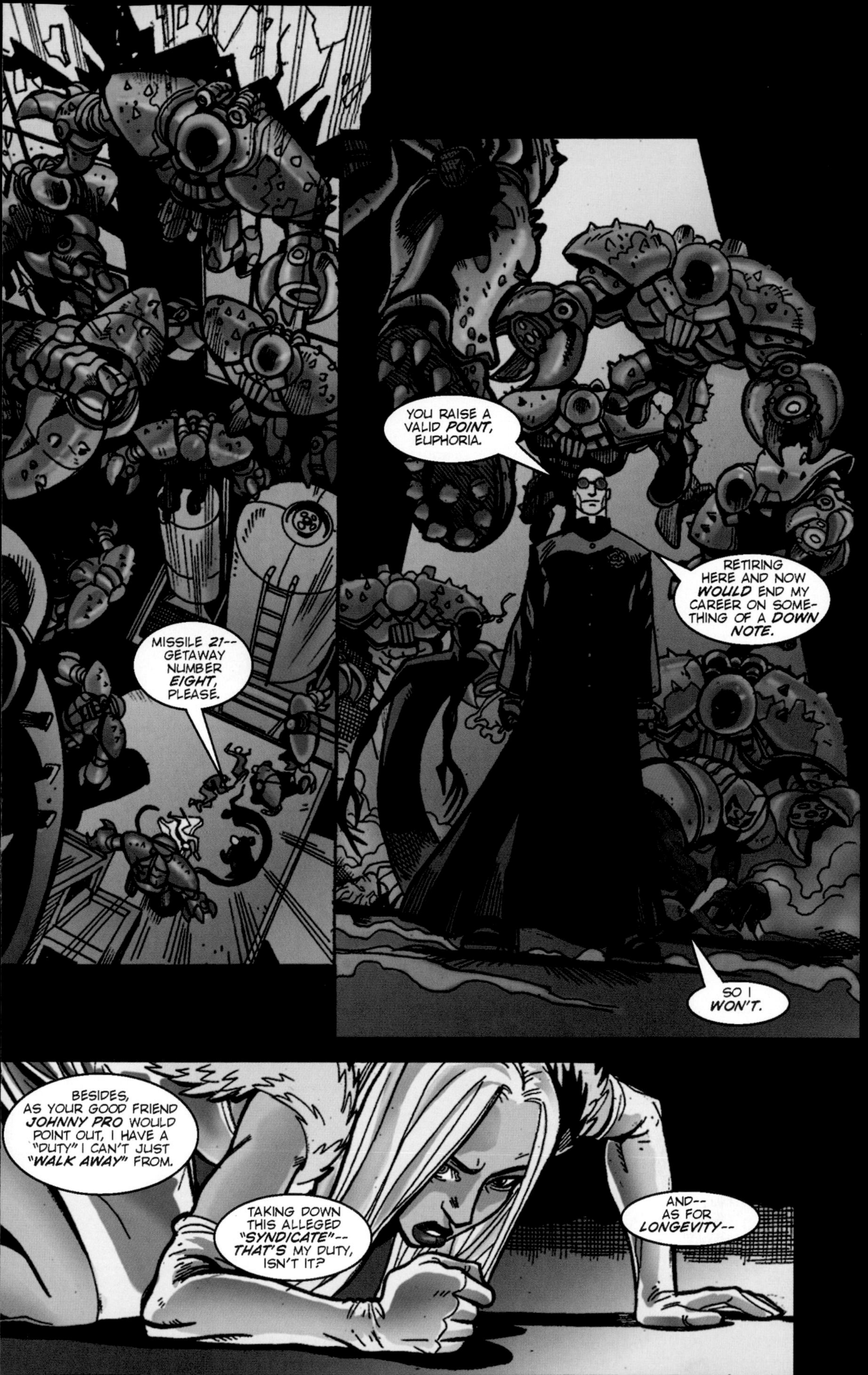
MISSILE 21--GETAWAY NUMBER EIGHT, PLEASE.
YOU RAISE A VALID POINT, EUPHORIA.
RETIRING HERE AND NOW WOULD END MY CAREER ON SOME-THING OF A DOWN NOTE.
SO I WON'T.
BESIDES, AS YOUR GOOD FRIEND JOHNNY PRO WOULD POINT OUT, I HAVE A "DUTY" I CAN'T JUST "WALK AWAY" FROM.
TAKING DOWN THIS ALLEGED "SYNDICATE"--THAT'S MY DUTY, ISN'T IT?
AND--AS FOR LONGEVITY--

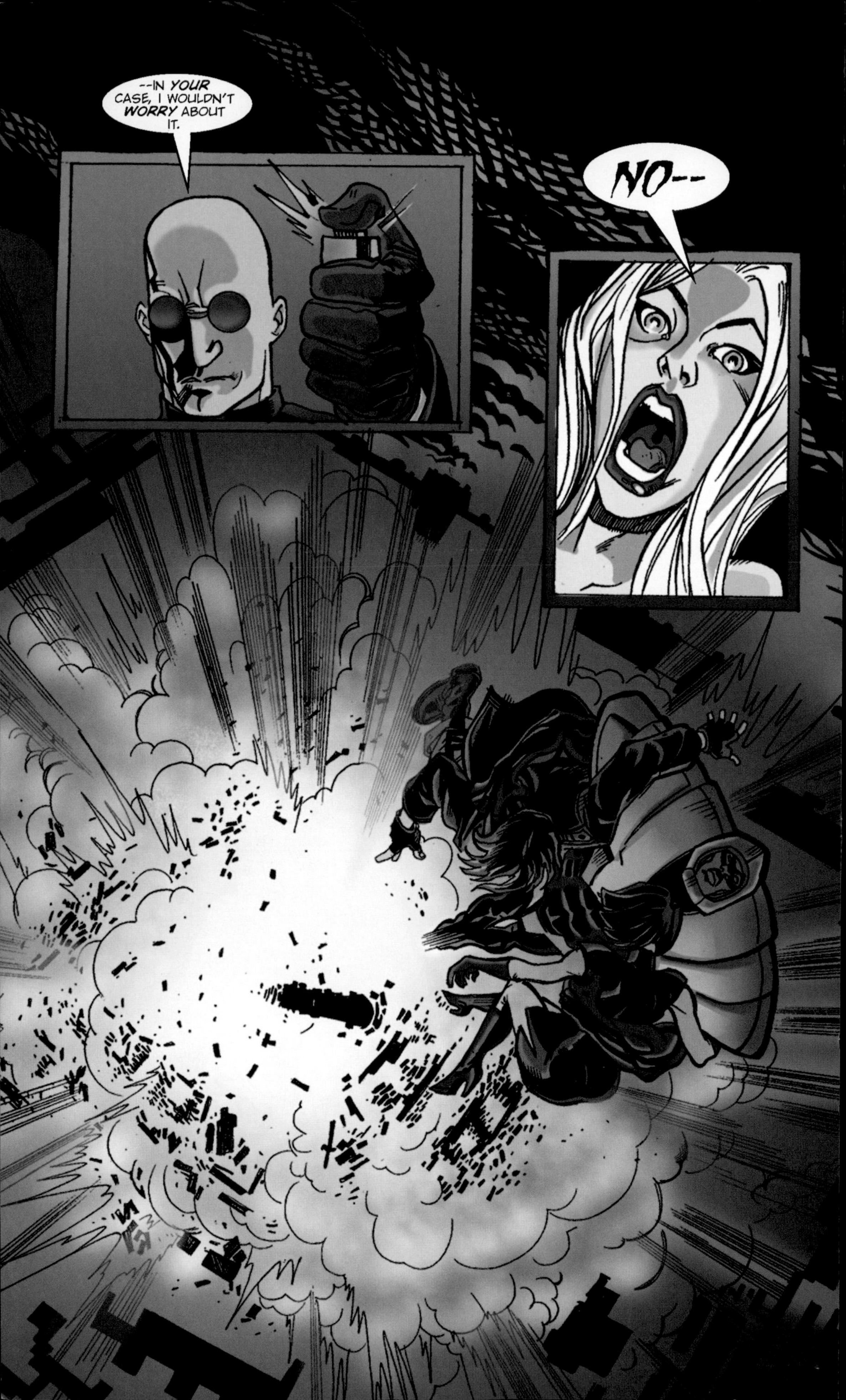
--IN YOUR CASE, I WOULDN'T WORRY ABOUT IT.
NO--

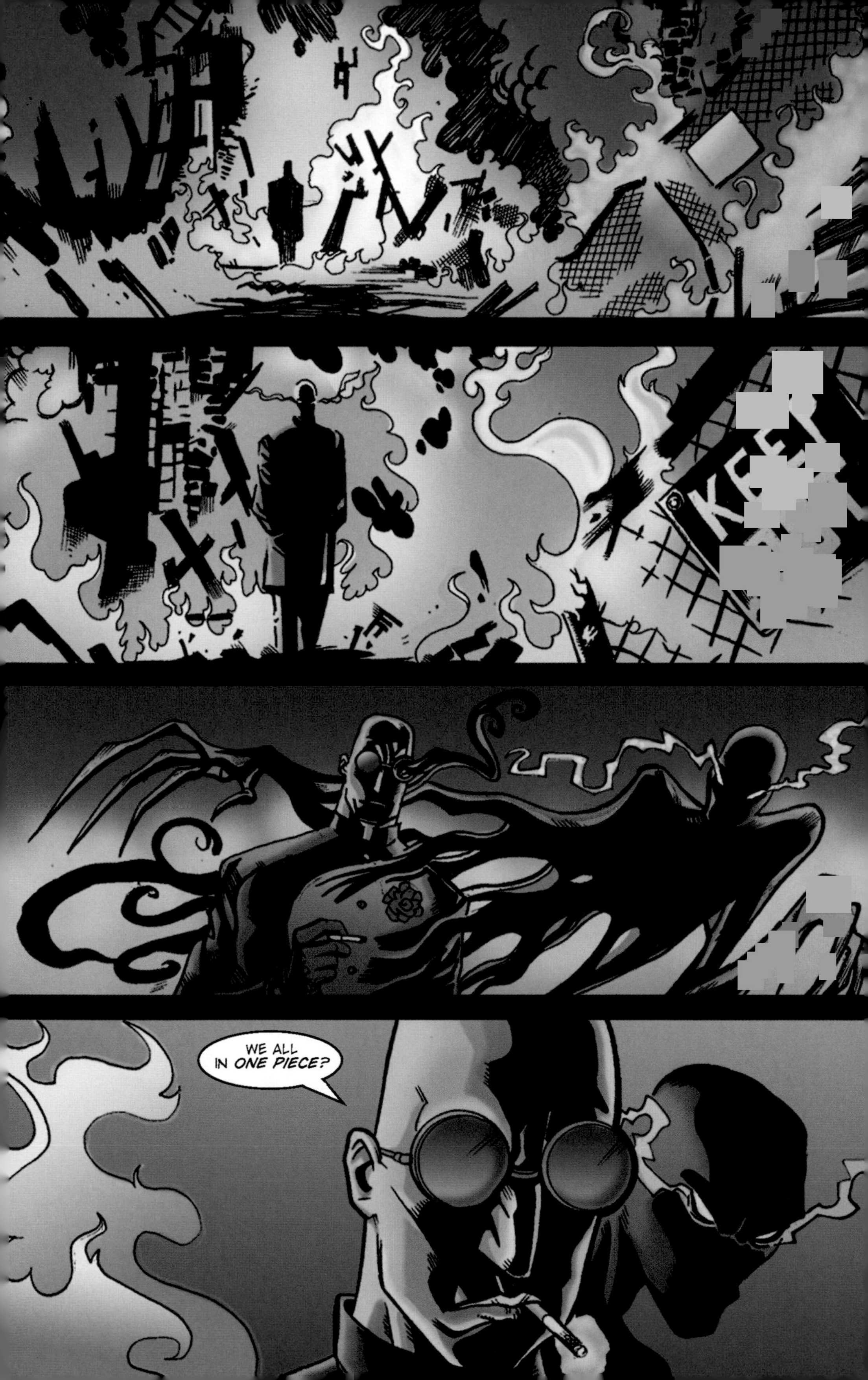
WE ALL IN ONE PIECE?

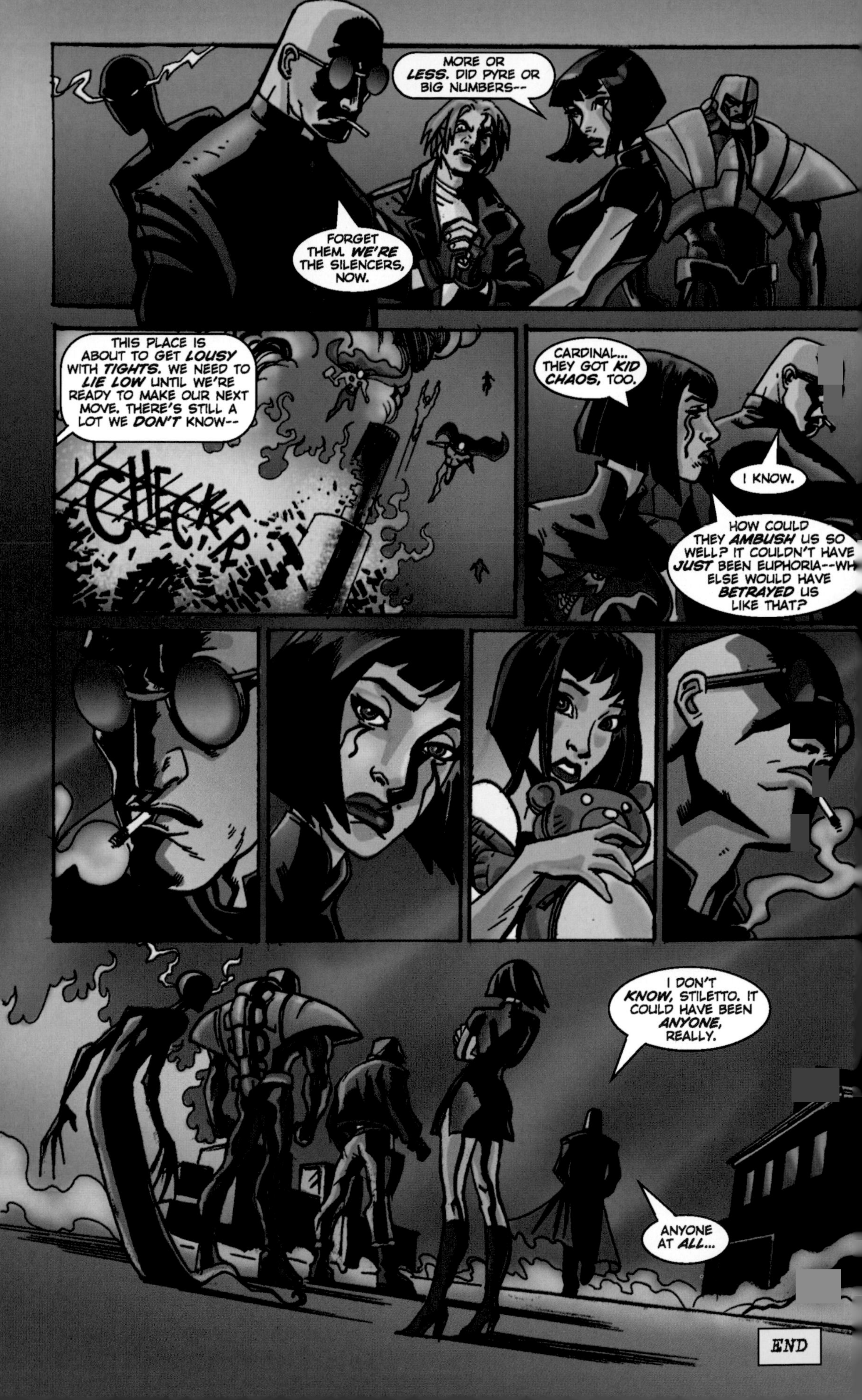
MORE OR LESS. DID PYRE OR BIG NUMBERS--
FORGET THEM. WE'RE THE SILENCERS, NOW.
THIS PLACE IS ABOUT TO GET LOUSY WITH TIGHTS. WE NEED TO LIE LOW UNTIL WE'RE READY TO MAKE OUR NEXT MOVE. THERE'S STILL A LOT WE DON'T KNOW--
CARDINAL... THEY GOT KID CHAOS, TOO.
I KNOW.
HOW COULD THEY AMBUSH US SO WELL? IT COULDN'T HAVE JUST BEEN EUPHORIA--WH ELSE WOULD HAVE BETRAYED US LIKE THAT?
I DON'T KNOW, STILETTO. IT COULD HAVE BEEN ANYONE, REALLY.
ANYONE AT ALL...
END

SPREE

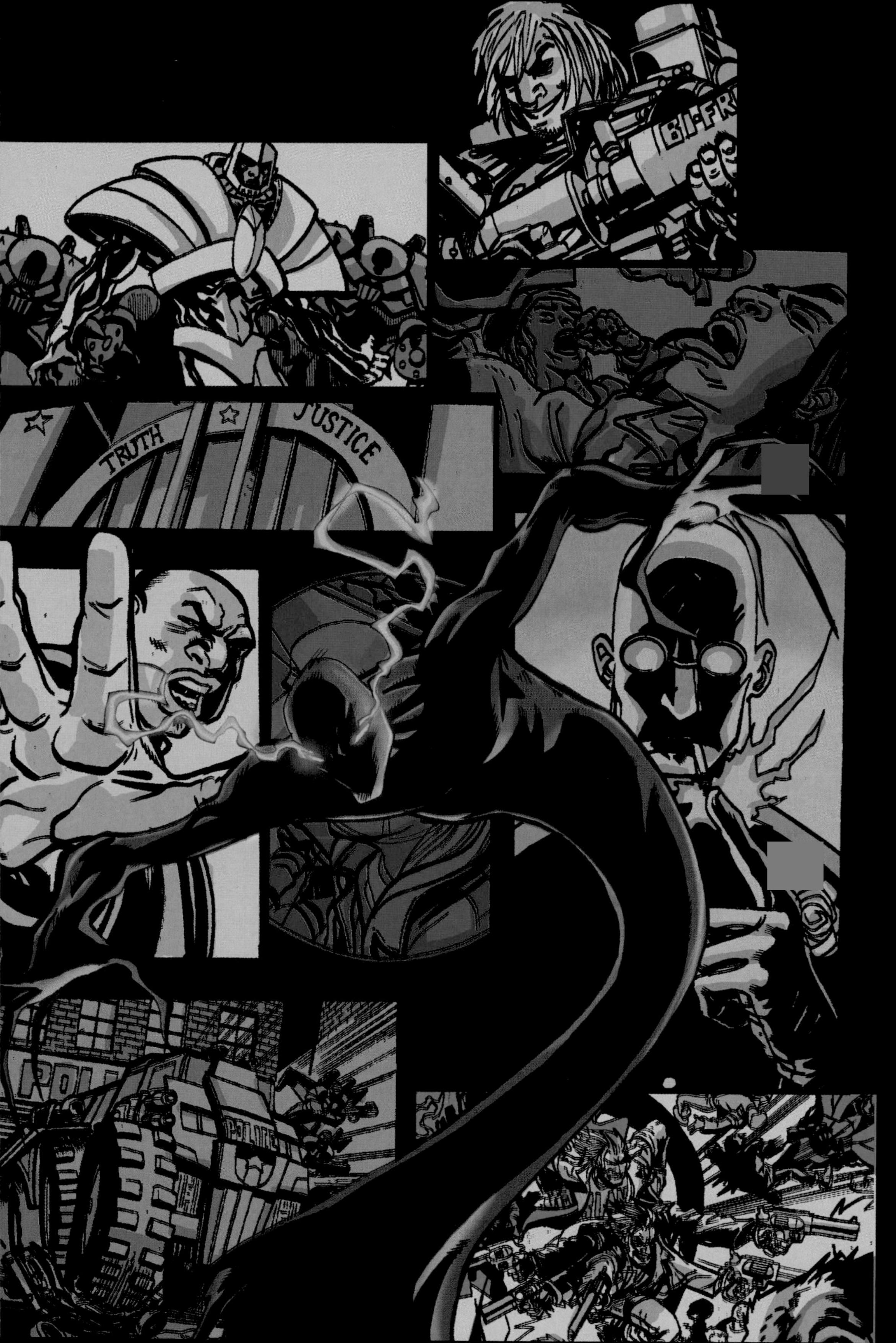
TRUTH
JUSTICE
POLICE

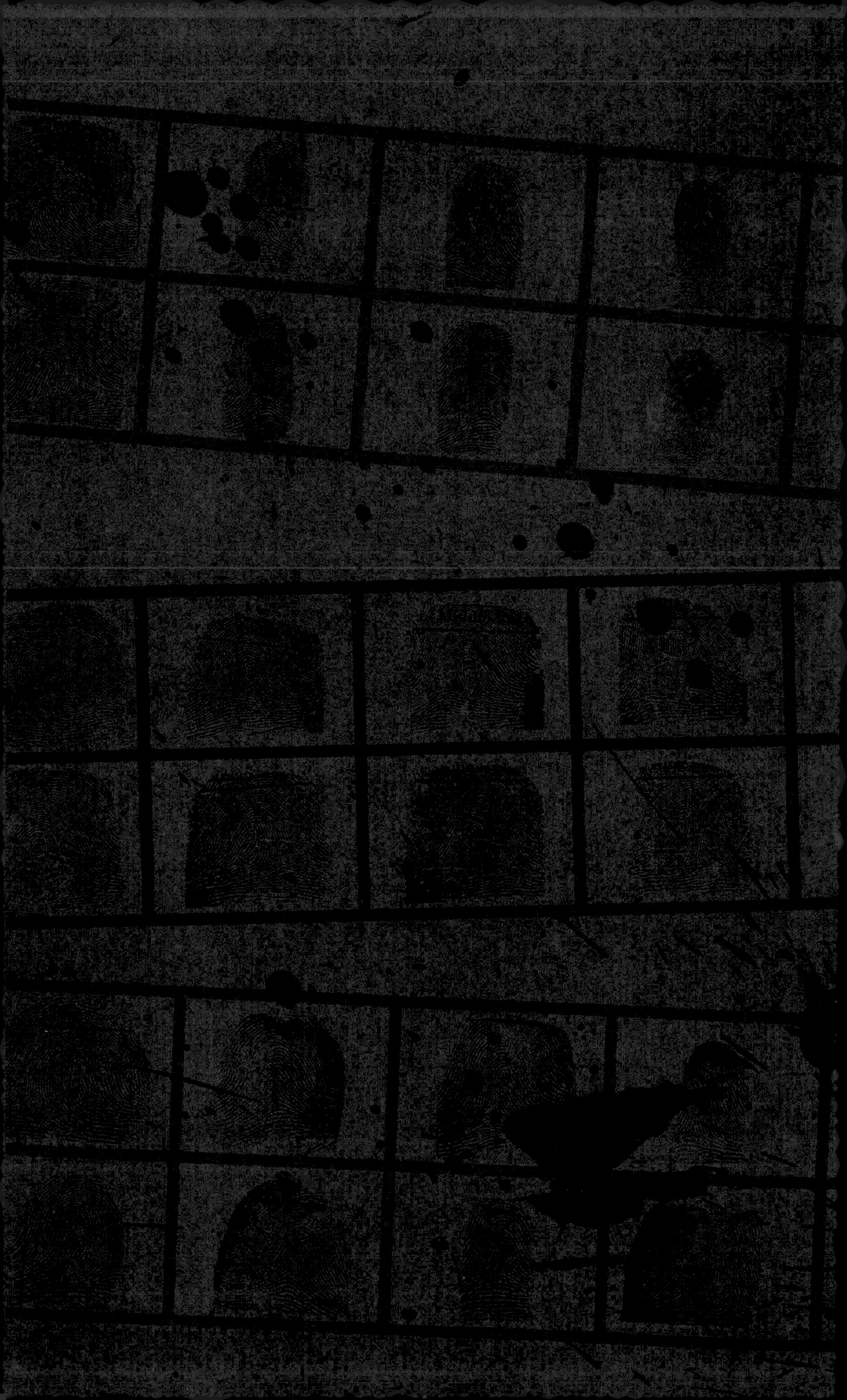

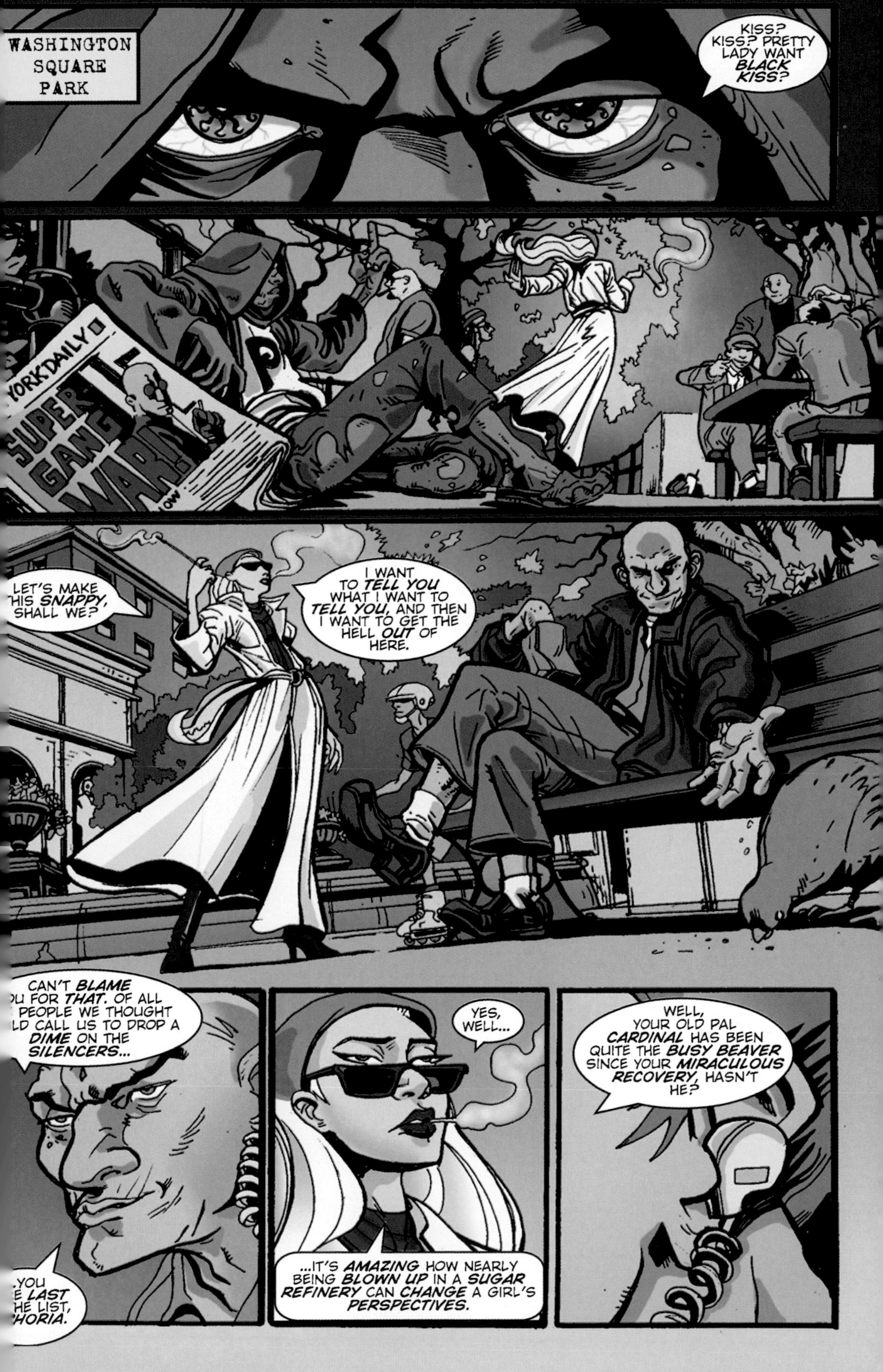
WASHINGTON SQUARE PARK
KISS? KISS? PRETTY LADY WANT BLACK KISS?
YORK DAILY
SUPER GANG WAR!
LET'S MAKE THIS SNAPPY, SHALL WE?
I WANT TO TELL YOU WHAT I WANT TO TELL YOU, AND THEN I WANT TO GET THE HELL OUT OF HERE.
CAN'T BLAME OU FOR THAT. OF ALL PEOPLE WE THOUGHT LD CALL US TO DROP A DIME ON THE SILENCERS...
YES, WELL...
WELL, YOUR OLD PAL CARDINAL HAS BEEN QUITE THE BUSY BEAVER SINCE YOUR MIRACULOUS RECOVERY, HASN'T HE?
...YOU LAST HE LIST, HORIA.
...IT'S AMAZING HOW NEARLY BEING BLOWN UP IN A SUGAR REFINERY CAN CHANGE A GIRL'S PERSPECTIVES.

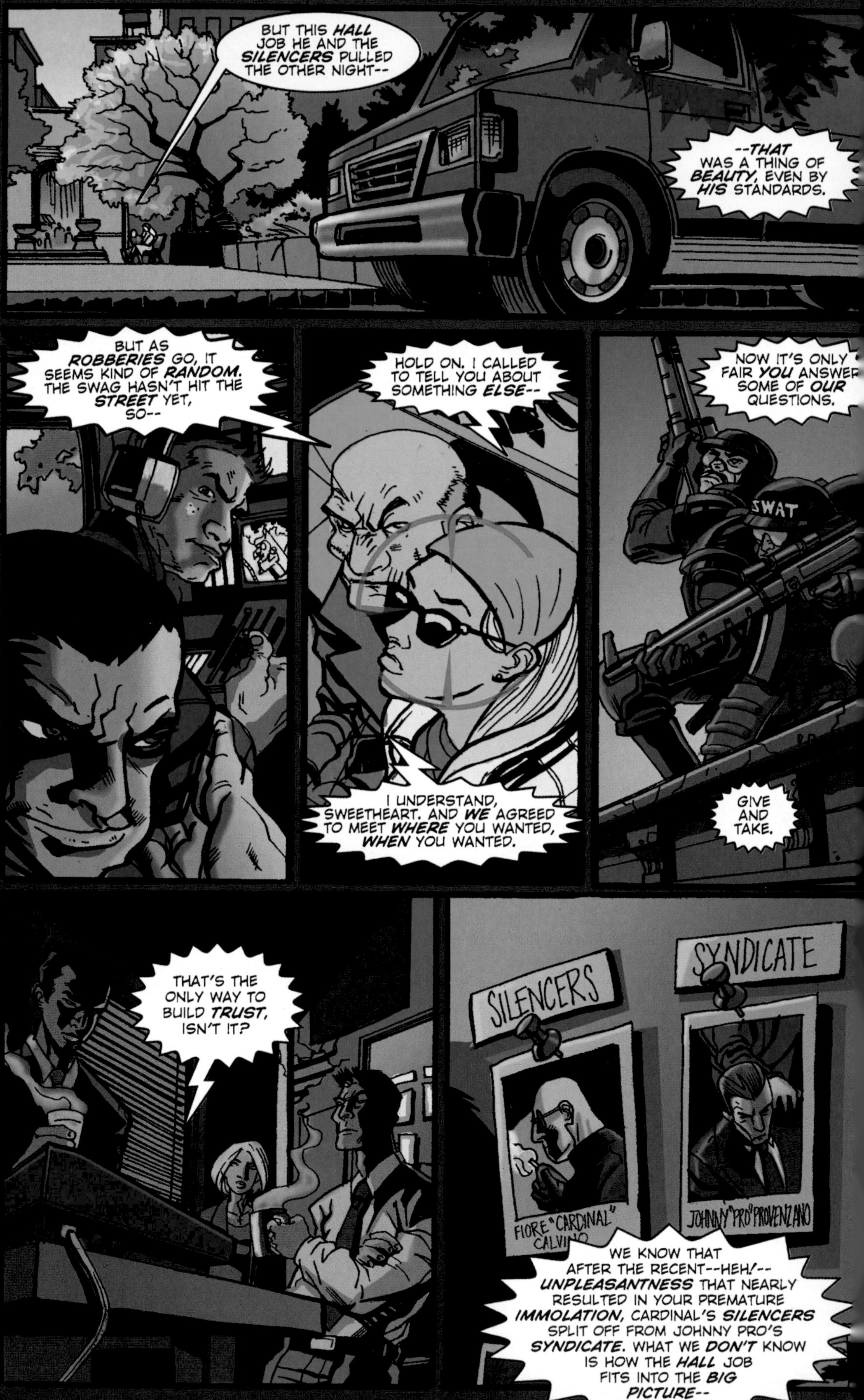
BUT THIS HALL JOB HE AND THE SILENCERS PULLED THE OTHER NIGHT--
--THAT WAS A THING OF BEAUTY, EVEN BY HIS STANDARDS.
BUT AS ROBBERIES GO, IT SEEMS KIND OF RANDOM. THE SWAG HASN'T HIT THE STREET YET, SO--
HOLD ON. I CALLED TO TELL YOU ABOUT SOMETHING ELSE--
I UNDERSTAND, SWEETHEART. AND WE AGREED TO MEET WHERE YOU WANTED, WHEN YOU WANTED.
NOW IT'S ONLY FAIR YOU ANSWER SOME OF OUR QUESTIONS.
SWAT
GIVE AND TAKE.
THAT'S THE ONLY WAY TO BUILD TRUST, ISN'T IT?
SYNDICATE
SILENCERS
FIORE "CARDINAL" CALVINO
JOHNNY "PRO" PROVENZANO
WE KNOW THAT AFTER THE RECENT--HEH!--UNPLEASANTNESS THAT NEARLY RESULTED IN YOUR PREMATURE IMMOLATION, CARDINAL'S SILENCERS SPLIT OFF FROM JOHNNY PRO'S SYNDICATE. WHAT WE DON'T KNOW IS HOW THE HALL JOB FITS INTO THE BIG PICTURE--

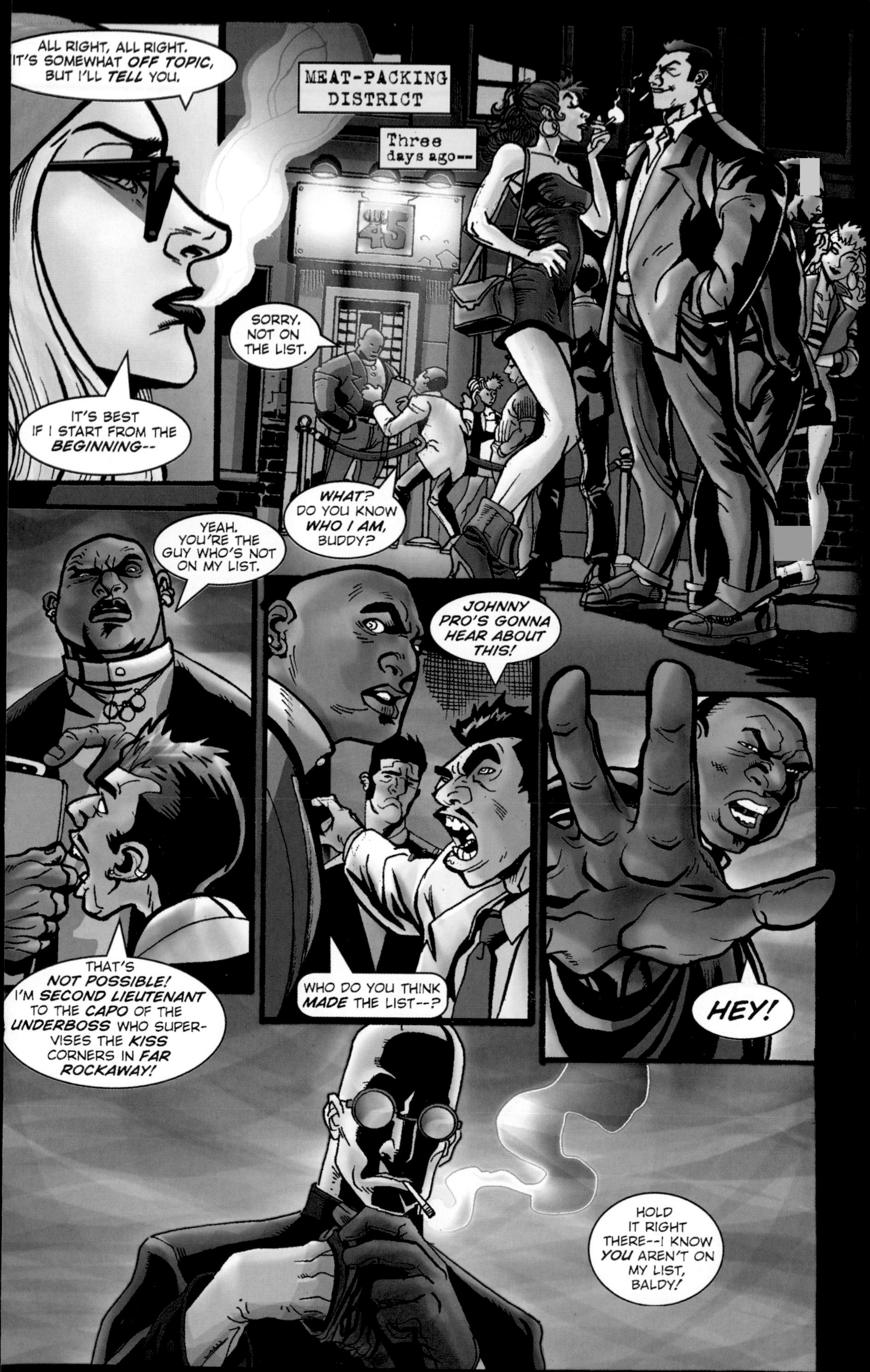
ALL RIGHT, ALL RIGHT. IT'S SOMEWHAT OFF TOPIC, BUT I'LL TELL YOU.
IT'S BEST IF I START FROM THE BEGINNING--
MEAT-PACKING DISTRICT
Three days ago--
45
SORRY. NOT ON THE LIST.
WHAT? DO YOU KNOW WHO I AM, BUDDY?
YEAH. YOU'RE THE GUY WHO'S NOT ON MY LIST.
THAT'S NOT POSSIBLE! I'M SECOND LIEUTENANT TO THE CAPO OF THE UNDERBOSS WHO SUPERVISES THE KISS CORNERS IN FAR ROCKAWAY!
JOHNNY PRO'S GONNA HEAR ABOUT THIS!
WHO DO YOU THINK MADE THE LIST--?
HEY!
HOLD IT RIGHT THERE--I KNOW YOU AREN'T ON MY LIST, BALDY!

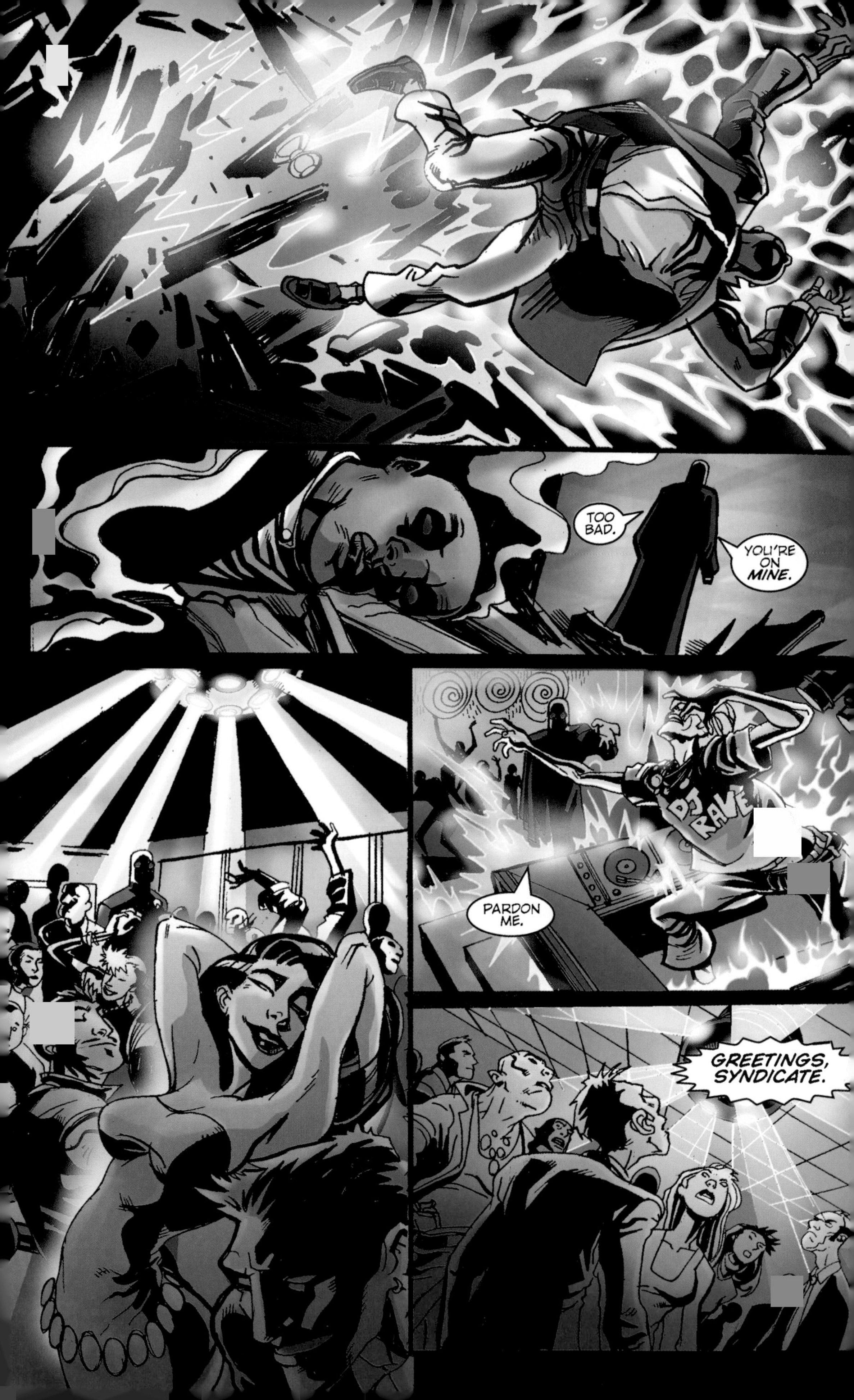
TOO BAD.
YOU'RE ON MINE.
DJ RAVE
PARDON ME.
GREETINGS, SYNDICATE.

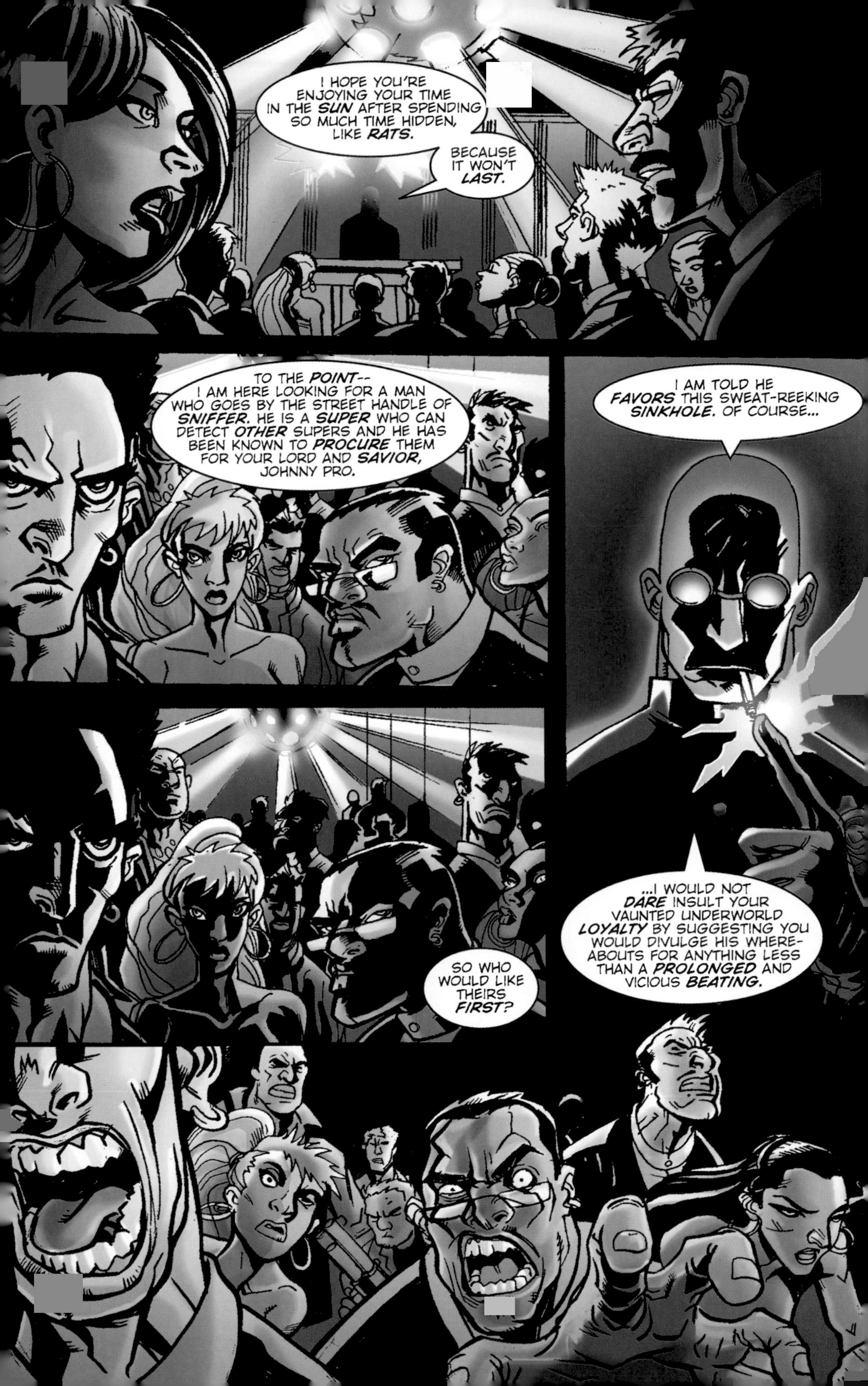
I HOPE YOU'RE ENJOYING YOUR TIME IN THE SUN AFTER SPENDING SO MUCH TIME HIDDEN, LIKE RATS.
BECAUSE IT WON'T LAST.
TO THE POINT-- I AM HERE LOOKING FOR A MAN WHO GOES BY THE STREET HANDLE OF SNIFFER. HE IS A SUPER WHO CAN DETECT OTHER SUPERS AND HE HAS BEEN KNOWN TO PROCURE THEM FOR YOUR LORD AND SAVIOR, JOHNNY PRO.
I AM TOLD HE FAVORS THIS SWEAT-REEKING SINKHOLE. OF COURSE...
...I WOULD NOT DARE INSULT YOUR VAUNTED UNDERWORLD LOYALTY BY SUGGESTING YOU WOULD DIVULGE HIS WHERE-ABOUTS FOR ANYTHING LESS THAN A PROLONGED AND VICIOUS BEATING.
SO WHO WOULD LIKE THEIRS FIRST?

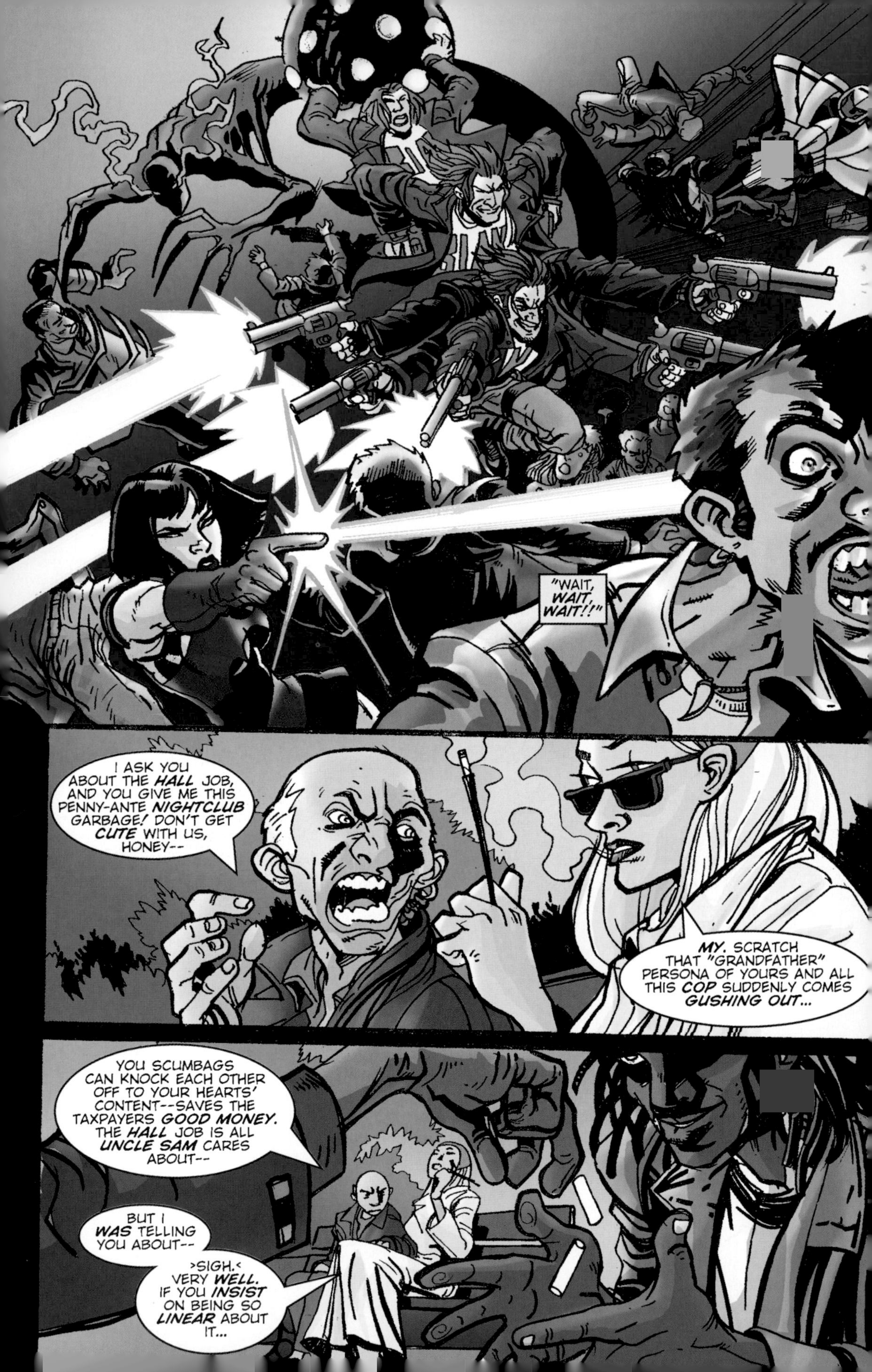
"WAIT, WAIT, WAIT!!"
I ASK YOU ABOUT THE HALL JOB, AND YOU GIVE ME THIS PENNY-ANTE NIGHTCLUB GARBAGE! DON'T GET CUTE WITH US, HONEY--
MY. SCRATCH THAT "GRANDFATHER" PERSONA OF YOURS AND ALL THIS COP SUDDENLY COMES GUSHING OUT...
YOU SCUMBAGS CAN KNOCK EACH OTHER OFF TO YOUR HEARTS' CONTENT--SAVES THE TAXPAYERS GOOD MONEY. THE HALL JOB IS ALL UNCLE SAM CARES ABOUT--
BUT I WAS TELLING YOU ABOUT--
>SIGH.< VERY WELL. IF YOU INSIST ON BEING SO LINEAR ABOUT IT...

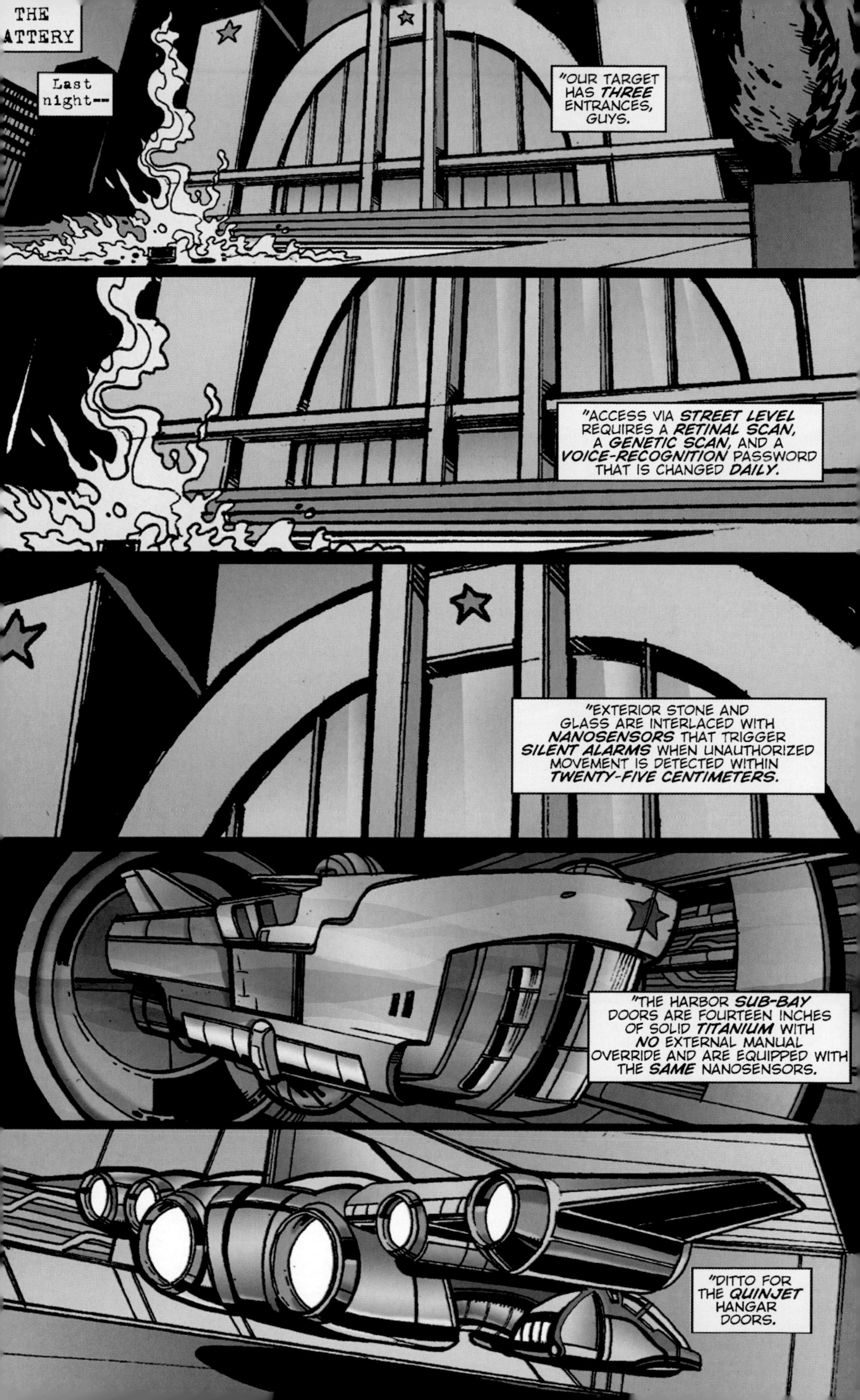
THE ATTERY
Last night--
"OUR TARGET HAS THREE ENTRANCES, GUYS.
"ACCESS VIA STREET LEVEL REQUIRES A RETINAL SCAN, A GENETIC SCAN, AND A VOICE-RECOGNITION PASSWORD THAT IS CHANGED DAILY.
"EXTERIOR STONE AND GLASS ARE INTERLACED WITH NANOSENSORS THAT TRIGGER SILENT ALARMS WHEN UNAUTHORIZED MOVEMENT IS DETECTED WITHIN TWENTY-FIVE CENTIMETERS.
"THE HARBOR SUB-BAY DOORS ARE FOURTEEN INCHES OF SOLID TITANIUM WITH NO EXTERNAL MANUAL OVERRIDE AND ARE EQUIPPED WITH THE SAME NANOSENSORS.
"DITTO FOR THE QUINJET HANGAR DOORS.

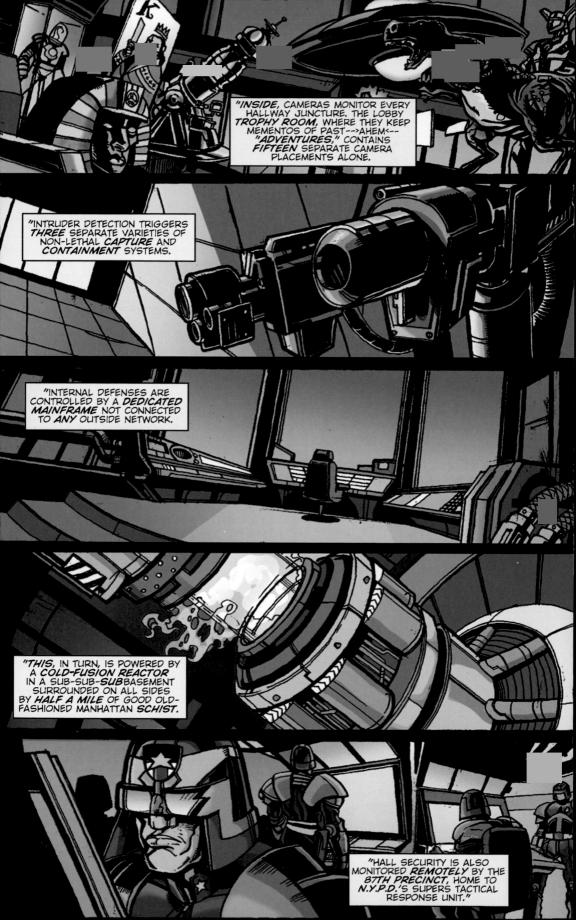

"INSIDE, CAMERAS MONITOR EVERY HALLWAY JUNCTURE. THE LOBBY *TROPHY ROOM,* WHERE THEY KEEP MEMENTOS OF PAST-->*AHEM*<-- *"ADVENTURES,"* CONTAINS *FIFTEEN* SEPARATE CAMERA PLACEMENTS ALONE.

"INTRUDER DETECTION TRIGGERS *THREE* SEPARATE VARIETIES OF NON-LETHAL *CAPTURE* AND *CONTAINMENT* SYSTEMS.

"INTERNAL DEFENSES ARE CONTROLLED BY A *DEDICATED MAINFRAME* NOT CONNECTED TO *ANY* OUTSIDE NETWORK.

"*THIS,* IN TURN, IS POWERED BY A *COLD-FUSION REACTOR* IN A SUB-SUB-*SUB*BASEMENT SURROUNDED ON ALL SIDES BY *HALF A MILE* OF GOOD OLD-FASHIONED MANHATTAN *SCHIST.*

"HALL SECURITY IS ALSO MONITORED *REMOTELY* BY THE *87TH PRECINCT,* HOME TO *N.Y.P.D.'S* SUPERS TACTICAL RESPONSE UNIT."

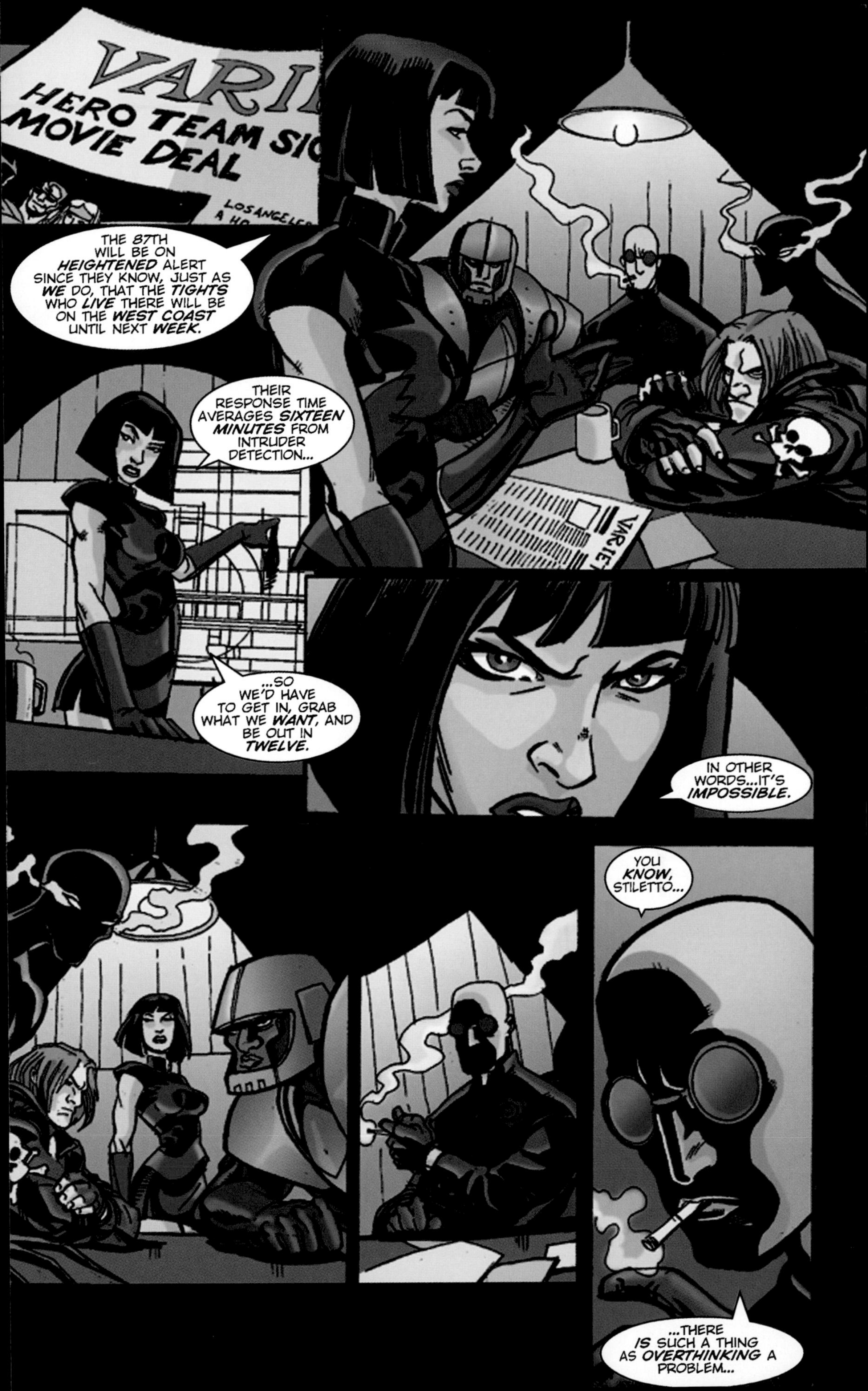
VARI
HERO TEAM SIG
MOVIE DEAL
LOS ANGELES
A HO
THE 87TH WILL BE ON HEIGHTENED ALERT SINCE THEY KNOW, JUST AS WE DO, THAT THE TIGHTS WHO LIVE THERE WILL BE ON THE WEST COAST UNTIL NEXT WEEK.
THEIR RESPONSE TIME AVERAGES SIXTEEN MINUTES FROM INTRUDER DETECTION...
VARIET
...SO WE'D HAVE TO GET IN, GRAB WHAT WE WANT, AND BE OUT IN TWELVE.
IN OTHER WORDS...IT'S IMPOSSIBLE.
YOU KNOW, STILETTO...
...THERE IS SUCH A THING AS OVERTHINKING A PROBLEM...

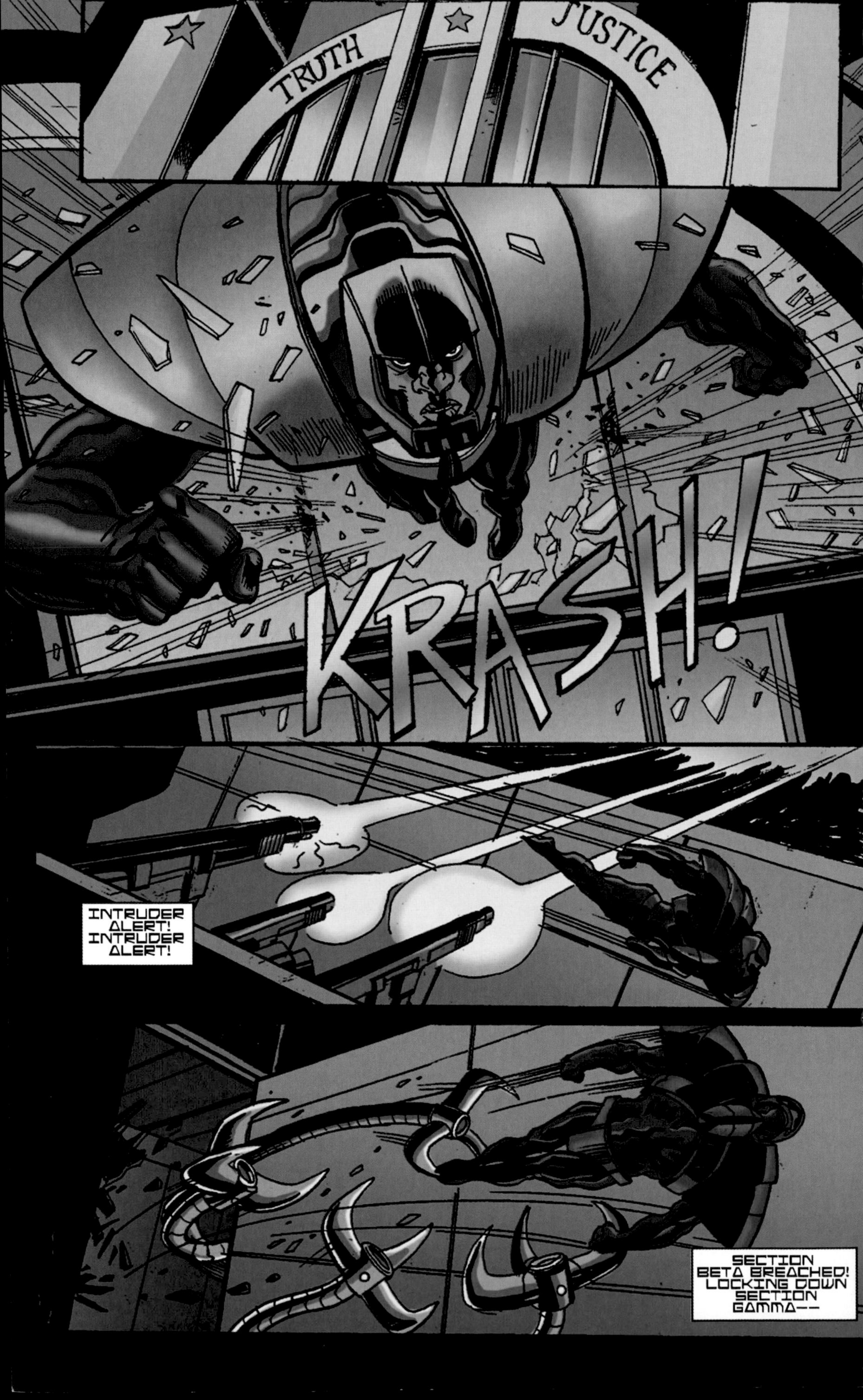
TRUTH JUSTICE
KRASH!
INTRUDER ALERT! INTRUDER ALERT!
SECTION BETA BREACHED! LOCKING DOWN SECTION GAMMA--

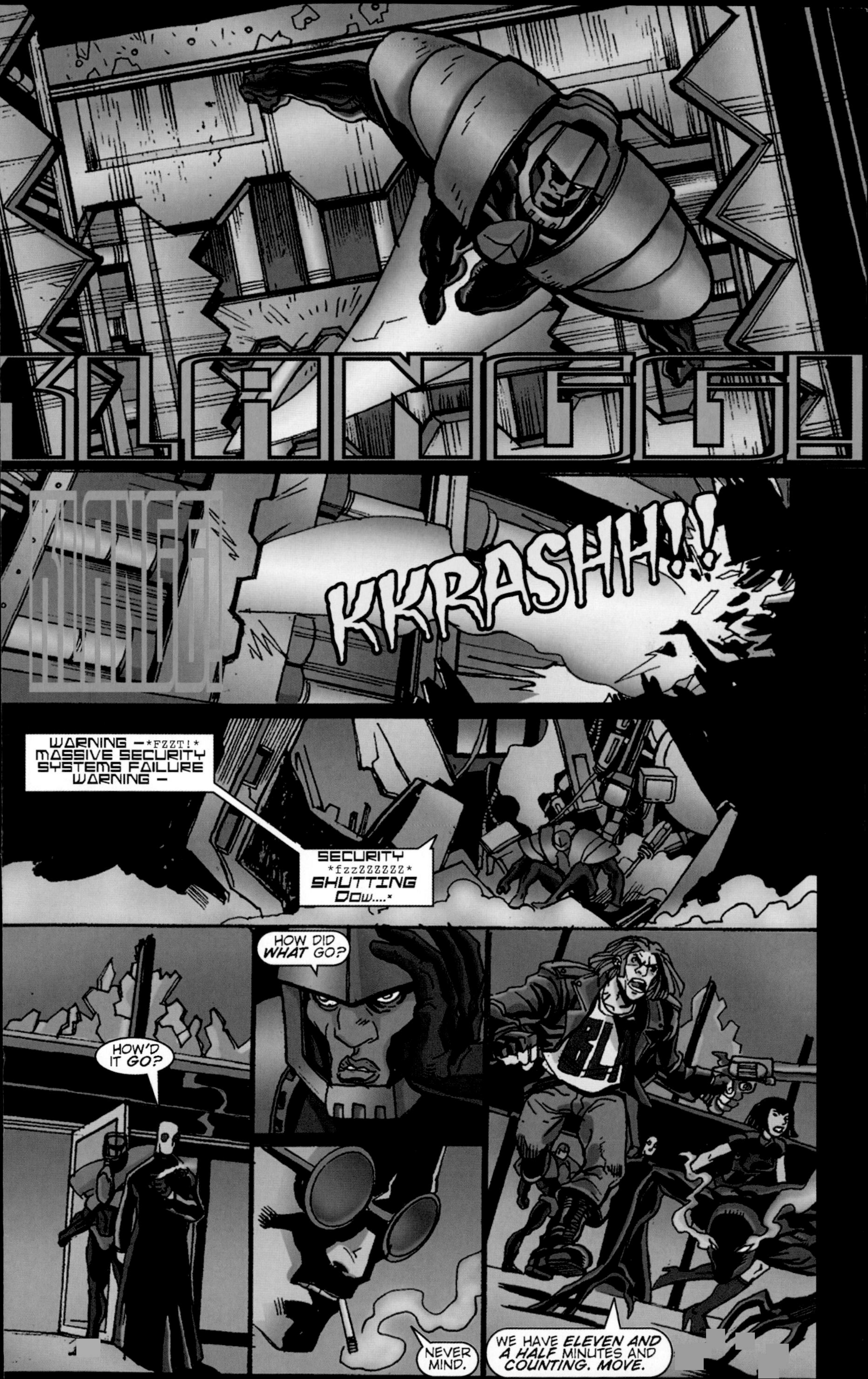
KLANGGG!!
KKRASHH!!
WARNING —*FZZT!* MASSIVE SECURITY SYSTEMS FAILURE WARNING —
SECURITY *fzzZZZZZZ* SHUTTING Dow....*
HOW'D IT GO?
HOW DID WHAT GO?
NEVER MIND.
WE HAVE ELEVEN AND A HALF MINUTES AND COUNTING. MOVE.

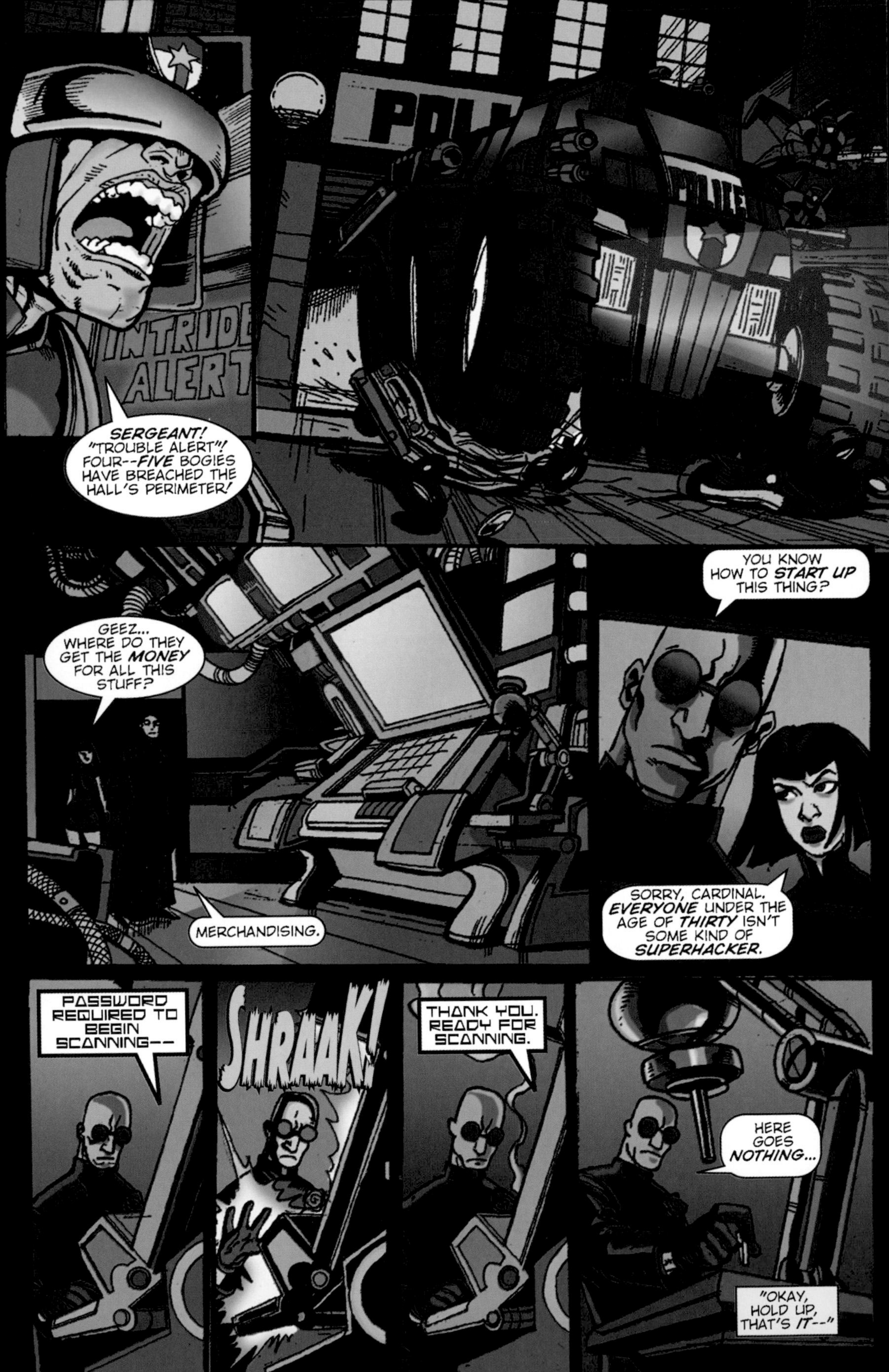
INTRUDE ALERT
POLICE
SERGEANT! "TROUBLE ALERT"! FOUR--FIVE BOGIES HAVE BREACHED THE HALL'S PERIMETER!
GEEZ... WHERE DO THEY GET THE MONEY FOR ALL THIS STUFF?
MERCHANDISING.
YOU KNOW HOW TO START UP THIS THING?
SORRY, CARDINAL. EVERYONE UNDER THE AGE OF THIRTY ISN'T SOME KIND OF SUPERHACKER.
PASSWORD REQUIRED TO BEGIN SCANNING--
SHRAAK!
THANK YOU. READY FOR SCANNING.
HERE GOES NOTHING...
"OKAY, HOLD UP, THAT'S IT--"

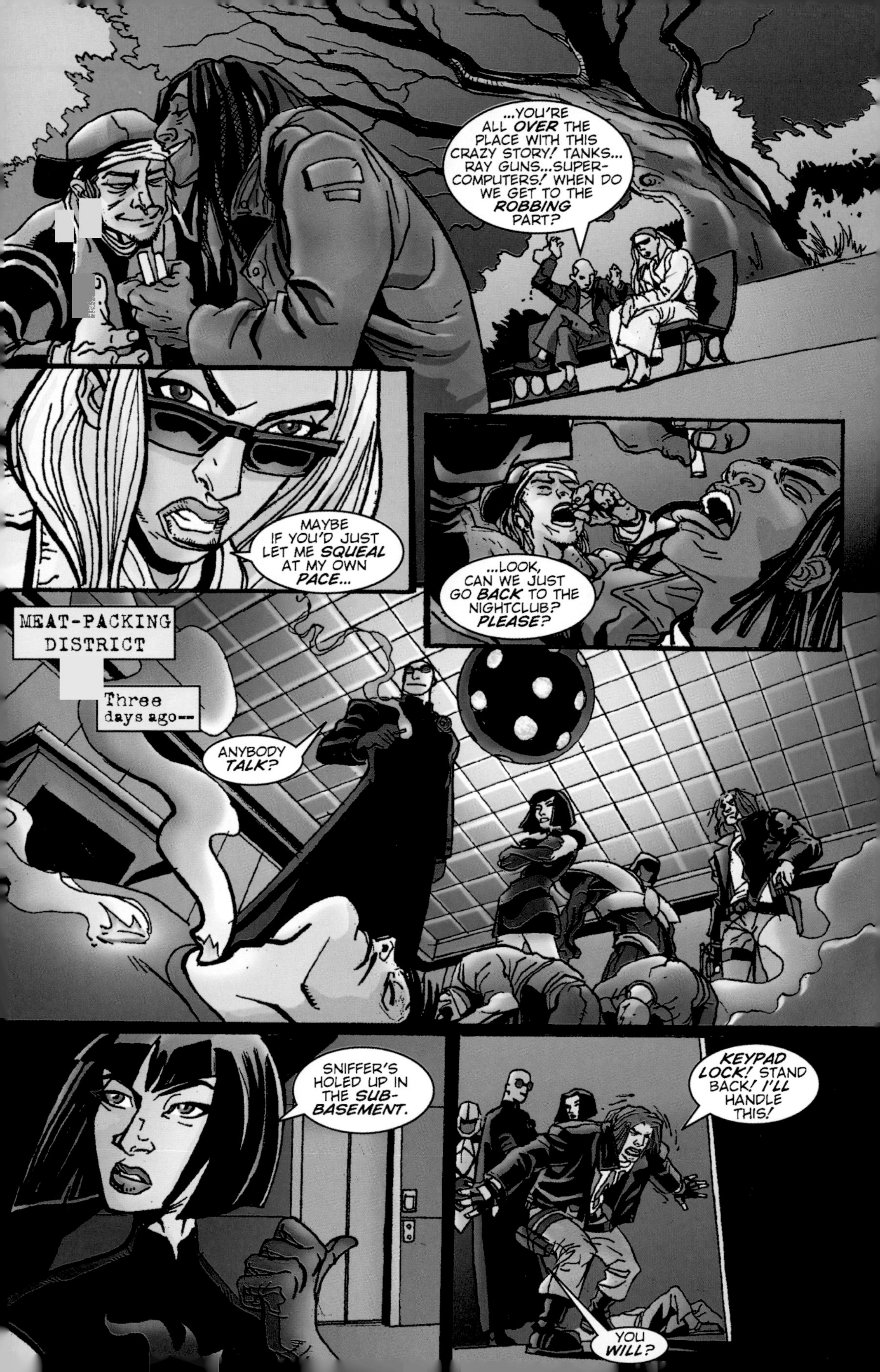
...YOU'RE ALL OVER THE PLACE WITH THIS CRAZY STORY! TANKS... RAY GUNS...SUPER-COMPUTERS! WHEN DO WE GET TO THE ROBBING PART?
MAYBE IF YOU'D JUST LET ME SQUEAL AT MY OWN PACE...
...LOOK, CAN WE JUST GO BACK TO THE NIGHTCLUB? PLEASE?
MEAT-PACKING DISTRICT
Three days ago--
ANYBODY TALK?
SNIFFER'S HOLED UP IN THE SUB-BASEMENT.
KEYPAD LOCK! STAND BACK! I'LL HANDLE THIS!
YOU WILL?

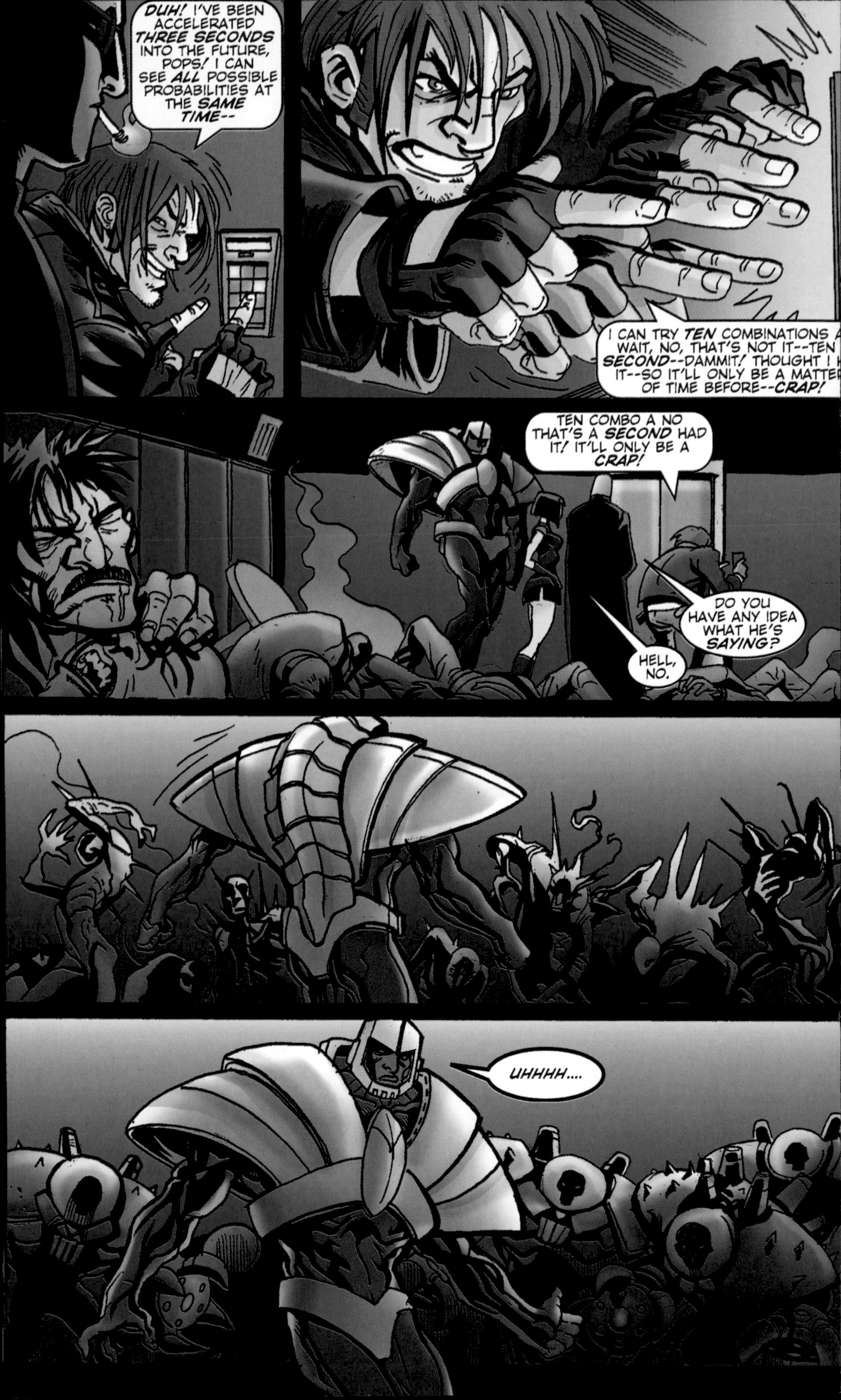
DUH! I'VE BEEN ACCELERATED THREE SECONDS INTO THE FUTURE, POPS! I CAN SEE ALL POSSIBLE PROBABILITIES AT THE SAME TIME--
I CAN TRY TEN COMBINATIONS A WAIT, NO, THAT'S NOT IT--TEN SECOND--DAMMIT! THOUGHT I H IT--SO IT'LL ONLY BE A MATTE OF TIME BEFORE--CRAP!
TEN COMBO A NO THAT'S A SECOND HAD IT! IT'LL ONLY BE A CRAP!
DO YOU HAVE ANY IDEA WHAT HE'S SAYING?
HELL, NO.
UHHHH....

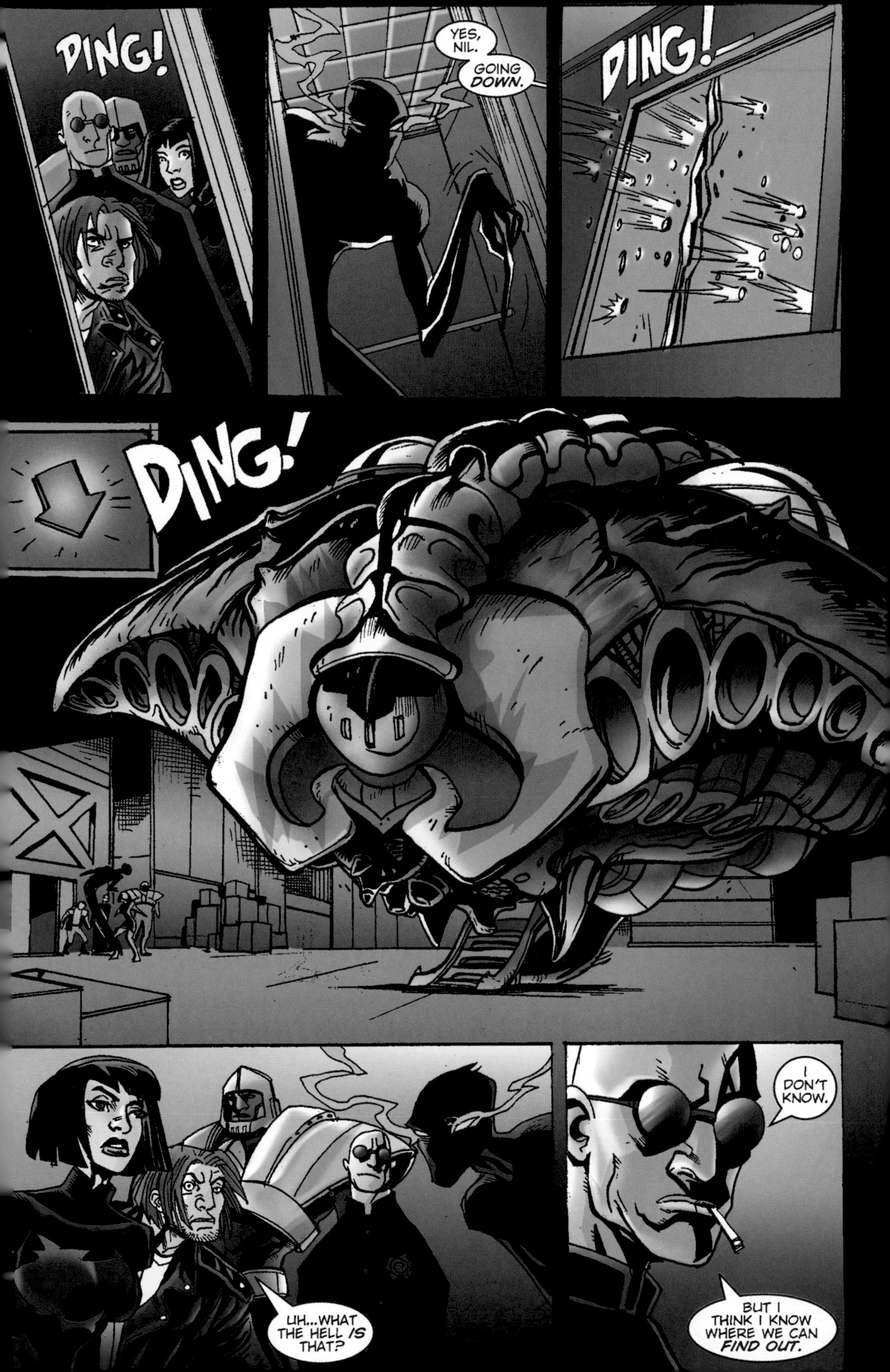
DING!
YES, NIL.
GOING DOWN.
DING!
DING!
UH...WHAT THE HELL IS THAT?
I DON'T KNOW.
BUT I THINK I KNOW WHERE WE CAN FIND OUT.

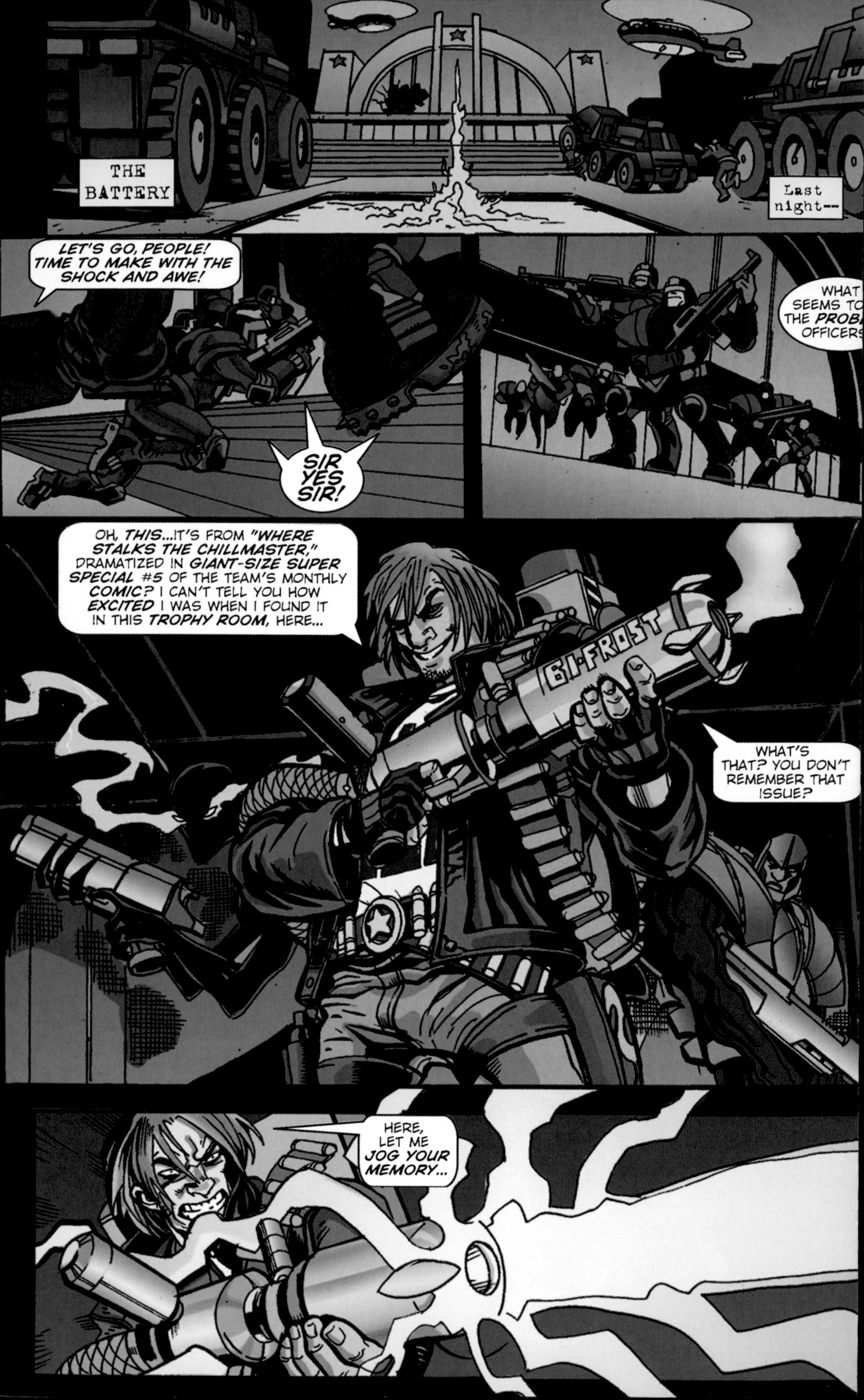
THE BATTERY
Last night--
LET'S GO, PEOPLE! TIME TO MAKE WITH THE SHOCK AND AWE!
SIR YES SIR!
WHAT SEEMS TO THE PROBL OFFICERS
OH, THIS...IT'S FROM "WHERE STALKS THE CHILLMASTER," DRAMATIZED IN GIANT-SIZE SUPER SPECIAL #5 OF THE TEAM'S MONTHLY COMIC? I CAN'T TELL YOU HOW EXCITED I WAS WHEN I FOUND IT IN THIS TROPHY ROOM, HERE...
GI-FROST
WHAT'S THAT? YOU DON'T REMEMBER THAT ISSUE?
HERE, LET ME JOG YOUR MEMORY...

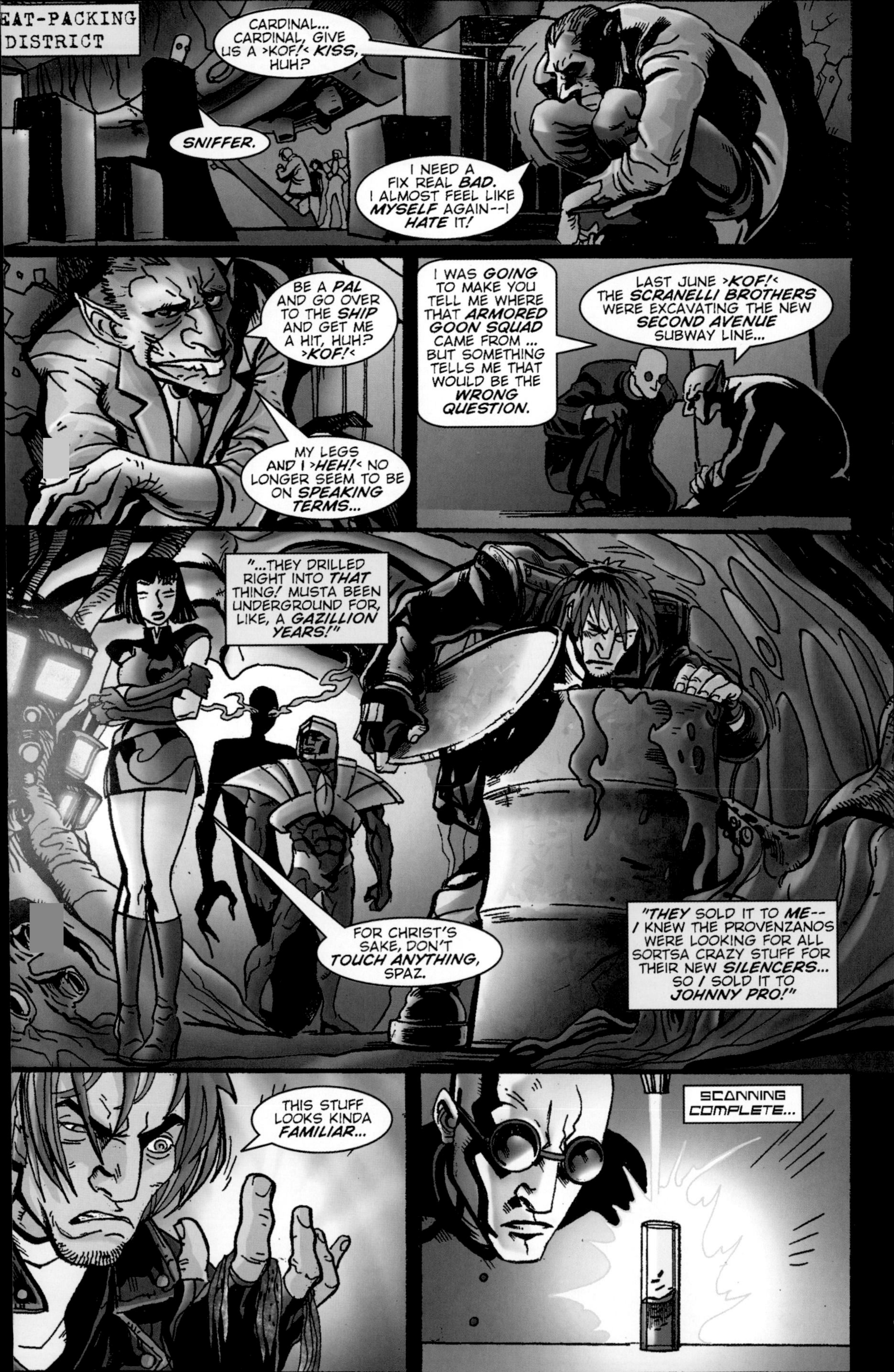
EAT-PACKING DISTRICT
CARDINAL... CARDINAL, GIVE US A >KOF!< KISS, HUH?
SNIFFER.
I NEED A FIX REAL BAD. I ALMOST FEEL LIKE MYSELF AGAIN--I HATE IT!
BE A PAL AND GO OVER TO THE SHIP AND GET ME A HIT, HUH? >KOF!<
MY LEGS AND I >HEH!< NO LONGER SEEM TO BE ON SPEAKING TERMS...
I WAS GOING TO MAKE YOU TELL ME WHERE THAT ARMORED GOON SQUAD CAME FROM ... BUT SOMETHING TELLS ME THAT WOULD BE THE WRONG QUESTION.
LAST JUNE >KOF!< THE SCRANELLI BROTHERS WERE EXCAVATING THE NEW SECOND AVENUE SUBWAY LINE...
"...THEY DRILLED RIGHT INTO THAT THING! MUSTA BEEN UNDERGROUND FOR, LIKE, A GAZILLION YEARS!"
FOR CHRIST'S SAKE, DON'T TOUCH ANYTHING, SPAZ.
"THEY SOLD IT TO ME-- I KNEW THE PROVENZANOS WERE LOOKING FOR ALL SORTSA CRAZY STUFF FOR THEIR NEW SILENCERS... SO I SOLD IT TO JOHNNY PRO!"
THIS STUFF LOOKS KINDA FAMILIAR...
SCANNING COMPLETE...

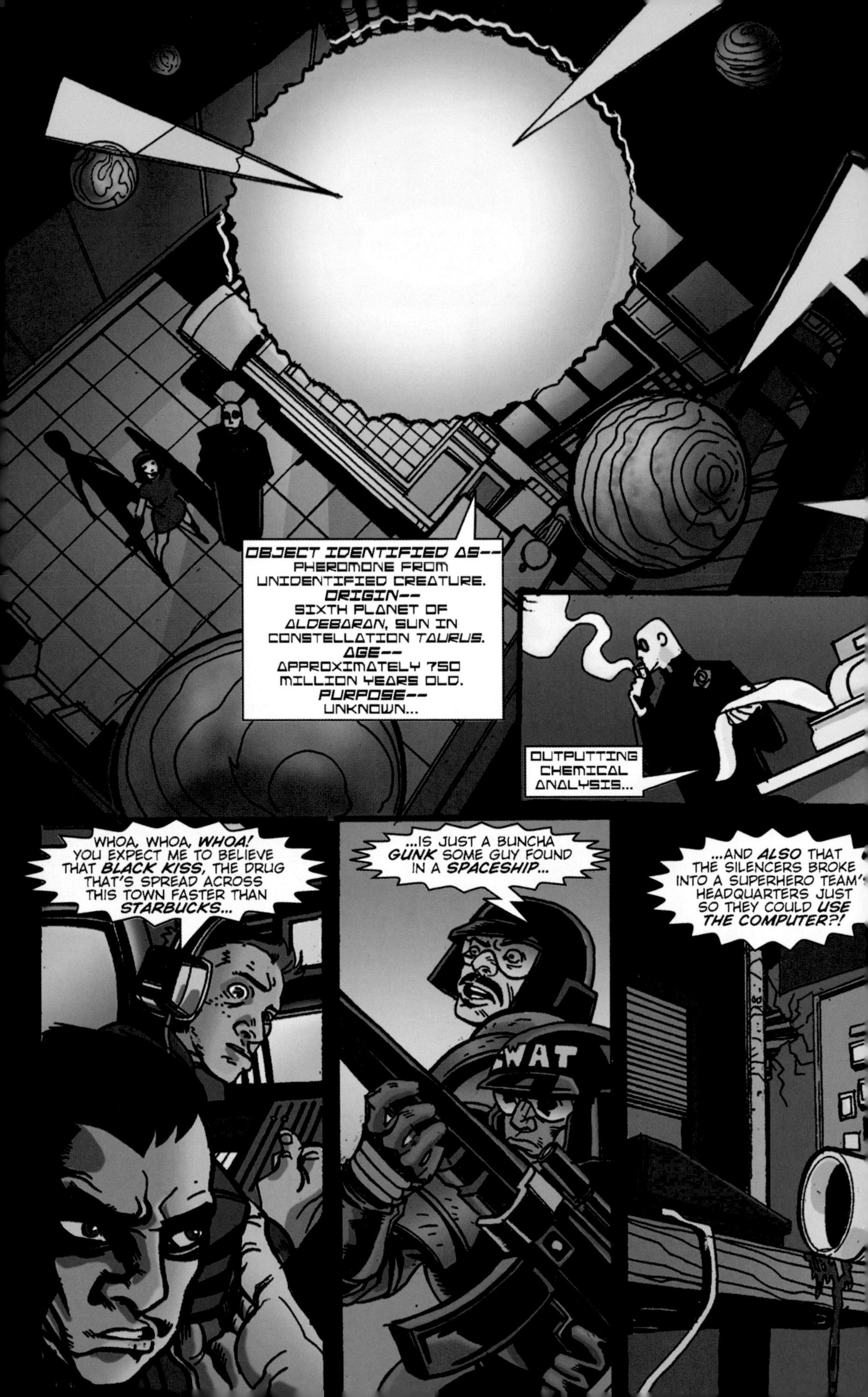
OBJECT IDENTIFIED AS-- PHEROMONE FROM UNIDENTIFIED CREATURE. ORIGIN-- SIXTH PLANET OF ALDEBARAN, SUN IN CONSTELLATION TAURUS. AGE-- APPROXIMATELY 750 MILLION YEARS OLD. PURPOSE-- UNKNOWN...
OUTPUTTING CHEMICAL ANALYSIS...
WHOA, WHOA, WHOA! YOU EXPECT ME TO BELIEVE THAT BLACK KISS, THE DRUG THAT'S SPREAD ACROSS THIS TOWN FASTER THAN STARBUCKS...
...IS JUST A BUNCHA GUNK SOME GUY FOUND IN A SPACESHIP...
...AND ALSO THAT THE SILENCERS BROKE INTO A SUPERHERO TEAM' HEADQUARTERS JUST SO THEY COULD USE THE COMPUTER?!
SWAT

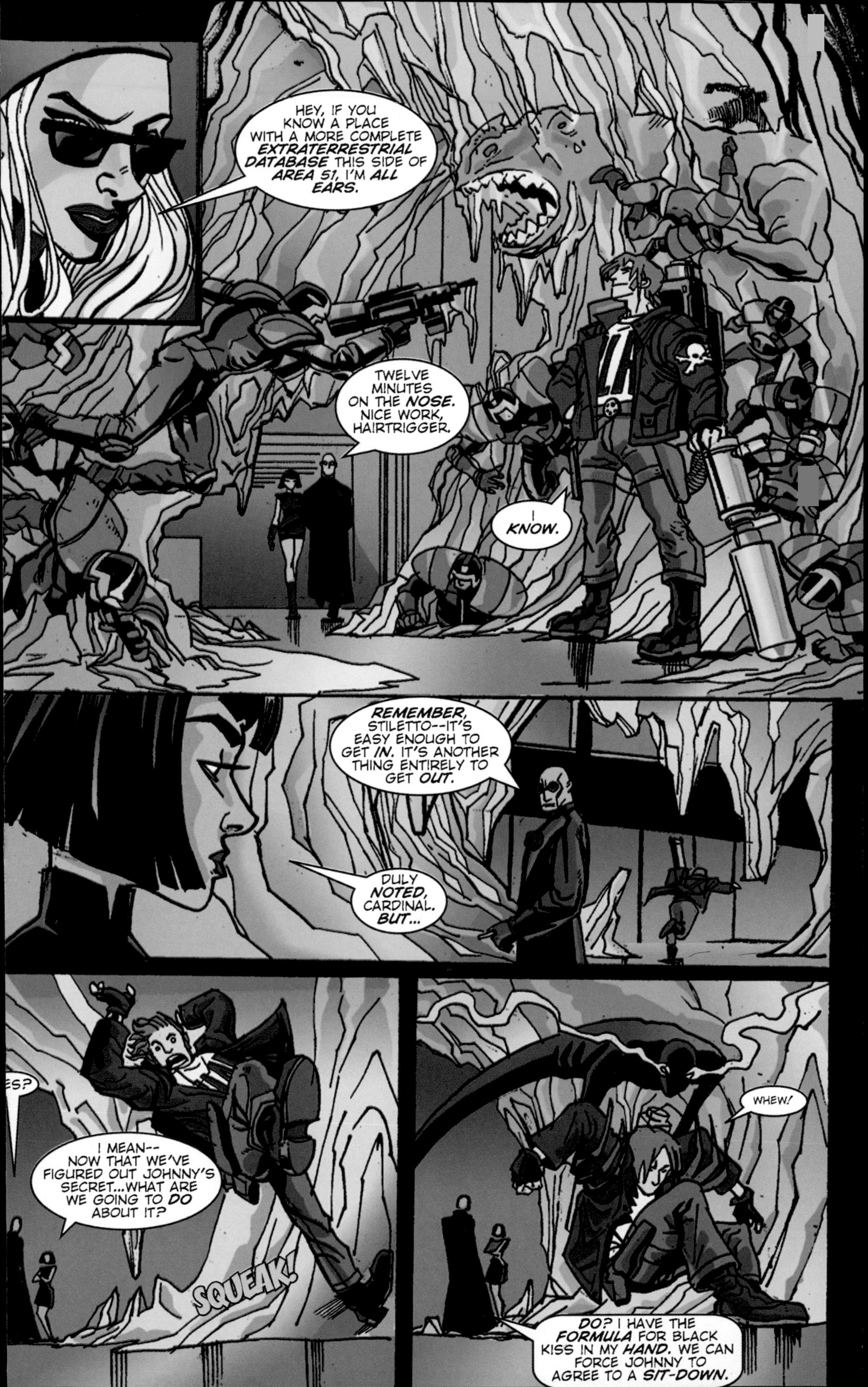
HEY, IF YOU KNOW A PLACE WITH A MORE COMPLETE EXTRATERRESTRIAL DATABASE THIS SIDE OF AREA 51, I'M ALL EARS.
TWELVE MINUTES ON THE NOSE. NICE WORK, HAIRTRIGGER.
I KNOW.
REMEMBER, STILETTO--IT'S EASY ENOUGH TO GET IN. IT'S ANOTHER THING ENTIRELY TO GET OUT.
DULY NOTED, CARDINAL. BUT...
I MEAN-- NOW THAT WE'VE FIGURED OUT JOHNNY'S SECRET...WHAT ARE WE GOING TO DO ABOUT IT?
SQUEAK!
WHEW!
DO? I HAVE THE FORMULA FOR BLACK KISS IN MY HAND. WE CAN FORCE JOHNNY TO AGREE TO A SIT-DOWN.

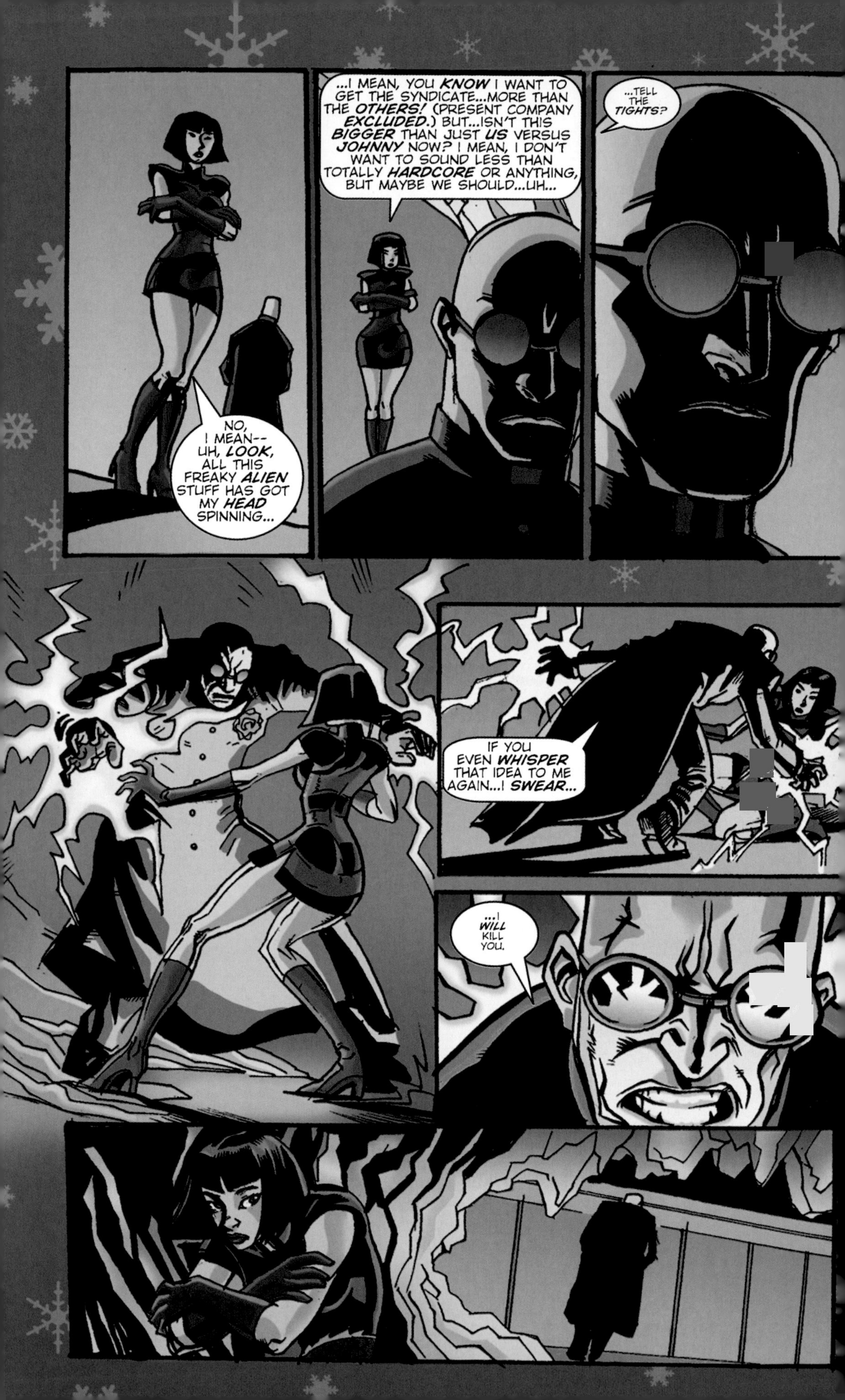
NO, I MEAN-- UH, LOOK, ALL THIS FREAKY ALIEN STUFF HAS GOT MY HEAD SPINNING...
...I MEAN, YOU KNOW I WANT TO GET THE SYNDICATE...MORE THAN THE OTHERS! (PRESENT COMPANY EXCLUDED.) BUT...ISN'T THIS BIGGER THAN JUST US VERSUS JOHNNY NOW? I MEAN, I DON'T WANT TO SOUND LESS THAN TOTALLY HARDCORE OR ANYTHING, BUT MAYBE WE SHOULD...UH...
...TELL THE TIGHTS?
IF YOU EVEN WHISPER THAT IDEA TO ME AGAIN...I SWEAR...
...I WILL KILL YOU.

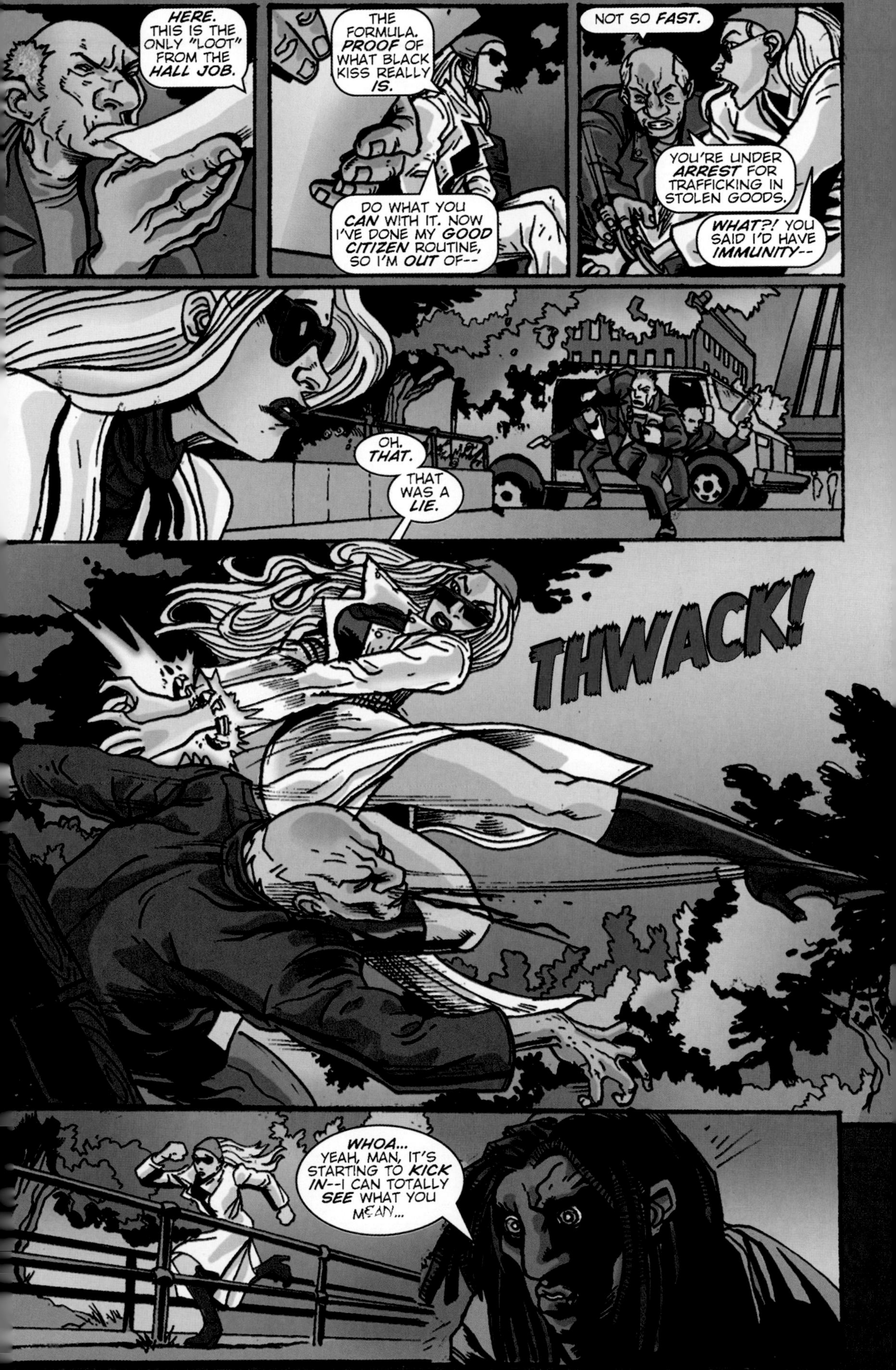

HERE. THIS IS THE ONLY "LOOT" FROM THE HALL JOB.
THE FORMULA. PROOF OF WHAT BLACK KISS REALLY IS.
DO WHAT YOU CAN WITH IT. NOW I'VE DONE MY GOOD CITIZEN ROUTINE, SO I'M OUT OF--
NOT SO FAST.
YOU'RE UNDER ARREST FOR TRAFFICKING IN STOLEN GOODS.
WHAT?! YOU SAID I'D HAVE IMMUNITY--
OH. THAT.
THAT WAS A LIE.
THWACK!
WHOA... YEAH, MAN, IT'S STARTING TO KICK IN--I CAN TOTALLY SEE WHAT YOU MEAN...

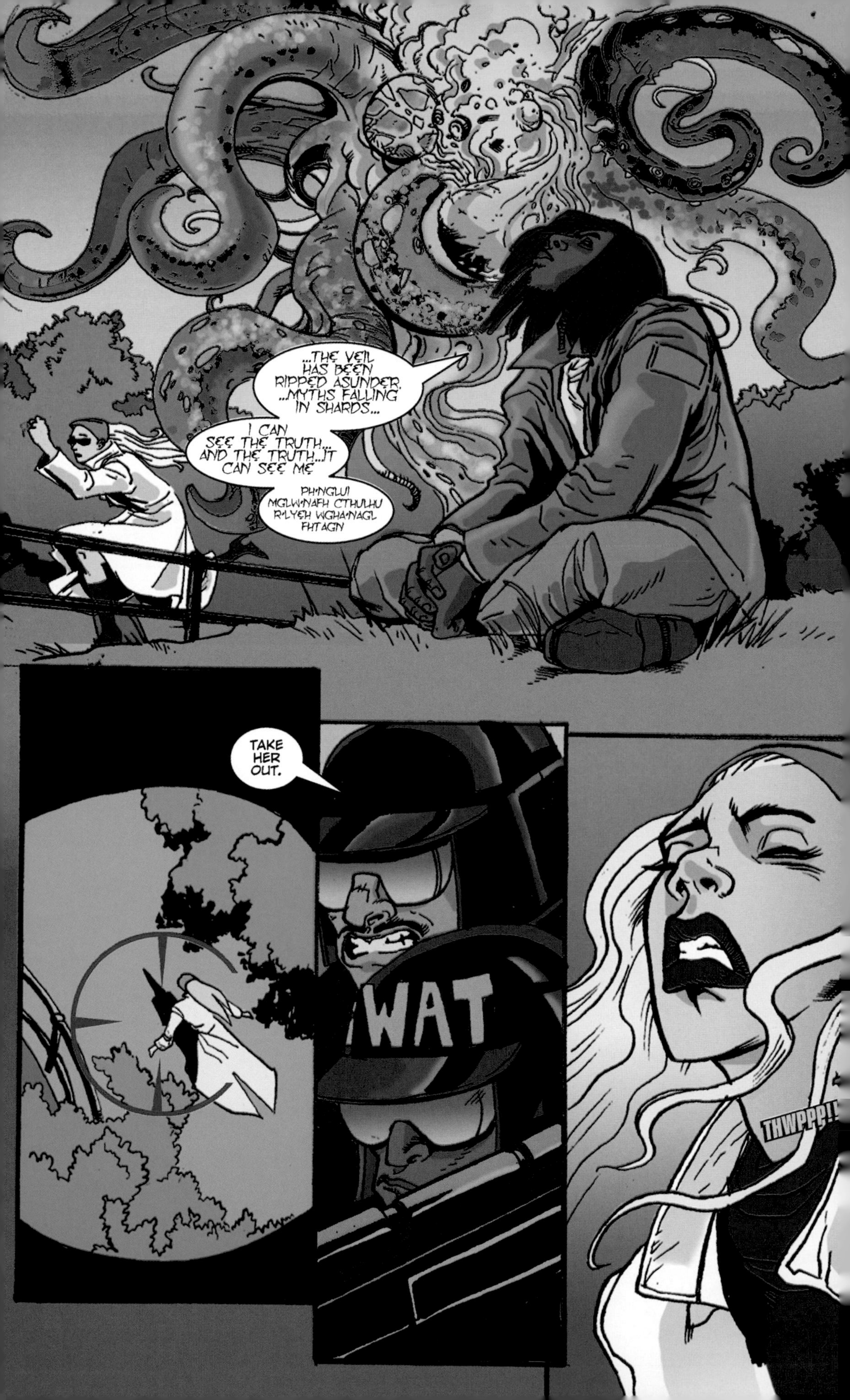
...THE VEIL HAS BEEN RIPPED ASUNDER. ...MYTHS FALLING IN SHARDS...
I CAN SEE THE TRUTH... AND THE TRUTH...IT CAN SEE ME
PH'NGLUI MGLW'NAFH CTHULHU R'LYEH WGAH'NAGL FHTAGN
TAKE HER OUT.
SWAT
THWPPP!!

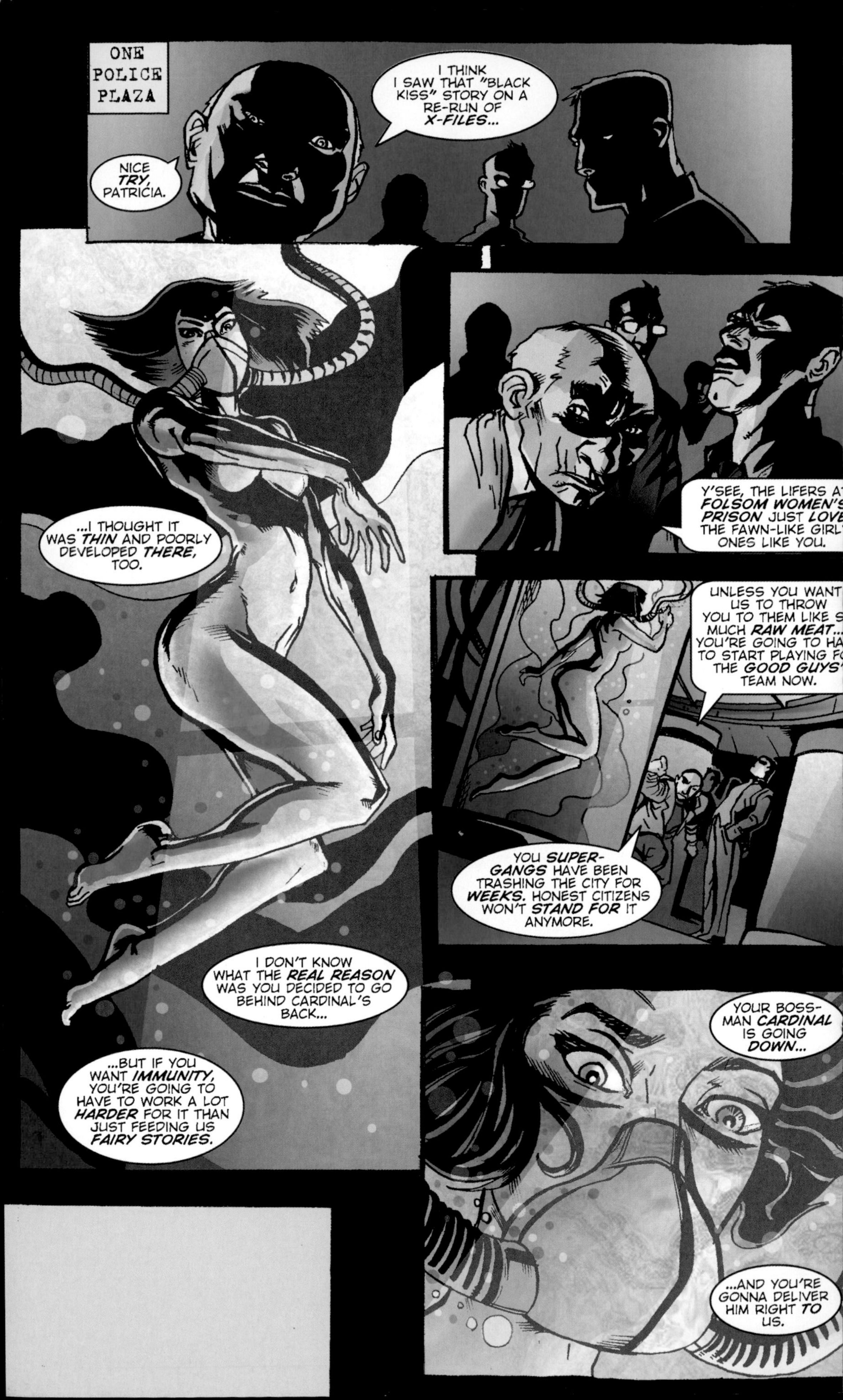

ONE POLICE PLAZA
I THINK I SAW THAT "BLACK KISS" STORY ON A RE-RUN OF X-FILES...
NICE TRY, PATRICIA.
...I THOUGHT IT WAS THIN AND POORLY DEVELOPED THERE, TOO.
Y'SEE, THE LIFERS AT FOLSOM WOMEN'S PRISON JUST LOVE THE FAWN-LIKE GIRL ONES LIKE YOU.
UNLESS YOU WANT US TO THROW YOU TO THEM LIKE SO MUCH RAW MEAT... YOU'RE GOING TO HA TO START PLAYING FO THE GOOD GUYS' TEAM NOW.
YOU SUPER-GANGS HAVE BEEN TRASHING THE CITY FOR WEEKS. HONEST CITIZENS WON'T STAND FOR IT ANYMORE.
I DON'T KNOW WHAT THE REAL REASON WAS YOU DECIDED TO GO BEHIND CARDINAL'S BACK...
...BUT IF YOU WANT IMMUNITY, YOU'RE GOING TO HAVE TO WORK A LOT HARDER FOR IT THAN JUST FEEDING US FAIRY STORIES.
YOUR BOSS-MAN CARDINAL IS GOING DOWN...
...AND YOU'RE GONNA DELIVER HIM RIGHT TO US.

TÊTE-À-TÊTE

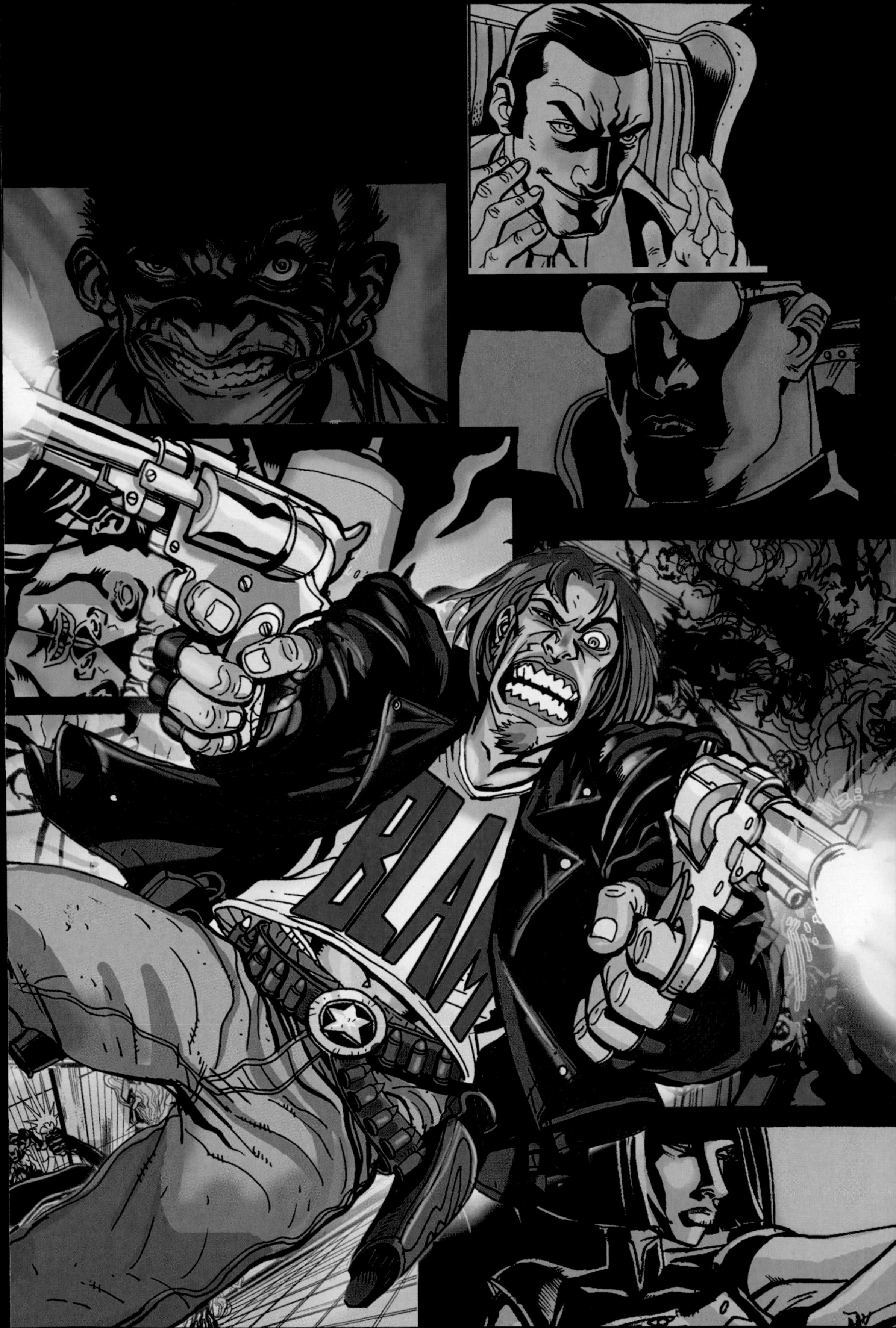
BLAM

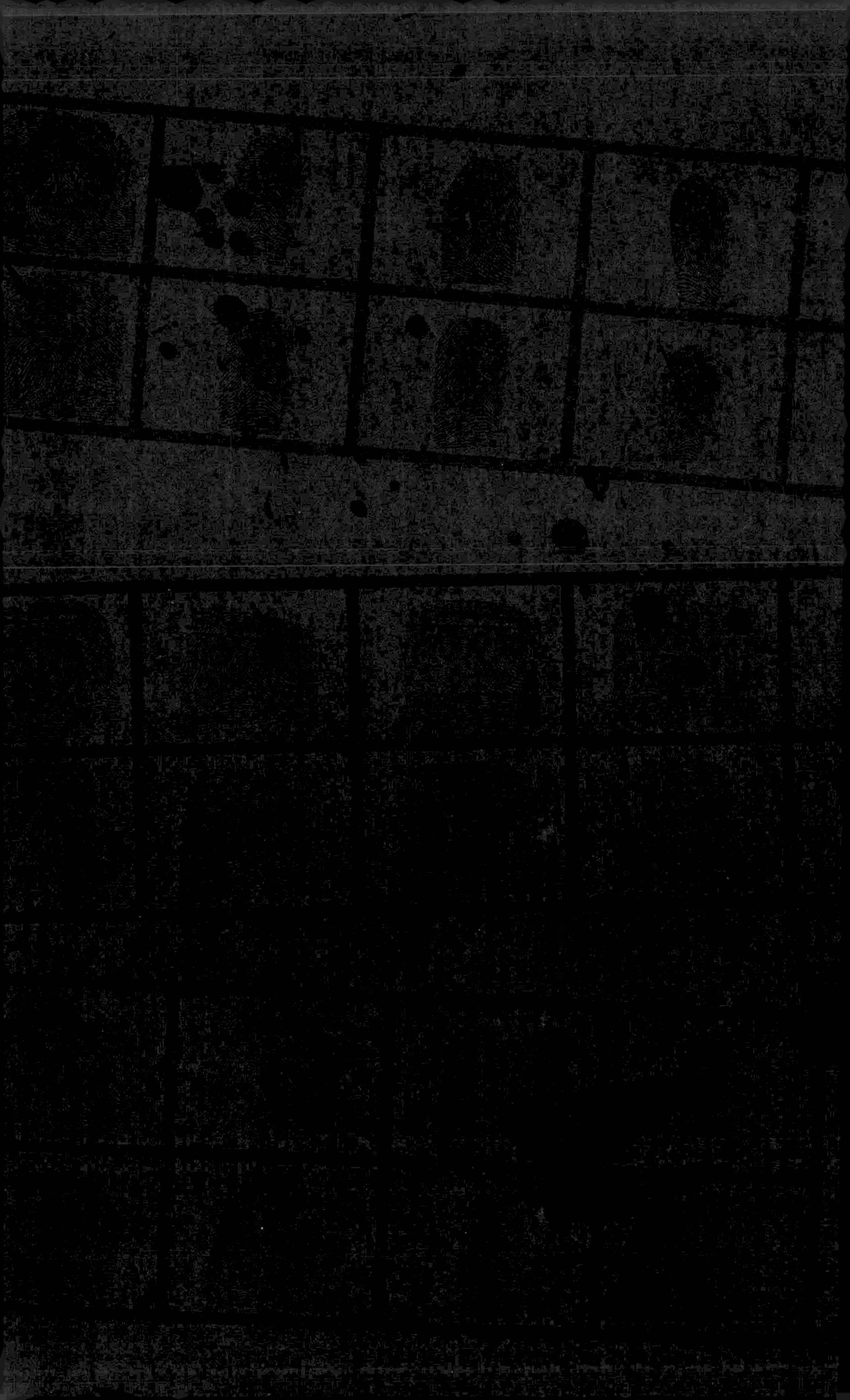

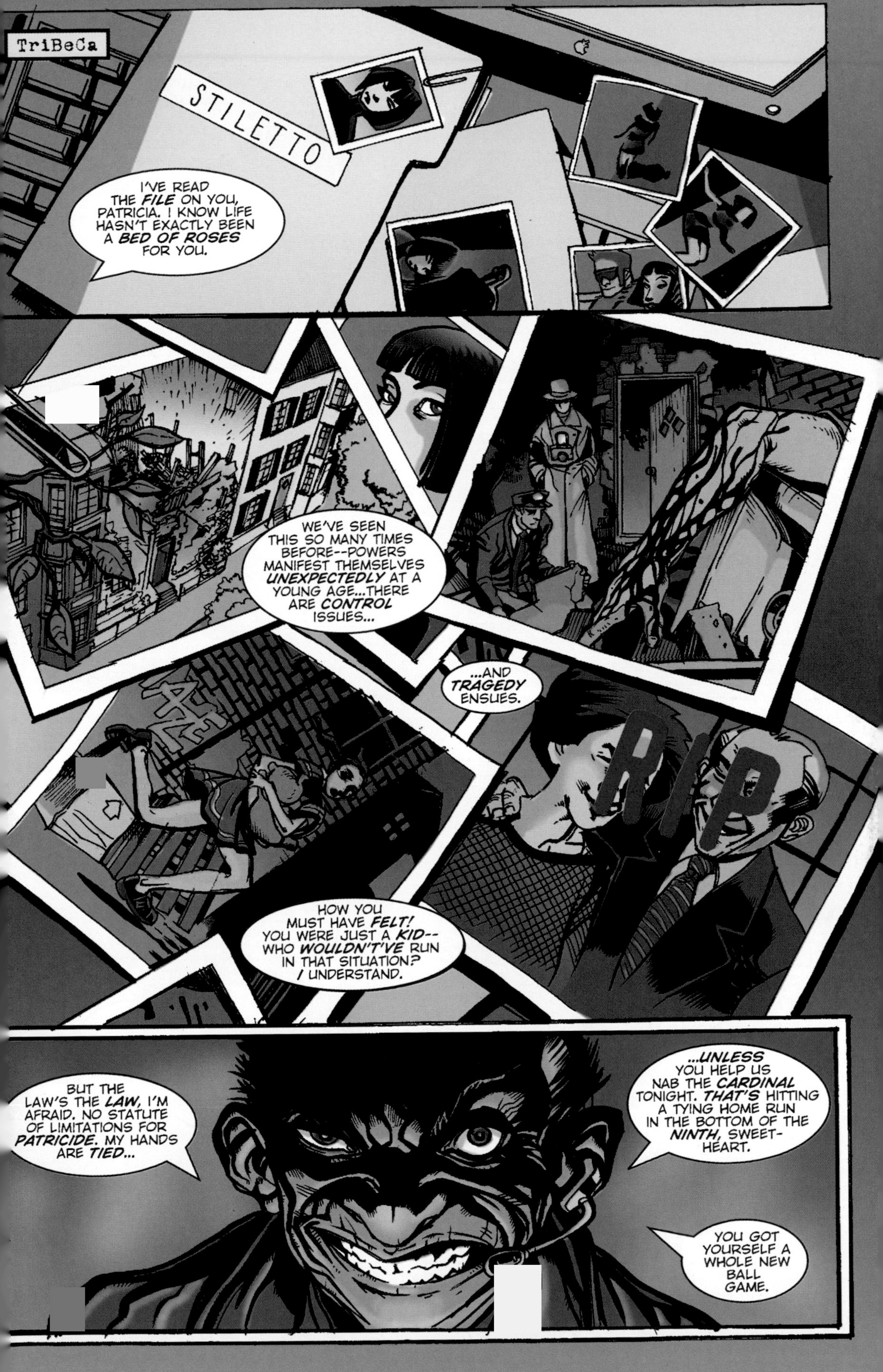
TriBeCa
STILETTO
I'VE READ THE FILE ON YOU, PATRICIA. I KNOW LIFE HASN'T EXACTLY BEEN A BED OF ROSES FOR YOU.
WE'VE SEEN THIS SO MANY TIMES BEFORE--POWERS MANIFEST THEMSELVES UNEXPECTEDLY AT A YOUNG AGE...THERE ARE CONTROL ISSUES...
...AND TRAGEDY ENSUES.
RIP
HOW YOU MUST HAVE FELT! YOU WERE JUST A KID--WHO WOULDN'T'VE RUN IN THAT SITUATION? I UNDERSTAND.
BUT THE LAW'S THE LAW, I'M AFRAID. NO STATUTE OF LIMITATIONS FOR PATRICIDE. MY HANDS ARE TIED...
...UNLESS YOU HELP US NAB THE CARDINAL TONIGHT. THAT'S HITTING A TYING HOME RUN IN THE BOTTOM OF THE NINTH, SWEET-HEART.
YOU GOT YOURSELF A WHOLE NEW BALL GAME.

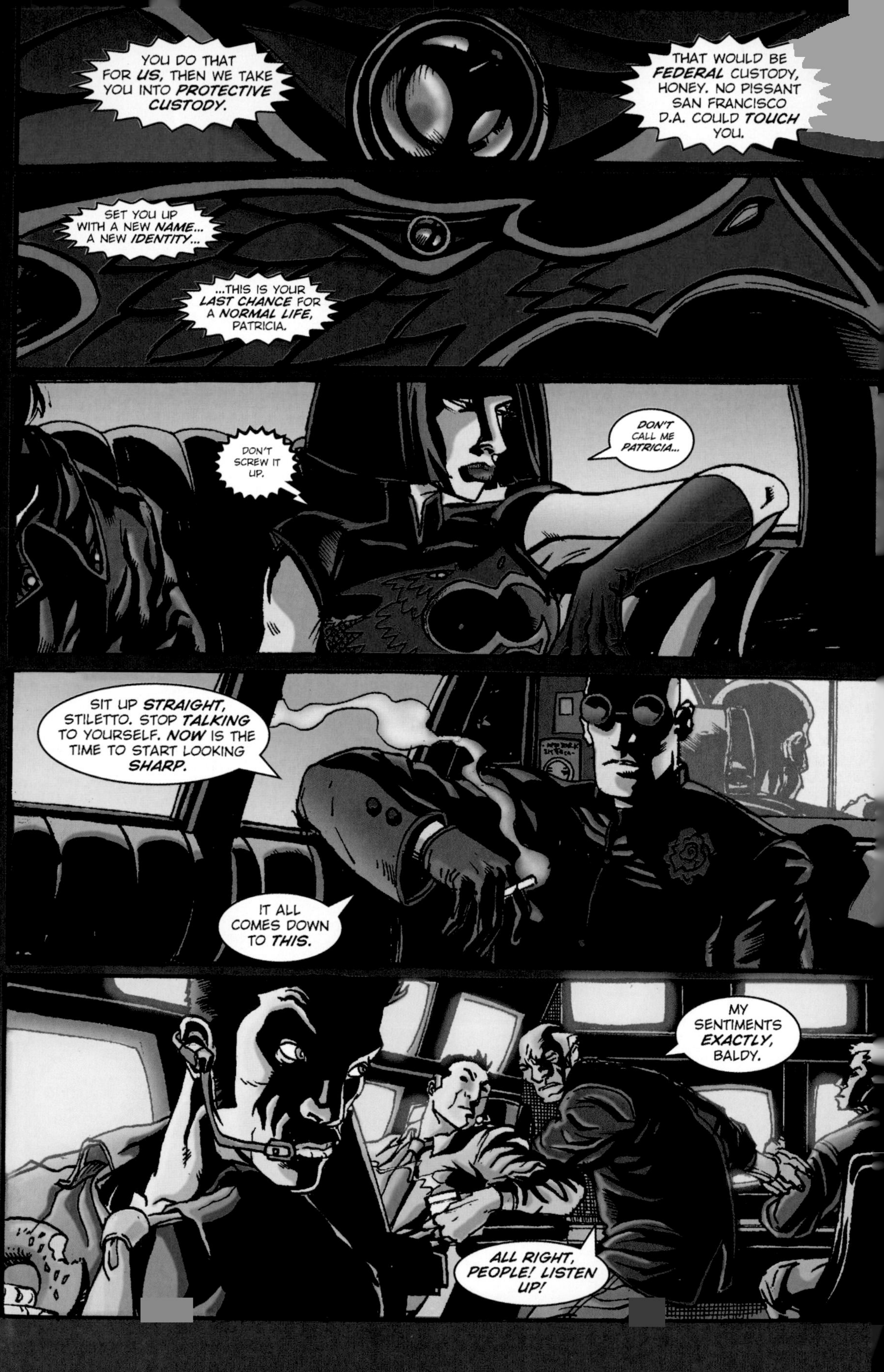
YOU DO THAT FOR US, THEN WE TAKE YOU INTO PROTECTIVE CUSTODY.
THAT WOULD BE FEDERAL CUSTODY, HONEY. NO PISSANT SAN FRANCISCO D.A. COULD TOUCH YOU.
SET YOU UP WITH A NEW NAME... A NEW IDENTITY...
...THIS IS YOUR LAST CHANCE FOR A NORMAL LIFE, PATRICIA.
DON'T SCREW IT UP.
DON'T CALL ME PATRICIA...
SIT UP STRAIGHT, STILETTO. STOP TALKING TO YOURSELF. NOW IS THE TIME TO START LOOKING SHARP.
IT ALL COMES DOWN TO THIS.
MY SENTIMENTS EXACTLY, BALDY.
ALL RIGHT, PEOPLE! LISTEN UP!

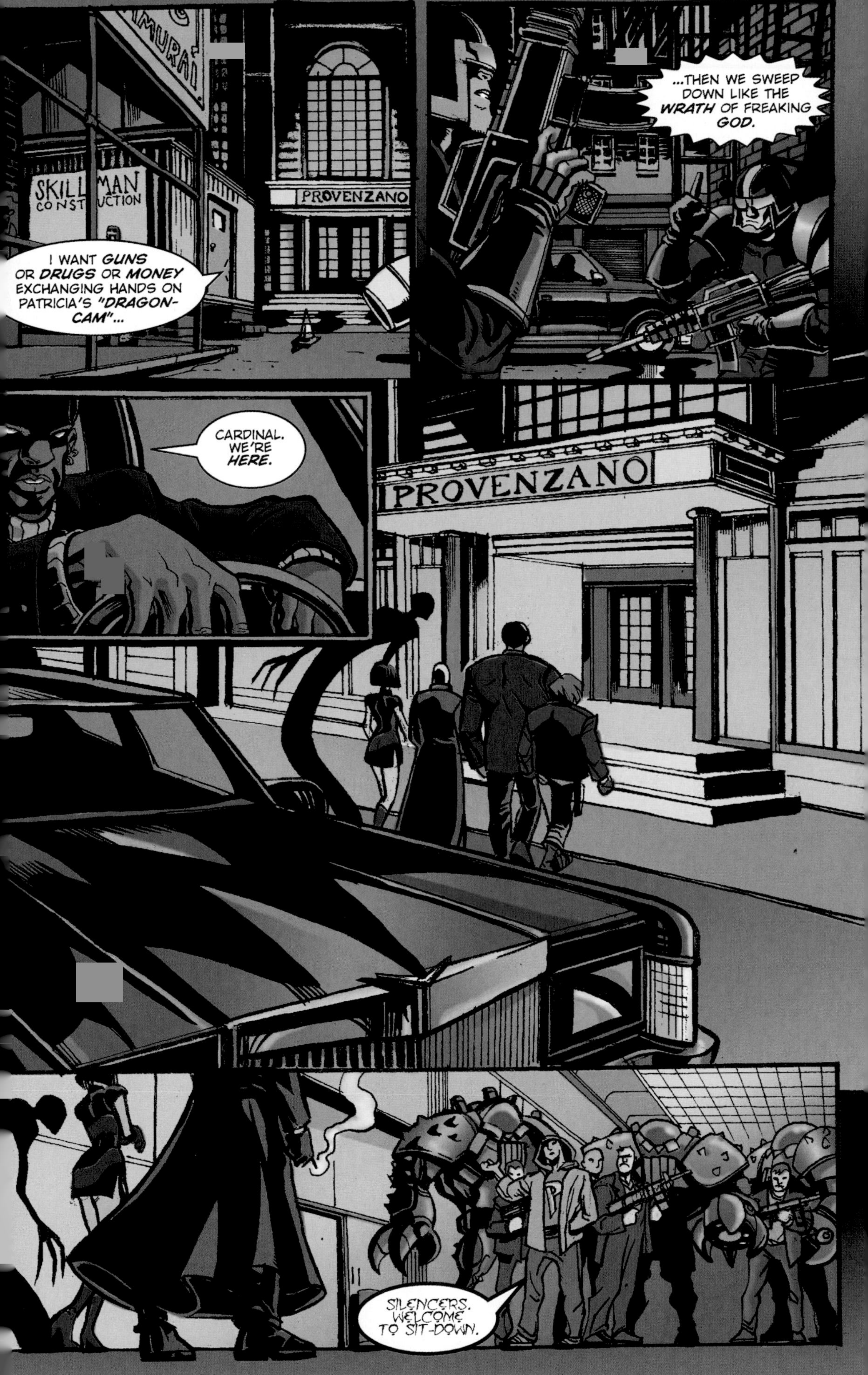
PROVENZANO
I WANT GUNS OR DRUGS OR MONEY EXCHANGING HANDS ON PATRICIA'S "DRAGON-CAM"...
...THEN WE SWEEP DOWN LIKE THE WRATH OF FREAKING GOD.
CARDINAL. WE'RE HERE.
PROVENZANO
SILENCERS. WELCOME TO SIT-DOWN.

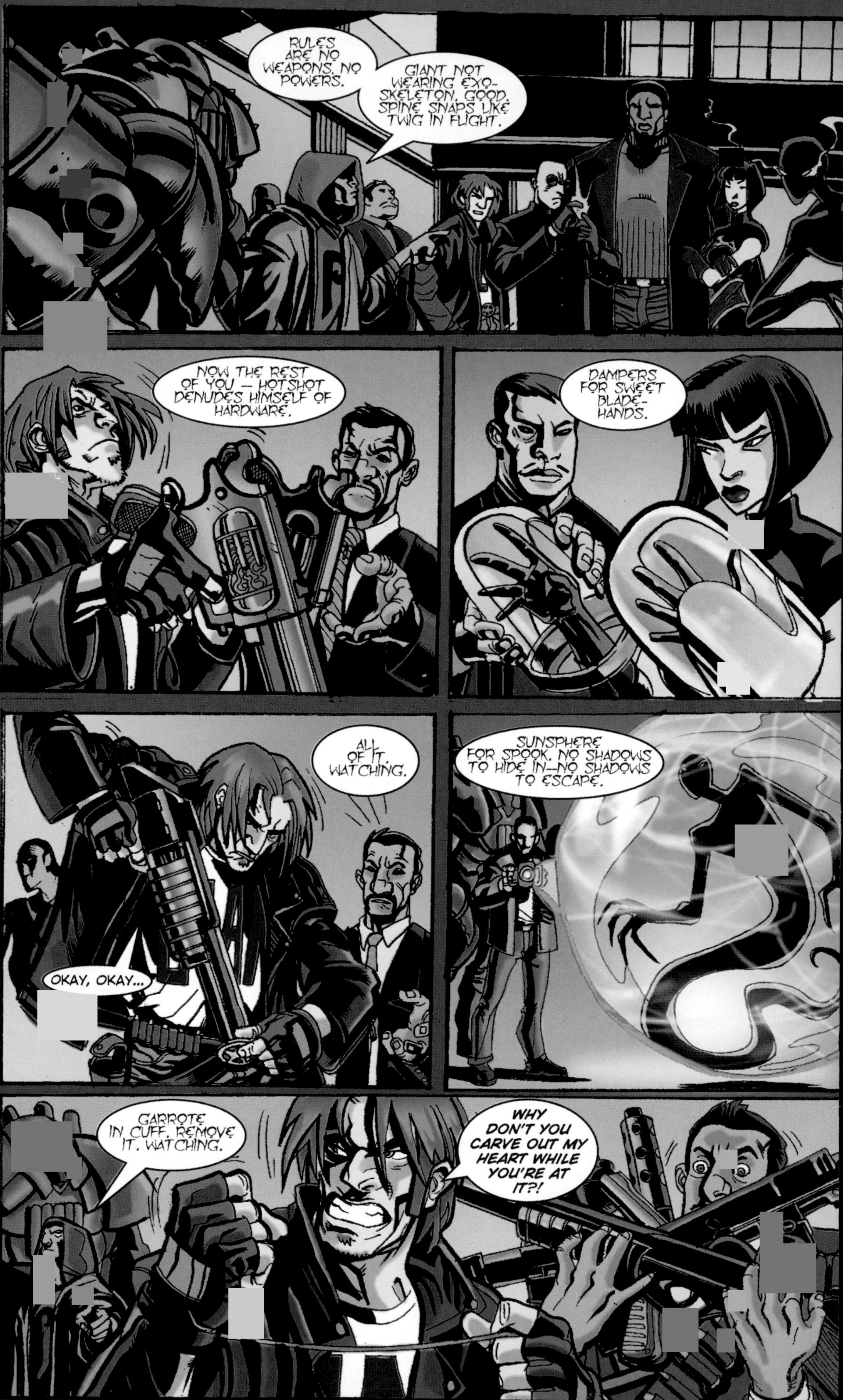
RULES ARE NO WEAPONS, NO POWERS.
GIANT NOT WEARING EXO-SKELETON. GOOD. SPINE SNAPS LIKE TWIG IN FLIGHT.
NOW THE REST OF YOU -- HOTSHOT DENUDES HIMSELF OF HARDWARE.
DAMPERS FOR SWEET BLADE-HANDS.
ALL OF IT. WATCHING.
OKAY, OKAY...
SUNSPHERE FOR SPOOK. NO SHADOWS TO HIDE IN--NO SHADOWS TO ESCAPE.
GARROTE IN CUFF. REMOVE IT. WATCHING.
WHY DON'T YOU CARVE OUT MY HEART WHILE YOU'RE AT IT?!

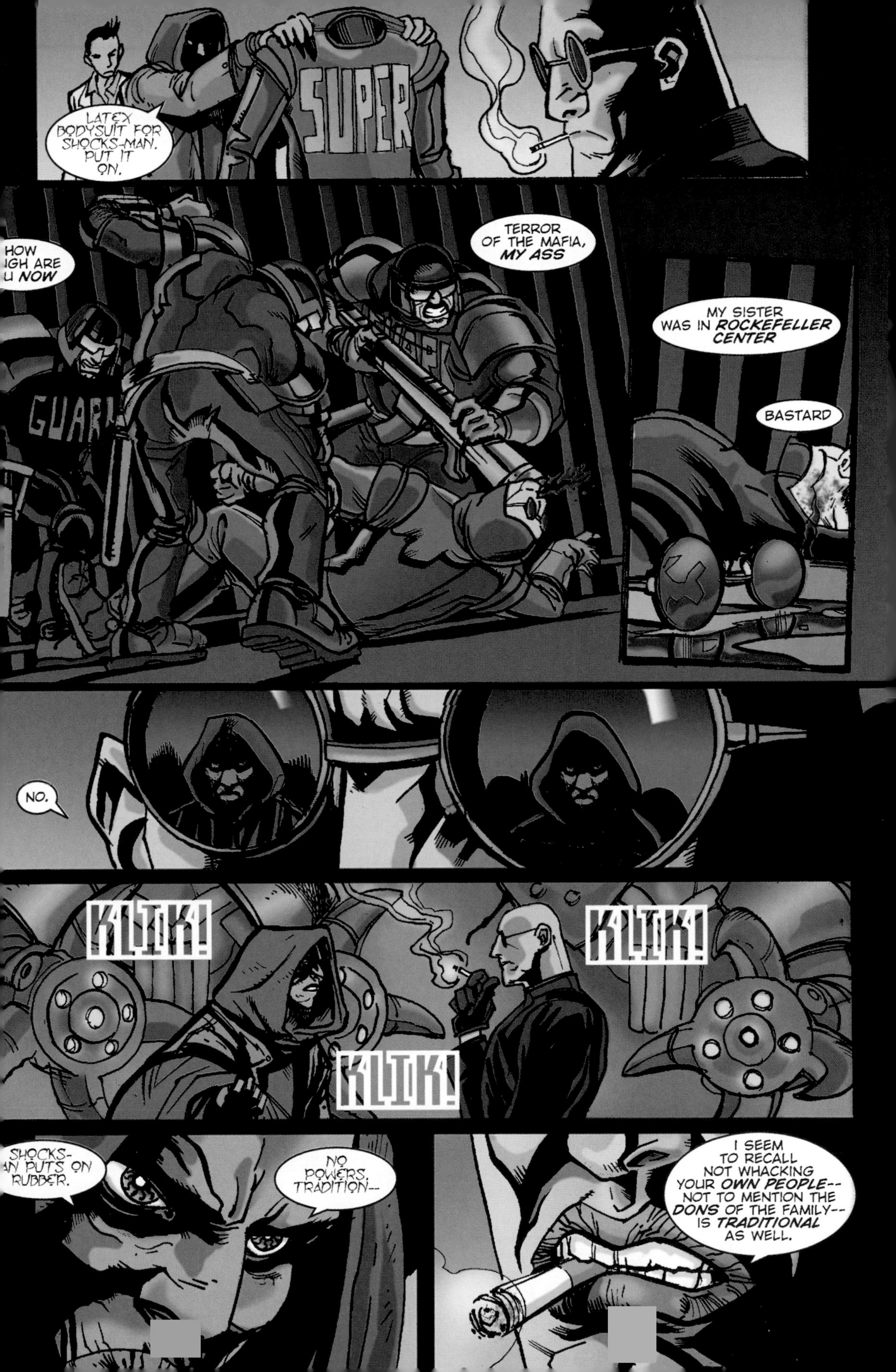

LATEX BODYSUIT FOR SHOCKS-MAN. PUT IT ON.
HOW IGH ARE U NOW
TERROR OF THE MAFIA, MY ASS
MY SISTER WAS IN ROCKEFELLER CENTER
BASTARD
NO.
KLIK!
KLIK!
KLIK!
SHOCKS- AN PUTS ON RUBBER.
NO POWERS. TRADITION--
I SEEM TO RECALL NOT WHACKING YOUR OWN PEOPLE-- NOT TO MENTION THE DONS OF THE FAMILY-- IS TRADITIONAL AS WELL.

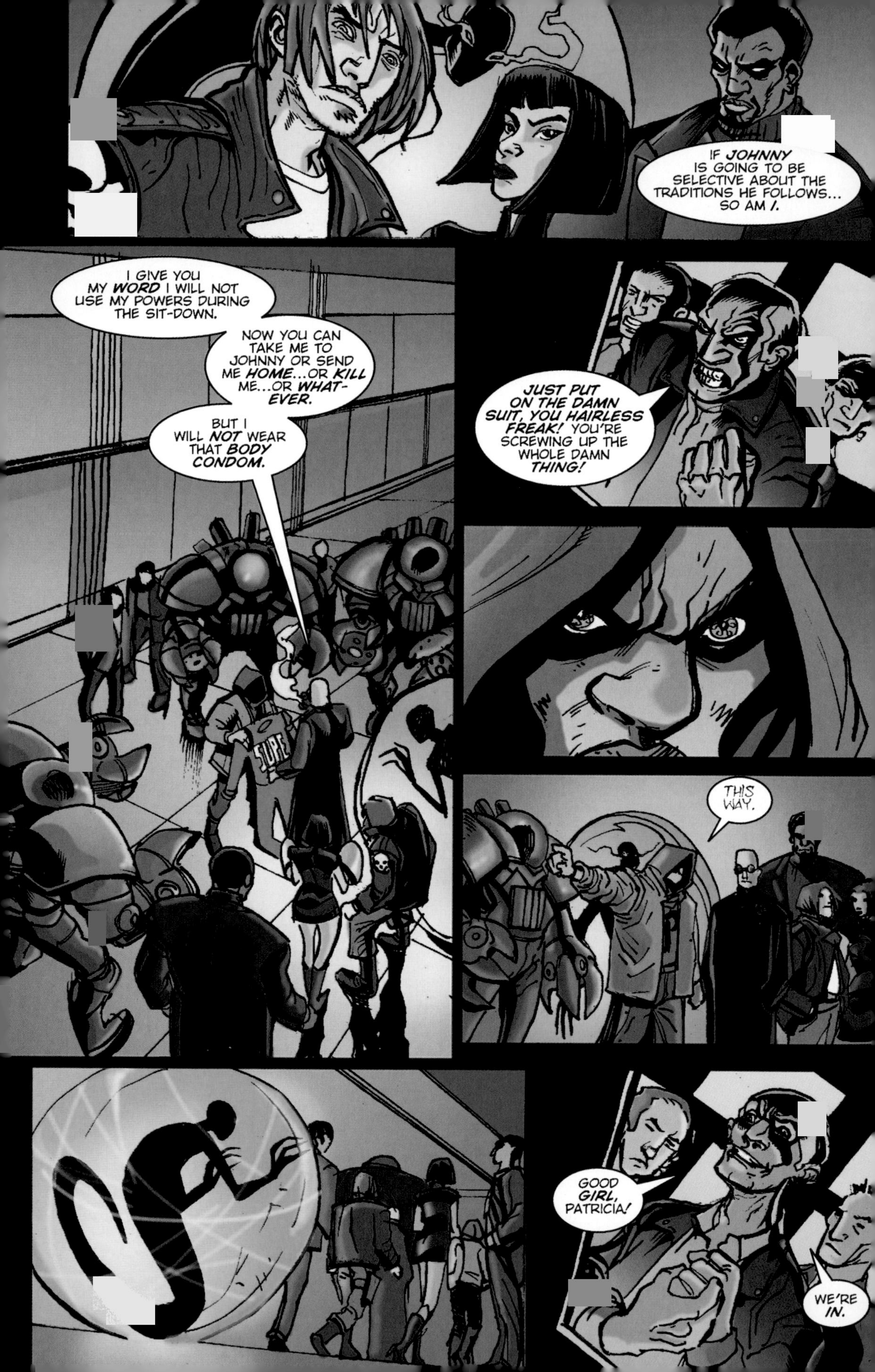
IF JOHNNY IS GOING TO BE SELECTIVE ABOUT THE TRADITIONS HE FOLLOWS... SO AM I.
I GIVE YOU MY WORD I WILL NOT USE MY POWERS DURING THE SIT-DOWN.
NOW YOU CAN TAKE ME TO JOHNNY OR SEND ME HOME...OR KILL ME...OR WHATEVER.
BUT I WILL NOT WEAR THAT BODY CONDOM.
JUST PUT ON THE DAMN SUIT, YOU HAIRLESS FREAK! YOU'RE SCREWING UP THE WHOLE DAMN THING!
THIS WAY.
GOOD GIRL, PATRICIA!
WE'RE IN.

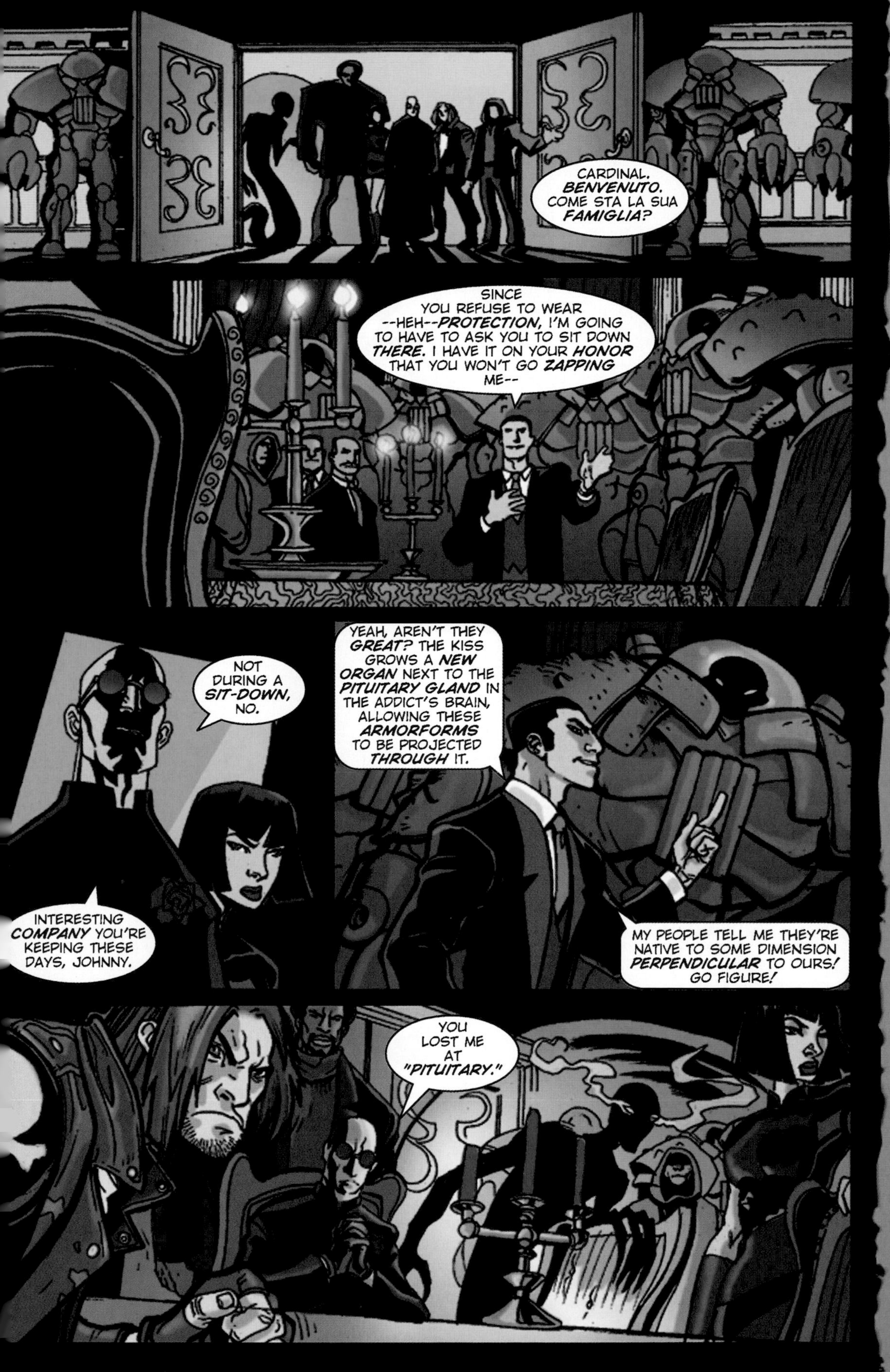
CARDINAL. BENVENUTO. COME STA LA SUA FAMIGLIA?
SINCE YOU REFUSE TO WEAR --HEH--PROTECTION, I'M GOING TO HAVE TO ASK YOU TO SIT DOWN THERE. I HAVE IT ON YOUR HONOR THAT YOU WON'T GO ZAPPING ME--
NOT DURING A SIT-DOWN, NO.
INTERESTING COMPANY YOU'RE KEEPING THESE DAYS, JOHNNY.
YEAH, AREN'T THEY GREAT? THE KISS GROWS A NEW ORGAN NEXT TO THE PITUITARY GLAND IN THE ADDICT'S BRAIN, ALLOWING THESE ARMORFORMS TO BE PROJECTED THROUGH IT.
MY PEOPLE TELL ME THEY'RE NATIVE TO SOME DIMENSION PERPENDICULAR TO OURS! GO FIGURE!
YOU LOST ME AT "PITUITARY."

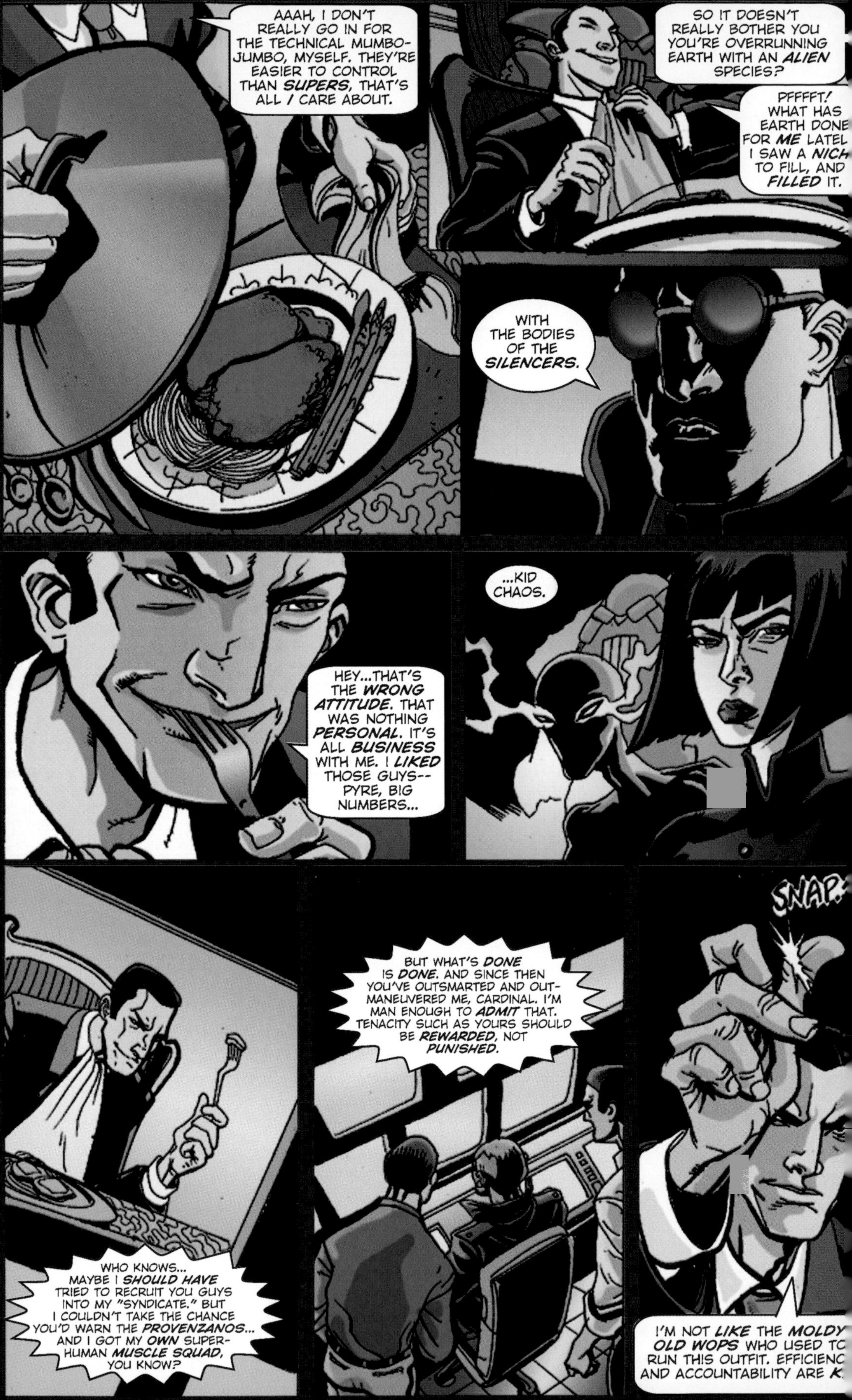
AAAH, I DON'T REALLY GO IN FOR THE TECHNICAL MUMBO-JUMBO, MYSELF. THEY'RE EASIER TO CONTROL THAN SUPERS, THAT'S ALL I CARE ABOUT.
SO IT DOESN'T REALLY BOTHER YOU YOU'RE OVERRUNNING EARTH WITH AN ALIEN SPECIES?
PFFFFT! WHAT HAS EARTH DONE FOR ME LATEL I SAW A NICH TO FILL, AND FILLED IT.
WITH THE BODIES OF THE SILENCERS.
HEY...THAT'S THE WRONG ATTITUDE. THAT WAS NOTHING PERSONAL. IT'S ALL BUSINESS WITH ME. I LIKED THOSE GUYS-- PYRE, BIG NUMBERS...
...KID CHAOS.
WHO KNOWS... MAYBE I SHOULD HAVE TRIED TO RECRUIT YOU GUYS INTO MY "SYNDICATE." BUT I COULDN'T TAKE THE CHANCE YOU'D WARN THE PROVENZANOS... AND I GOT MY OWN SUPER-HUMAN MUSCLE SQUAD, YOU KNOW?
BUT WHAT'S DONE IS DONE. AND SINCE THEN YOU'VE OUTSMARTED AND OUT-MANEUVERED ME, CARDINAL. I'M MAN ENOUGH TO ADMIT THAT. TENACITY SUCH AS YOURS SHOULD BE REWARDED, NOT PUNISHED.
SNAP
I'M NOT LIKE THE MOLDY OLD WOPS WHO USED TC RUN THIS OUTFIT. EFFICIENC AND ACCOUNTABILITY ARE K

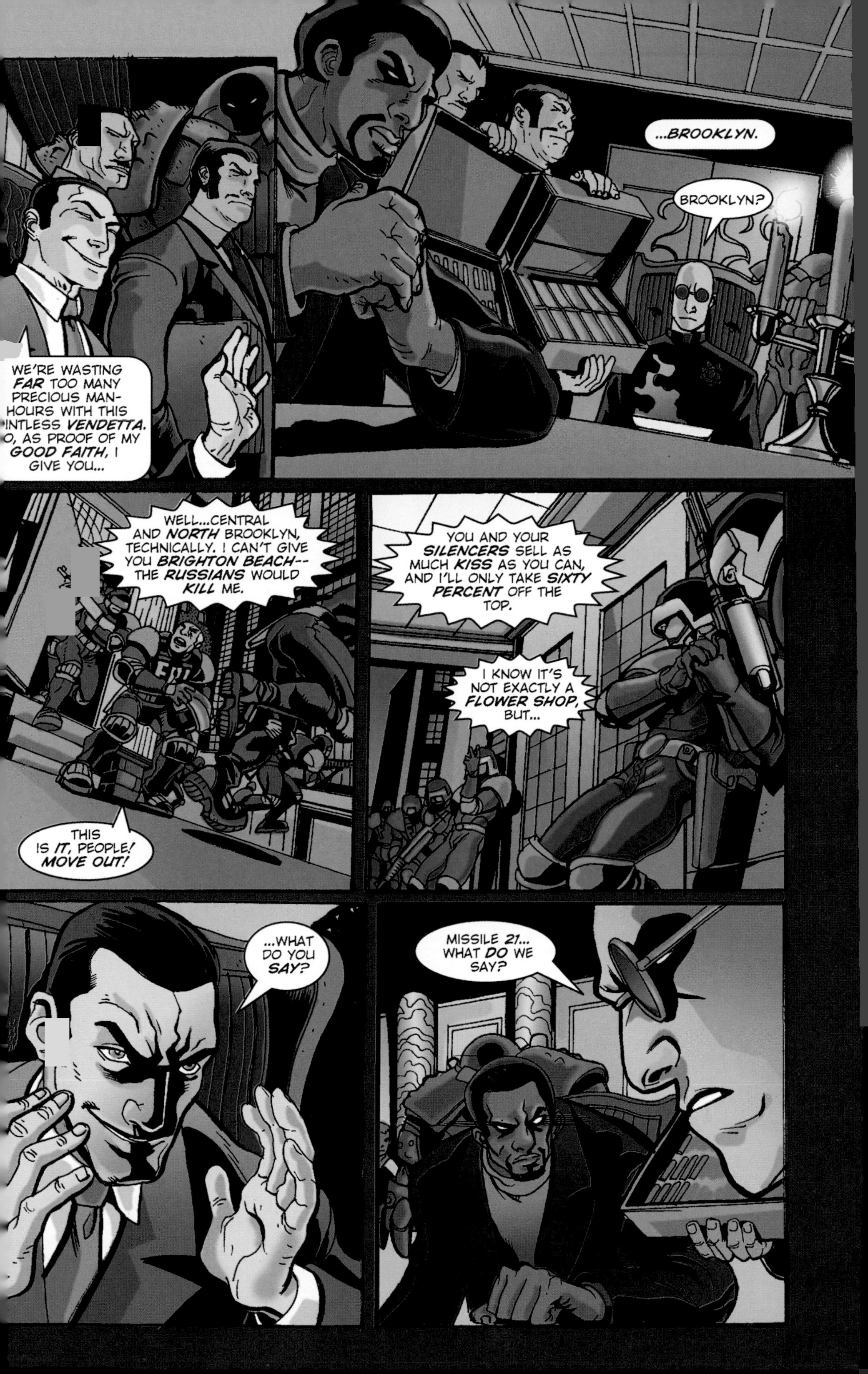
WE'RE WASTING FAR TOO MANY PRECIOUS MAN-HOURS WITH THIS
INTLESS VENDETTA.
O, AS PROOF OF MY GOOD FAITH, I GIVE YOU...
...BROOKLYN.
BROOKLYN?
WELL...CENTRAL AND NORTH BROOKLYN, TECHNICALLY. I CAN'T GIVE YOU BRIGHTON BEACH--THE RUSSIANS WOULD KILL ME.
THIS IS IT, PEOPLE! MOVE OUT!
YOU AND YOUR SILENCERS SELL AS MUCH KISS AS YOU CAN, AND I'LL ONLY TAKE SIXTY PERCENT OFF THE TOP.
I KNOW IT'S NOT EXACTLY A FLOWER SHOP, BUT...
...WHAT DO YOU SAY?
MISSILE 21... WHAT DO WE SAY?

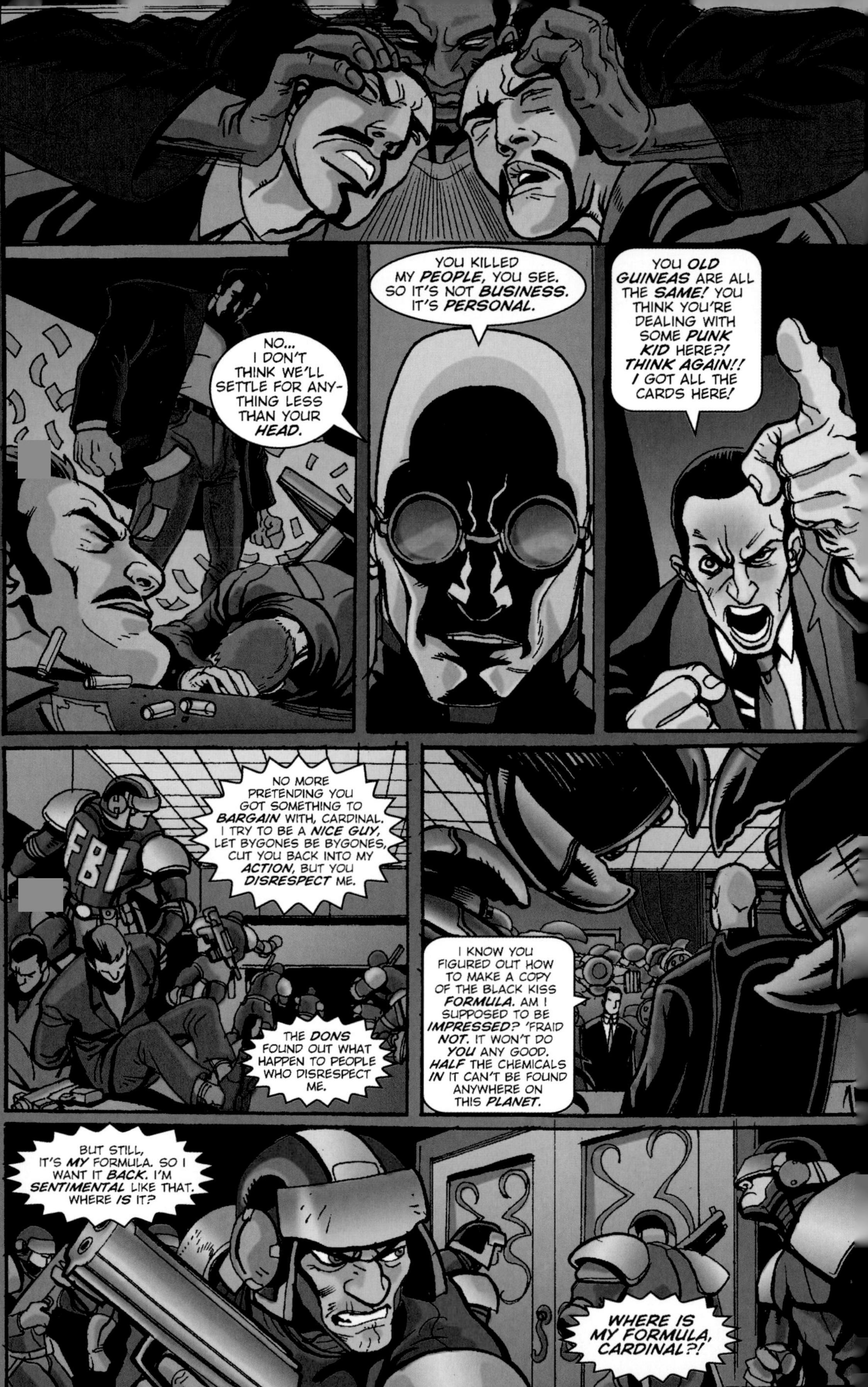
NO... I DON'T THINK WE'LL SETTLE FOR ANYTHING LESS THAN YOUR HEAD.
YOU KILLED MY PEOPLE, YOU SEE. SO IT'S NOT BUSINESS. IT'S PERSONAL.
YOU OLD GUINEAS ARE ALL THE SAME! YOU THINK YOU'RE DEALING WITH SOME PUNK KID HERE?! THINK AGAIN!! I GOT ALL THE CARDS HERE!
NO MORE PRETENDING YOU GOT SOMETHING TO BARGAIN WITH, CARDINAL. I TRY TO BE A NICE GUY, LET BYGONES BE BYGONES, CUT YOU BACK INTO MY ACTION, BUT YOU DISRESPECT ME.
THE DONS FOUND OUT WHAT HAPPEN TO PEOPLE WHO DISRESPECT ME.
I KNOW YOU FIGURED OUT HOW TO MAKE A COPY OF THE BLACK KISS FORMULA. AM I SUPPOSED TO BE IMPRESSED? 'FRAID NOT. IT WON'T DO YOU ANY GOOD. HALF THE CHEMICALS IN IT CAN'T BE FOUND ANYWHERE ON THIS PLANET.
BUT STILL, IT'S MY FORMULA. SO I WANT IT BACK. I'M SENTIMENTAL LIKE THAT. WHERE IS IT?
WHERE IS MY FORMULA, CARDINAL?!

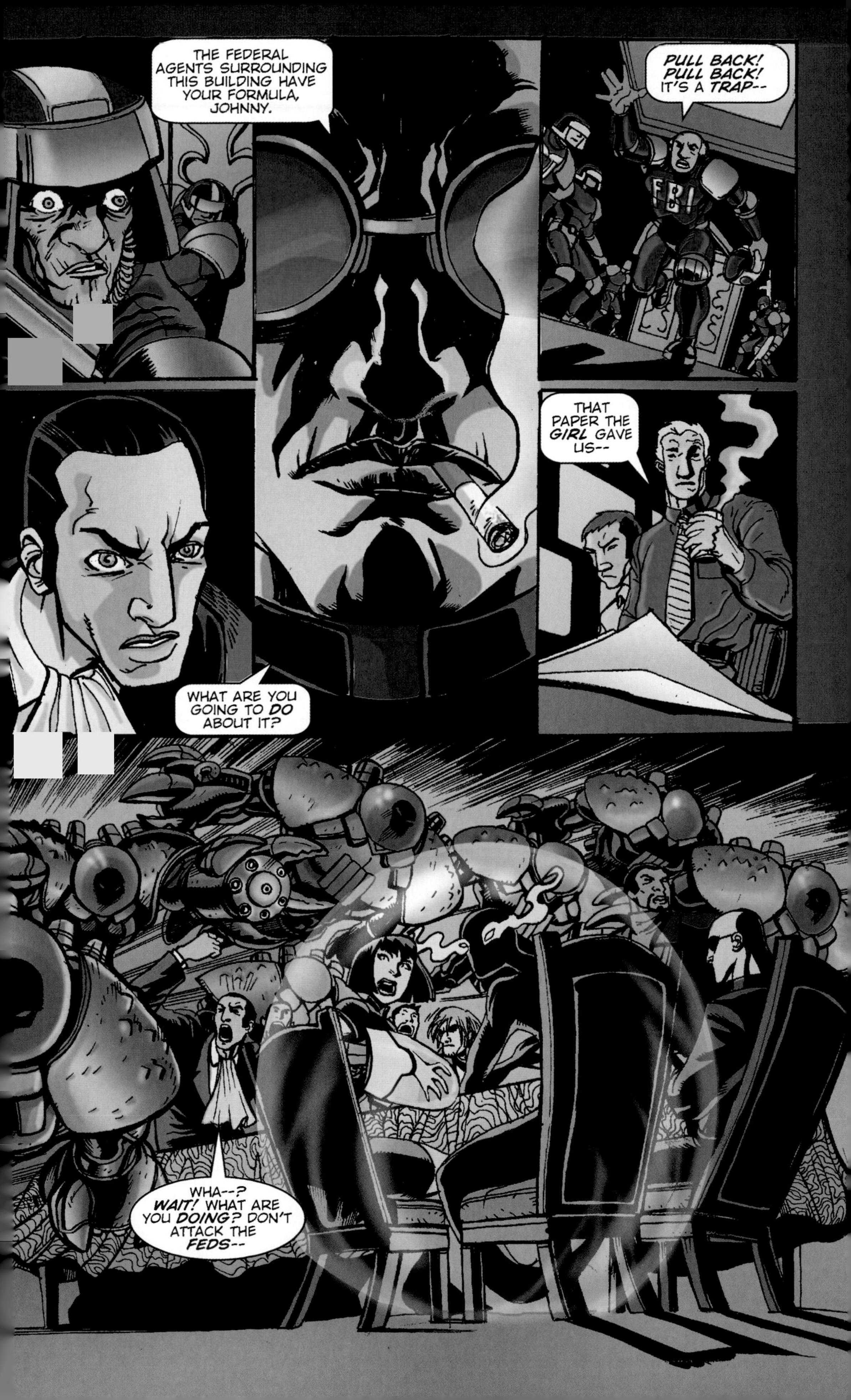
THE FEDERAL AGENTS SURROUNDING THIS BUILDING HAVE YOUR FORMULA, JOHNNY.
PULL BACK! PULL BACK! IT'S A TRAP--
WHAT ARE YOU GOING TO DO ABOUT IT?
THAT PAPER THE GIRL GAVE US--
WHA--? WAIT! WHAT ARE YOU DOING? DON'T ATTACK THE FEDS--

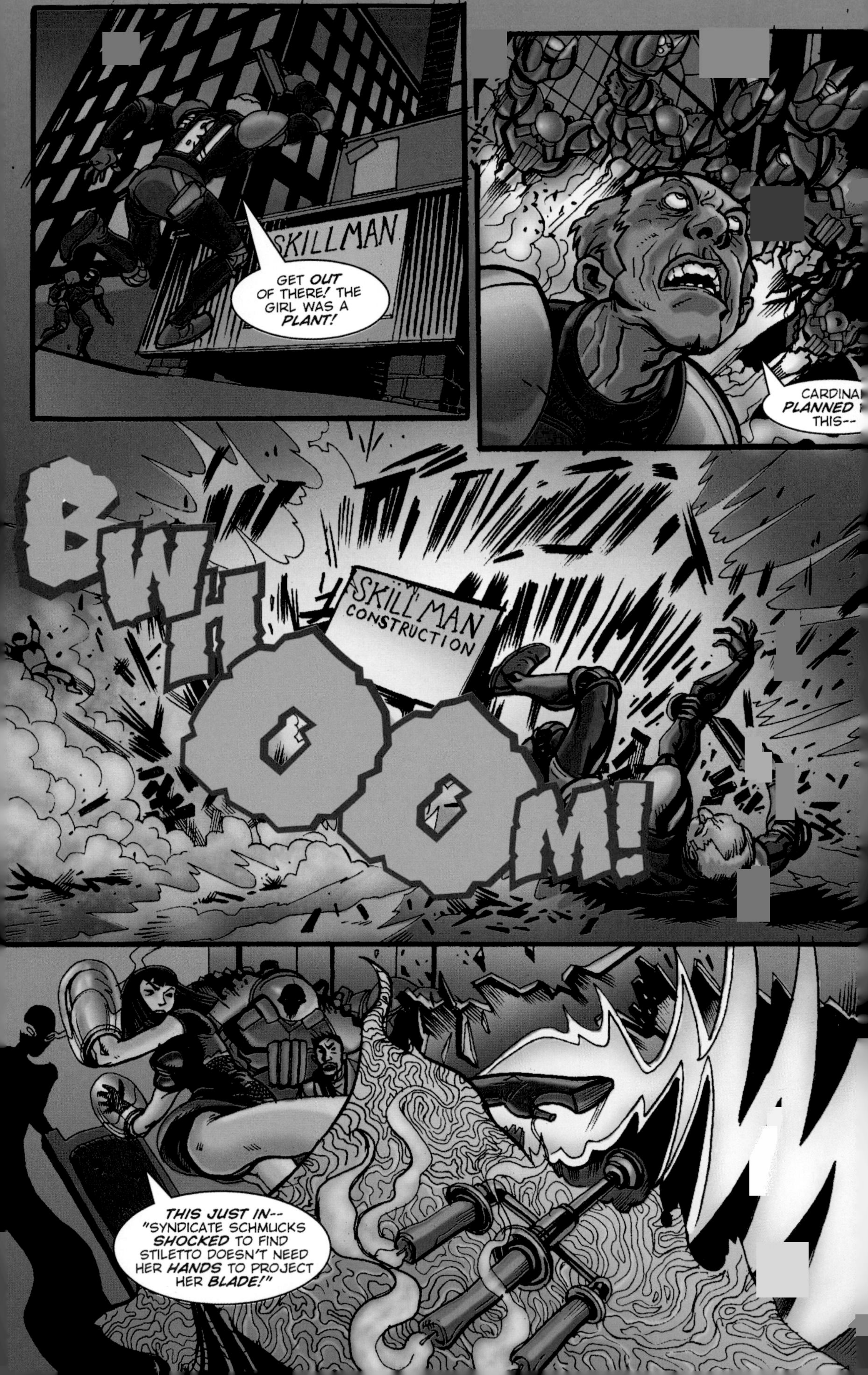
SKILLMAN
GET OUT OF THERE! THE GIRL WAS A PLANT!
CARDINA
PLANNED
THIS--
BWHOOM!
SKILLMAN CONSTRUCTION
THIS JUST IN-- "SYNDICATE SCHMUCKS SHOCKED TO FIND STILETTO DOESN'T NEED HER HANDS TO PROJECT HER BLADE!"

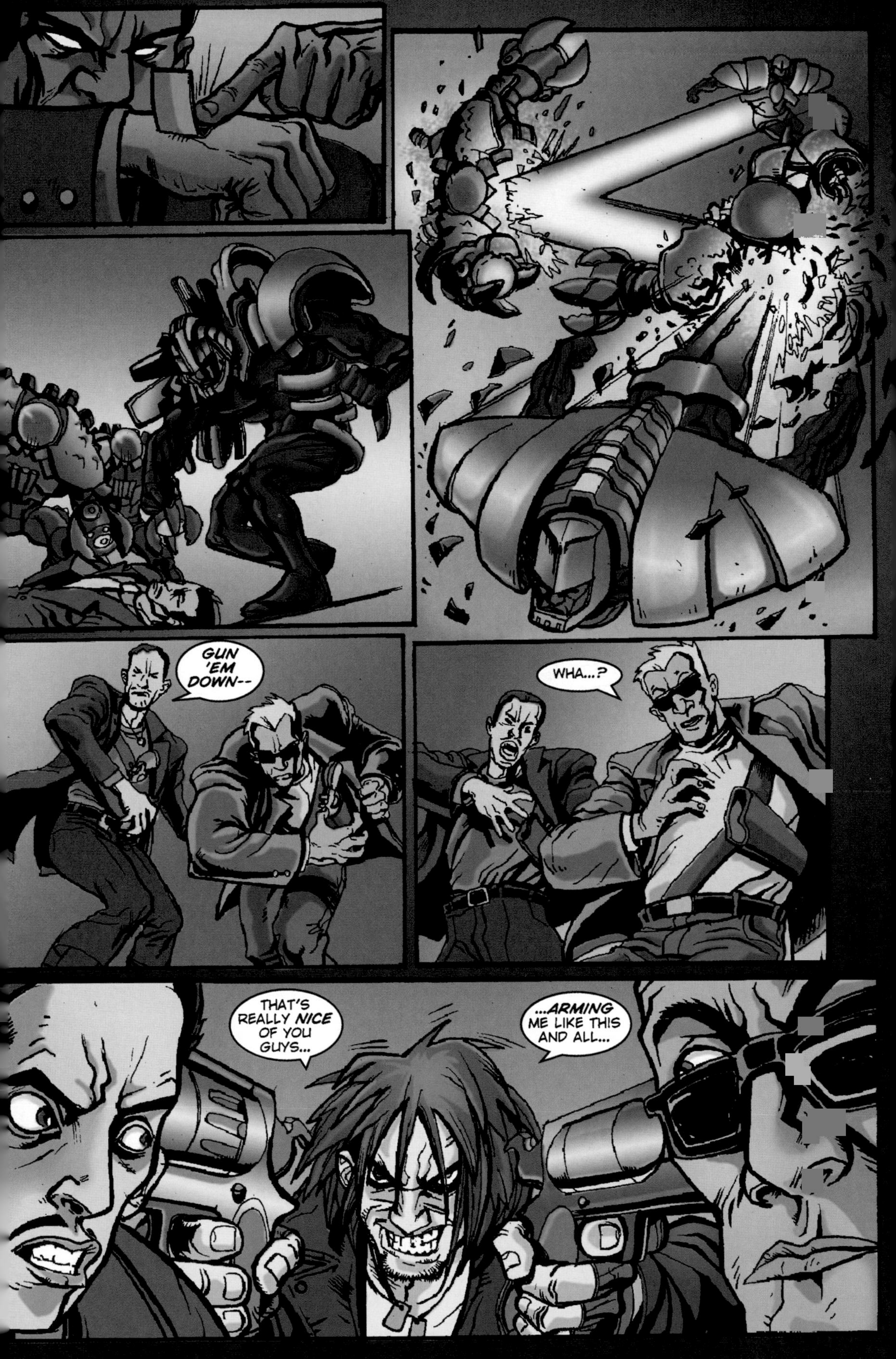
GUN 'EM DOWN--
WHA...?
THAT'S REALLY NICE OF YOU GUYS...
...ARMING ME LIKE THIS AND ALL...

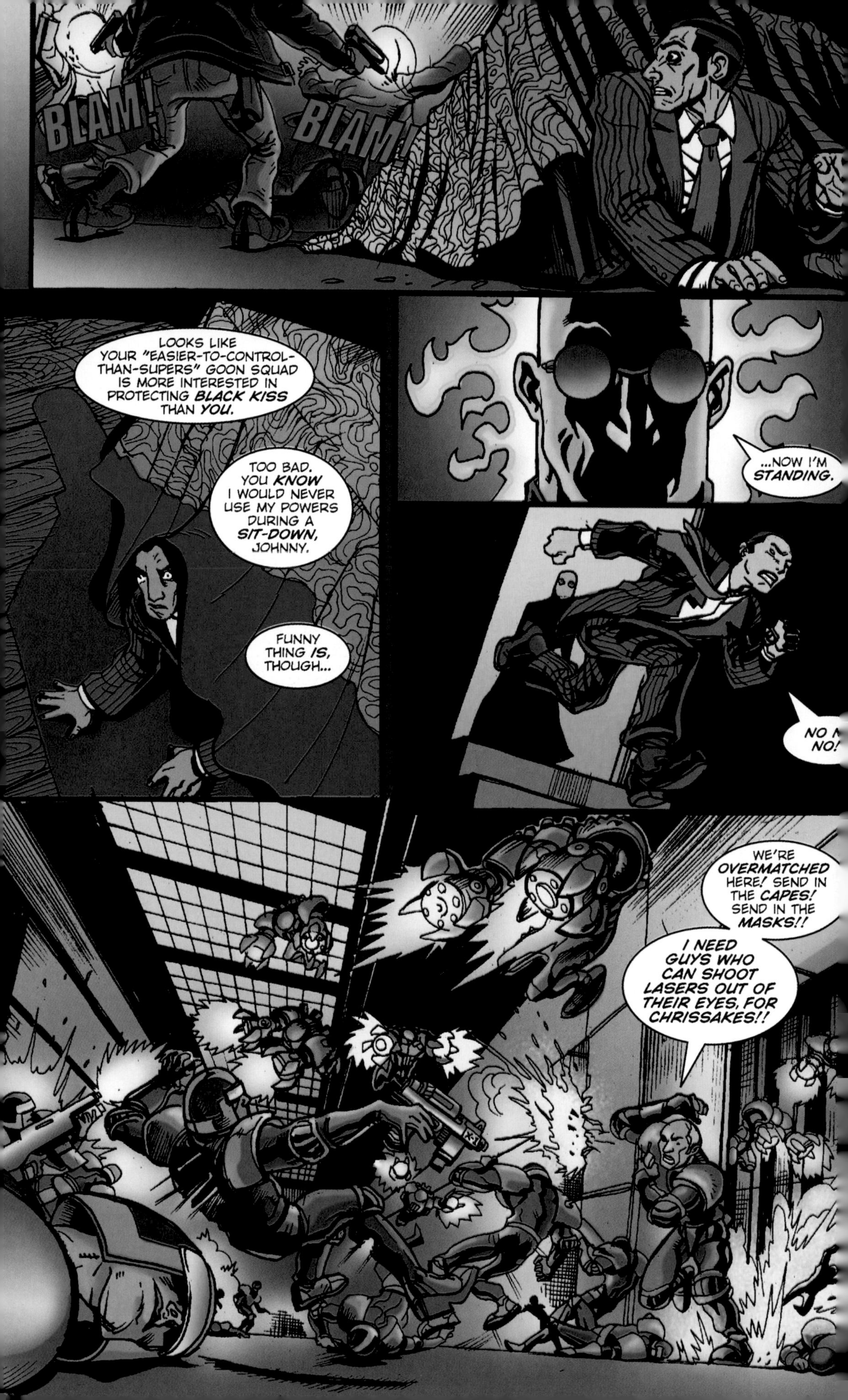
BLAM!
BLAM!
LOOKS LIKE YOUR "EASIER-TO-CONTROL-THAN-SUPERS" GOON SQUAD IS MORE INTERESTED IN PROTECTING BLACK KISS THAN YOU.
TOO BAD. YOU KNOW I WOULD NEVER USE MY POWERS DURING A SIT-DOWN, JOHNNY.
FUNNY THING IS, THOUGH...
...NOW I'M STANDING.
WE'RE OVERMATCHED HERE! SEND IN THE CAPES! SEND IN THE MASKS!!
I NEED GUYS WHO CAN SHOOT LASERS OUT OF THEIR EYES, FOR CHRISSAKES!!

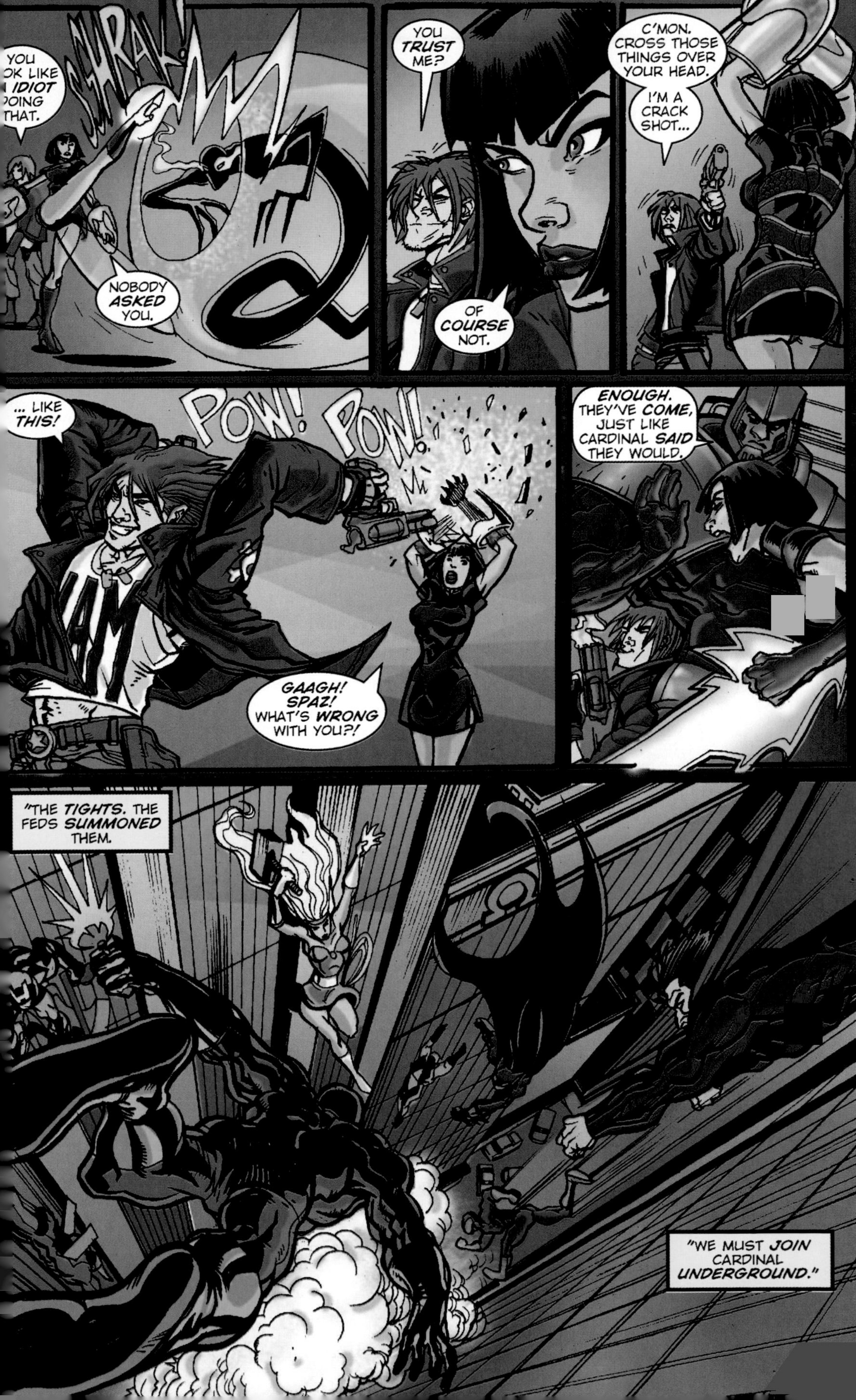
YOU
OK LIKE
IDIOT
OING
THAT.
SHRAK!
NOBODY ASKED YOU.
YOU TRUST ME?
OF COURSE NOT.
C'MON. CROSS THOSE THINGS OVER YOUR HEAD.
I'M A CRACK SHOT...
... LIKE THIS!
POW! POW!
GAAGH! SPAZ! WHAT'S WRONG WITH YOU?!
ENOUGH. THEY'VE COME, JUST LIKE CARDINAL SAID THEY WOULD.
"THE TIGHTS. THE FEDS SUMMONED THEM.
"WE MUST JOIN CARDINAL UNDERGROUND."

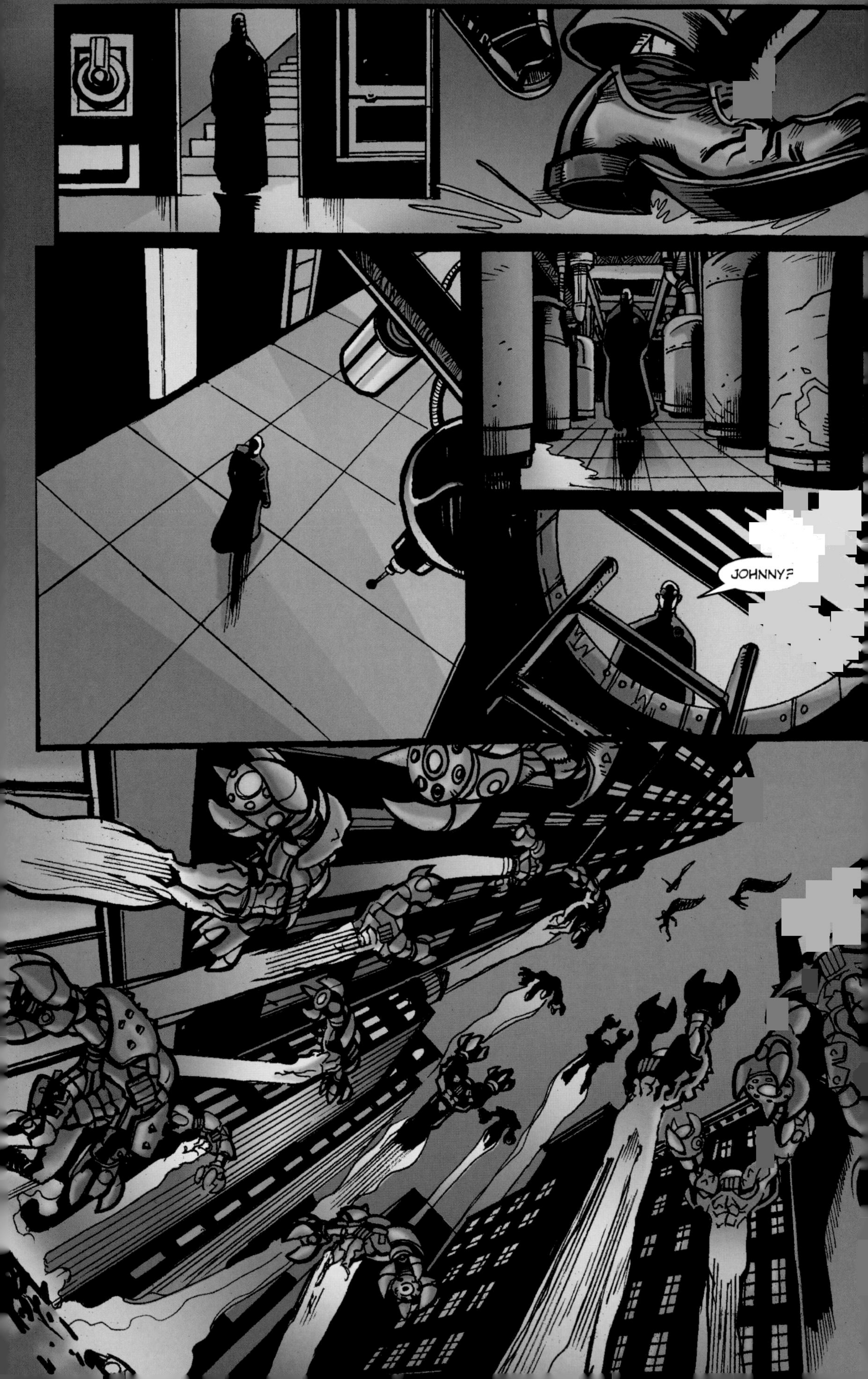
JOHNNY?

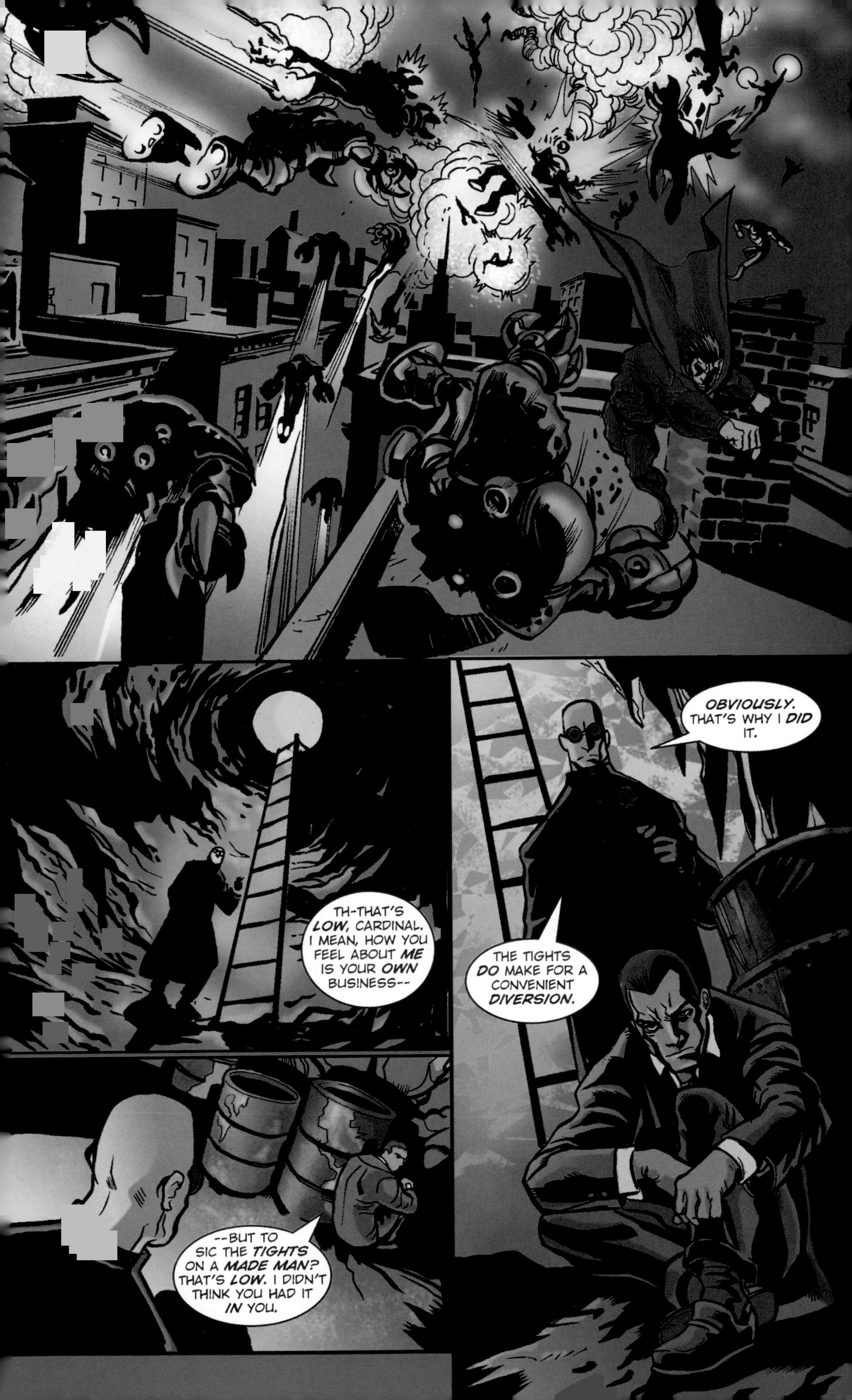
TH-THAT'S LOW, CARDINAL. I MEAN, HOW YOU FEEL ABOUT ME IS YOUR OWN BUSINESS--
--BUT TO SIC THE TIGHTS ON A MADE MAN? THAT'S LOW. I DIDN'T THINK YOU HAD IT IN YOU.
OBVIOUSLY. THAT'S WHY I DID IT.
THE TIGHTS DO MAKE FOR A CONVENIENT DIVERSION.

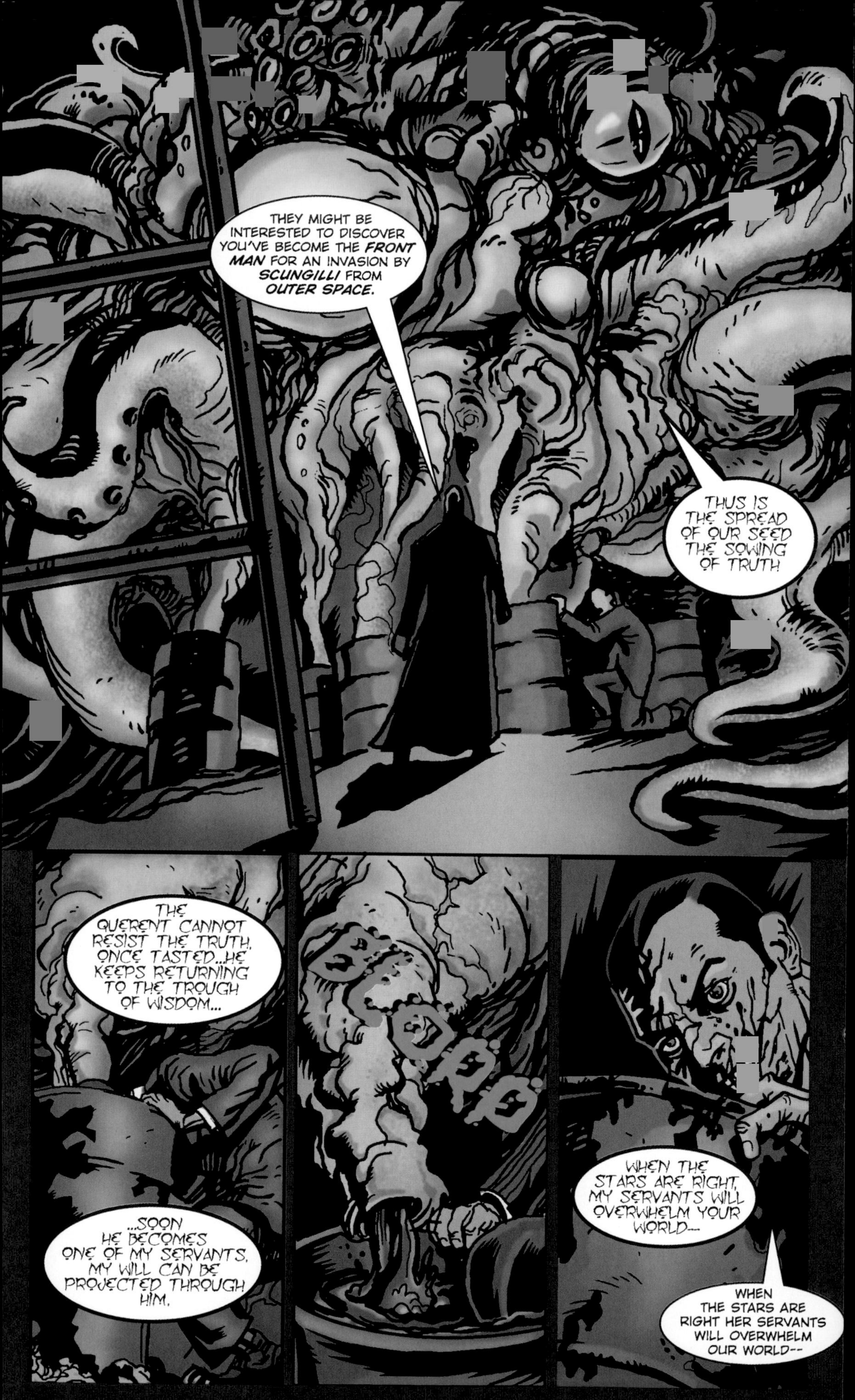
THEY MIGHT BE INTERESTED TO DISCOVER YOU'VE BECOME THE **FRONT MAN** FOR AN INVASION BY ***SCUNGILLI*** FROM ***OUTER SPACE.***
THUS IS THE SPREAD OF OUR SEED THE SOWING OF TRUTH
THE QUERENT CANNOT RESIST THE TRUTH, ONCE TASTED...HE KEEPS RETURNING TO THE TROUGH OF WISDOM...
...SOON HE BECOMES ONE OF MY SERVANTS, MY WILL CAN BE PROJECTED THROUGH HIM.
WHEN THE STARS ARE RIGHT, MY SERVANTS WILL OVERWHELM YOUR WORLD--
WHEN THE STARS ARE RIGHT HER SERVANTS WILL OVERWHELM OUR WORLD--

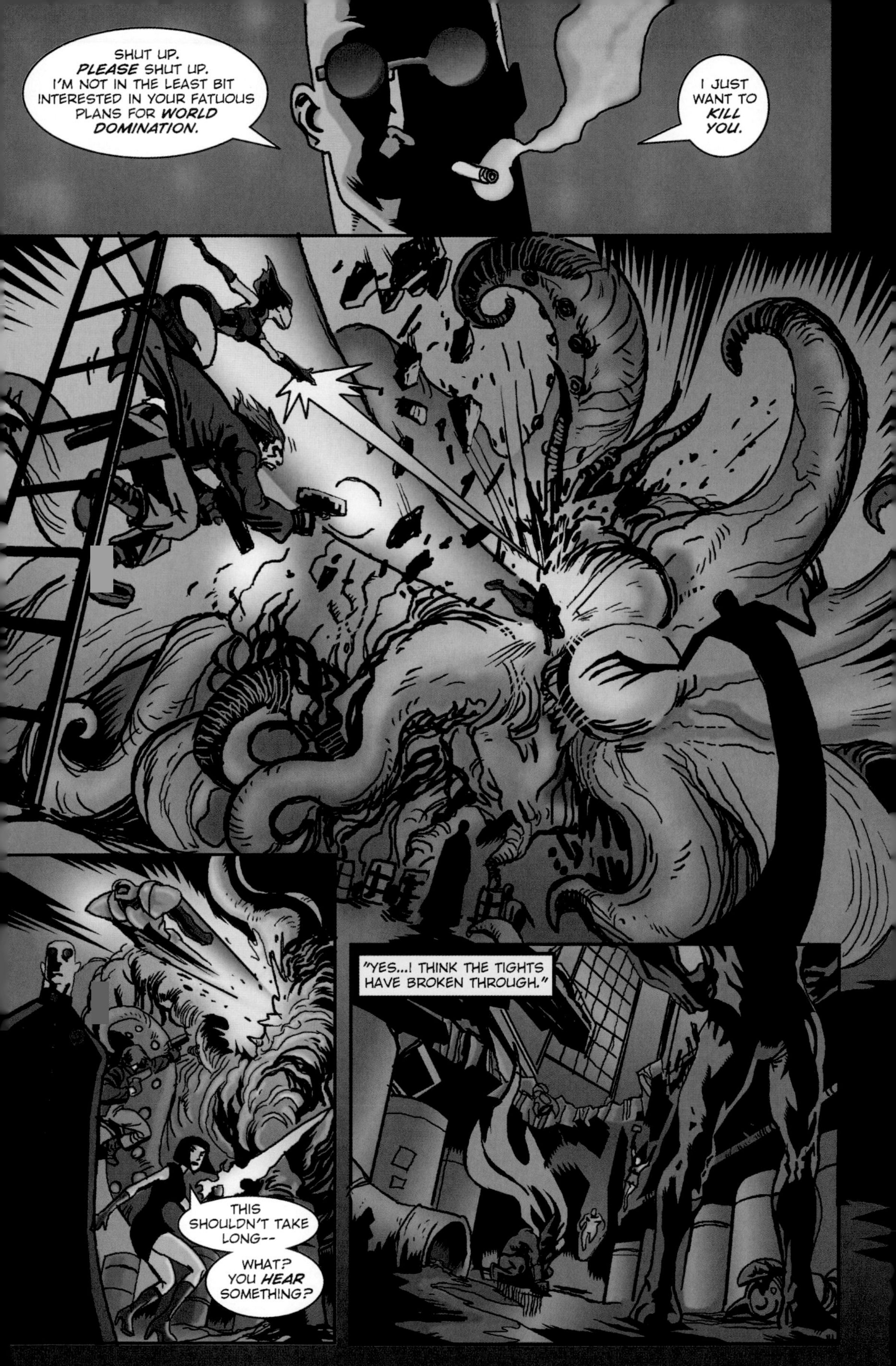
SHUT UP.
PLEASE SHUT UP.
I'M NOT IN THE LEAST BIT INTERESTED IN YOUR FATUOUS PLANS FOR *WORLD DOMINATION*.
I JUST WANT TO *KILL YOU*.
"YES...I THINK THE TIGHTS HAVE BROKEN THROUGH."
THIS SHOULDN'T TAKE LONG--
WHAT? YOU *HEAR* SOMETHING?

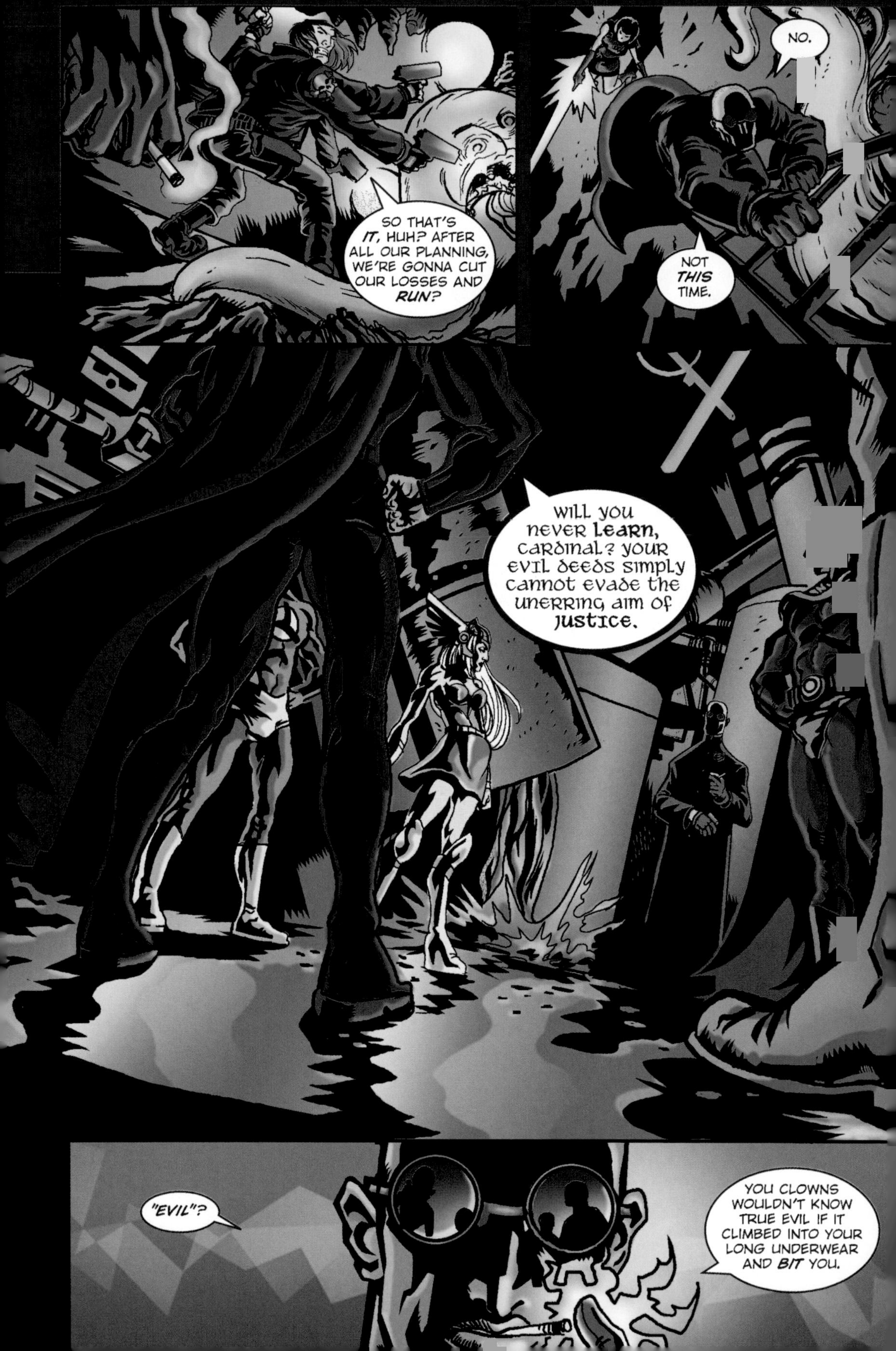
SO THAT'S *IT*, HUH? AFTER ALL OUR PLANNING, WE'RE GONNA CUT OUR LOSSES AND *RUN*?
NO.
NOT *THIS* TIME.
WILL YOU NEVER **LEARN**, CARDINAL? YOUR EVIL DEEDS SIMPLY CANNOT EVADE THE UNERRING AIM OF **JUSTICE**.
"EVIL"?
YOU CLOWNS WOULDN'T KNOW TRUE EVIL IF IT CLIMBED INTO YOUR LONG UNDERWEAR AND *BIT* YOU.

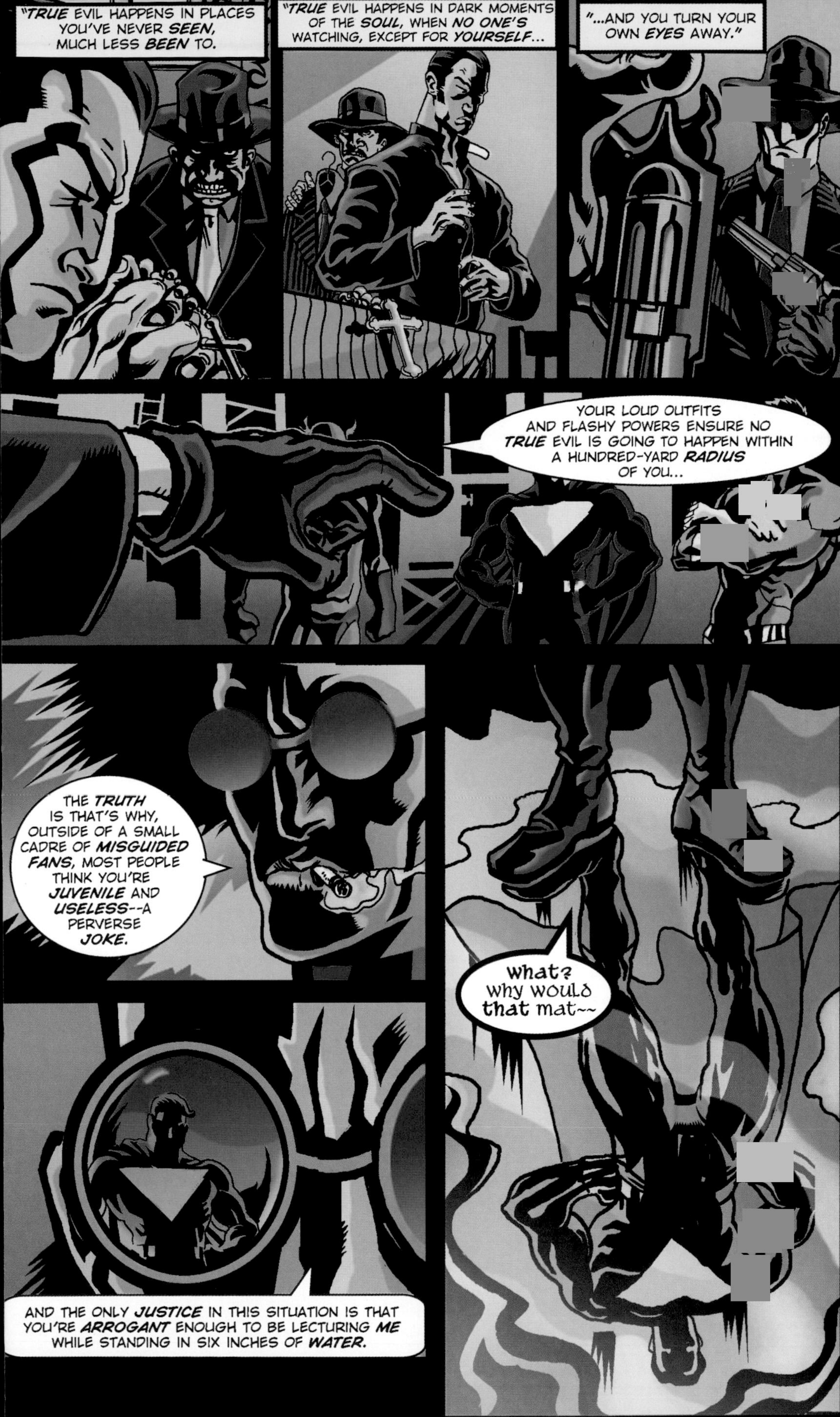
"TRUE EVIL HAPPENS IN PLACES YOU'VE NEVER SEEN, MUCH LESS BEEN TO.
"TRUE EVIL HAPPENS IN DARK MOMENTS OF THE SOUL, WHEN NO ONE'S WATCHING, EXCEPT FOR YOURSELF...
"...AND YOU TURN YOUR OWN EYES AWAY."
YOUR LOUD OUTFITS AND FLASHY POWERS ENSURE NO TRUE EVIL IS GOING TO HAPPEN WITHIN A HUNDRED-YARD RADIUS OF YOU...
THE TRUTH IS THAT'S WHY, OUTSIDE OF A SMALL CADRE OF MISGUIDED FANS, MOST PEOPLE THINK YOU'RE JUVENILE AND USELESS--A PERVERSE JOKE.
what? why would that mat~~
AND THE ONLY JUSTICE IN THIS SITUATION IS THAT YOU'RE ARROGANT ENOUGH TO BE LECTURING ME WHILE STANDING IN SIX INCHES OF WATER.

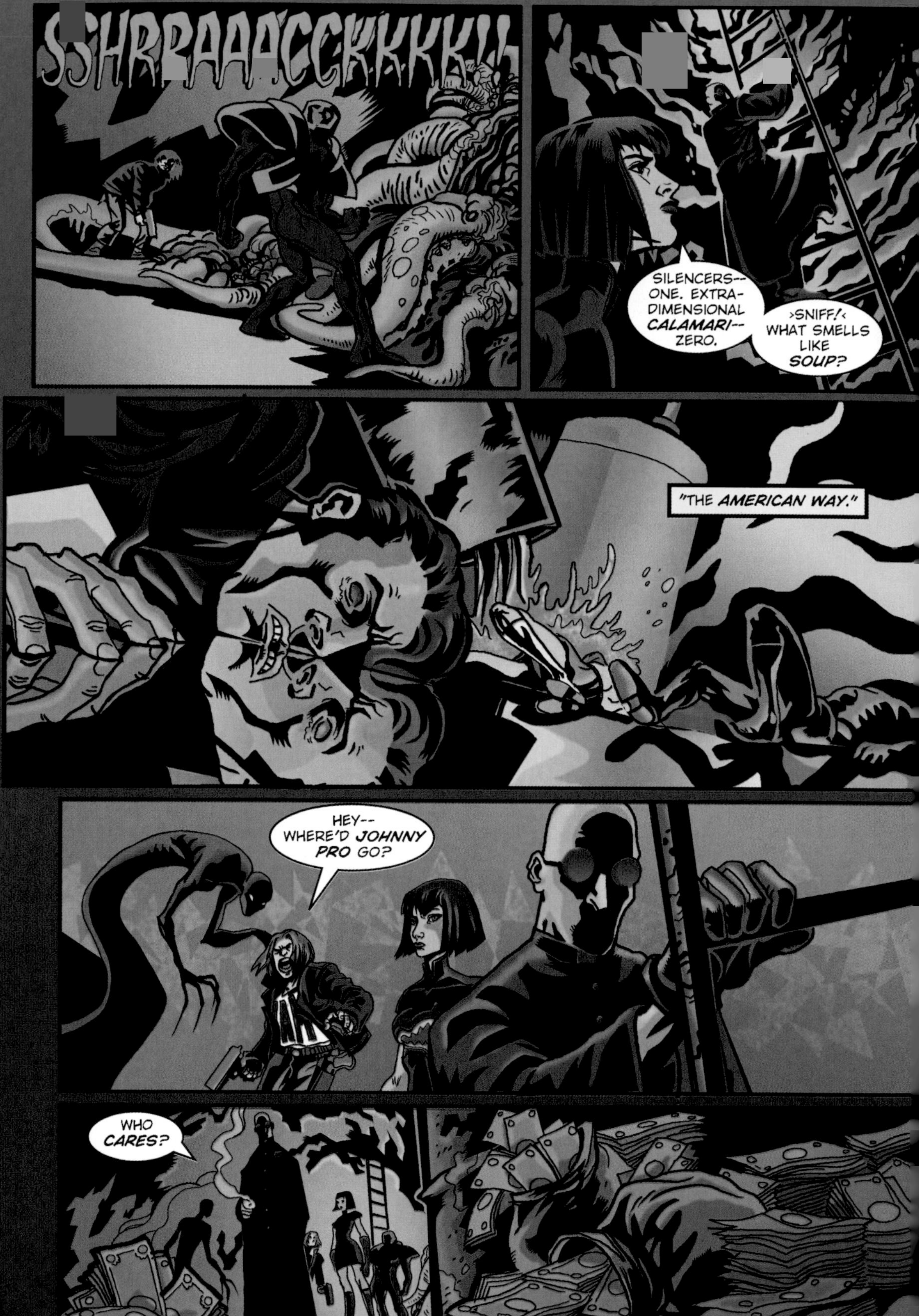
SSHRRAAACCCKKKKK!!
SILENCERS-- ONE. EXTRA-DIMENSIONAL CALAMARI-- ZERO.
>SNIFF!< WHAT SMELLS LIKE SOUP?
"THE AMERICAN WAY."
HEY-- WHERE'D JOHNNY PRO GO?
WHO CARES?

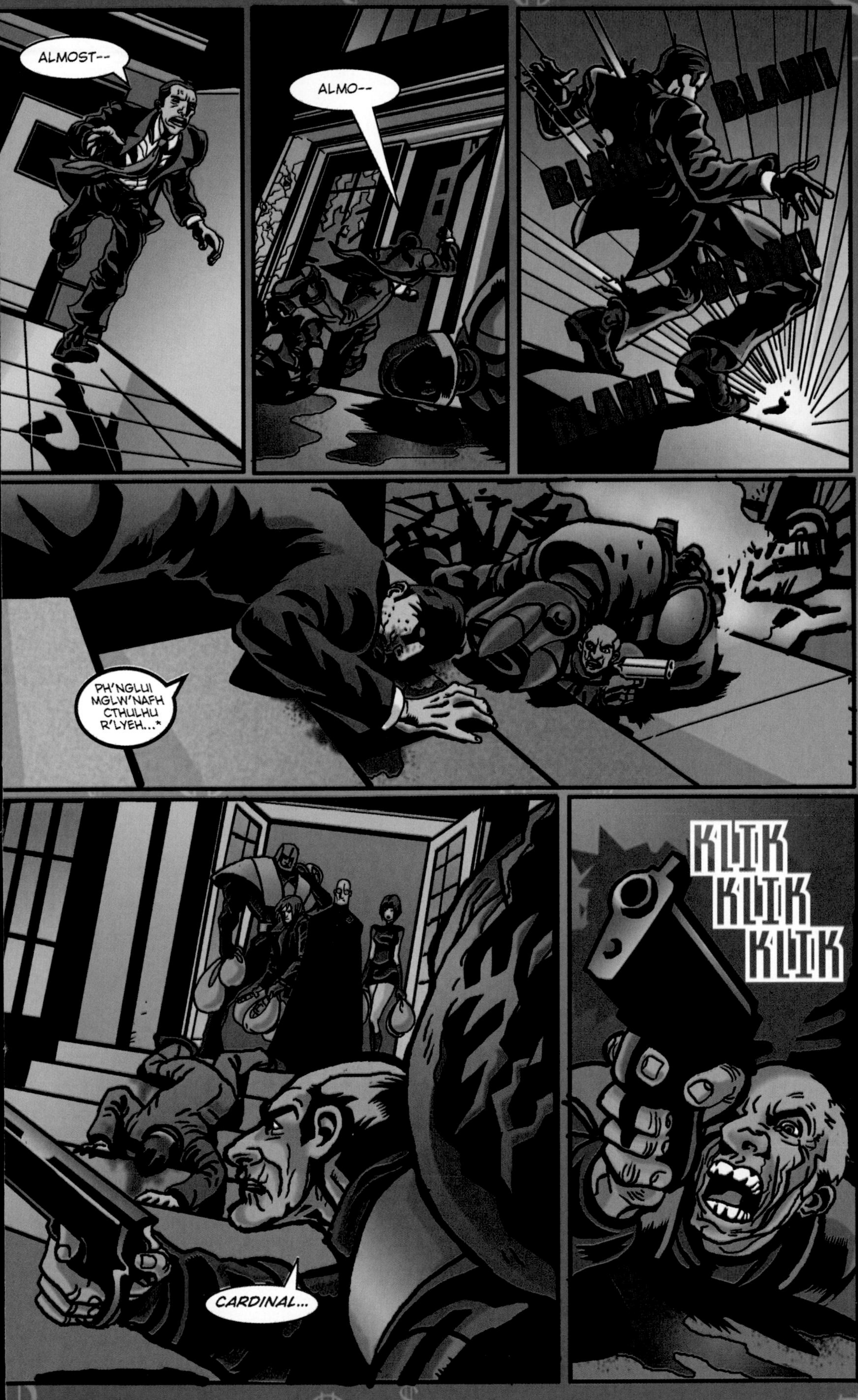
ALMOST--
ALMO--
BLAM!
BLAM!
BLAM!
BLAM!
PH'NGLUI MGLW'NAFH CTHULHU R'LYEH...*
CARDINAL...
KLIK KLIK KLIK

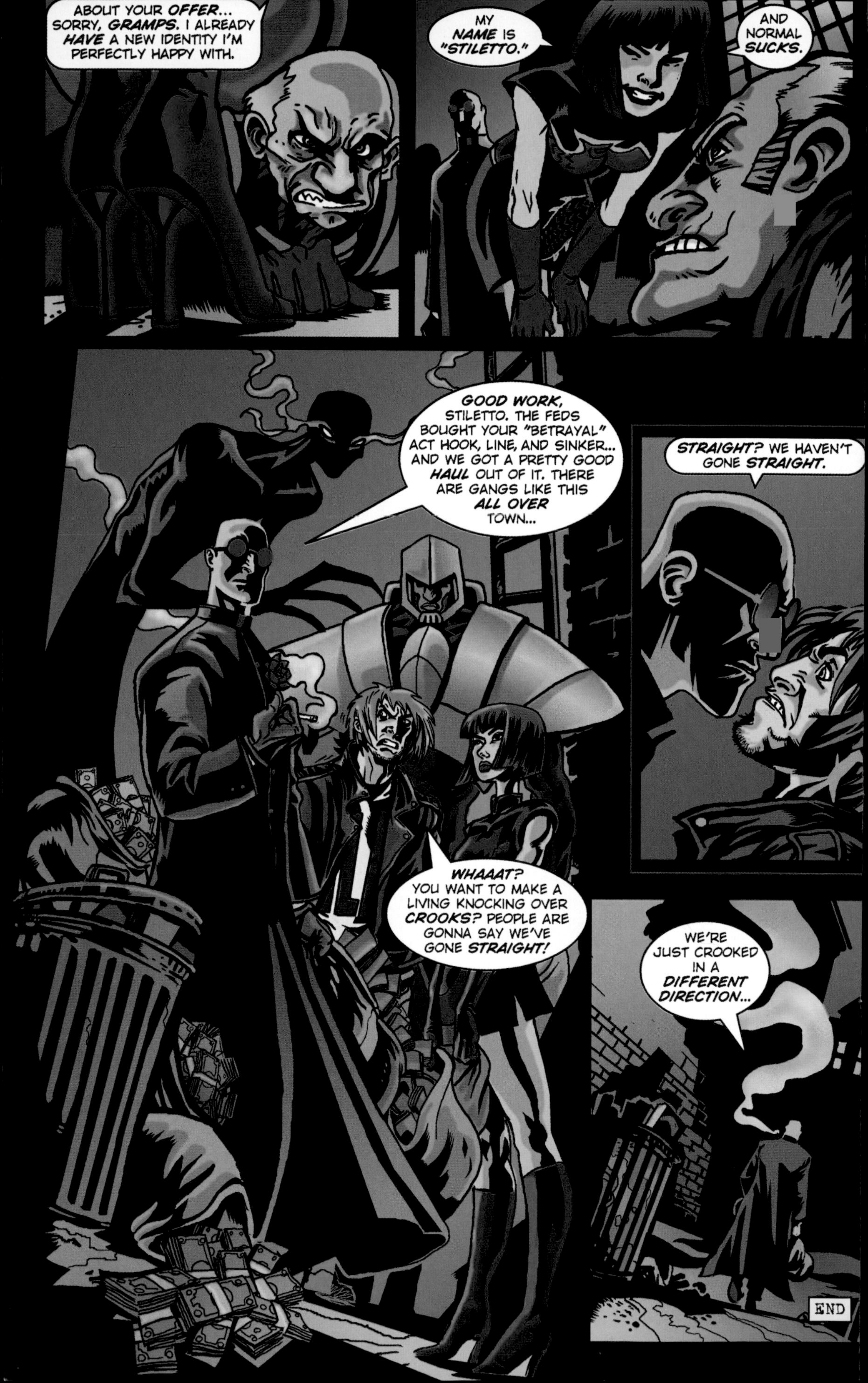
ABOUT YOUR OFFER... SORRY, GRAMPS. I ALREADY HAVE A NEW IDENTITY I'M PERFECTLY HAPPY WITH.
MY NAME IS "STILETTO."
AND NORMAL SUCKS.
GOOD WORK, STILETTO. THE FEDS BOUGHT YOUR "BETRAYAL" ACT HOOK, LINE, AND SINKER... AND WE GOT A PRETTY GOOD HAUL OUT OF IT. THERE ARE GANGS LIKE THIS ALL OVER TOWN...
WHAAAT? YOU WANT TO MAKE A LIVING KNOCKING OVER CROOKS? PEOPLE ARE GONNA SAY WE'VE GONE STRAIGHT!
STRAIGHT? WE HAVEN'T GONE STRAIGHT.
WE'RE JUST CROOKED IN A DIFFERENT DIRECTION...
END

SPAZ

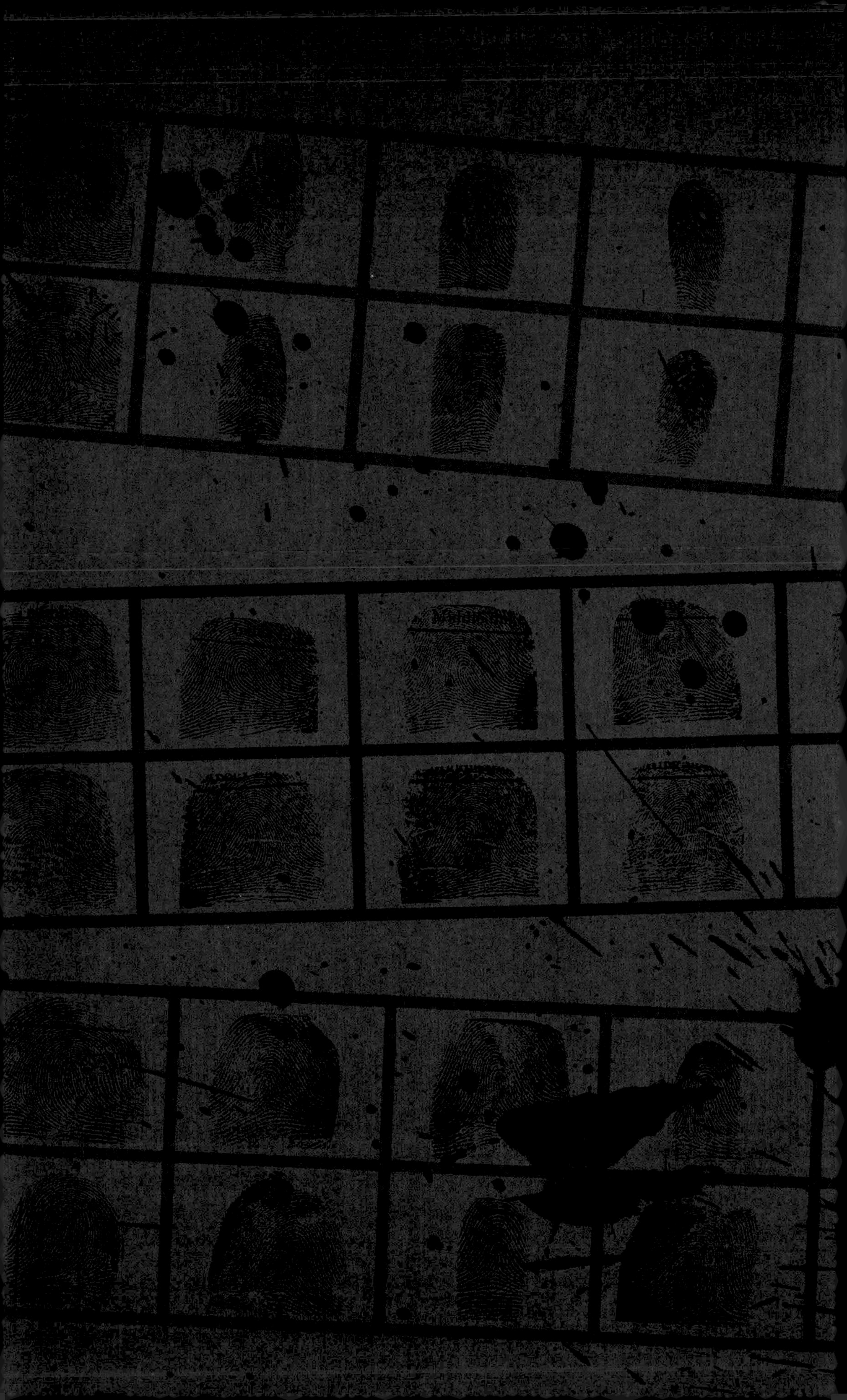

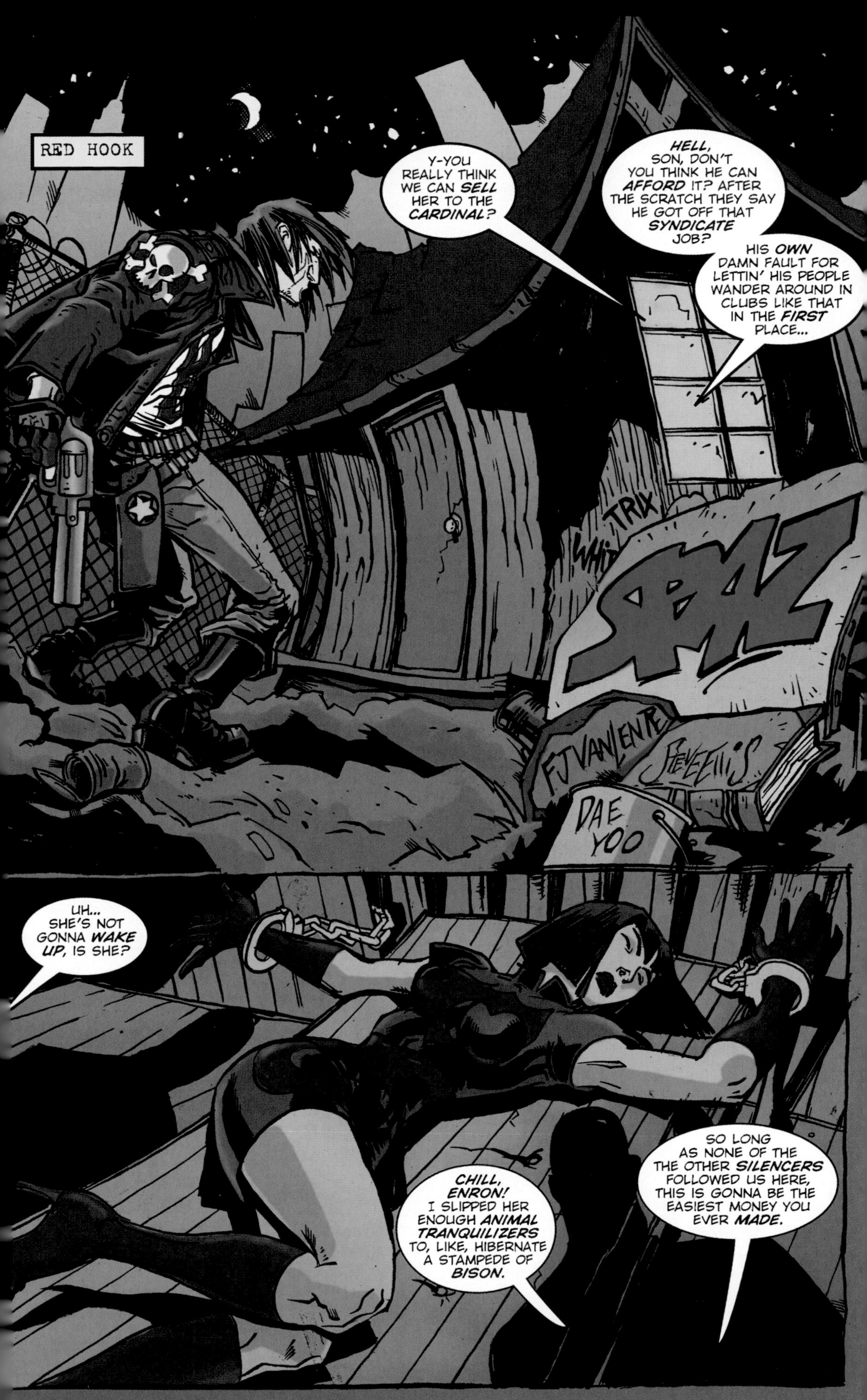
RED HOOK
Y-YOU REALLY THINK WE CAN SELL HER TO THE CARDINAL?
HELL, SON, DON'T YOU THINK HE CAN AFFORD IT? AFTER THE SCRATCH THEY SAY HE GOT OFF THAT SYNDICATE JOB?
HIS OWN DAMN FAULT FOR LETTIN' HIS PEOPLE WANDER AROUND IN CLUBS LIKE THAT IN THE FIRST PLACE...
TRIX
SPAZ
FJ VANLENTE
STEVE ELLIS
DAE YOO
UH... SHE'S NOT GONNA WAKE UP, IS SHE?
CHILL, ENRON! I SLIPPED HER ENOUGH ANIMAL TRANQUILIZERS TO, LIKE, HIBERNATE A STAMPEDE OF BISON.
SO LONG AS NONE OF THE THE OTHER SILENCERS FOLLOWED US HERE, THIS IS GONNA BE THE EASIEST MONEY YOU EVER MADE.

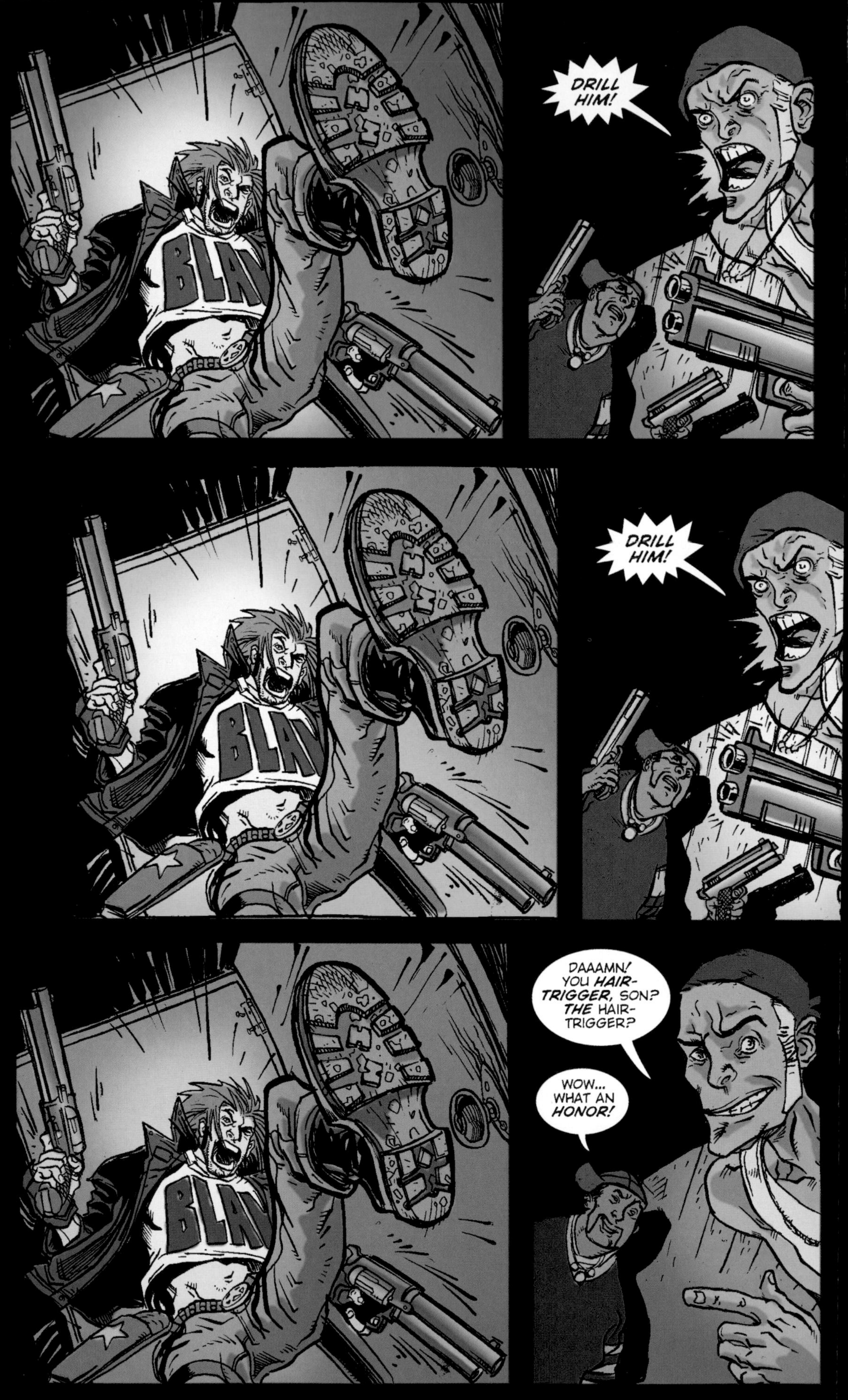
DRILL HIM!
DRILL HIM!
DAAAMN! YOU HAIR-TRIGGER, SON? THE HAIR-TRIGGER?
WOW... WHAT AN HONOR!

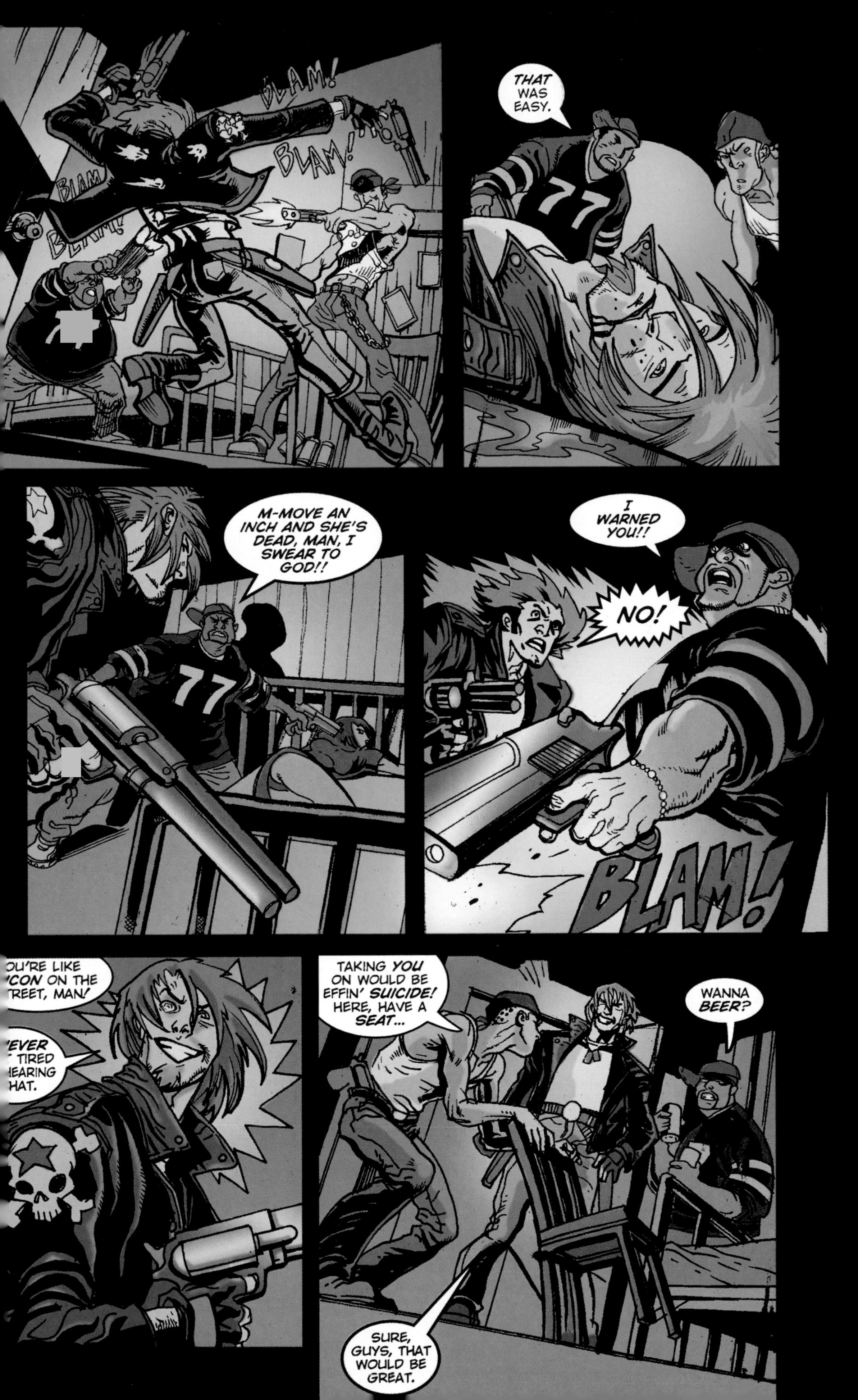
BLAM!
BLAM!
BLAM
BLAM!
THAT WAS EASY.
M-MOVE AN INCH AND SHE'S DEAD, MAN, I SWEAR TO GOD!!
I WARNED YOU!!
NO!
BLAM!
OU'RE LIKE
CON ON THE
TREET, MAN!
EVER
TIRED
HEARING
HAT.
TAKING YOU ON WOULD BE EFFIN' SUICIDE! HERE, HAVE A SEAT...
WANNA BEER?
SURE, GUYS, THAT WOULD BE GREAT.

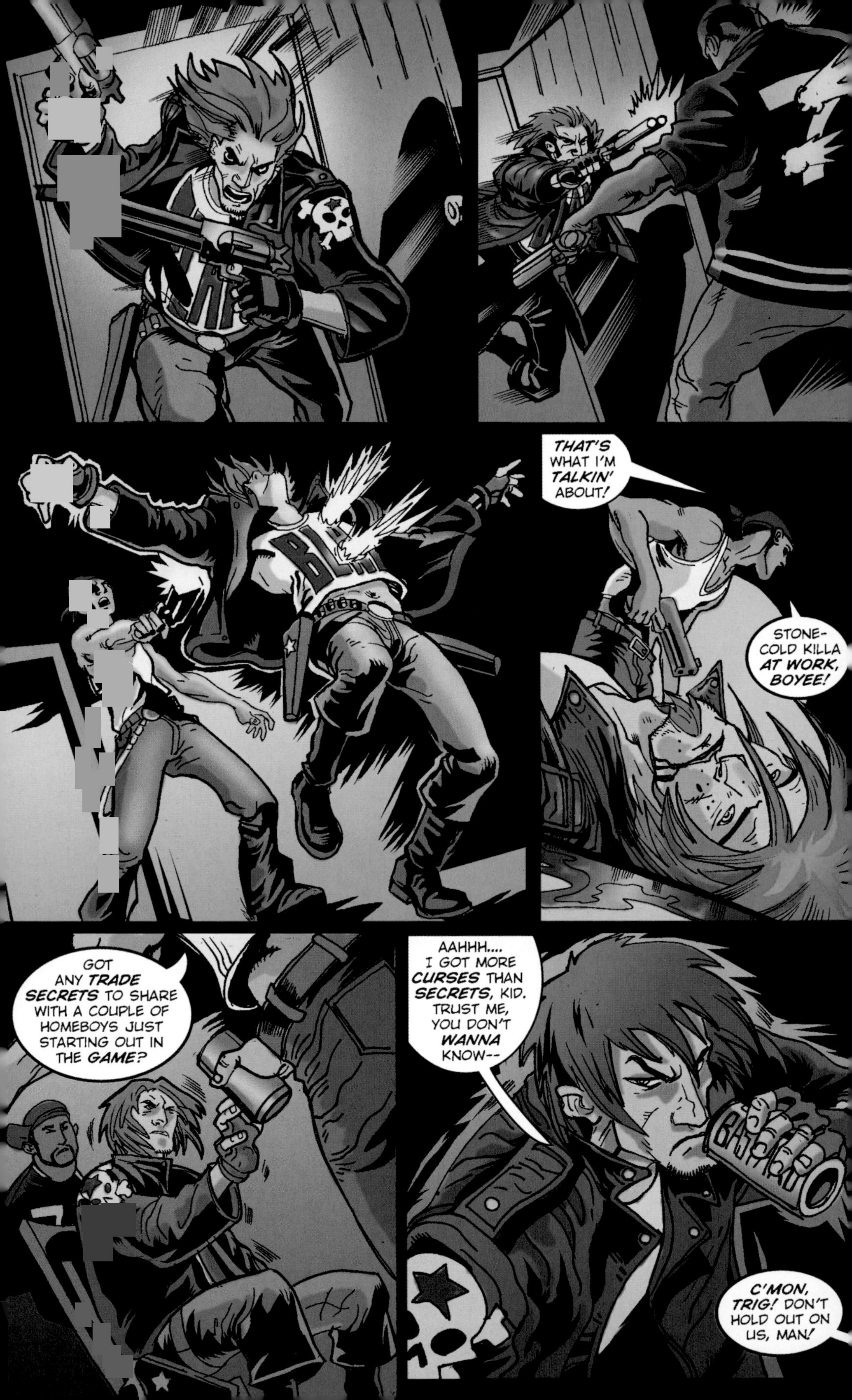
THAT'S WHAT I'M TALKIN' ABOUT!
STONE-COLD KILLA AT WORK, BOYEE!
GOT ANY TRADE SECRETS TO SHARE WITH A COUPLE OF HOMEBOYS JUST STARTING OUT IN THE GAME?
AAHHH.... I GOT MORE CURSES THAN SECRETS, KID. TRUST ME, YOU DON'T WANNA KNOW--
C'MON, TRIG! DON'T HOLD OUT ON US, MAN!

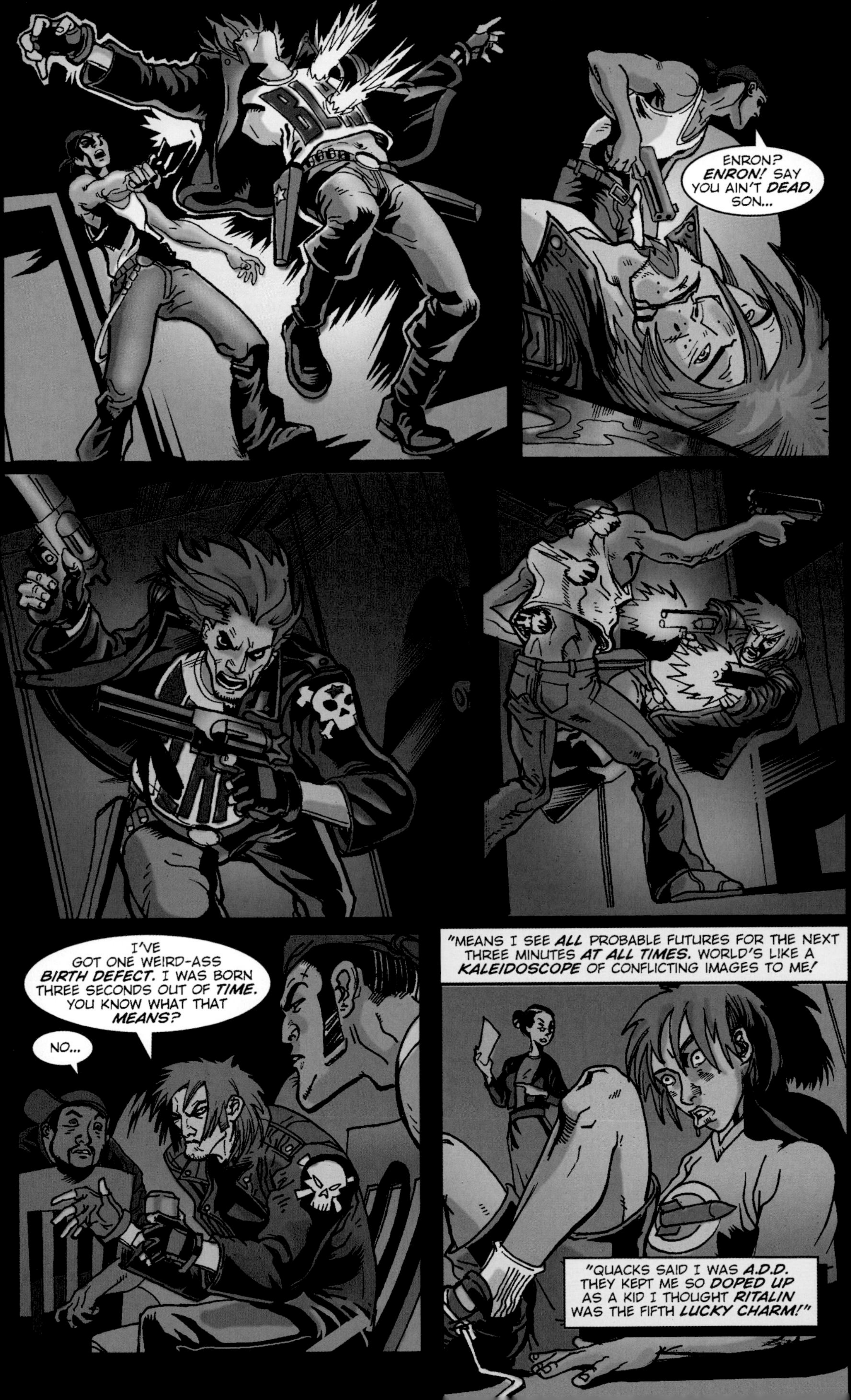
ENRON? ENRON! SAY YOU AIN'T DEAD, SON...
I'VE GOT ONE WEIRD-ASS BIRTH DEFECT. I WAS BORN THREE SECONDS OUT OF TIME. YOU KNOW WHAT THAT MEANS?
NO...
"MEANS I SEE ALL PROBABLE FUTURES FOR THE NEXT THREE MINUTES AT ALL TIMES. WORLD'S LIKE A KALEIDOSCOPE OF CONFLICTING IMAGES TO ME!
"QUACKS SAID I WAS A.D.D. THEY KEPT ME SO DOPED UP AS A KID I THOUGHT RITALIN WAS THE FIFTH LUCKY CHARM!"

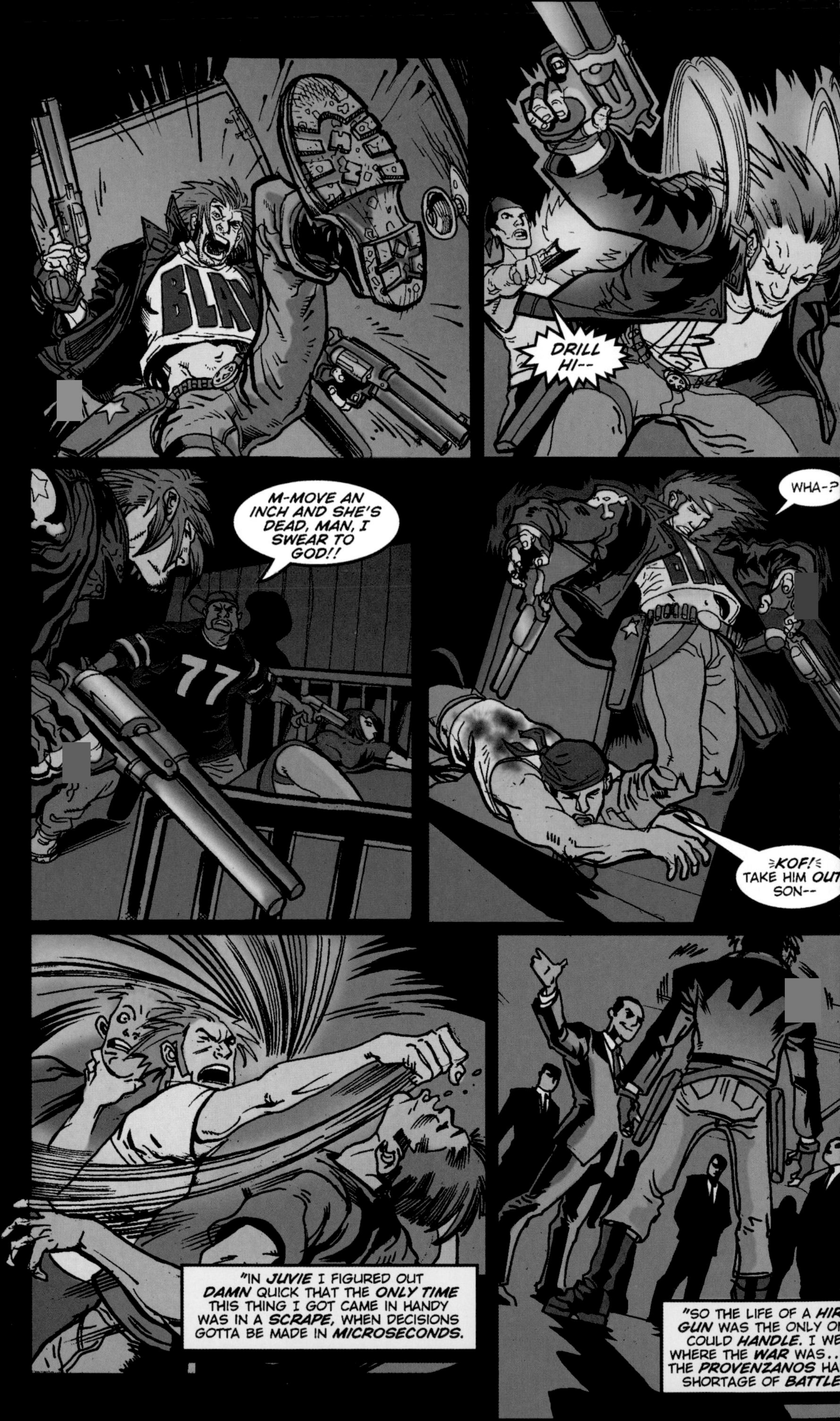

DRILL HI--
M-MOVE AN INCH AND SHE'S DEAD, MAN, I SWEAR TO GOD!!
WHA-?
KOF! TAKE HIM OUT SON--
"IN JUVIE I FIGURED OUT DAMN QUICK THAT THE ONLY TIME THIS THING I GOT CAME IN HANDY WAS IN A SCRAPE, WHEN DECISIONS GOTTA BE MADE IN MICROSECONDS.
"SO THE LIFE OF A HIR GUN WAS THE ONLY ON COULD HANDLE. I WE WHERE THE WAR WAS.. THE PROVENZANOS HA SHORTAGE OF BATTLE

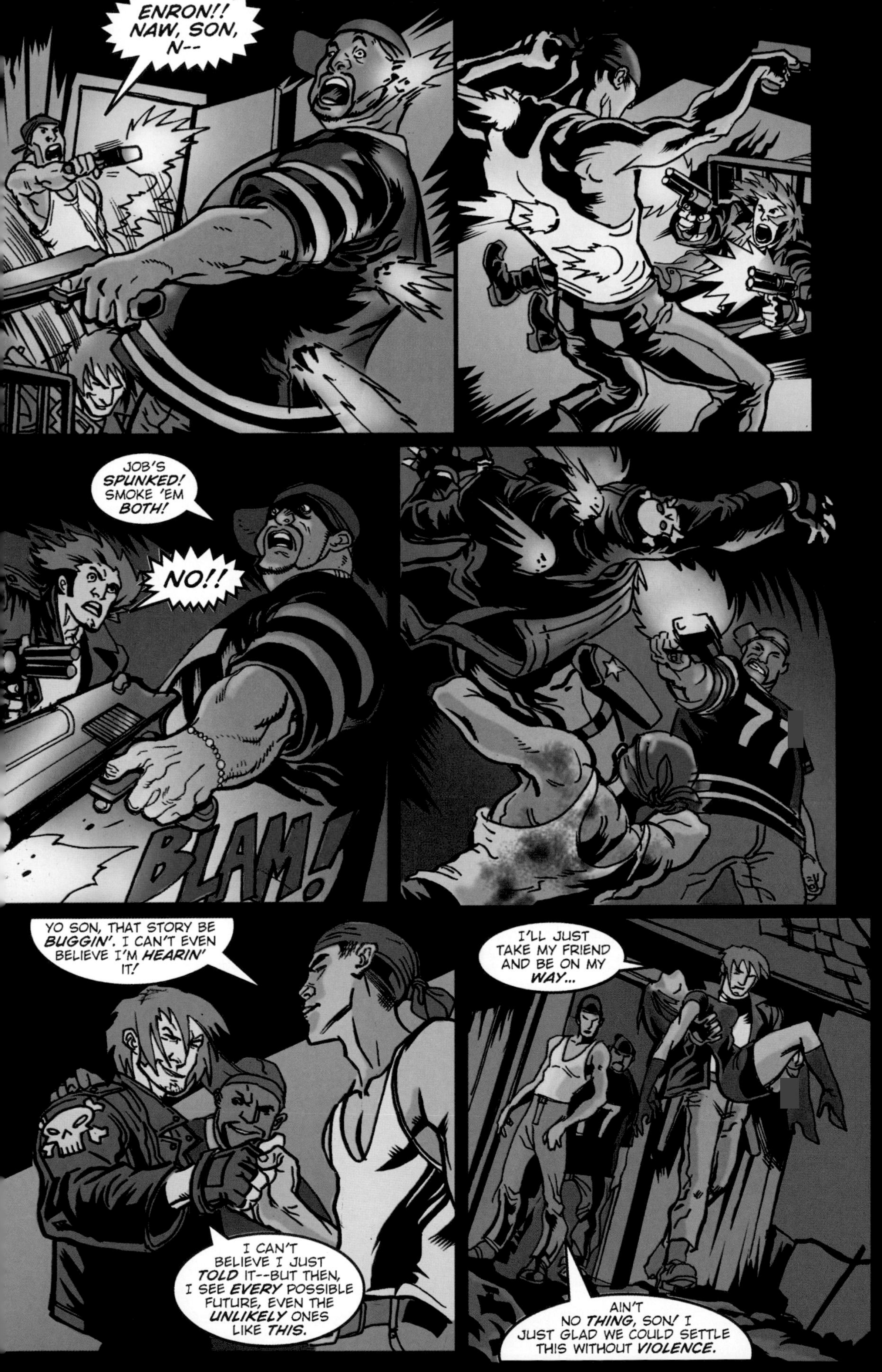

ENRON!! NAW, SON, N--
JOB'S SPUNKED! SMOKE 'EM BOTH!
NO!!
BLAM!
YO SON, THAT STORY BE BUGGIN'. I CAN'T EVEN BELIEVE I'M HEARIN' IT!
I CAN'T BELIEVE I JUST TOLD IT--BUT THEN, I SEE EVERY POSSIBLE FUTURE, EVEN THE UNLIKELY ONES LIKE THIS.
I'LL JUST TAKE MY FRIEND AND BE ON MY WAY...
AIN'T NO THING, SON! I JUST GLAD WE COULD SETTLE THIS WITHOUT VIOLENCE.

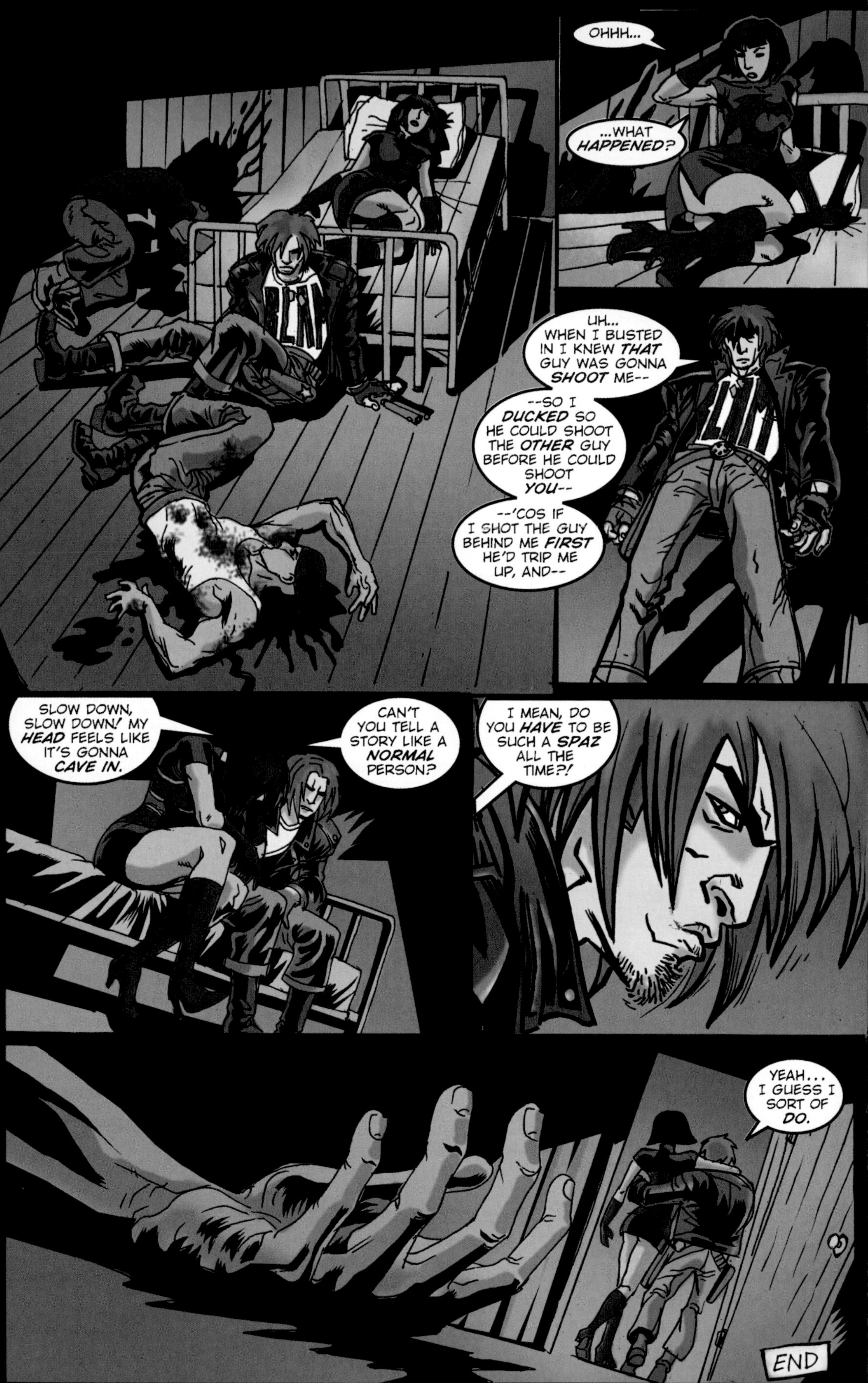
OHHH...
...WHAT HAPPENED?
UH... WHEN I BUSTED IN I KNEW THAT GUY WAS GONNA SHOOT ME--
--SO I DUCKED SO HE COULD SHOOT THE OTHER GUY BEFORE HE COULD SHOOT YOU--
--'COS IF I SHOT THE GUY BEHIND ME FIRST HE'D TRIP ME UP, AND--
SLOW DOWN, SLOW DOWN! MY HEAD FEELS LIKE IT'S GONNA CAVE IN.
CAN'T YOU TELL A STORY LIKE A NORMAL PERSON?
I MEAN, DO YOU HAVE TO BE SUCH A SPAZ ALL THE TIME?!
YEAH... I GUESS I SORT OF DO.
END

POWERED AND DANGEROUS

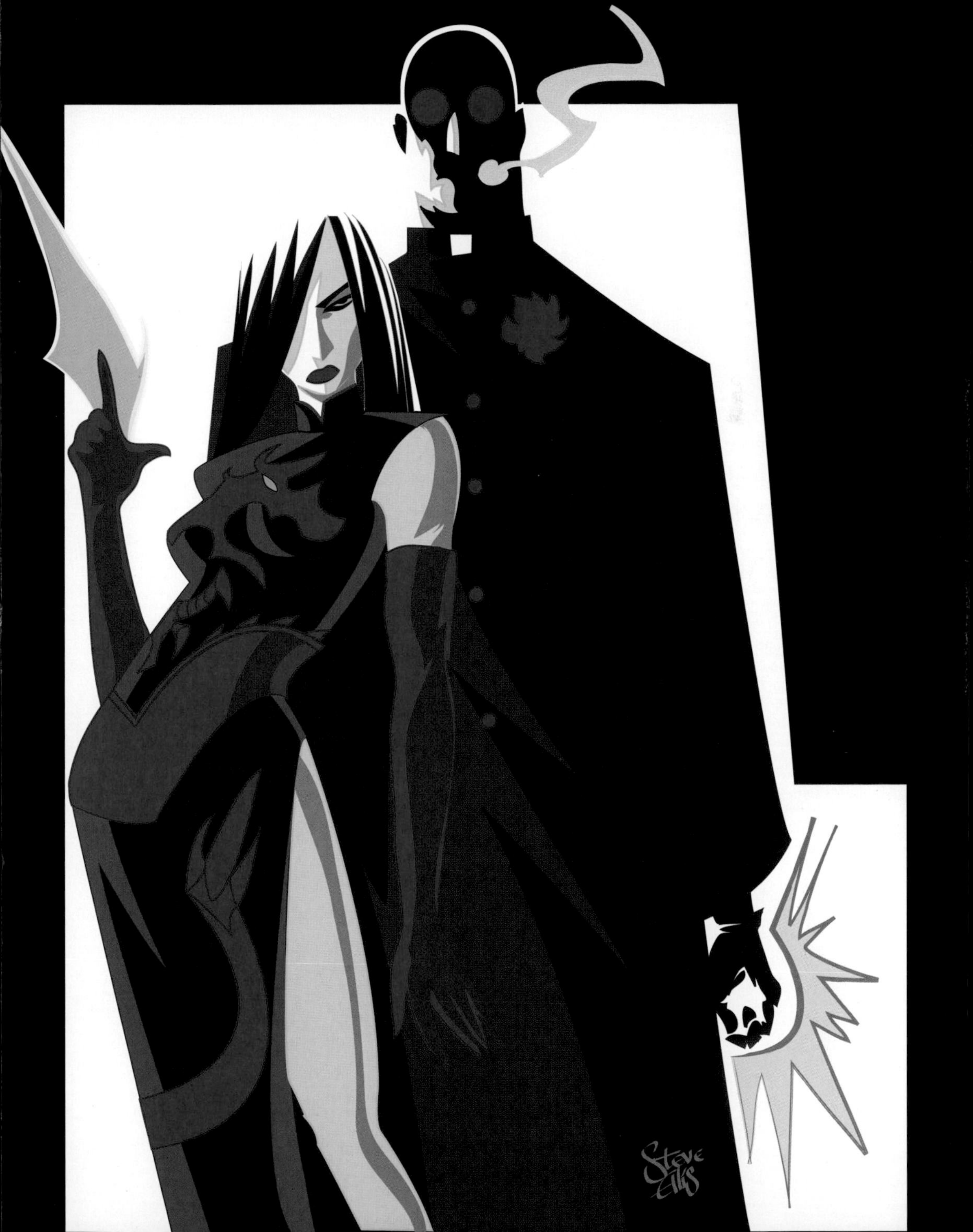
Steve Ellis

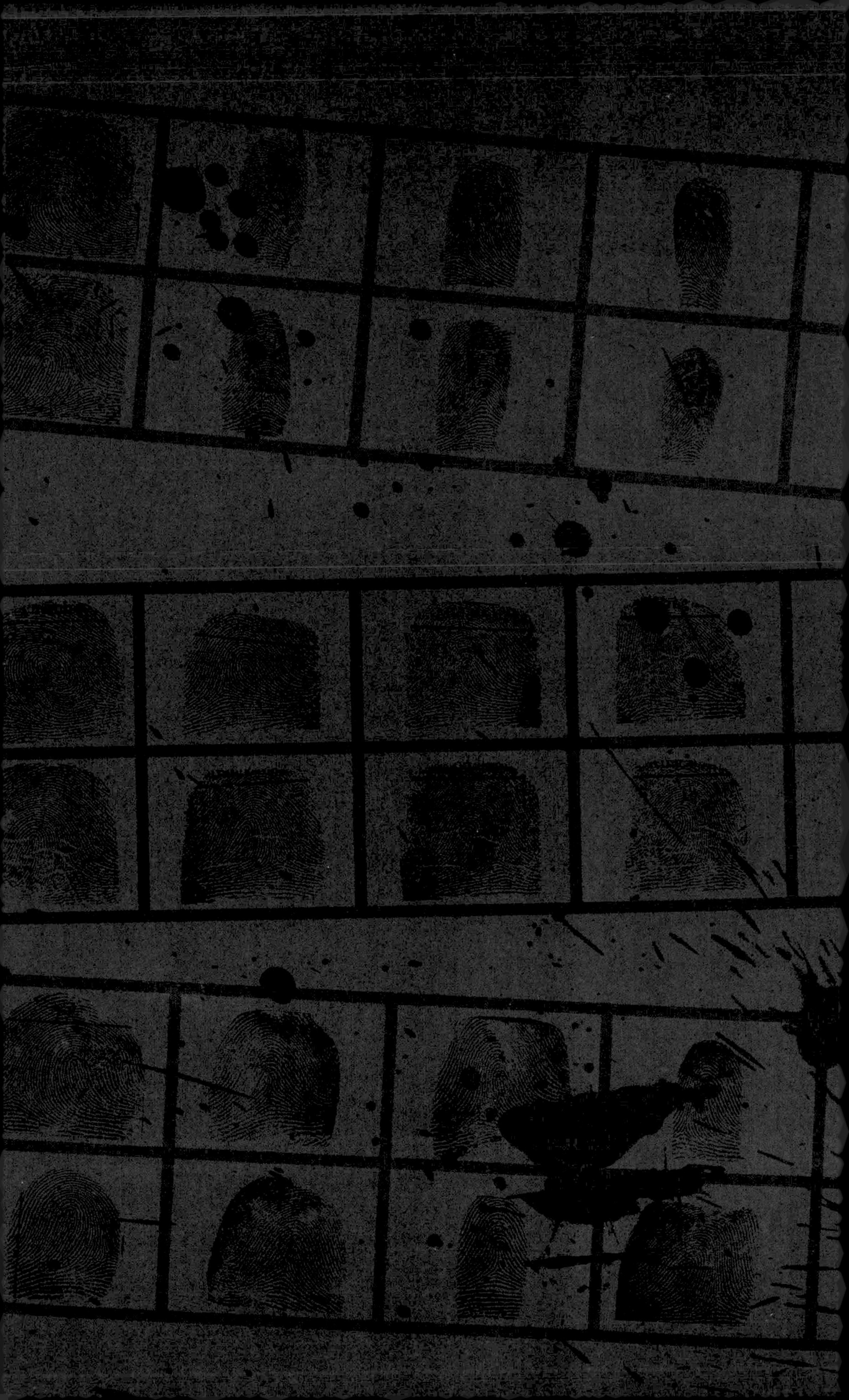

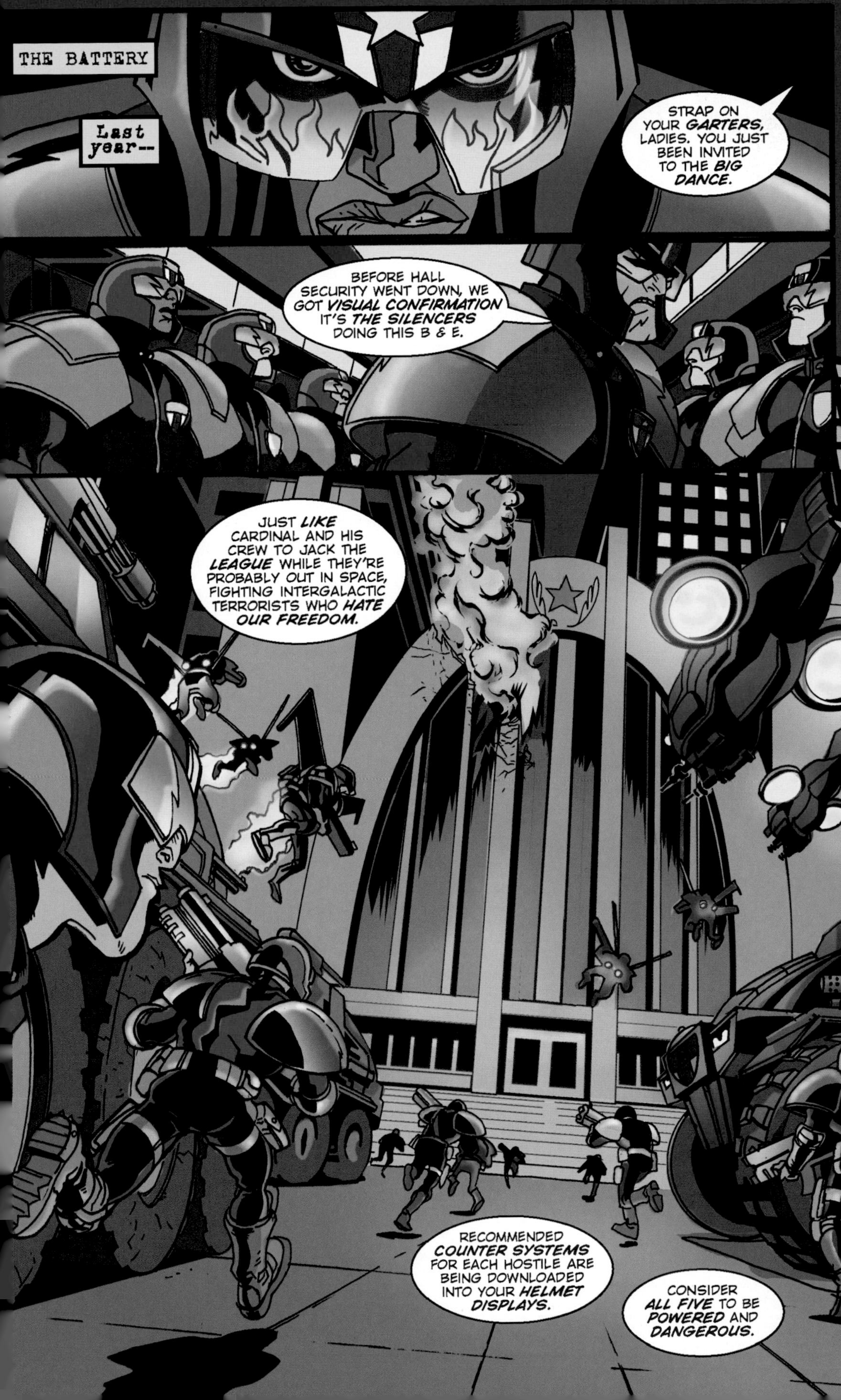
THE BATTERY
Last year--
STRAP ON YOUR GARTERS, LADIES. YOU JUST BEEN INVITED TO THE BIG DANCE.
BEFORE HALL SECURITY WENT DOWN, WE GOT VISUAL CONFIRMATION IT'S THE SILENCERS DOING THIS B & E.
JUST LIKE CARDINAL AND HIS CREW TO JACK THE LEAGUE WHILE THEY'RE PROBABLY OUT IN SPACE, FIGHTING INTERGALACTIC TERRORISTS WHO HATE OUR FREEDOM.
RECOMMENDED COUNTER SYSTEMS FOR EACH HOSTILE ARE BEING DOWNLOADED INTO YOUR HELMET DISPLAYS.
CONSIDER ALL FIVE TO BE POWERED AND DANGEROUS.

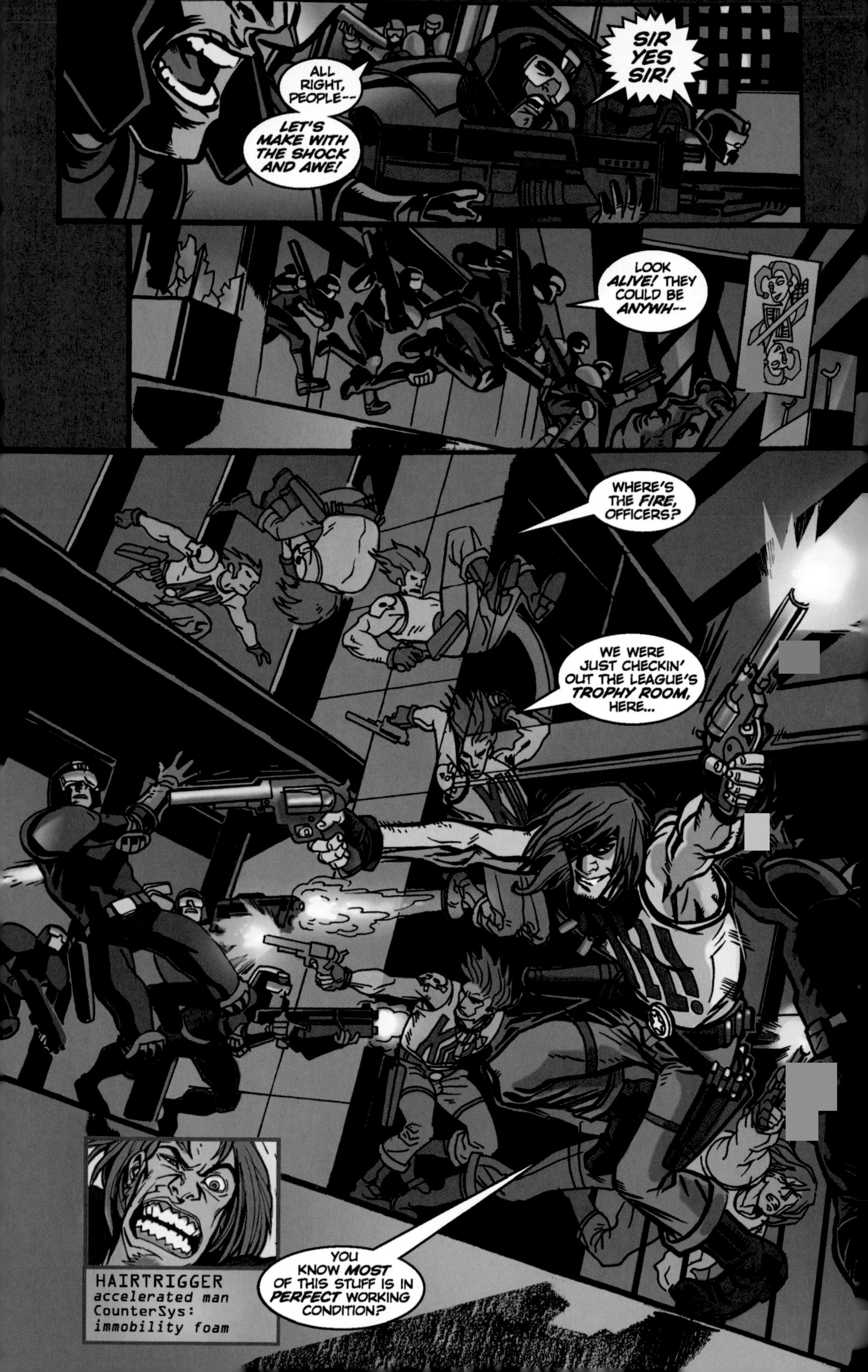
ALL RIGHT, PEOPLE--
LET'S MAKE WITH THE SHOCK AND AWE!
SIR YES SIR!
LOOK ALIVE! THEY COULD BE ANYWH--
WHERE'S THE FIRE, OFFICERS?
WE WERE JUST CHECKIN' OUT THE LEAGUE'S TROPHY ROOM, HERE...
HAIRTRIGGER
accelerated man
CounterSys:
immobility foam
YOU KNOW MOST OF THIS STUFF IS IN PERFECT WORKING CONDITION?

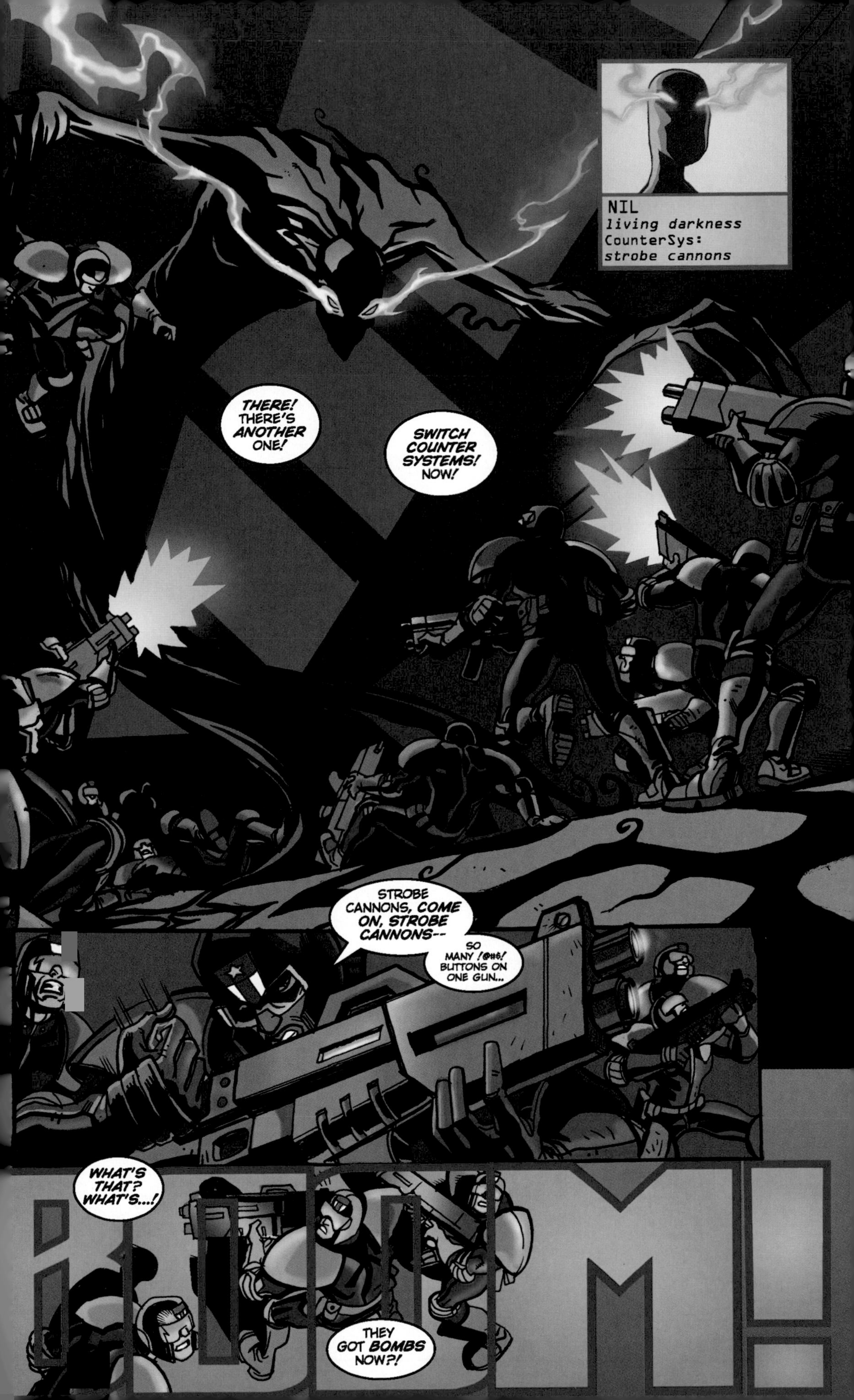
NIL
living darkness
CounterSys:
strobe cannons
THERE! THERE'S ANOTHER ONE!
SWITCH COUNTER SYSTEMS! NOW!
STROBE CANNONS, COME ON, STROBE CANNONS--
SO MANY !@#$! BUTTONS ON ONE GUN...
WHAT'S THAT? WHAT'S...!
THEY GOT BOMBS NOW?!

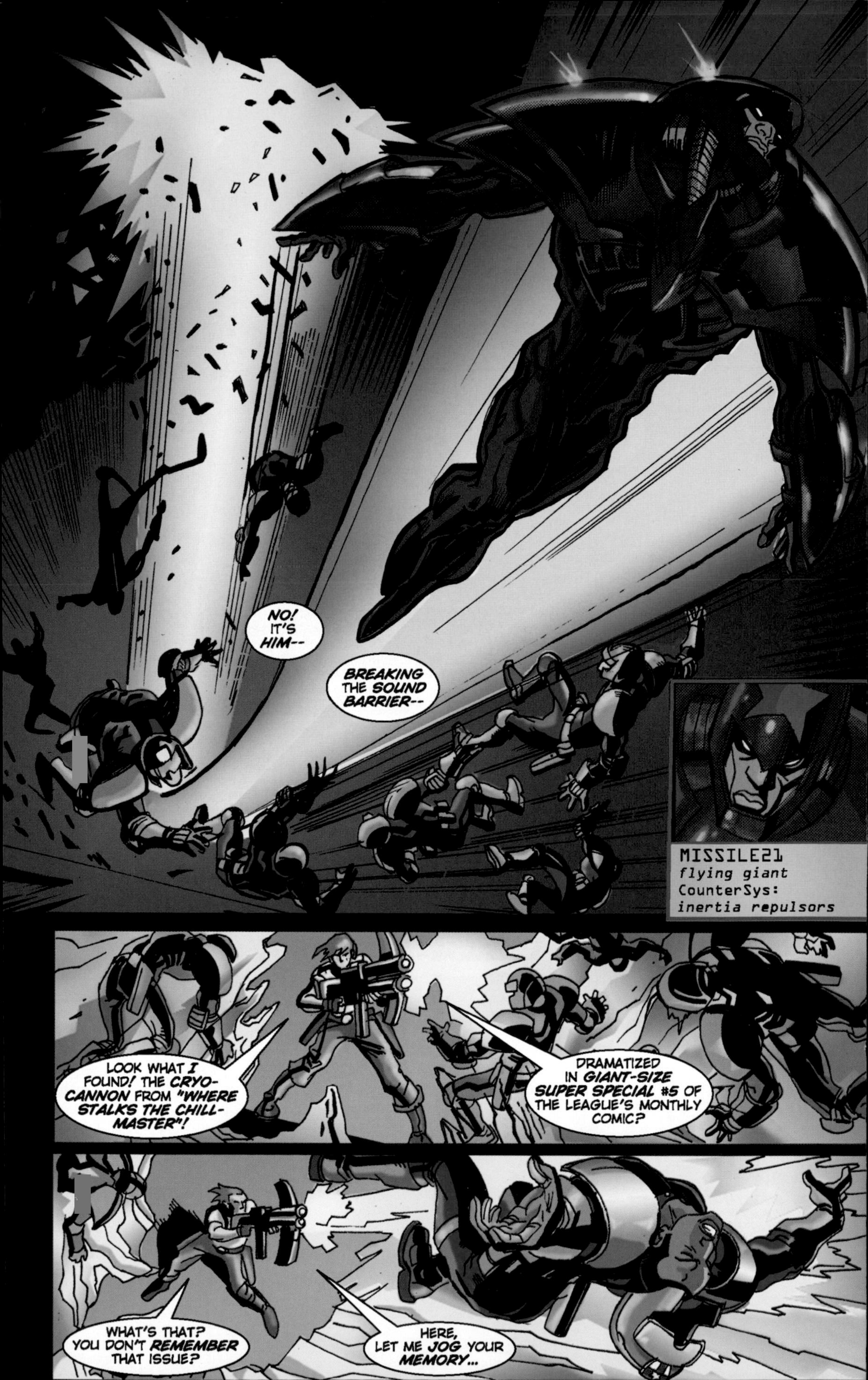
NO! IT'S HIM--
BREAKING THE SOUND BARRIER--
MISSILE21
flying giant
CounterSys:
inertia repulsors
LOOK WHAT I FOUND! THE CRYO-CANNON FROM "WHERE STALKS THE CHILL-MASTER"!
DRAMATIZED IN GIANT-SIZE SUPER SPECIAL #5 OF THE LEAGUE'S MONTHLY COMIC?
WHAT'S THAT? YOU DON'T REMEMBER THAT ISSUE?
HERE, LET ME JOG YOUR MEMORY...

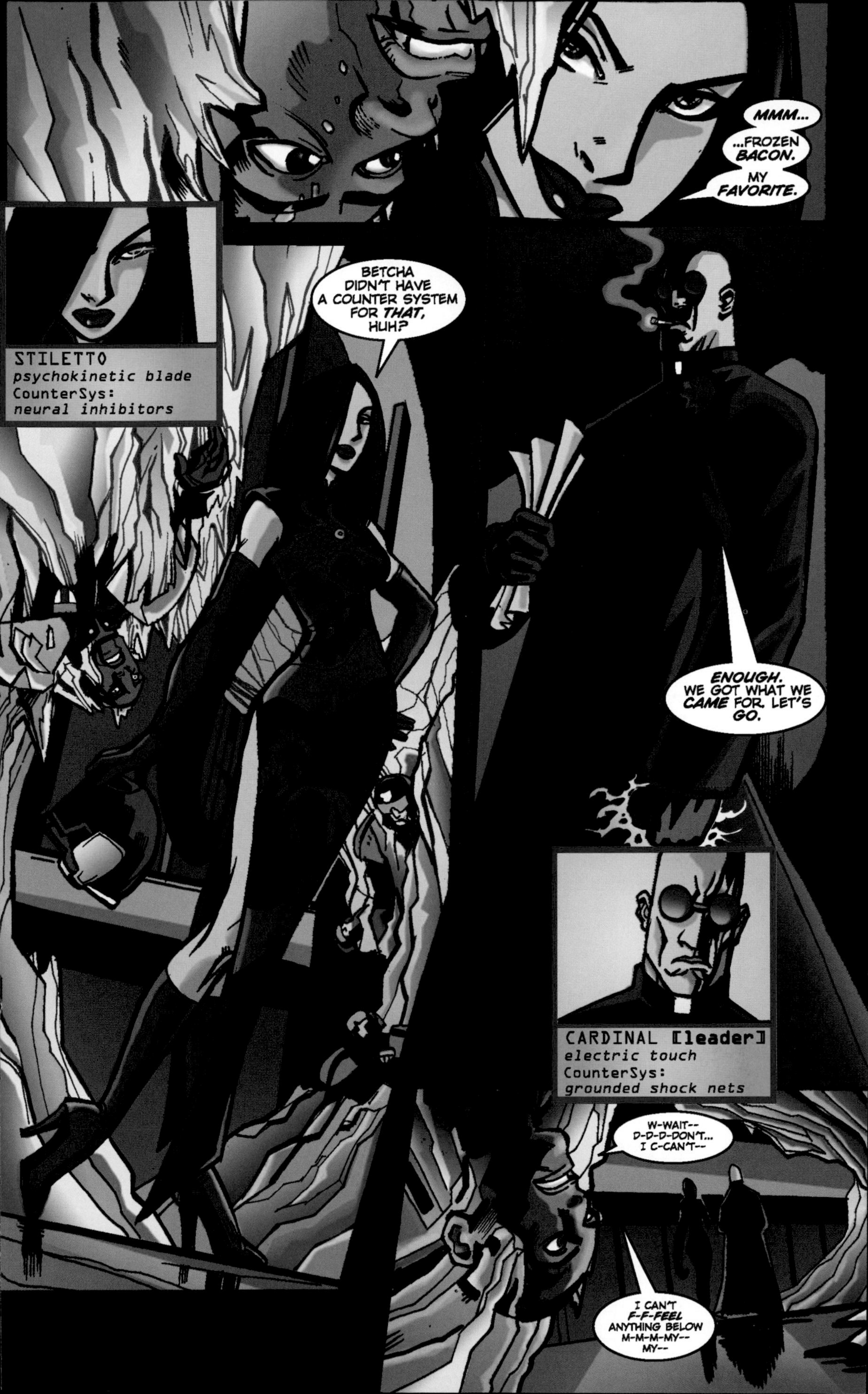
MMM...
...FROZEN BACON.
MY FAVORITE.
STILETTO
psychokinetic blade
CounterSys:
neural inhibitors
BETCHA DIDN'T HAVE A COUNTER SYSTEM FOR THAT, HUH?
ENOUGH. WE GOT WHAT WE CAME FOR. LET'S GO.
CARDINAL [leader]
electric touch
CounterSys:
grounded shock nets
W-WAIT-- D-D-D-DON'T... I C-CAN'T--
I CAN'T F-F-FEEL ANYTHING BELOW M-M-M-MY-- MY--

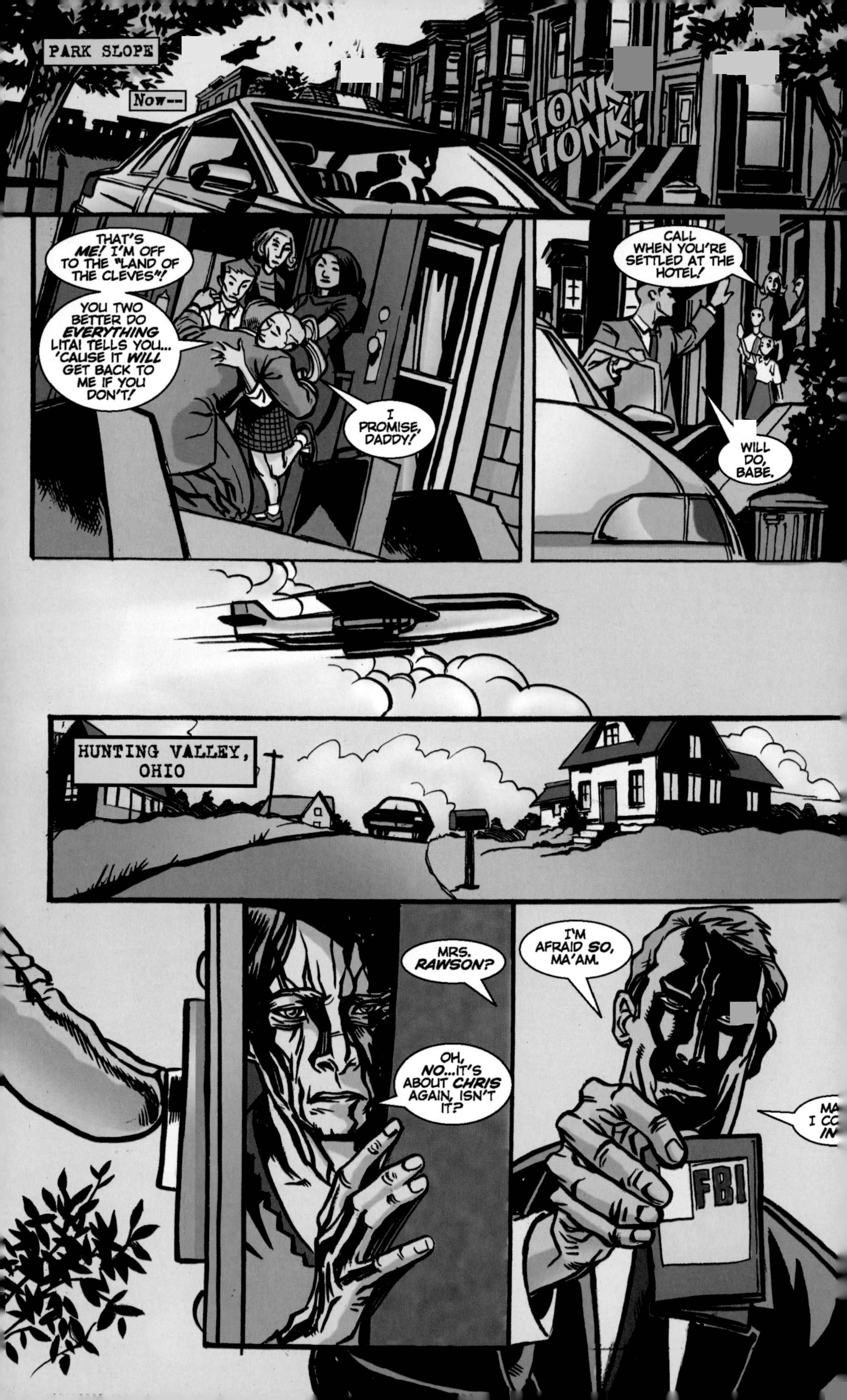
PARK SLOPE
Now--
HONK HONK!
THAT'S ME! I'M OFF TO THE "LAND OF THE CLEVES"!
YOU TWO BETTER DO EVERYTHING LITAI TELLS YOU... 'CAUSE IT WILL GET BACK TO ME IF YOU DON'T!
I PROMISE, DADDY!
CALL WHEN YOU'RE SETTLED AT THE HOTEL!
WILL DO, BABE.
HUNTING VALLEY, OHIO
MRS. RAWSON?
I'M AFRAID SO, MA'AM.
OH, NO...IT'S ABOUT CHRIS AGAIN, ISN'T IT?
FBI

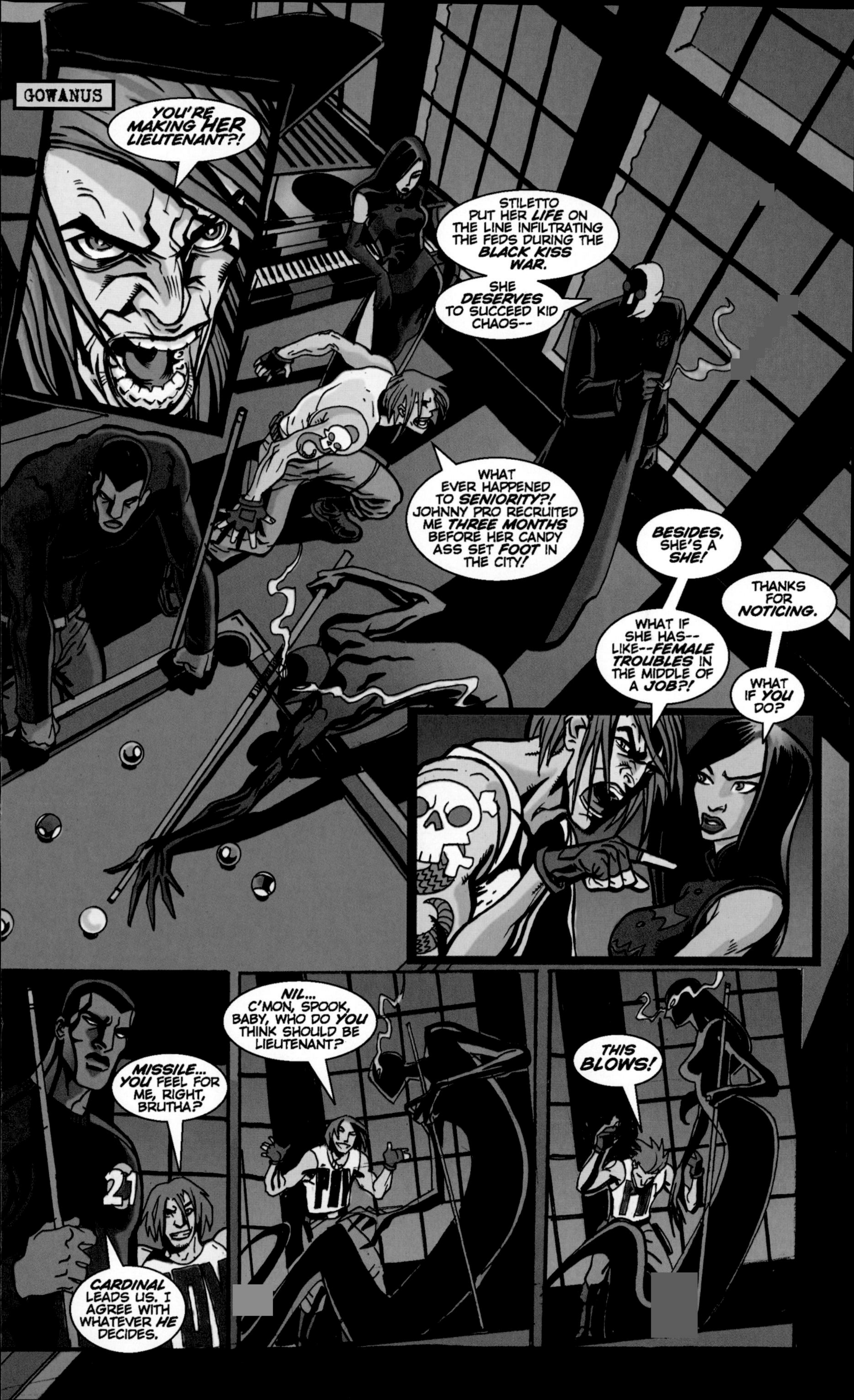
GOWANUS
YOU'RE MAKING HER LIEUTENANT?!
STILETTO PUT HER LIFE ON THE LINE INFILTRATING THE FEDS DURING THE BLACK KISS WAR.
SHE DESERVES TO SUCCEED KID CHAOS--
WHAT EVER HAPPENED TO SENIORITY?! JOHNNY PRO RECRUITED ME THREE MONTHS BEFORE HER CANDY ASS SET FOOT IN THE CITY!
BESIDES, SHE'S A SHE!
WHAT IF SHE HAS--LIKE--FEMALE TROUBLES IN THE MIDDLE OF A JOB?!
THANKS FOR NOTICING.
WHAT IF YOU DO?
MISSILE... YOU FEEL FOR ME, RIGHT, BRUTHA?
CARDINAL LEADS US. I AGREE WITH WHATEVER HE DECIDES.
NIL... C'MON, SPOOK, BABY, WHO DO YOU THINK SHOULD BE LIEUTENANT?
THIS BLOWS!

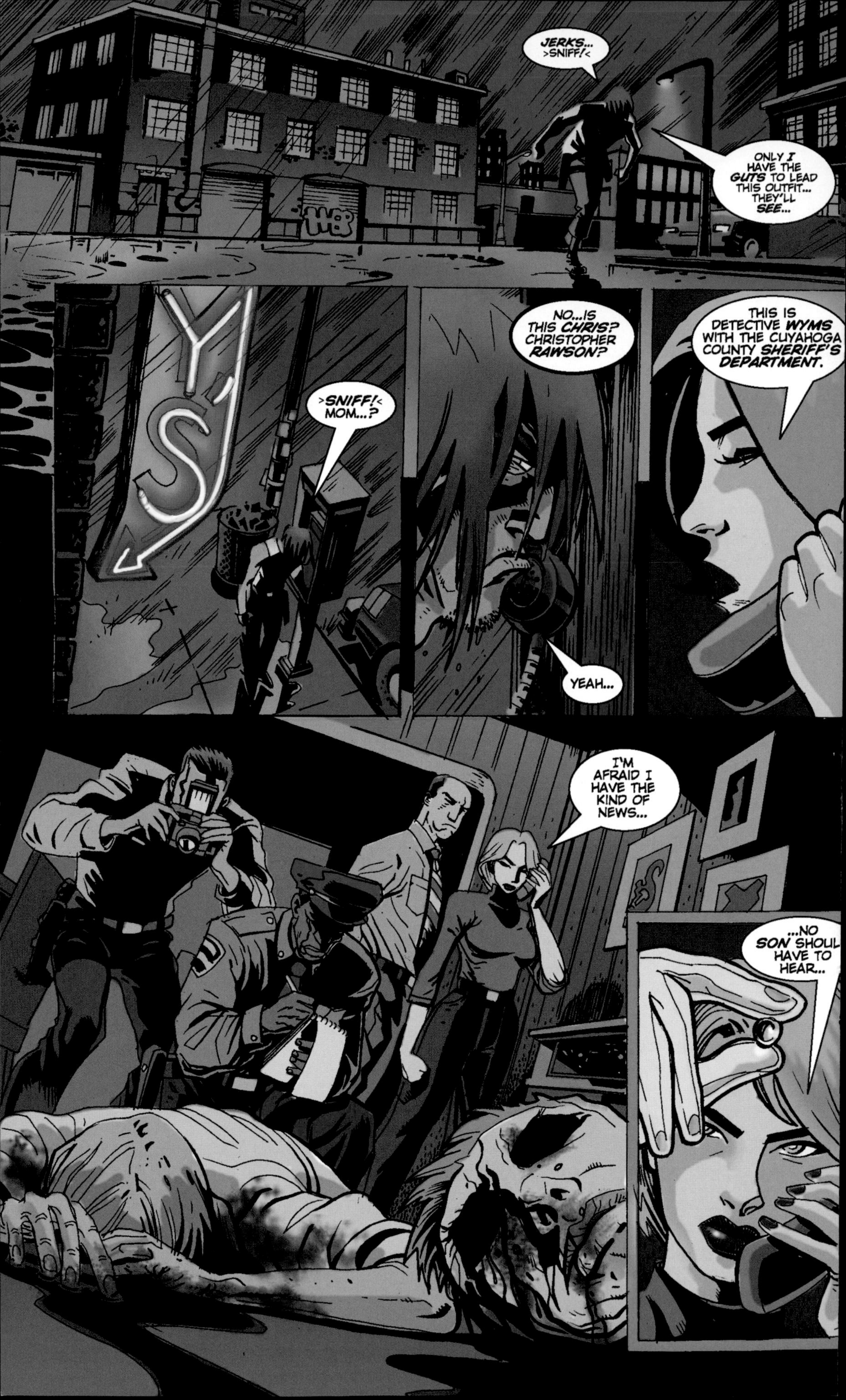
JERKS... >SNIFF!<
ONLY I HAVE THE GUTS TO LEAD THIS OUTFIT... THEY'LL SEE...
>SNIFF!< MOM...?
NO...IS THIS CHRIS? CHRISTOPHER RAWSON?
YEAH...
THIS IS DETECTIVE WYMS WITH THE CUYAHOGA COUNTY SHERIFF'S DEPARTMENT.
I'M AFRAID I HAVE THE KIND OF NEWS...
...NO SON SHOUL HAVE TO HEAR...

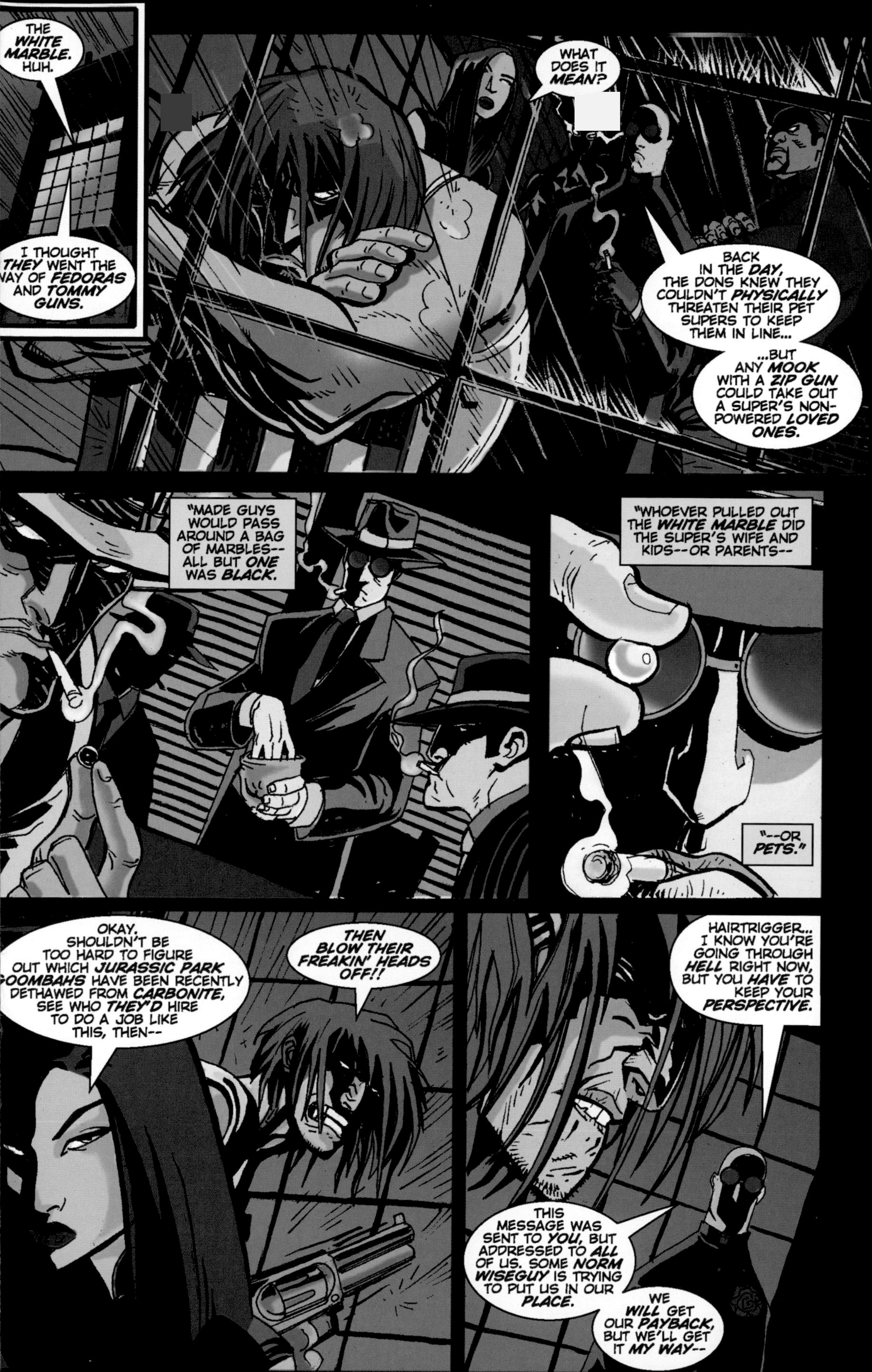
THE WHITE MARBLE. HUH.
I THOUGHT THEY WENT THE WAY OF FEDORAS AND TOMMY GUNS.
WHAT DOES IT MEAN?
BACK IN THE DAY, THE DONS KNEW THEY COULDN'T PHYSICALLY THREATEN THEIR PET SUPERS TO KEEP THEM IN LINE...
...BUT ANY MOOK WITH A ZIP GUN COULD TAKE OUT A SUPER'S NON-POWERED LOVED ONES.
"MADE GUYS WOULD PASS AROUND A BAG OF MARBLES--ALL BUT ONE WAS BLACK.
"WHOEVER PULLED OUT THE WHITE MARBLE DID THE SUPER'S WIFE AND KIDS--OR PARENTS--
"--OR PETS."
OKAY. SHOULDN'T BE TOO HARD TO FIGURE OUT WHICH JURASSIC PARK GOOMBAHS HAVE BEEN RECENTLY DETHAWED FROM CARBONITE, SEE WHO THEY'D HIRE TO DO A JOB LIKE THIS, THEN--
THEN BLOW THEIR FREAKIN' HEADS OFF!!
HAIRTRIGGER... I KNOW YOU'RE GOING THROUGH HELL RIGHT NOW, BUT YOU HAVE TO KEEP YOUR PERSPECTIVE.
THIS MESSAGE WAS SENT TO YOU, BUT ADDRESSED TO ALL OF US. SOME NORM WISEGUY IS TRYING TO PUT US IN OUR PLACE.
WE WILL GET OUR PAYBACK, BUT WE'LL GET IT MY WAY--

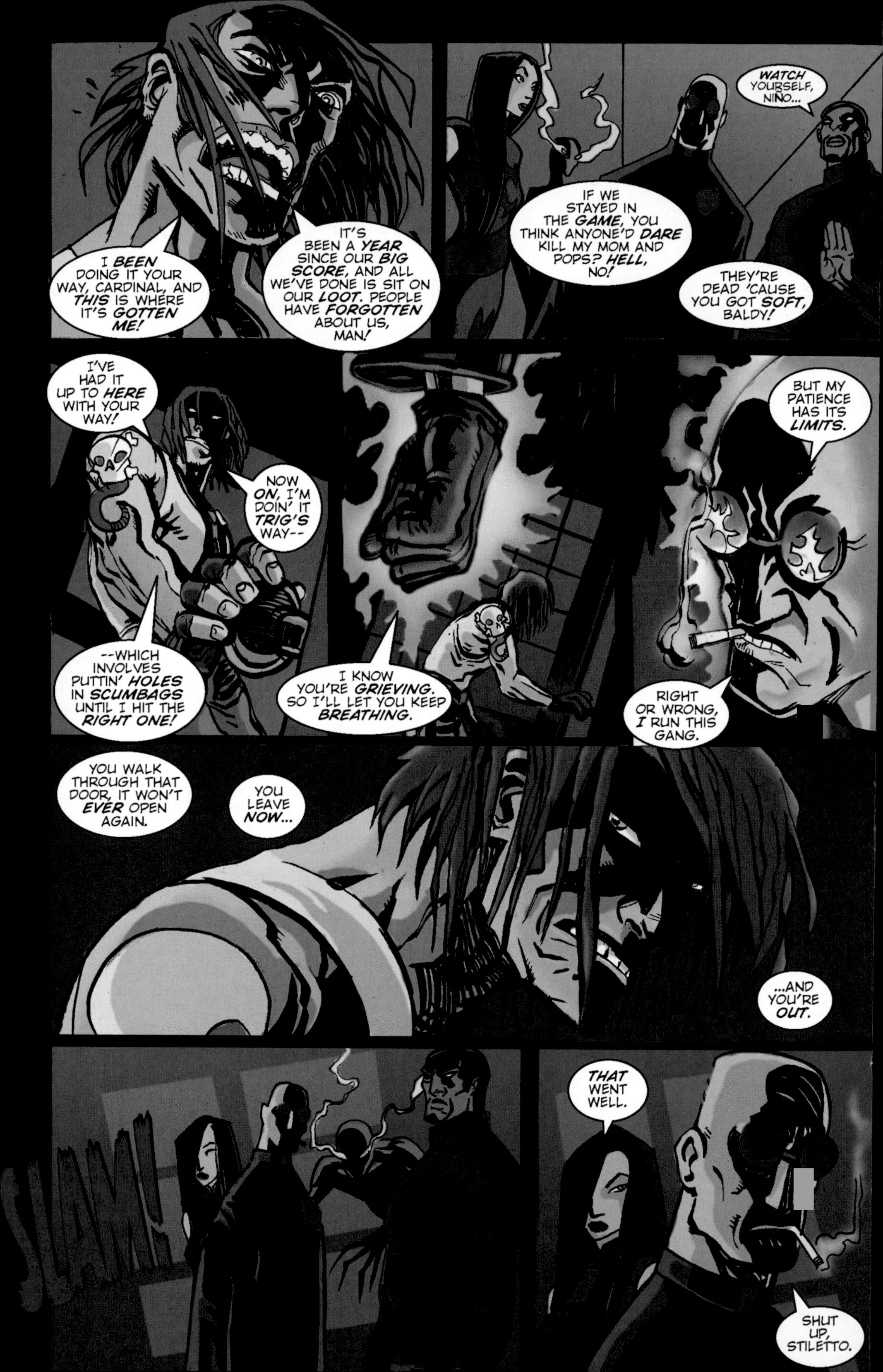

I BEEN DOING IT YOUR WAY, CARDINAL, AND THIS IS WHERE IT'S GOTTEN ME!
IT'S BEEN A YEAR SINCE OUR BIG SCORE, AND ALL WE'VE DONE IS SIT ON OUR LOOT. PEOPLE HAVE FORGOTTEN ABOUT US, MAN!
WATCH YOURSELF, NIÑO...
IF WE STAYED IN THE GAME, YOU THINK ANYONE'D DARE KILL MY MOM AND POPS? HELL, NO!
THEY'RE DEAD 'CAUSE YOU GOT SOFT, BALDY!
I'VE HAD IT UP TO HERE WITH YOUR WAY!
NOW ON, I'M DOIN' IT TRIG'S WAY--
--WHICH INVOLVES PUTTIN' HOLES IN SCUMBAGS UNTIL I HIT THE RIGHT ONE!
I KNOW YOU'RE GRIEVING. SO I'LL LET YOU KEEP BREATHING.
BUT MY PATIENCE HAS ITS LIMITS.
RIGHT OR WRONG, I RUN THIS GANG.
YOU WALK THROUGH THAT DOOR, IT WON'T EVER OPEN AGAIN.
YOU LEAVE NOW...
...AND YOU'RE OUT.
SLAM!
THAT WENT WELL.
SHUT UP, STILETTO.

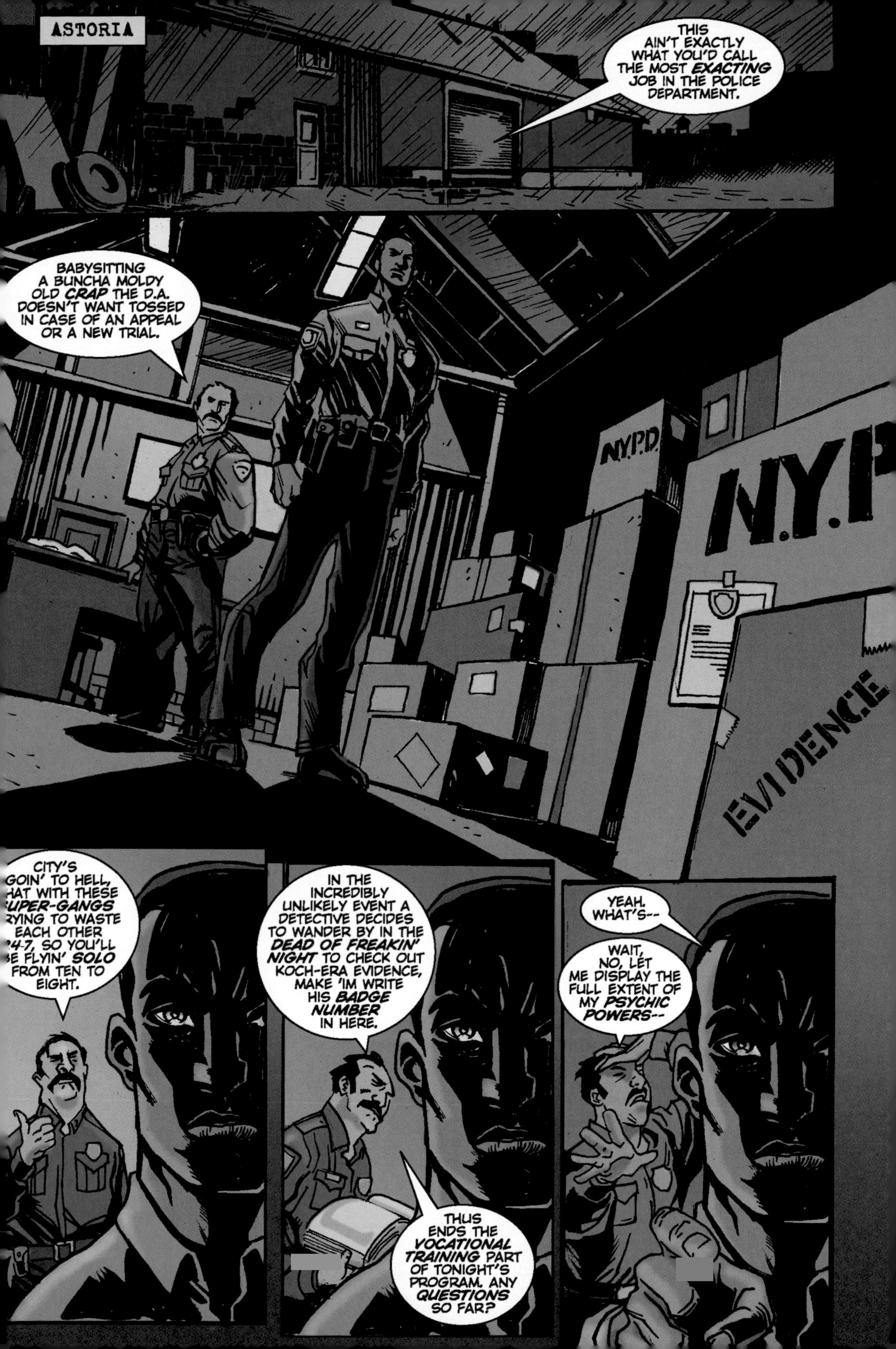
ASTORIA
THIS AIN'T EXACTLY WHAT YOU'D CALL THE MOST EXACTING JOB IN THE POLICE DEPARTMENT.
BABYSITTING A BUNCHA MOLDY OLD CRAP THE D.A. DOESN'T WANT TOSSED IN CASE OF AN APPEAL OR A NEW TRIAL.
N.Y.P.D.
N.Y.P
EVIDENCE
CITY'S GOIN' TO HELL, HAT WITH THESE UPER-GANGS RYING TO WASTE EACH OTHER 24-7, SO YOU'LL E FLYIN' SOLO FROM TEN TO EIGHT.
IN THE INCREDIBLY UNLIKELY EVENT A DETECTIVE DECIDES TO WANDER BY IN THE DEAD OF FREAKIN' NIGHT TO CHECK OUT KOCH-ERA EVIDENCE, MAKE 'IM WRITE HIS BADGE NUMBER IN HERE.
THUS ENDS THE VOCATIONAL TRAINING PART OF TONIGHT'S PROGRAM. ANY QUESTIONS SO FAR?
YEAH, WHAT'S--
WAIT, NO, LET ME DISPLAY THE FULL EXTENT OF MY PSYCHIC POWERS--

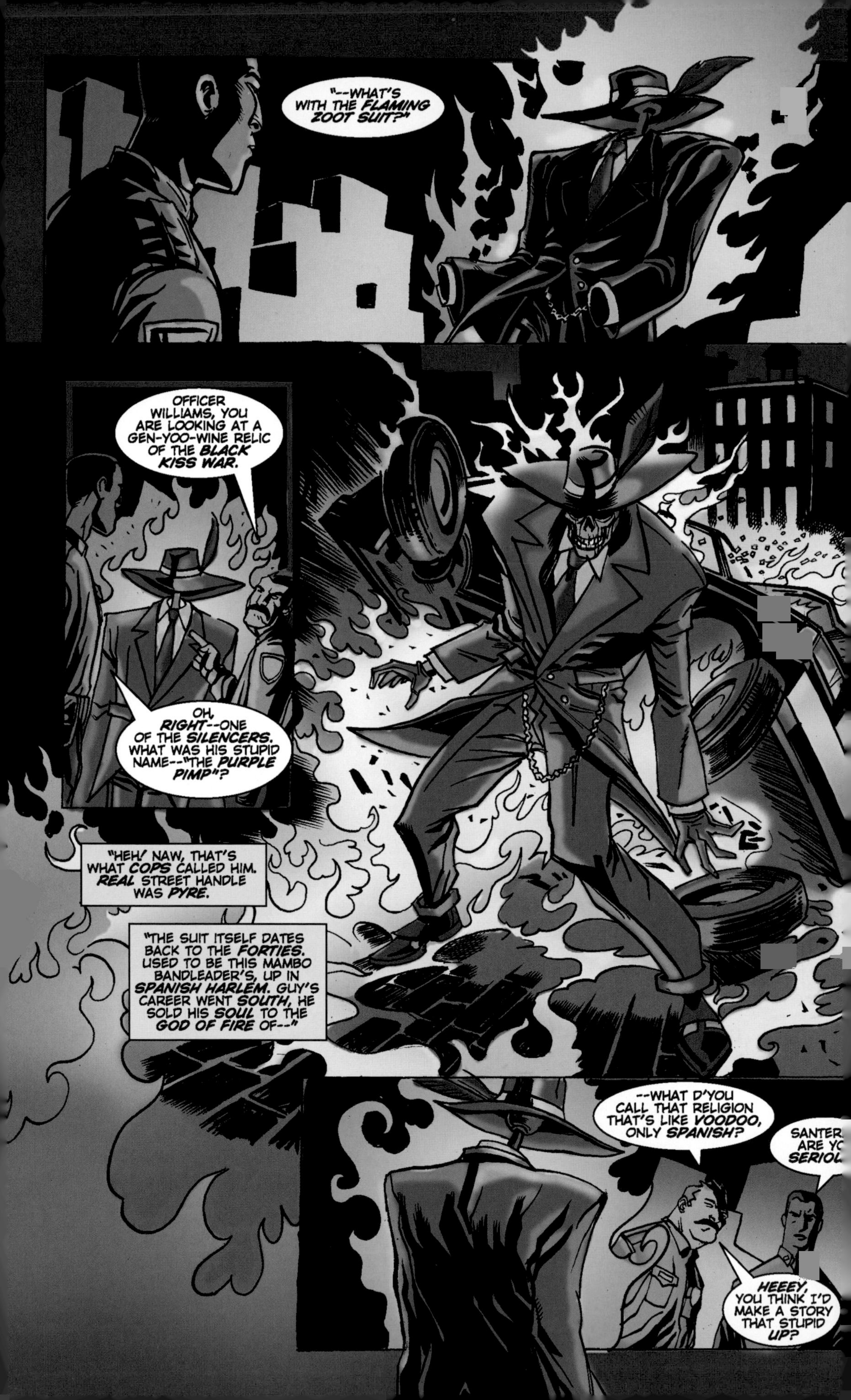
"--WHAT'S WITH THE *FLAMING ZOOT SUIT?*"
OFFICER WILLIAMS, YOU ARE LOOKING AT A GEN-YOO-WINE RELIC OF THE *BLACK KISS WAR.*
OH, *RIGHT*--ONE OF THE *SILENCERS.* WHAT WAS HIS STUPID NAME--"THE *PURPLE PIMP*"?
"HEH! NAW, THAT'S WHAT *COPS* CALLED HIM. *REAL* STREET HANDLE WAS *PYRE.*
"THE SUIT ITSELF DATES BACK TO THE *FORTIES.* USED TO BE THIS MAMBO BANDLEADER'S, UP IN *SPANISH HARLEM.* GUY'S CAREER WENT *SOUTH,* HE SOLD HIS *SOUL* TO THE *GOD OF FIRE* OF--"
--WHAT D'YOU CALL THAT RELIGION THAT'S LIKE *VOODOO,* ONLY *SPANISH?*
SANTER ARE YO *SERIOU*
HEEEY, YOU THINK I'D MAKE A STORY THAT STUPID *UP?*

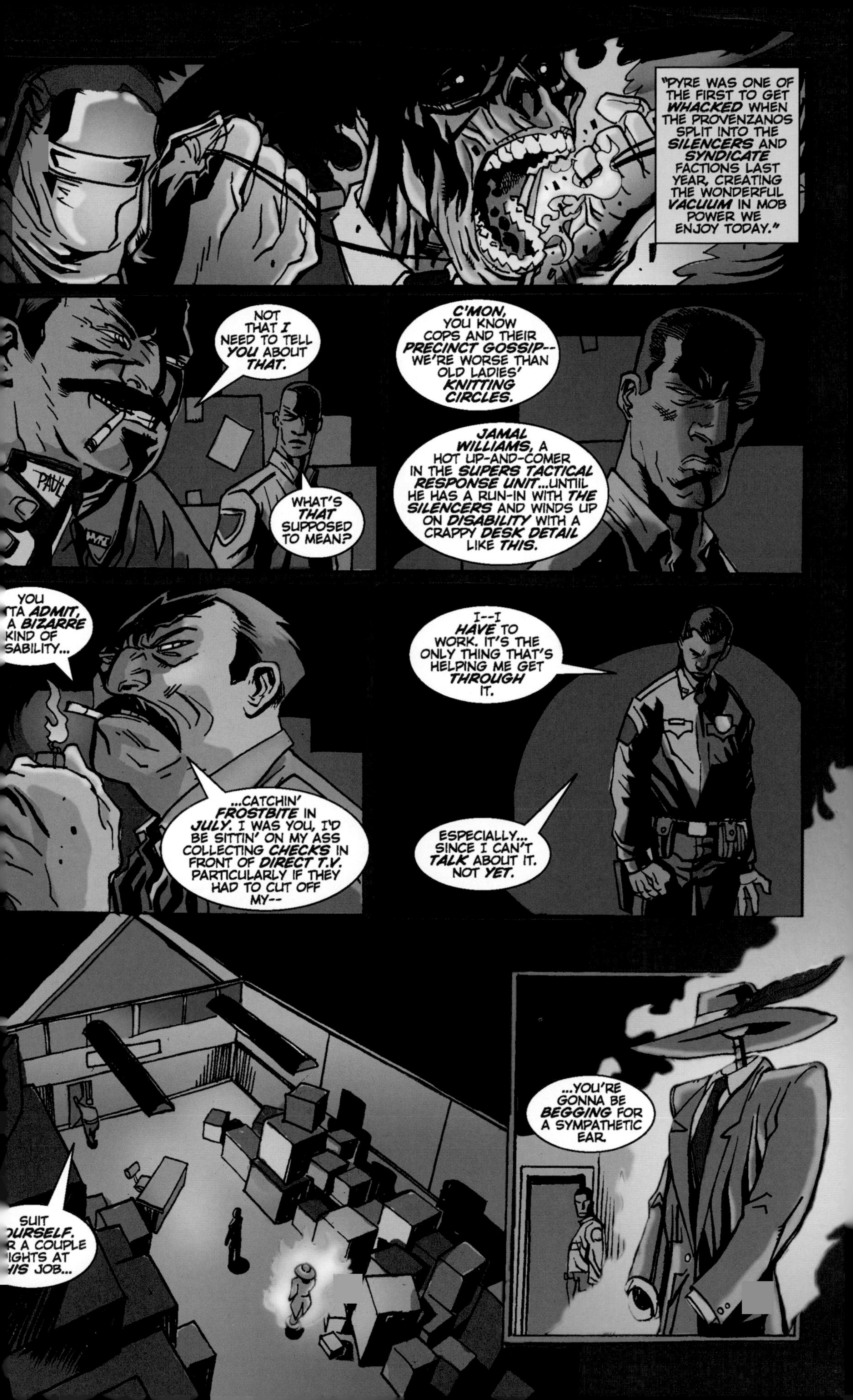
"PYRE WAS ONE OF THE FIRST TO GET WHACKED WHEN THE PROVENZANOS SPLIT INTO THE SILENCERS AND SYNDICATE FACTIONS LAST YEAR, CREATING THE WONDERFUL VACUUM IN MOB POWER WE ENJOY TODAY."
NOT THAT I NEED TO TELL YOU ABOUT THAT.
WHAT'S THAT SUPPOSED TO MEAN?
C'MON, YOU KNOW COPS AND THEIR PRECINCT GOSSIP-- WE'RE WORSE THAN OLD LADIES' KNITTING CIRCLES.
JAMAL WILLIAMS, A HOT UP-AND-COMER IN THE SUPERS TACTICAL RESPONSE UNIT...UNTIL HE HAS A RUN-IN WITH THE SILENCERS AND WINDS UP ON DISABILITY WITH A CRAPPY DESK DETAIL LIKE THIS.
YOU TTA ADMIT, A BIZARRE KIND OF SABILITY...
...CATCHIN' FROSTBITE IN JULY. I WAS YOU, I'D BE SITTIN' ON MY ASS COLLECTING CHECKS IN FRONT OF DIRECT T.V. PARTICULARLY IF THEY HAD TO CUT OFF MY--
I--I HAVE TO WORK. IT'S THE ONLY THING THAT'S HELPING ME GET THROUGH IT.
ESPECIALLY... SINCE I CAN'T TALK ABOUT IT. NOT YET.
SUIT OURSELF. R A COUPLE IGHTS AT IS JOB...
...YOU'RE GONNA BE BEGGING FOR A SYMPATHETIC EAR.

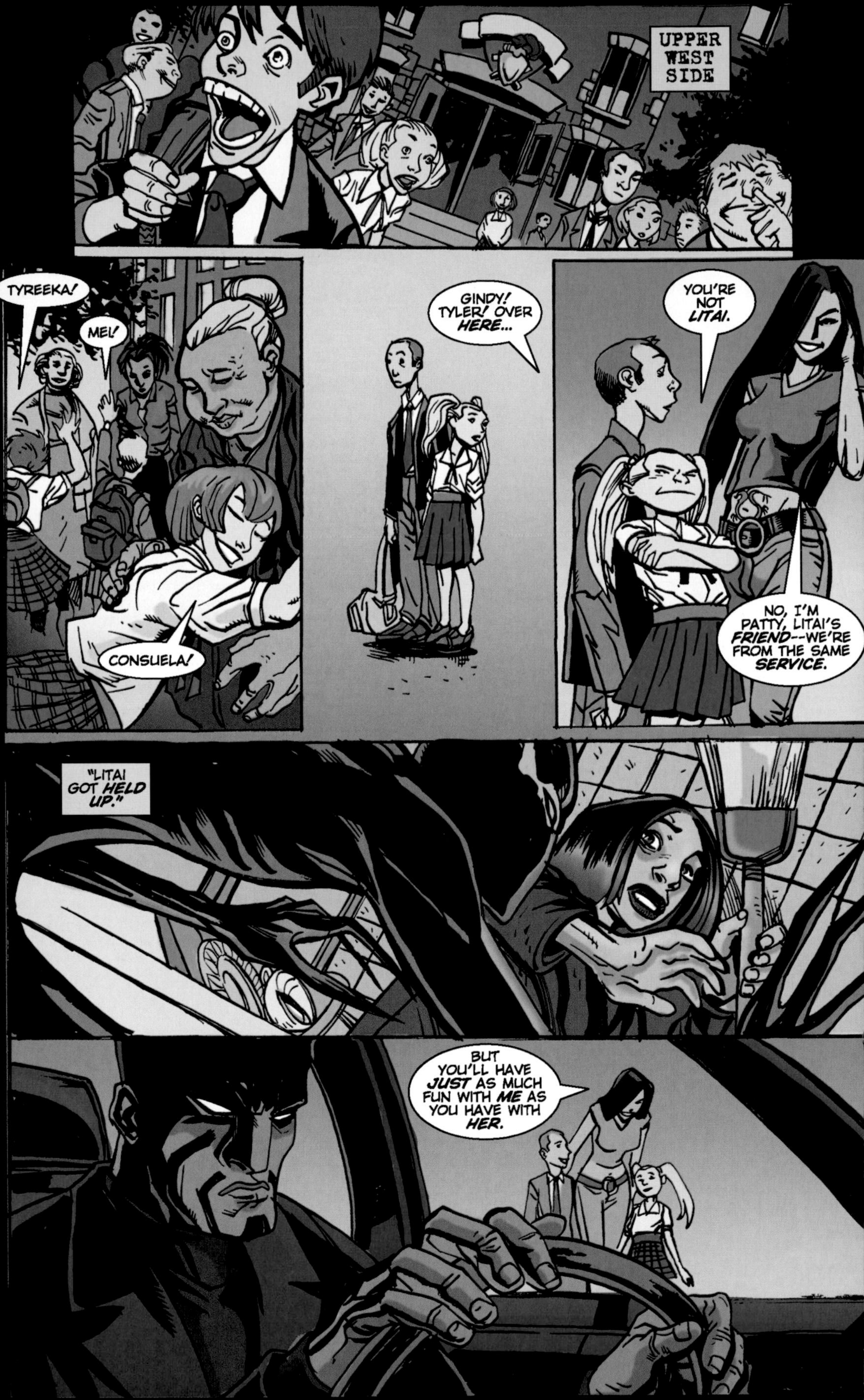
UPPER WEST SIDE
TYREEKA!
MEI!
CONSUELA!
GINDY! TYLER! OVER HERE...
YOU'RE NOT LITAI.
NO, I'M PATTY, LITAI'S FRIEND--WE'RE FROM THE SAME SERVICE.
"LITAI GOT HELD UP."
BUT YOU'LL HAVE JUST AS MUCH FUN WITH ME AS YOU HAVE WITH HER.

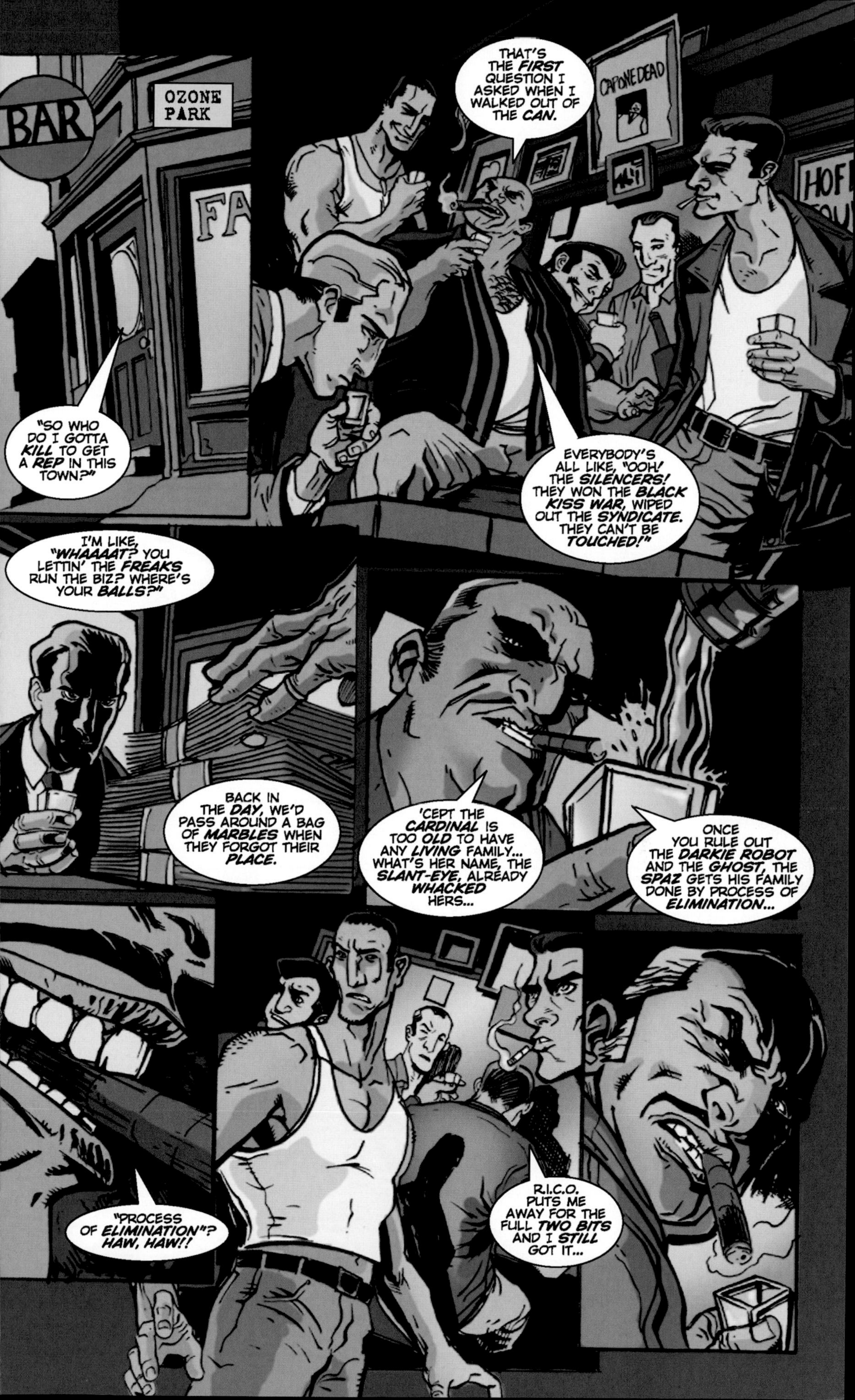
BAR
OZONE PARK
FA
THAT'S THE FIRST QUESTION I ASKED WHEN I WALKED OUT OF THE CAN.
CAPONE DEAD
"SO WHO DO I GOTTA KILL TO GET A REP IN THIS TOWN?"
EVERYBODY'S ALL LIKE, "OOH! THE SILENCERS! THEY WON THE BLACK KISS WAR, WIPED OUT THE SYNDICATE. THEY CAN'T BE TOUCHED!"
I'M LIKE, "WHAAAAT? YOU LETTIN' THE FREAKS RUN THE BIZ? WHERE'S YOUR BALLS?"
BACK IN THE DAY, WE'D PASS AROUND A BAG OF MARBLES WHEN THEY FORGOT THEIR PLACE.
'CEPT THE CARDINAL IS TOO OLD TO HAVE ANY LIVING FAMILY... WHAT'S HER NAME, THE SLANT-EYE, ALREADY WHACKED HERS...
ONCE YOU RULE OUT THE DARKIE ROBOT AND THE GHOST, THE SPAZ GETS HIS FAMILY DONE BY PROCESS OF ELIMINATION...
"PROCESS OF ELIMINATION"? HAW, HAW!!
R.I.C.O. PUTS ME AWAY FOR THE FULL TWO BITS AND I STILL GOT IT...

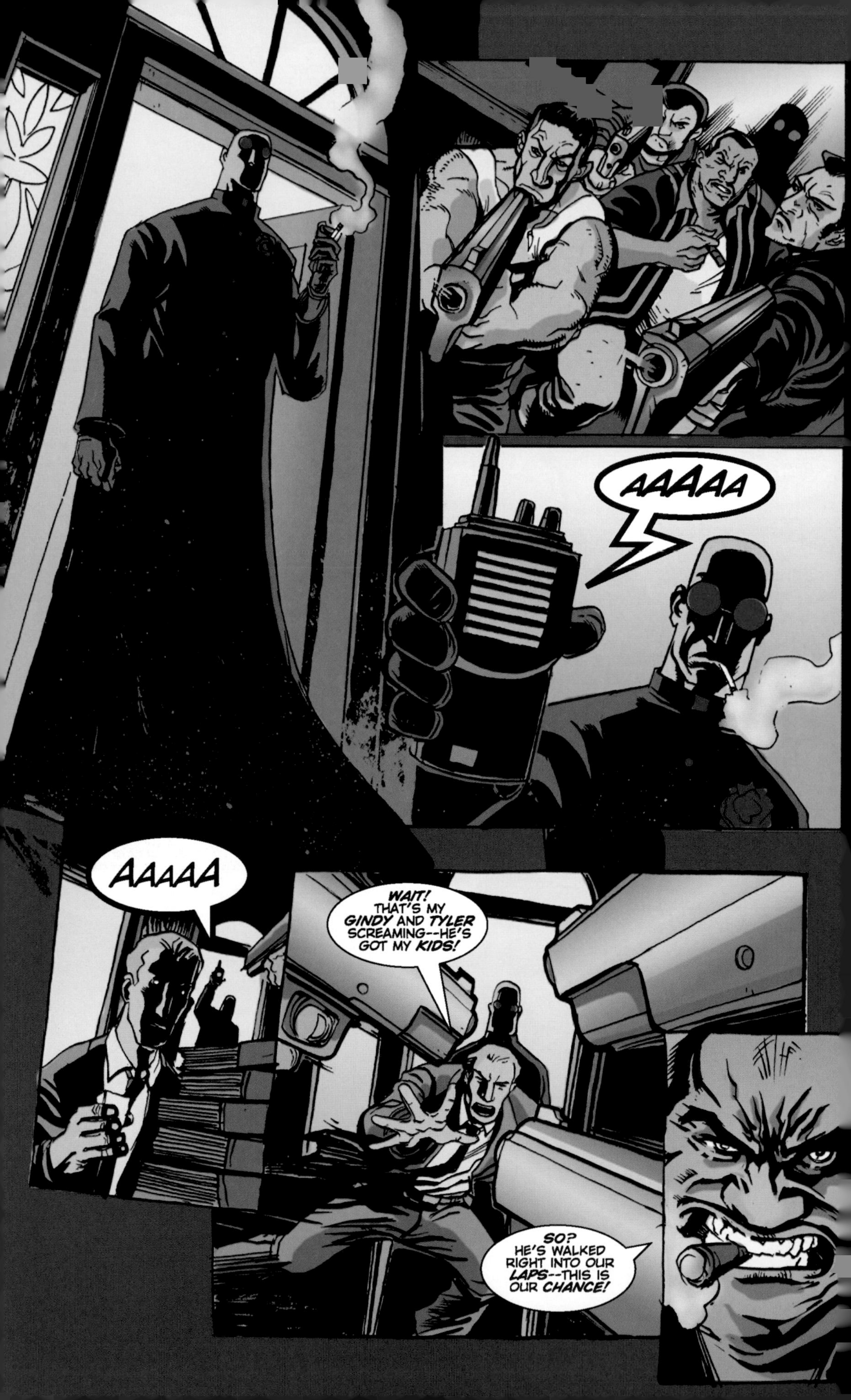
AAAAA
AAAAA
WAIT! THAT'S MY GINDY AND TYLER SCREAMING--HE'S GOT MY KIDS!
SO? HE'S WALKED RIGHT INTO OUR LAPS--THIS IS OUR CHANCE!

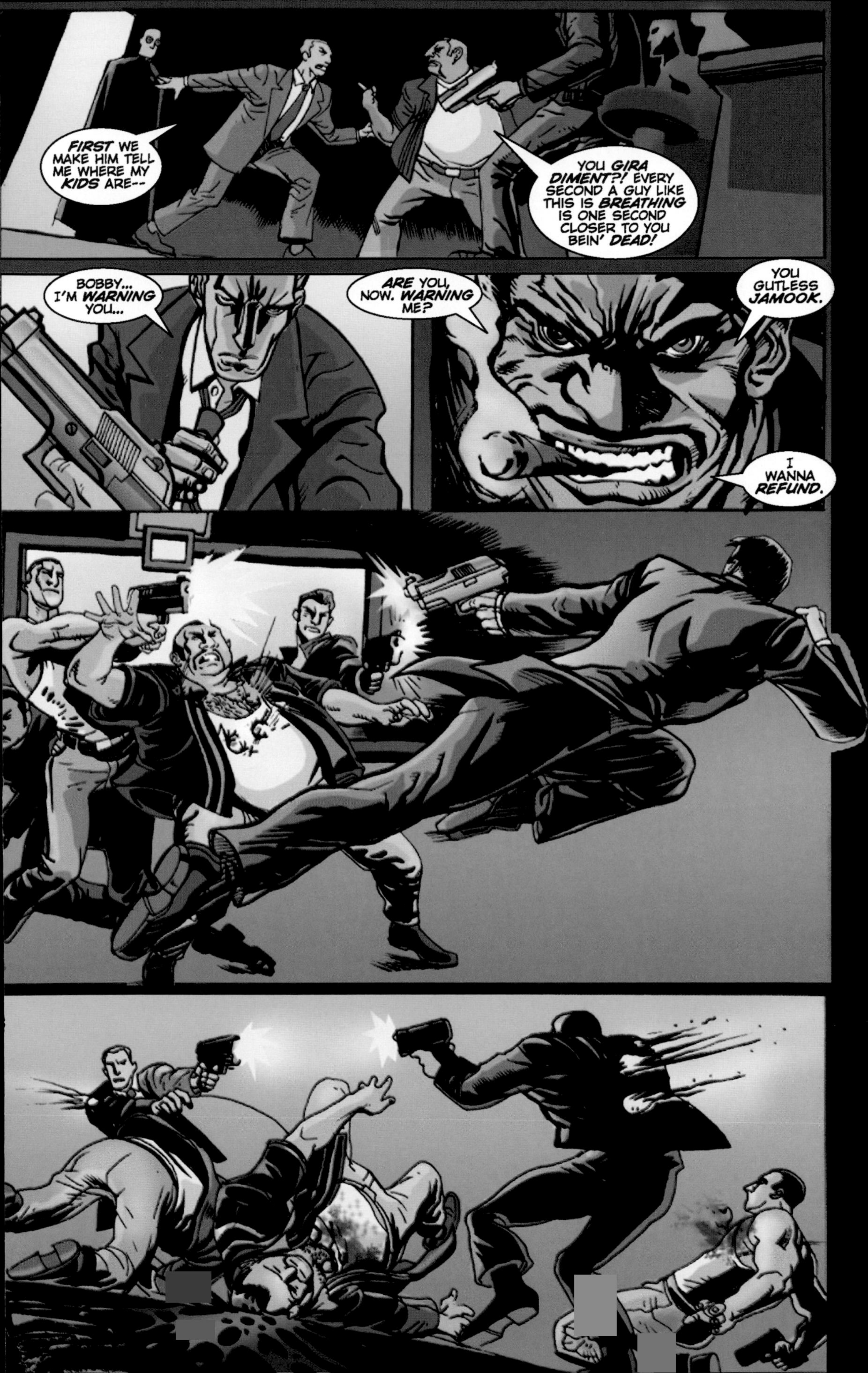

FIRST WE MAKE HIM TELL ME WHERE MY KIDS ARE--
YOU GIRA DIMENT?! EVERY SECOND A GUY LIKE THIS IS BREATHING IS ONE SECOND CLOSER TO YOU BEIN' DEAD!
BOBBY... I'M WARNING YOU...
ARE YOU, NOW. WARNING ME?
YOU GUTLESS JAMOOK.
I WANNA REFUND.

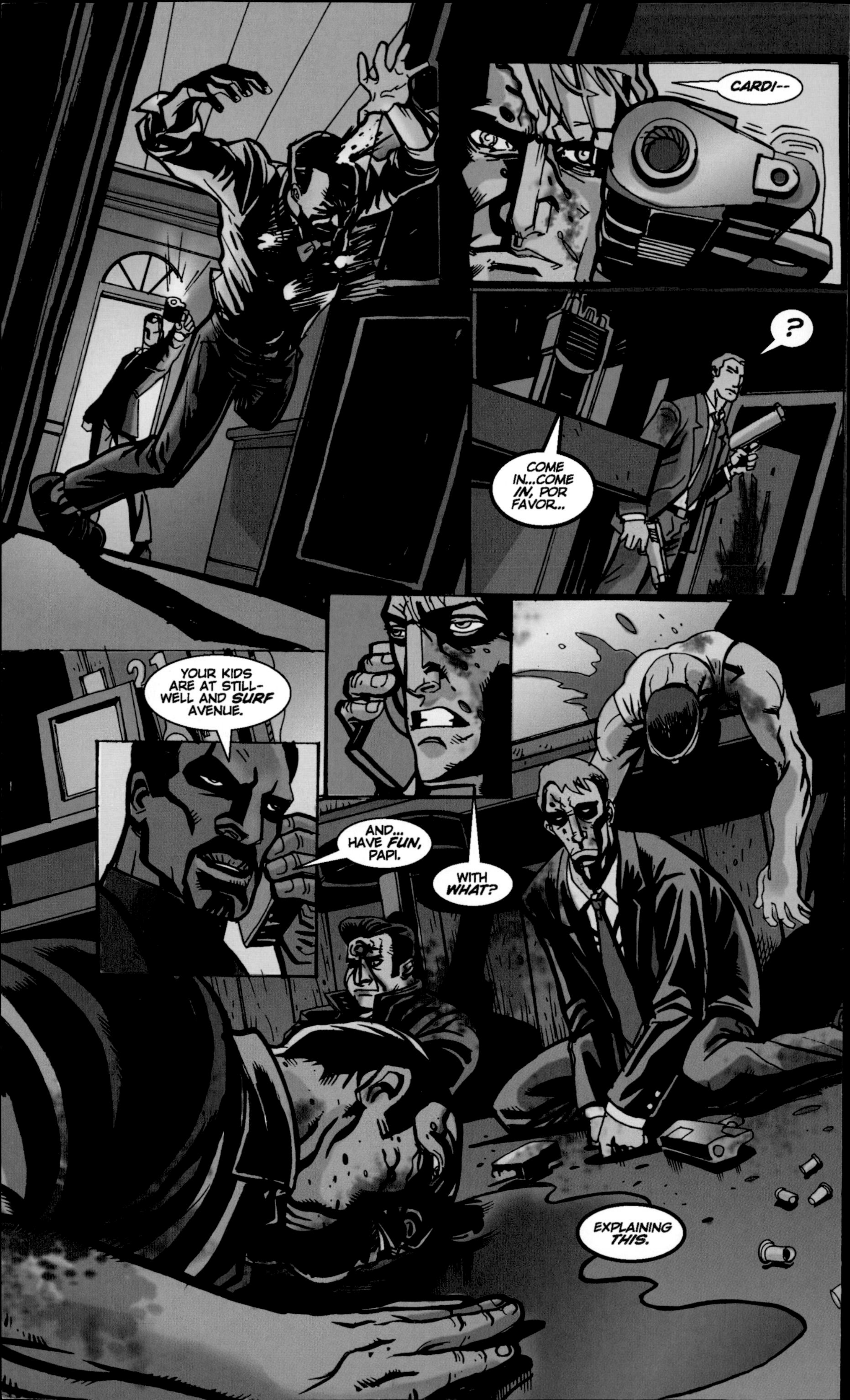
CARDI--
?
COME IN...COME IN, POR FAVOR...
YOUR KIDS ARE AT STILL-WELL AND SURF AVENUE.
AND... HAVE FUN, PAPI.
WITH WHAT?
EXPLAINING THIS.

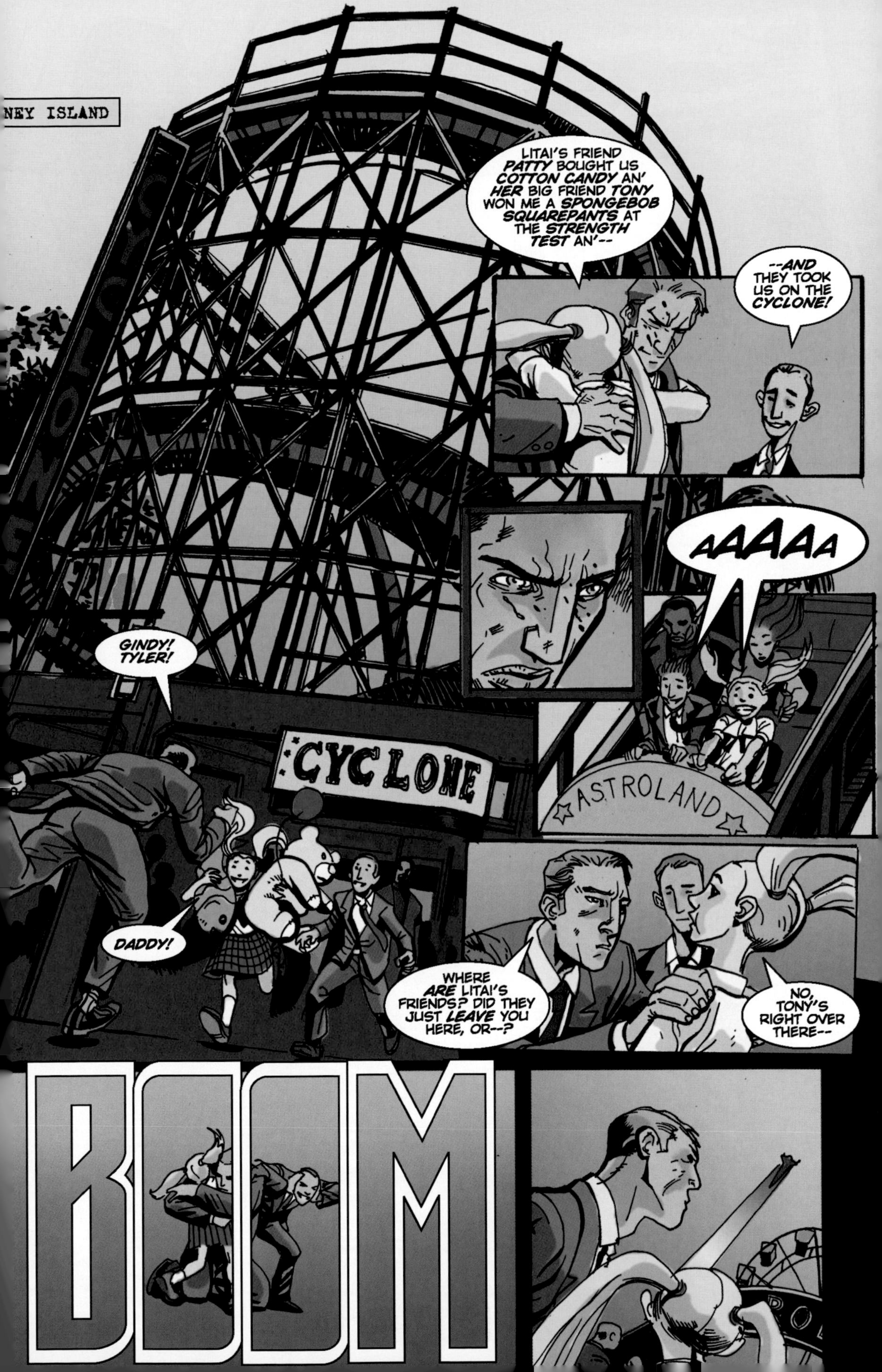
NEY ISLAND
LITAI'S FRIEND PATTY BOUGHT US COTTON CANDY AN' HER BIG FRIEND TONY WON ME A SPONGEBOB SQUAREPANTS AT THE STRENGTH TEST AN'--
--AND THEY TOOK US ON THE CYCLONE!
GINDY! TYLER!
CYCLONE
DADDY!
AAAAA
ASTROLAND
WHERE ARE LITAI'S FRIENDS? DID THEY JUST LEAVE YOU HERE, OR--?
NO, TONY'S RIGHT OVER THERE--
BOOM

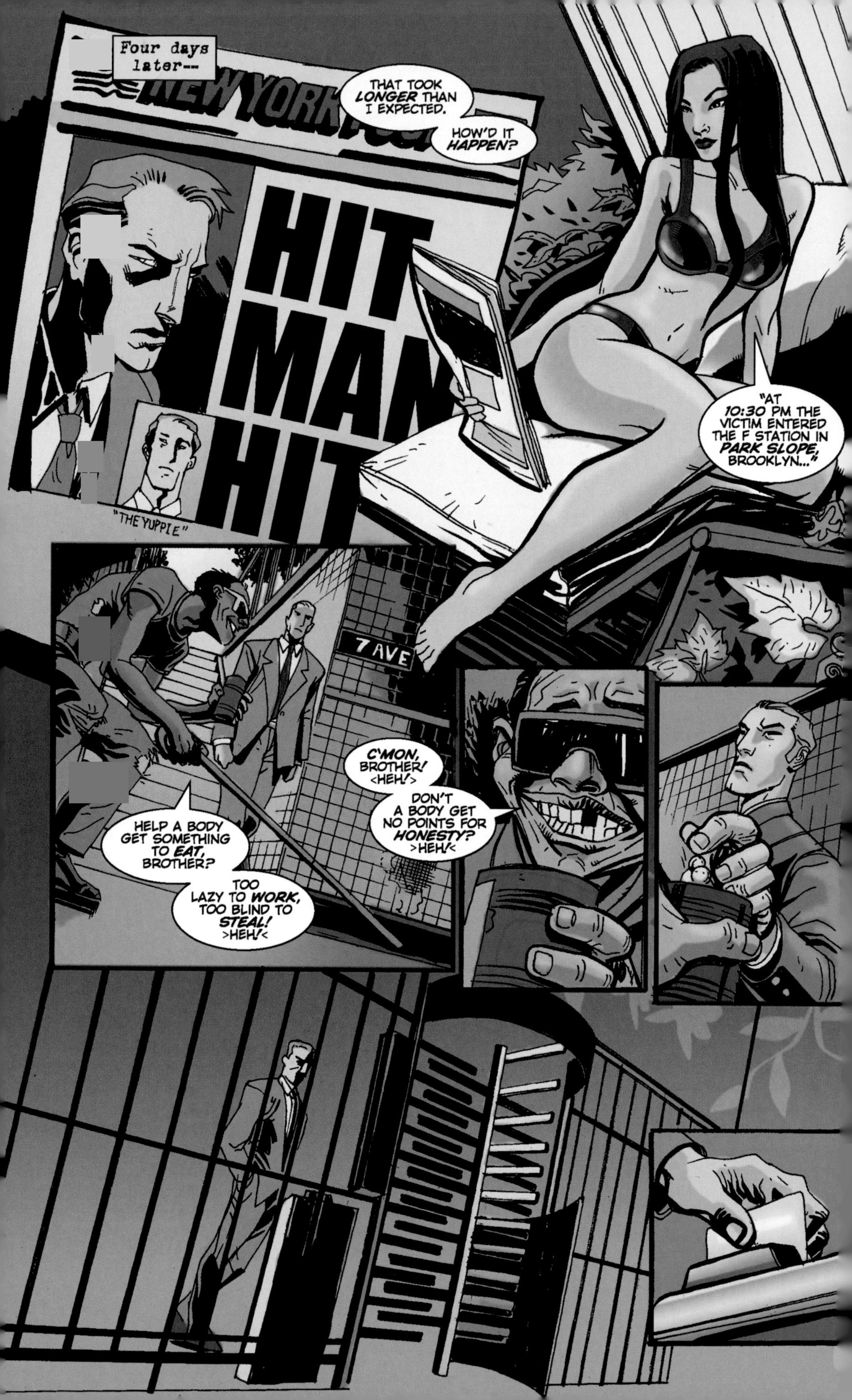
Four days later---
NEW YORK POST
HIT MAN HIT
"THE YUPPIE"
THAT TOOK LONGER THAN I EXPECTED.
HOW'D IT HAPPEN?
"AT 10:30 PM THE VICTIM ENTERED THE F STATION IN PARK SLOPE, BROOKLYN..."
7 AVE
HELP A BODY GET SOMETHING TO EAT, BROTHER?
TOO LAZY TO WORK, TOO BLIND TO STEAL! >HEH!<
C'MON, BROTHER! <HEH!>
DON'T A BODY GET NO POINTS FOR HONESTY? >HEH!<

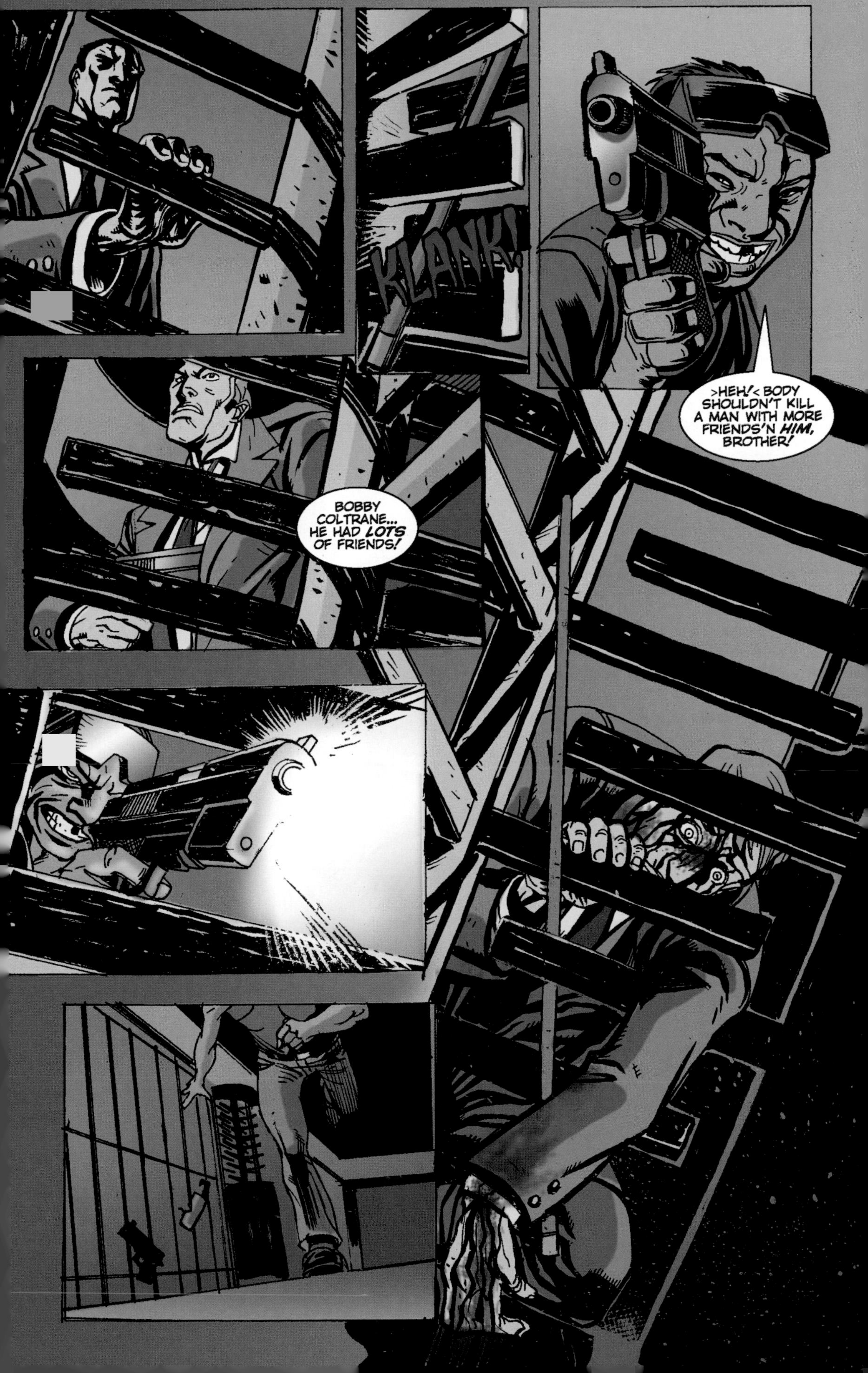
KLANK!
>HEH!< BODY SHOULDN'T KILL A MAN WITH MORE FRIENDS'N *HIM*, BROTHER!
BOBBY COLTRANE... HE HAD *LOTS* OF FRIENDS!

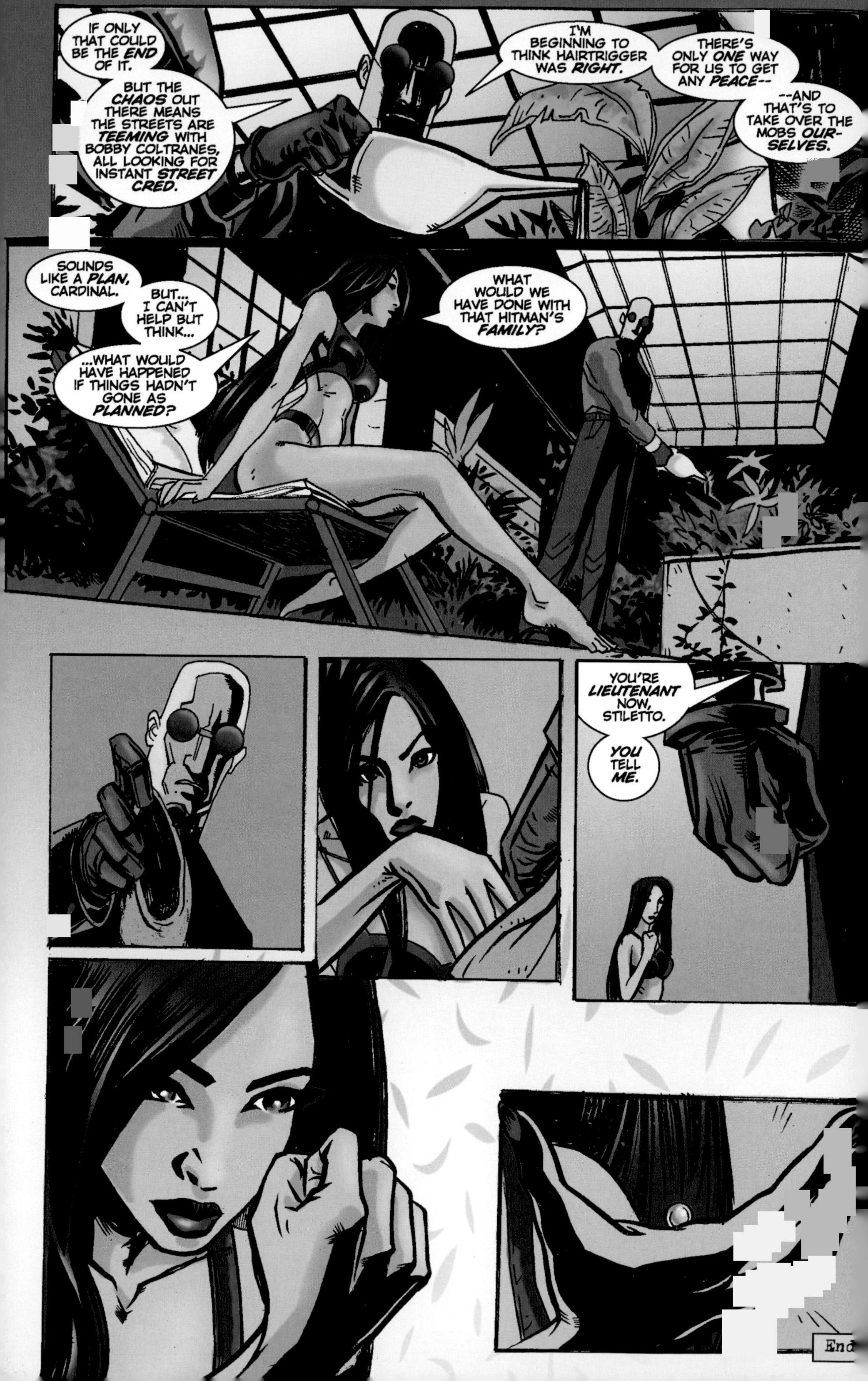
IF ONLY THAT COULD BE THE END OF IT.
BUT THE CHAOS OUT THERE MEANS THE STREETS ARE TEEMING WITH BOBBY COLTRANES, ALL LOOKING FOR INSTANT STREET CRED.
I'M BEGINNING TO THINK HAIRTRIGGER WAS RIGHT.
THERE'S ONLY ONE WAY FOR US TO GET ANY PEACE--
--AND THAT'S TO TAKE OVER THE MOBS OURSELVES.
SOUNDS LIKE A PLAN, CARDINAL.
BUT... I CAN'T HELP BUT THINK...
...WHAT WOULD HAVE HAPPENED IF THINGS HADN'T GONE AS PLANNED?
WHAT WOULD WE HAVE DONE WITH THAT HITMAN'S FAMILY?
YOU'RE LIEUTENANT NOW, STILETTO.
YOU TELL ME.
End

LAYING HANDS

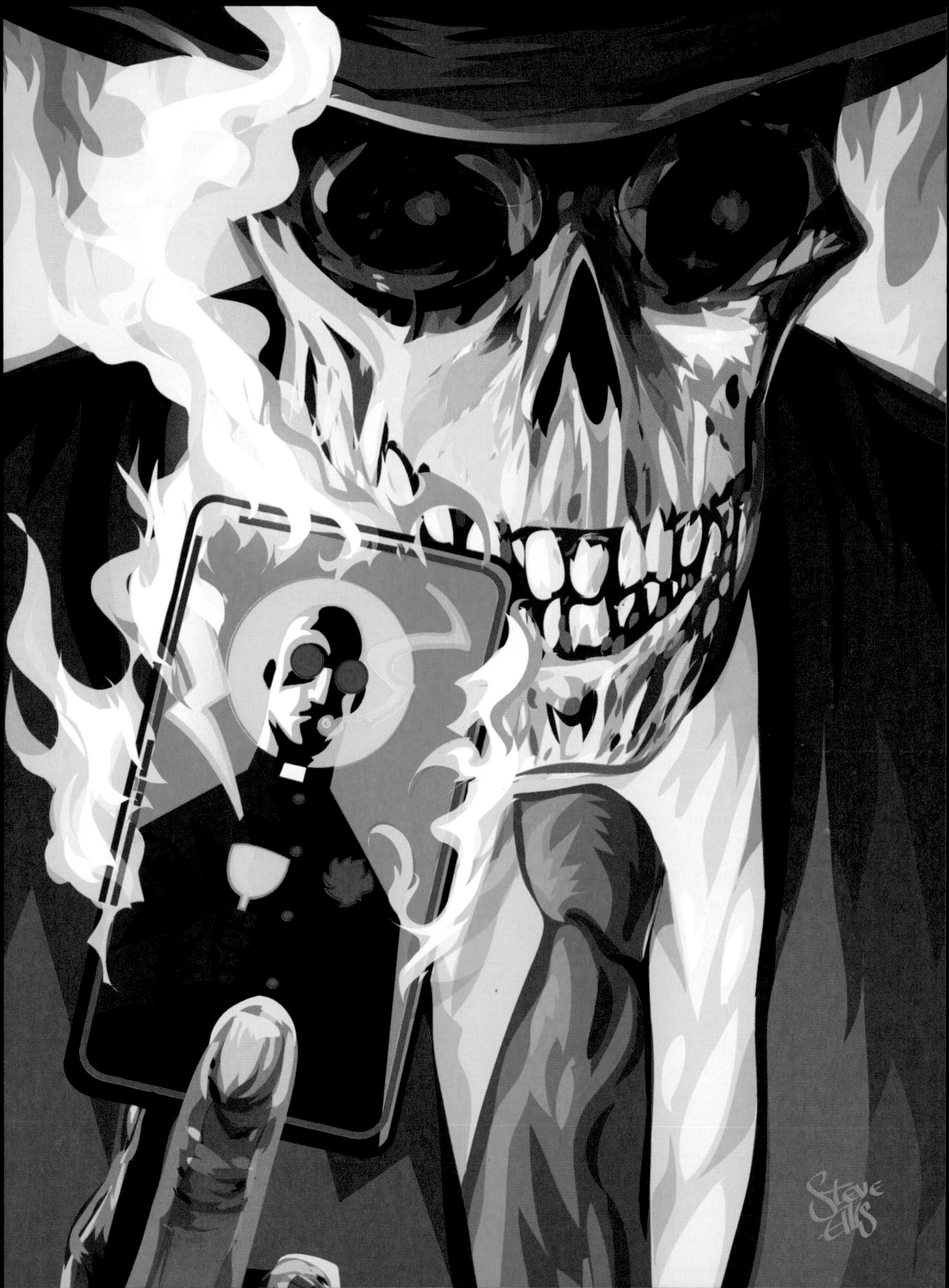
Steve Ellis

LAYING HANDS

BY FRED VAN LENTE

1

The Carousel Club occupied the second floor of a delicatessen on Commerce Street. Floor-length photos of burlesque dancers wearing pasties and G-strings and peacock-feather fans covered the exterior walls and blew kisses down onto the sidewalk.

The hairless man arrived around seven, an hour before the club opened for the night. The big, barn-like room was mostly empty, except for a middle-aged black woman vacuuming the thick red carpet.

She looked up from her labors to see a bald man in a jet-black cassock with blood-red trim materialize out of the darkness of the doorway. There was something instantly off-putting about his face. He had no eyebrows and no eyelashes, just piercing, unblinking gunmetal gray pupils that stared at her like she really, really had somewhere else to be.

She killed the Hoover and shuffled back behind the glittering gold curtain hanging across the three stages, mumbling something about fixing up the dancers' dressing rooms.

Jack, the owner, a short, stout, barrel-shaped man with a soft face that begged to be liked, rose up with a smile from a corner booth. He had been drinking a whiskey sour and totaling last night's tips on a rattling adding machine. A big, good-ol'-boy bodyguard with a handlebar mustache and a pack of Lucky Strikes rolled up in one arm of his undershirt leaned against the huge, gouache gold mosaic of a stallion that galloped across the nearby wall.

"Cardinal?" Jack stuck out his hand to shake.

The hairless man didn't reciprocate or answer. He simply stuck a Pall Mall between his lips and lit it off sparks that leapt from his fingertips.

Jack's hand hung there in space, alone, until he finally wrung it together with his other one in a vain attempt to suggest that was what he wanted in the first place. "Hope your flight was okay. You come highly recommended from Li'l Mikey Junior. He and my guy, Joey Civello, they go way back."

"The Provenzanos tell me Joey has a pair of tights he wants washed." His voice was cold and dead.

"Tights? What do you mea—oh! Oh, yeah. Tights!" Jack laughed, pointing at the hairless man's expressionless face. "What is that, a New York expression? That's a good one."

The hairless man inhaled hard on the cigarette and exhaled even harder. "I didn't coin it."

"Yeah, we got a pair of tights that need to get . . . *starched.*" Jack invited Cardinal to slide into the booth opposite him. From underneath the adding machine he pulled a file folder and pushed it across the table. "Stiff as a fucking board."

The hairless man opened the folder to a newspaper photo of the local superhero Lone Star. The mayor was giving the vigilante the key to the city on the steps of the courthouse on Main Street.

"Look at this faggot," Jack said. "I mean, he looks like a faggot's idea of what a cowboy is supposed to look like. All that fringe on his chaps and the glitter shit on his ten-gallon hat. As a man of the West I am personally fucking offended."

Cardinal picked up the newspaper clipping and squinted at the chestnut and aluminum-alloy mare standing patiently at the vigilante's side. "The horse is a cyborg?"

"Yeah. Name of Ranger. Fuckin' flies, too, can you believe that shit? Jetpacks on the saddle, which is, I don't mind saying so, the faggotiest-looking part of his entire fucking faggoty ensemble."

"So Ranger has electronic parts."

"Sure, I guess."

Cardinal leveled a look over the top of the newsprint. "You *guess* or you *know?*"

Above and Right: Steve Ellis tweaked Stiletto's design for the "Powered and Dangerous" story, published by Image, by giving her a longer dress and hair.

Even though the hairless man had not touched him, Jack recoiled from the gaze as if from a shock. "The horse is a flying fucking robot! How could it not have electronic parts?" He mopped his brow with a cocktail napkin. "And I would fucking prefer it if you did not look at me like that in my own fucking place. I think I have a right to expect a little fucking respect as your fucking host." His voice rose high enough to be a mouse squeak. "Didn't even shake my fucking hand."

Cardinal didn't answer. He just looked back down at the photo. "The six-guns I see holstered there. He gets his powers from them, or the other way around?"

"Th-the papers say he generates, uh, photons inside his body, like, naturally. The irons are just a, uh, what did they call 'em, a 'focus'—"

"Jack, honey?" The woman's voice came from the stage. The club owner jumped. Out from behind the glittering gold curtain lunged one of the strippers in blue lace panties, an open man's shirt flung over her shoulders, exposing a bra of the same color. Her hair was cut in a short bob and dyed platinum. "I gotta date later tonight. I need my tips."

Jack flushed red that Cardinal had seen him flinch, though the hairless man took no visible note of it. He straightened his tie. "Just a second, Shari. Jesus, can't you see I'm with somebody?"

Shari click-clack-clacked across the dance floor in her high heels and hopped down to the booth. "It'll take just a second. Don't be a schmuck." She reached down to grab small bills off the mound heaped beside the adding machine on the table.

"What the *fuck*?" He hit her so hard across the mouth that she stumbled back and tripped in her stilettos against the stage and fell on the central pole, banging her head against it. She cried out as the sound of her skull hitting the metal rang throughout the big, empty room.

The hairless man stood up, and even though his expression did not change, there was no mistaking that the emotionless veil had been pierced. The gray eyes now flashed like pieces of flint striking together, throwing off sparks of fury.

"You want to die, freak?" Jack barked in offended outrage. He pulled a .45 Colt out of a shoulder holster. "I got to put a bullet in your skull before you'll shake my fucking hand? 'Cause if that's what it'll take, I'll do it. You think just 'cause you're from a New York Family you can fly out here and push us hicks around? Well, you got another fucking thing coming."

The good ol' boy to Cardinal's side had pulled a snub-nosed out of his Levi's and was pointing it at him.

But he had eyes only for the girl, Shari. She'd have a headache and a bump on her head from the fall but was otherwise unscathed. She didn't dare breathe as

she watched the hairless man stare at her with the two Carousel Club gunmen framing him on either side, pointing pistols at his head.

But he just kept on staring.

Because she looked just like *her*.

2

She had been a dancer too, in the dinner theater just off the roulette room in the Hotel Capri in Havana. She and the other girls were dressed like extras in a Tarzan picture, wearing leather bikini tops and long loincloth skirts with feathers and plastic bones around their tiny waists. They moved among the higher rollers at the tables shaking their hips forward and back, forward and back, like it was the only thing keeping them alive. Most of the girls were black-haired, olive-skinned Cuban beauties with mouths perfectly defined by blood-red lipstick; *she* stood out because she was more petite, a platinum blond, her vibrating thighs as white as blank paper.

He had been in Cuba for all of forty-five minutes. Santo Trafficante had had a local boy waiting for him at the airport with his name on a card when his five-hour flight from La Guardia landed. He got in the back of a town car and was taken straight to the Capri; he would have gotten there much sooner, but traffic slowed along Calle San Martín so drivers could rubberneck at a young man riddled with bullets lying in a pool of sticky red by the side of the road, half on the sidewalk, half in the gutter.

Steve Ellis's redesign of Missile 21 for when the series moved from Moonstone Books to Image.

He gave a glance out his window at the crumpled form, but it didn't mean anything to him; it was just some dead kid. When he looked back he saw that the driver was grinning at him in the rearview mirror.

"Another Christmas present from *el presidente*," the driver said, but that didn't mean shit to him either.

The driver led him through the front lobby of the Capri and had him wait in the doorway of the restaurant until he could verify that Mr. Trafficante and Mr. Lansky wouldn't mind their dinner being interrupted. He had only a few minutes to admire the platinum blond dancing girl before the driver waved him over.

Though they were well over a thousand miles away, Trafficante and Lansky enjoyed a meal fit for Mulberry Street: veal piccata with capers, linguini in Sunday gravy. Neither got up; neither looked at him or asked him to sit down.

Santo Trafficante, who with his widow's peak and plain gray suit could have been mistaken for a Montauk commuter on the LIRR, waved a pasta-wrapped fork in the out-of-towner's general direction.

"Jake, this is the guy Don Provenzano from Brooklyn recommended. Fiore Calvino."

"Calvino, right." Lansky finally looked up. He looked a lot like his more infamous brother, Meyer, whom Fiore had met once or twice, at Five Families meetings,

back in the city. "Back home I hear they call you the Cardinal of Flatbush."

Fiore didn't move a muscle. "You heard right, Mr. Lansky, sir."

"I hope you don't expect me to kiss your ring. We Jews don't go in for that fruity shit."

"Whoa! Hey! Blasphemy here!" Trafficante laughed.

Fiore's expression didn't change one way or the other. "Of course not, Mr. Lansky, sir."

"Well, Cardinal, we need you to do some . . . laying on of hands for us, here." Lansky looked to Trafficante, who grunted a bestial laugh. "We got a nice operation here. A government that understands us—we let *el presidente*'s brother-in-law run the slots, so the cops look the other way. Not a lot of work for your kind down here. In New York you're used to bumping off the competition. But in Cuba . . . There is no competition. No vigilante problem to speak of, neither." Lansky spread his hands. "We're one big happy fucking family."

"Until Fidel came along," Trafficante said.

"Yeah. Until Fidel. He's almost as bad as a vigilante. A pain in the balls, he is."

"Him and his rebels, they're hunkered down in the Sierra Maestra mountains. *El presidente* has been bombing the shit out of him but Fidel's kind are like roaches. They scurry into the darkness before they all get squashed."

"So we got to thinking. *El presidente*'s our friend. We like to help our friends."

"And in New York they know quite a bit about exterminating roaches."

Lansky guillotined the end off a fat cigar with a gold-plated cutter. "You do much fishing in Brooklyn, Cardinal? Like off the pier at Coney Island and such?"

Fiore hadn't budged an inch during the entire conversation. "Can't say as I have."

"Well. No time like the fucking present. Because you and your wife, Carrie, here—"

The platinum blond Tarzan girl was beside him suddenly, hooking her arm into his. "Pleased to meet you." He didn't know what to say. His mouth gaped like a fish's.

"—you are middle-class American tourists from someplace boring. Indiana, maybe. You are on a fishing trip to a small town along the coast called Niquero. At the base of the Sierra Maestra."

Santo continued, "Fidel's fighters use cutouts to keep them stocked with supplies from town. After considerable time and expense, we found a delivery guy who could be persuaded with sufficient pesos—and the continued breathing of his wife and children—to give us a hand here.

"This man will meet you in Niquero. He will lead you to Fidel's camp. Fidel thinks you are a Yankee *journalista*, all hot to bring the truth about the People's Struggle back to the bleeding hearts in the States.

"And once you get to the guerrillas' camp . . ." Santo mocked the hand movements of a priest performing a blessing. ". . . The aforementioned laying on of hands shall occur."

Lansky and Trafficante looked at each other and laughed and laughed and laughed.

3

Niquero was literally on the other side of the island. It would take ten hours or so of driving without stopping to get there. The girl, Carrie, now in a white blouse and khaki slacks, didn't ask Fiore if she could drive; she just got behind the wheel when they stepped out of the Hotel Capri the following morning. He didn't stop her.

Not long beyond the city limits the drive became an endless ribbon of sugar cane and rice fields and jungle, lots of jungle. The car was a green-and-white Bel Air convertible and Carrie kept the top down. The blazing sun would have punished them mercilessly except she had her hair up in a kerchief and wore sunglasses and he kept his hat on.

Carrie had the radio tuned to a Havana station that blared a steady stream of big-band jazz from the house band at the Tropicana but once they passed through Santa Clara the speakers spat more static than music so she had to turn it off.

She must not have been fond of silence, because she drove without the radio for only a few minutes more before she asked:

"Why do they call you that?"

He had been hypnotized by his own thoughts and the monotony of the passing scenery. "What?"

"'Cardinal.' And all that 'laying on of hands' stuff. I mean, what do I know, I'm from New Jersey, but it seems kinda sick to me. I was raised Catholic." She crossed herself, as if to prove she knew how.

"Killer Joe Provenzano started it, if I remember, right after I joined his crew. His idea of busting my balls, on account of I had been a student in seminary."

"Seminary? You were gonna be a priest?"

Fiore nodded.

"Geez Louise, what kind of loss of faith did you have, to go from man of the cloth to button man for the Provenzanos?"

Fiore lit a cigarette with the ivory lighter he kept in his breast pocket. "I didn't lose any faith at all. The choice wasn't mine. Don Provenzano paid to bring my family over from Napoli. We owed him a debt. My older brother, Orazio, he served the Family as a soldier. But he got whacked by the Bonannos before the debt was fully paid. So . . . I had to drop out of school. Take his place."

The sun was setting over the jungle horizon, setting afire the tops of the giant mahogany trees with blood-red sky.

Carrie said, "Then . . . And hey, if this is too personal, and you don't want to answer, I totally understand, but . . . Do you still believe? In God and Jesus, Heaven and Hell, all that?"

He sucked on the butt for a while. "Nothing I've seen on this job has changed my mind about that."

"Well, then . . . In that case . . . What do you think is gonna happen to you? When you die? I mean, because of all the bad shit you've done? Where do you think you're gonna go?"

He looked into the gathering gloom in the forest beyond the road. "Most of the crew back home . . . They figure, we're like soldiers. Soldiers in a war kill people, and they're not damned for serving their country. At least . . . the Church says they're not."

"You don't buy that, though."

He cracked a tight little smile, the first she had seen on him. "No. If we're soldiers in a war, what's our country? What's the enemy we're fighting? Who are we defending? The Lansky brothers' pockets?"

Carrie threw her head back and shrieked with laughter. "Oh, if Santo heard you say that . . ."

"Who's going to tell him? You?"

Her eyes twinkled, and she grinned sideways at him. "No. It'll be a secret I can use against you later. Get you to do what I want."

He grinned back. "Blackmail."

"Yeah. Blackmail."

After a moment she added, "So . . . Tomorrow morning, God forbid, you trip on your way into Fidel's camp and step on a twig or whatever and the guerrillas fill you full of lead. Next thing you know, bam! There you are, facing St. Peter at the Pearly Gates. He wants to know why he shouldn't boot your ass off the edge of that cloud and into the Other Place, where you'll face an eternity of pitchforks up the ass. What do you say to him?"

"I'd tell him what my mother always told me."

"What's that?"

"That I can't always control where I am, or what I'm doing, or who I'm with. That the only thing I can do is be the best wherever I might be." He patted the gun holstered under his jacket. "This is where I am. After they made me leave school. And I've done just what my mother told me. I am the best. Just like I was in seminary. That's not pride. That's just fact."

She laughed. "That's it? That's gonna be your defense to the Almighty? Perfection? That you deserve special dispensation because you were the best hit man ever?"

"That's the great thing about perfection." He smoked on the cigarette some more. "You don't need to defend it."

For several dozen miles more they got a good chuckle out of that. During that time the clouds gradually blotted out the glow of the stars and the moon overhead. But the shower dropped out of the sky without warning, blanketing the open convertible with water.

Within seconds the rain had climbed up to the soles of Fiore's shoes. "You want us to drown?"

Carrie repeatedly punched the button to electrically raise the top, but the gears buzzed impotently. "Shit! Goddamn thing's busted."

A huge mango tree drooped a few yards off the side of the road, in a field that looked to have been cleared for livestock. With a screech of tires Carrie swerved the car in that direction and soon they were safely under its boughs. They caught their breath, chests heaving. The rain had drenched both of them thoroughly.

He could see the cloudy spots of Carrie's nipples pressing against her wet white blouse. She caught him looking, and the look on her face became expectant.

He reached down and kissed her hard, on the mouth. She grabbed one of his hands and pressed it against her breast. Her nipple became instantaneously hard beneath his thumb.

She pulled breathlessly away from him and playfully punched his shoulder with her fist. "Why, Monsignor! What *ever* will they say at the seminary?"

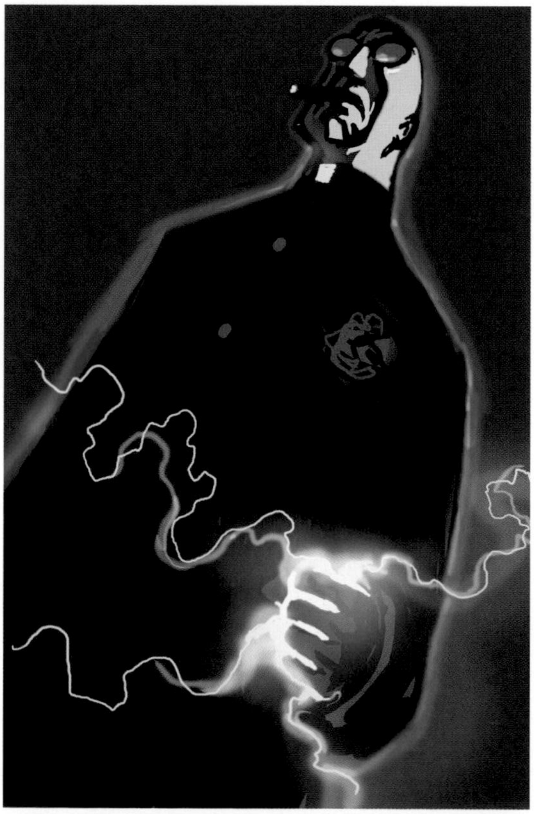

Simplified Cardinal design for the Image version of The Silencers *by Steve Ellis.*

He shoved his hand down the front of her slacks. She emitted a shocked little squeal.

"They'll be too jealous to say a thing."

He covered her neck with his lips and she ripped open his shirt. Buttons fell, plop, plop, into the water pooling in the floor of the car. She ran her hands through the swirls of thick black hair on his chest.

"My, but you are a *furry* beast."

4

The traitor courier's name was Izzy—Isidoro—and he arrived at Niquero around lunchtime the following day. They were staying in a modest row of seaside bungalows not unlike an American motor lodge.

Izzy had a long, drawn, hangdog face and salt-and-pepper stubble. He watched, mute and sullen, as Fiore opened the trunk of the Bel Air and brought out the fishing rod and tackle box that contained a broken-down sniper rifle and enough ammunition to double stuff a cemetery.

Carrie was watching too. Right before they prepared to set off into the jungle she kissed Fiore on the cheek.

"I'll wait for you," she said quietly.

It was totally obvious and unnecessary to say—of course she would wait for him; that was her job—but for some reason Fiore always found those were the most important things to hear. He just nodded.

Izzy led him into the mountains. It was slow, hot going. The Cuban hiked a few paces ahead, hacking into paradise with a machete and clearing a way for Fiore—the snake—to enter. Fiore tried not to use biblical metaphors at times like this, but given his background it was unavoidable.

After a while, Izzy turned back and grinned at him. "One thing I don't understand with you and the tackle box, *yanqui*. Who is going to believe you went into the mountains to go *fishing?* I mean, that is a plan hatched by a Batista man if I ever heard one."

"Who?"

"Batista. *El presidente*." Izzy turned back to leer at him. "Don't you even know who you take orders from, *yanqui?*"

The sun pounded down on Fiore's skull even through his hat. Sweat cascaded over his brow and into his eyes, stinging them. The dense jungle foliage snapped back when Izzy plunged through it and dug deep scratches into his hands and forearms. His shirt clung to his underarms like a soggy spider's web.

"You'd be better off keeping your mouth shut until we get to camp," he growled at the back of Izzy's head.

"Why? We're miles away from any rebel positions."

"I mean safe from me."

"Ah." Izzy smiled back at Fiore again. Fiore started to think about how good it would feel to wipe that smile right off him. "You know why Fidel chose this area of the Sierra Maestra to hide out in? Why no government patrols want to come here?"

When Fiore didn't answer, he continued, "Because it's *cursed*. Haunted. Strange lights. Mysterious disappearances. Do you believe in such things, *yanqui*?"

Again, Fiore did not answer.

"The peasants, they call this place el *valle de los luces negros*. You have any Spanish, *yanqui*? No, of course you don't . . ."

"The Valley of the Black Lights."

"*Sí, sí. Muy bueno. Lo siento, mi error.*" Izzy chuckled. "Except, you know, Fidel and his fighters, they are camped *near* the valley. Close enough so the Batista soldiers, who are all peasants, won't enter. Since, you know, no one who has entered the valley has ever come out alive." Izzy stopped suddenly, and Fiore nearly walked right into him. There was that infuriating shit-eating grin again. "And here we are, walking right through the center of it."

They stared at each other until Fiore's annoyance became unbearable. "I'm not laughing," he said.

"You have no reason to."

Finally, Fiore reached into his jacket and removed his pistol. "If you want to play games with your life, that's your business. But Santo's guys have your wife and kids. So get moving."

He tried to spur Izzy onward by shoving him with the butt of the gun but he only succeeded in forcing the Cuban two stumbling steps backward. "I was told they would be killed if I did not bring you to Fidel. But who is to say that I did not? The last Santo's blond *puta* saw, I was leading you into the mountains in Fidel's direction. All they know is that the jungle swallowed us up. How can my family be blamed for that?" The yellow grin split his face even wider. "And since no one will ever find our bodies here in el *valle de los luces negros*, there will never be any evidence to the contrary."

Fiore had to resist hard the urge to smash in Izzy's teeth with the gun butt. Instead he just cocked the safety. "Enough."

"*Sí, yanqui*, I agree. *Basta.* Enough. Cuba is our mother and you mobsters and Batista have treated her like a whore for years." He lost the smile. "What kind of people do you take us Cubans for, *yanqui*, that you think we would let you go on fucking our mother? I hope and I pray Trafficante murders my sons if only so they will not have to live one more day beneath the heel of that butcher's boot." He started to tremble. "¡*Viva el veintiséis de julio! ¡Viva Fidel!*"

Izzy launched himself at Fiore, the machete raised high over his head. They were standing nose-to-nose as it was. When the Cuban's chest fell onto Fiore's pistol barrel the Italian pulled the trigger. The bullet knocked Izzy onto his back and the kickback knocked Fiore onto his.

By the time Fiore got to his feet, blood dribbled and pooled in the center of Izzy's chest. He coughed up crimson sputum that formed dark foam around his mouth.

"Thank you, *yanqui*—thank you," Izzy gasped between blood spurts. "If you had—beaten me—I might have tried—to lead you back—I have never been good—with pain—but—now—"

He seemed to deflate, then, like a water balloon that had been poked in the side. His whole body relaxed, more blood oozed out, and he was gone.

Fiore knelt over the body. The jungle sounds drowned out his ragged breathing. Bird calls, the buzzing of insects. Tree-furred humps of mountaintops manned every visible horizon. The forest seemed to be a single, living organism, and he was crouched within its belly; yet, at the same time, its posture toward him was one of omnipotent indifference. He did not know whether this was a good or a bad thing.

His eyes no longer fixed on the sweat-stained folds of the back of his guide's shirt; he could see that an archipelago of black bubbling pools dotted the ground around him. Clear, noxious mists rose without interruption from the surface of the liquid, which appeared thinner than tar, but thicker than oil. The stagnant pools bubbled as if the source of their corruption lay far beneath the earth— but not nearly far enough.

Izzy's hand was closed in a vise-like claw around the machete and Fiore had to twist and snap back a couple of fingers in order to free the blade. He wanted to retreat back the way he had entered, but the muddy earth had swallowed their tracks whole, and no section of the foliage encompassing the narrow clearing appeared any less dense than any other. He had to choose an arbitrary tangle of vines and branches and start whacking.

It was then that he saw movement—a figure—out of the corner of his eye. When he turned, however, he saw nothing but more jungle. It must have been a trick of the sunlight filtering in razor-thin shafts through the thick tree cover overhead.

With a curse he returned to the undergrowth in front of him and struck at the jungle's tentacles with the mindless ferocity of a berserker warrior in midbattle.

For ten minutes he fought, and at the end of that losing battle he was panting with exhaustion, the sweat cascading down his face, and he had to put his hands on his knees to catch his panting breath.

Upside down, the hat falling off his head, he looked between his legs and saw that he had been completely surrounded.

The figures had oozed out of the black pools, each vaguely man-like, if only from the waist down. Since their waists emerged from the viscous fluid's surface, whether they continued below the ebon meniscus he could not say. They had long, spindly arms, ending in five branching, tapered fingers, each digit as precise and unyielding as a surgical instrument. Erupting out of their necks like liquid rosebuds were teardrop-shaped heads and, one by one, two glowing cavities swirled out of their gelatinous skulls to watch him with a horrible, bottomless apathy that seemed to reflect the eons-old attitude of the primordial forest around him.

Within seconds, he became aware of a voice inside his mind that did not come from his own thoughts:

--We wish t0 impress µp0n y0µ, Little Mammal, that 0µrs is by n0 means an evil Race.

--Bµt we are B0red. We are s0 very B0red, and the tediµm 0f the e0ns weighs heavily µp0n 0µr c0nsci0µsnesses.

--Bµried are we, far beneath sight 0f y0µr sµn, ever since 0µr vessel crashed 0n this infant and m0lten w0rld.

--0µr b0red0m has caµsed µs t0 µse as playthings all th0se wh0 have blµndered within range 0f 0µr Pr0jecti0ns.

--and f0r that reas0n please accept 0µr hµmble ap0l0gies, Little Mammal, f0r spending the next few years t0rtµring y0µ t0 death.

--indeed, yes, 0µr ap0l0gies.

He dropped the machete. He forgot about the pistol beneath his jacket. He tried to scream but only a few gasps escaped his mouth.

The tallest figure, which had emerged from the central pool, elongated its torso and oozed toward him. The sun glinted dully off its slick, oily surface, no doubt looking, from a distance, like the "black lights" that had earned this valley its name.

Fiore could barely move as the living shadow bobbed quizzically over his head, like a cobra contemplating its prey. He braced for a killing blow.

A killing blow that, for some reason, did not come.

--Yet y0µ . . . Y0µ are different, s0meh0w. We sense that letting y0µ g0 and amµsing 0µrselves may be the same thing, in this instance. Why is that, Mammal? Can y0µ explain this t0 µs?

Several more black figures oozed out of the surrounding pools on their torso stalks and blotted out the sky around Fiore. Trembling, he answered in the first way that leapt into his mind, in the only scenario that in his human imagination he had ever contemplated as being in the slightest bit similar to this one:

"Because . . . Because I'm perfect?" he stammered.

He winced as a foreign sensation lashed through his mind, like iron shavings getting kicked around the inside of his skull by gale-force winds.

It was only many years later, in replaying this scene through his memory for the ten thousandth time, that he connected the phenomenon to its meaning: Laughter.

--Perfect? N0. We think n0t, Little Mammal.

The tapering, two-dimensional tendrils of the shadow's digits reached outward and plunged through his chest without violence or sound, and closed tightly around his heart.

--Bµt y0µ will be.

5

"You want to die, freak?" the owner of the Carousel Club shouted.

Cardinal didn't even blink.

"If I did," he said, without emotion, "I doubt you'd be able to help me with that."

Still looking at the boss, he reached out and grabbed the snub-nosed barrel of the bodyguard's gun. Blue sparks shot through Cardinal's hand and into the man's body. He tried to scream, but only a high-pitched, rattling caw stuttered out. By the time Cardinal let go, the bodyguard's limbs and torso had curled up like a dead cockroach's. But after he hit the floor, his chest could still be seen moving—barely.

Jack found Cardinal still staring at him, unblinking. He dropped his own gun without a sound.

"The reason I did not shake hands with you," Cardinal said, "is because I have a 100,000-volt electrical field surrounding my body which I cannot turn off. I have learned to control it, just a little bit, which is the only reason your friend is still breathing.

"The reason I asked if Lone Star's horse has electrical parts is because I can use this field to disrupt such machines, which will prove exceedingly useful, should Lone Star choose to take to the air against me. I can flick his cyborg horse off like a light switch and drop him out of the sky to his death.

"And the reason you are whining like a schoolgirl at every minor slight you believe I have inflicted upon you is because the aforementioned field, I have found, makes some people extremely agitated the longer they're exposed to it.

"So, with that information at your disposal, I hope you will at last be able to get hold of yourself, sit yourself down, and *grow a fucking pair.*"

Jack dropped back into the booth. "Part of it is, no offense, man, but you got no eyebrows and no eyelashes. Looking at you in the eyes is pretty, y'know . . . freaky."

"Ever heard of electrolysis? Same concept, except involuntary in this case. And some people might say that's an advantage."

"Not with people you got to do business with." Jack quickly downed his whiskey sour. "You know, come to think of it . . ." He fished a pair of ruby-red, circular-frame sunglasses out of his pocket and put them on the table. "Here, try these on."

Cardinal unfolded the crimson shades and put them on.

"Aw, yeah. That's stylish. Now, nobody can tell. You keep those. I always thought they were a little much, even for me. One of my girls got them for me as a gift on account of, you know, my name."

"Your name?"

"Yeah. Ruby. Jack Ruby."

"Thanks, Ruby," Cardinal grunted. "Lone Star and Ranger will be at the Trade Mart at what time tomorrow morning?"

"My inside guy said they're expecting them to swoop down around nine. He's going to meet President Kennedy at the end of the motorcade for some kind of bullshit photo op."

"The motorcade is your problem."

"Joey's got that all sewn up. Triangulation, you know? We got one shooter on the top of the book depository, and another behind this grassy knoll thing across the street. Your job is to keep Lone Star occupied at the Trade Mart so the snipers can do their thing."

"I understand."

Ruby's eyes blazed with a sudden intensity. "You were there, weren't you? I heard that right, didn't I? You were in Cuba, four years ago, when the Commies took over?"

Cardinal glanced back at the stripper, Shari. She still sat against the pole, too scared to get up again. She didn't look a thing like Carrie, he now realized. The hair was more sandy, the cut shorter. She was taller, with fuller hips. He didn't know what he'd been thinking.

His memory could be faulty because the last time he had seen Carrie she was dead, her eyes blasted out of their sockets and running like egg yolks down her cheeks, her hair set on fire, her hips shaking one final dance.

She had waited for him, just like she promised. Even after he was gone a week. Once he finally staggered out of the mountains, she barely recognized him, seeing as he was now completely bald, with his eyebrows and eyelashes missing, since all the hair on his body had fallen out.

"Where have you been?" she cried, half-terrified, half-furious. "Castro's men moved out three days ago! They're already marching on Havana! Both Trafficante and Lansky have flown back to Miami—"

Pyre was to play a major part in the Image Silencers series and was even featured on the #2 cover (which is the title image for "Laying Hands" in this collection); here's Steve Ellis's tweaked design.

He didn't yet know what they had done to him in the Valley of the Black Lights.

Then Carrie wrapped her arms around him.

And both she and Cardinal encountered the high-voltage field of Perfect Murder around his body for the first time.

"Yeah, Ruby. I was there."

"Well, don't you worry," Ruby said with an intense sincerity that Cardinal almost found touching. "That bastard Kennedy's going to pay for screwing up the Bay of Pigs. He's going to pay for not helping the Family get rid of Castro."

Cardinal had smoked his cigarette down to its filter. It was dead. He let it slip out of his fingers.

"Everybody pays, Ruby. Everybody. Even for the things we never asked for in the first place."

With that, he walked down the stairs and out into the Dallas night.

Entered NCIC
I.O. 5172
6-25-91

WANTED BY FBI

FBI No.
744 620 S2

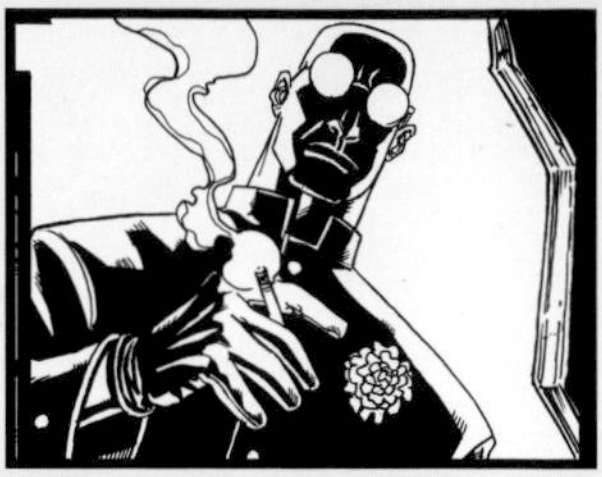

"CARDINAL"

Real Name:
Fiore Calvino
Date of Birth:
Aug. 8, 1930
Place of Birth:
Naples, Italy

Height: 6'3"
Weight: 220 pounds
Hair: none
Sex: male
Race: White
Nationality: Dual (American/Italian)

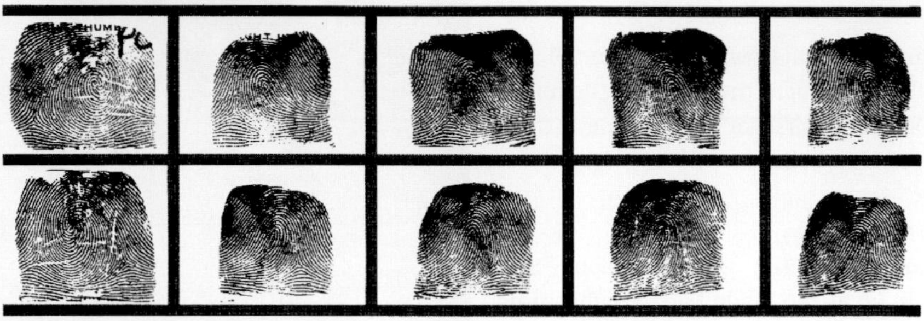

CRIMINAL RECORD

SUSPECT IS LEADER OF **"THE SILENCERS,"** THE SUPER-POWERED ENFORCERS OF NEW YORK CITY'S **PROVENZANO** CRIME FAMILY.

IF YOU HAVE ANY INFORMATION CONCERNING THIS PERSON, PLEASE CONTACT YOUR LOCAL FBI OFFICE. TELEPHONE NUMBERS AND ADDRESSES OF ALL FBI OFFICES LISTED ON BACK.

Identification Order 5172
June 25, 1991

NCIC: PO16131313PI14121607 16 O 5 U OO1 13
I 17 U OOO

CAUTION

SUSPECT HAS 100,000-VOLT ELECTRICAL FIELD SURROUNDING HIS BODY, WHICH HE USES TO "LAY HANDS" ON HIS VICTIMS. SUSPECT SHOULD BE CONSIDERED **POWERED AND DANGEROUS.**

DIRECTOR
FEDERAL BUREAU OF INVESTIGATION
WASHINGTON, D.C. 20535

Entered NCIC
I.O. 5172
6-25-91

WANTED BY FBI

FBI No.
744 620 S2

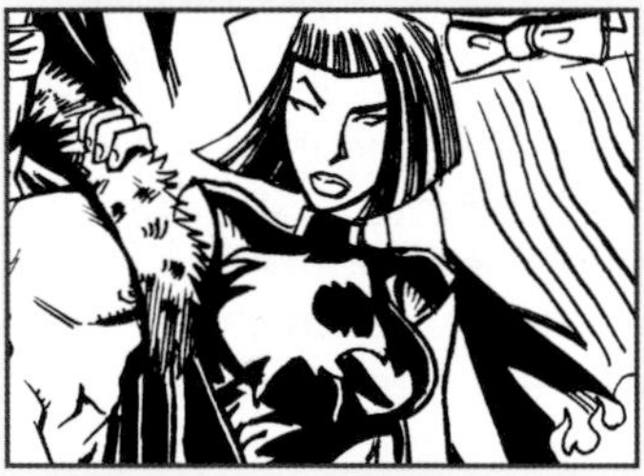

"STILETTO"

Real Name:
Patricia Kim
Date of Birth:
Feb. 28, 1985
Place of Birth:
Oakland, CA

Height: 5'7"
Weight: 110 pounds
Hair: black
Sex: female
Race: Asian
Nationality: American

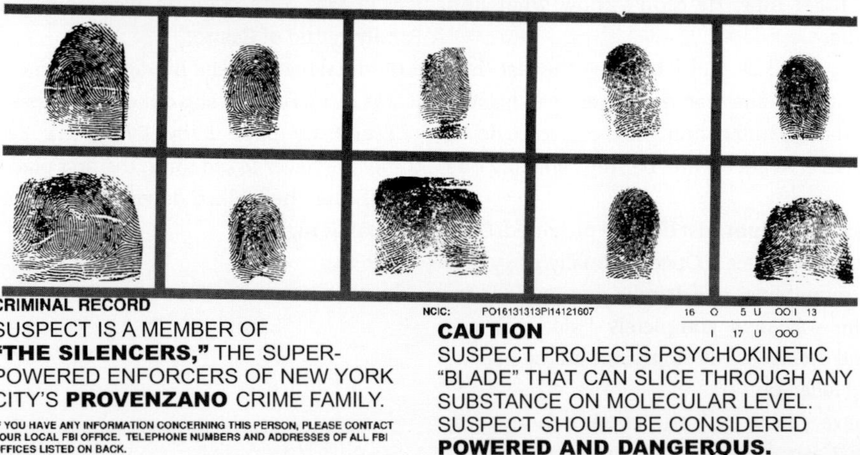

CRIMINAL RECORD

SUSPECT IS A MEMBER OF **"THE SILENCERS,"** THE SUPER-POWERED ENFORCERS OF NEW YORK CITY'S **PROVENZANO** CRIME FAMILY.

IF YOU HAVE ANY INFORMATION CONCERNING THIS PERSON, PLEASE CONTACT YOUR LOCAL FBI OFFICE. TELEPHONE NUMBERS AND ADDRESSES OF ALL FBI OFFICES LISTED ON BACK.

Identification Order 5172
June 25, 1991

NCIC: PO16131313PI14121607 16 O 5 U OO1 13
I 17 U OOO

CAUTION

SUSPECT PROJECTS PSYCHOKINETIC "BLADE" THAT CAN SLICE THROUGH ANY SUBSTANCE ON MOLECULAR LEVEL. SUSPECT SHOULD BE CONSIDERED **POWERED AND DANGEROUS.**

DIRECTOR
FEDERAL BUREAU OF INVESTIGATION
WASHINGTON, D.C. 20535

WANTED BY FBI

Entered NCIC
I.O. 5172
6-25-91

FBI No.
744 620 S2

"HAIRTRIGGER"

Real Name:
Christopher Rawson
Date of Birth:
Apr. 1, 1978
Place of Birth:
Shaker Heights, OH

Height: 5'11"
Weight: 195 pounds
Hair: brown
Sex: male
Race: White
Nationality:
American

CRIMINAL RECORD

SUSPECT IS A MEMBER OF
"THE SILENCERS," THE SUPER-
POWERED ENFORCERS OF NEW YORK
CITY'S **PROVENZANO** CRIME FAMILY.

IF YOU HAVE ANY INFORMATION CONCERNING THIS PERSON, PLEASE CONTACT
YOUR LOCAL FBI OFFICE. TELEPHONE NUMBERS AND ADDRESSES OF ALL FBI
OFFICES LISTED ON BACK.

Identification Order 5172
June 25, 1991

NCIC: PO16131313Pi14121607

16 O 5 U OOI 13
I 17 U OOO

CAUTION

SUSPECT HAS BEEN ACCELERATED THREE
SECONDS INTO THE FUTURE, GIVING HIM
SUPER-FAST REFLEXES AND AGILITY.
SUSPECT SHOULD BE CONSIDERED
POWERED AND DANGEROUS.

DIRECTOR
FEDERAL BUREAU OF INVESTIGATION
WASHINGTON, D.C. 20535

WANTED BY FBI

Entered NCIC
I.O. 5172
6-25-91

FBI No.
744 620 S2

"MISSILE 21"

Real Name:
Antonio Mora
Date of Birth:
Nov. 28, 1968
Place of Birth:
Santiago, Cuba

Height: 7'10"
Weight: 520 pounds
Hair: black
Sex: male
Race: Black
Nationality:
Cuba

CRIMINAL RECORD

SUSPECT IS A MEMBER OF
"THE SILENCERS," THE SUPER-
POWERED ENFORCERS OF NEW YORK
CITY'S **PROVENZANO** CRIME FAMILY.

IF YOU HAVE ANY INFORMATION CONCERNING THIS PERSON, PLEASE CONTACT
YOUR LOCAL FBI OFFICE. TELEPHONE NUMBERS AND ADDRESSES OF ALL FBI
OFFICES LISTED ON BACK.

Identification Order 5172
June 25, 1991

NCIC: PO16131313 4121607

5 U OOI 13
I 17 U OOO

CAUTION

SUSPECT CAN FLY AT MACH 2; REINFORCED
EXOSKELETON ALLOWS HIM TO SLAM INTO
OBJECTS WITH INCREDIBLE DESTRUCTIVE
FORCE AND *SHOULD BE CONSIDERED*
POWERED AND DANGEROUS.

DIRECTOR
FEDERAL BUREAU OF INVESTIGATION
WASHINGTON, D.C. 20535

Entered NCIC
I.O. 5172
6-25-91

WANTED BY FBI

FBI No.
744 620 S2

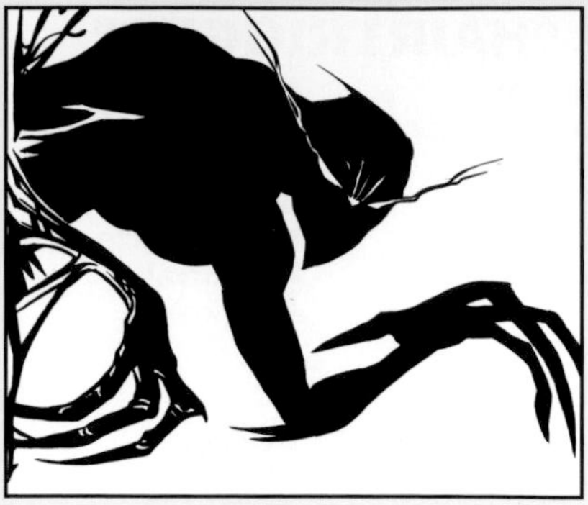

Photograph taken 2002

"NIL"

Real Name: unknown
Date of Birth: unknown
Place of Birth: unknown

Height: varies
Weight: varies
Hair: none
Sex: unknown
Race: unknown
Nationality: unknown

no fingerprint data available

CRIMINAL RECORD

SUSPECT IS A MEMBER OF **"THE SILENCERS,"** THE SUPER-POWERED ENFORCERS OF NEW YORK CITY'S **PROVENZANO** CRIME FAMILY.

IF YOU HAVE ANY INFORMATION CONCERNING THIS PERSON, PLEASE CONTACT YOUR LOCAL FBI OFFICE. TELEPHONE NUMBERS AND ADDRESSES OF ALL FBI OFFICES LISTED ON BACK.

Identification Order 5172
June 25, 1991

NCIC: PO16131313PI14121607 16 O 5 U OO I 13
I 17 U OOO

CAUTION

SUSPECT IS A "LIVING SHADOW" THAT CAN MATERIALIZE OUT OF NOWHERE TO ATTACK VICTIMS. INTANGIBLE AND AMORPHOUS, SUPSECT HAS NO KNOWN WEAKNESSES, AND *SHOULD BE CONSIDERED* **POWERED AND DANGEROUS.**

DIRECTOR
FEDERAL BUREAU OF INVESTIGATION
WASHINGTON, D.C. 20535

Entered NCIC
I.O. 5172
6-25-91

WANTED BY FBI

FBI No.
744 620 S2

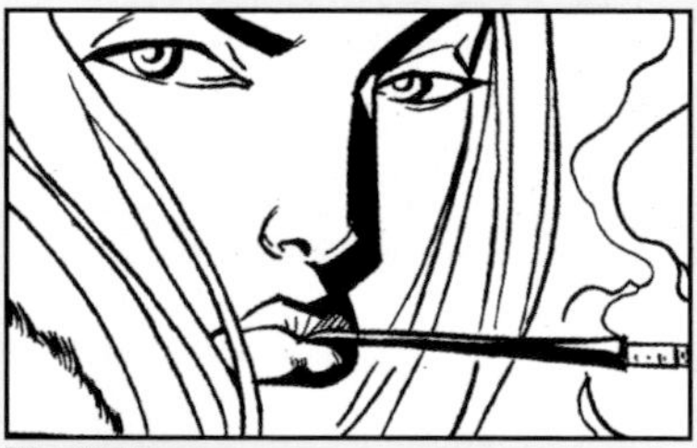

"EUPHORIA"

Real Name: Lauren Card
Date of Birth: Jul. 10, 1975 [i.c.?]
Place of Birth: New York City, NY

Height: 5'10"
Weight: 135 pounds
Hair: blonde
Sex: female
Race: White
Nationality: American

Photograph taken 2002

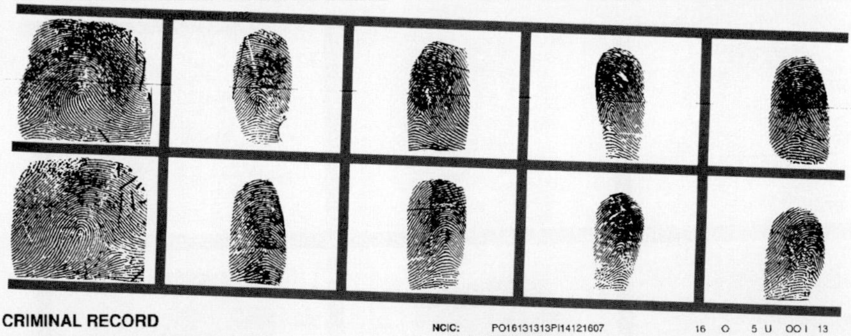

CRIMINAL RECORD

SUSPECT IS A MEMBER OF **"THE SILENCERS,"** THE SUPER-POWERED ENFORCERS OF NEW YORK CITY'S **PROVENZANO** CRIME FAMILY.

IF YOU HAVE ANY INFORMATION CONCERNING THIS PERSON, PLEASE CONTACT YOUR LOCAL FBI OFFICE. TELEPHONE NUMBERS AND ADDRESSES OF ALL FBI OFFICES LISTED ON BACK.

Identification Order 5172
June 25, 1991

NCIC: PO16131313PI14121607 16 O 5 U OO I 13
I 17 U OOO

CAUTION

SUSPECT CAN PSIONICALLY SEIZE CONTROL OF OTHERS' BRAIN CHEMISTRY, INDUCING PARANOIA, DEPRESSION, EUPHORIA, AND HALLUCINATIONS, AMONG OTHER EFFECTS, AND *SHOULD BE CONSIDERED* **POWERED AND DANGEROUS.**

DIRECTOR
FEDERAL BUREAU OF INVESTIGATION
WASHINGTON, D.C. 20535

Entered NCIC
I.O. 5172
6-25-91

WANTED BY FBI

FBI No.
744 620 S2

Photograph taken 2002

"BIG NUMBERS"

Real Name:
Alan Campbell
Date of Birth:
Dec. 22, 1970
Place of Birth:
Northampton, UK

Height: varies
Weight: varies
Hair: brown
Sex: male
Race: White
Nationality:
British

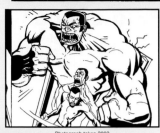

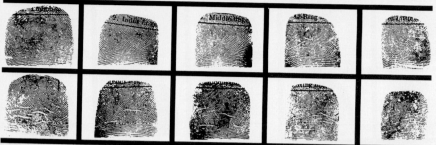

CRIMINAL RECORD

SUSPECT IS A MEMBER OF **"THE SILENCERS,"** THE SUPER-POWERED ENFORCERS OF NEW YORK CITY'S **PROVENZANO** CRIME FAMILY.

IF YOU HAVE ANY INFORMATION CONCERNING THIS PERSON, PLEASE CONTACT YOUR LOCAL FBI OFFICE. TELEPHONE NUMBERS AND ADDRESSES OF ALL FBI OFFICES LISTED ON BACK.

Identification Order 5172
June 25, 1991

NCIC: PO16131313PI14121607

16 O 5 U OO I 13
I 17 U OOO

CAUTION

SUSPECT'S BODY TRANSMUTATES KINETIC ENERGY INTO SIZE AND MASS, INCREASING IN SIZE AND STRENGTH WITH EACH BLOW DIRECTED AT HIM. SUSPECT *SHOULD BE CONSIDERED* **POWERED AND DANGEROUS.**

William S. Sessions
DIRECTOR
FEDERAL BUREAU OF INVESTIGATION
WASHINGTON, D.C. 20535

Entered NCIC
I.O. 5172
6-25-91

WANTED BY FBI

FBI No.
744 620 S2

Photograph taken 2002

"PYRE"

Real Name:
Reginal "Reggie" Wald
Date of Birth:
Oct. 17, 1971
Place of Birth:
Brooklyn, NY

Height: 5'9"
Weight: 190 pounds
Hair: black
Sex: male
Race: Black
Nationality:
American

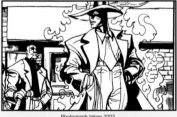

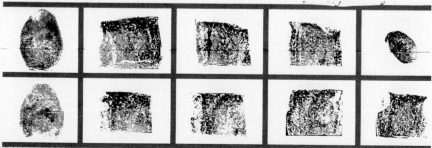

CRIMINAL RECORD

SUSPECT IS A MEMBER OF **"THE SILENCERS,"** THE SUPER-POWERED ENFORCERS OF NEW YORK CITY'S **PROVENZANO** CRIME FAMILY.

IF YOU HAVE ANY INFORMATION CONCERNING THIS PERSON, PLEASE CONTACT YOUR LOCAL FBI OFFICE. TELEPHONE NUMBERS AND ADDRESSES OF ALL FBI OFFICES LISTED ON BACK.

Identification Order 5172
June 25, 1991

NCIC: PO16131313PI14121607

16 O 5 U OO I 13
I 17 U OOO

CAUTION

SUSPECT WEARS ZOOT SUIT CURSED BY CHANGO, GOD IN AFRO-CUBAN SANTERIA RELIGION, GRANTING HIM A VARIETY OF FLAME-RELATED ABILITIES. SUSPECT *SHOULD BE CONSIDERED* **POWERED AND DANGEROUS.**

William S. Sessions
DIRECTOR
FEDERAL BUREAU OF INVESTIGATION
WASHINGTON, D.C. 20535

Entered NCIC
I.O. 5172
6-25-91

WANTED BY FBI

FBI No.
744 620 S2

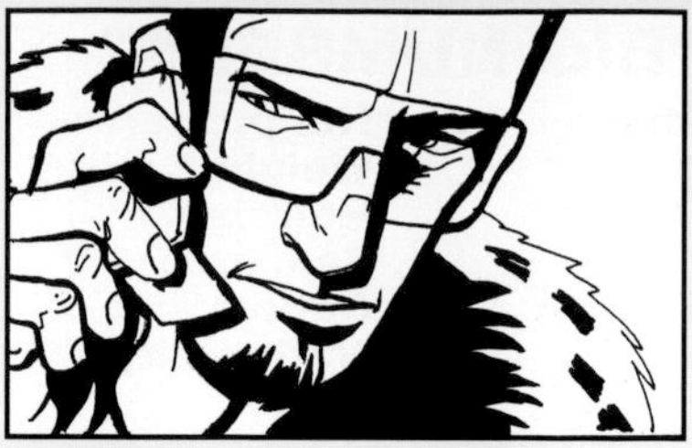

Photograph taken 2002

"KID CHAOS"

Real Name:
Charles "Chuck" Saxon
Date of Birth:
July 7, 1980
Place of Birth:
San Francisco, CA

Height: 6'
Weight: 175 pounds
Hair: brown
Sex: male
Race: White
Nationality:
American

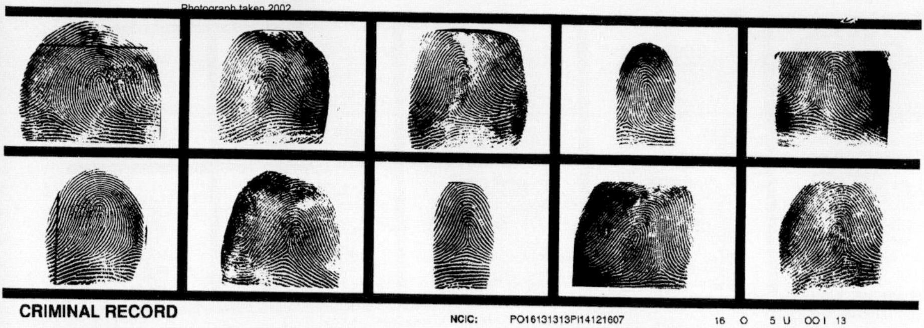

CRIMINAL RECORD

SUSPECT IS LIEUTENANT TO **CARDINAL** IN **"THE SILENCERS,"** THE SUPER-POWERED ENFORCERS OF NEW YORK CITY'S **PROVENZANO** CRIME FAMILY.

IF YOU HAVE ANY INFORMATION CONCERNING THIS PERSON, PLEASE CONTACT YOUR LOCAL FBI OFFICE. TELEPHONE NUMBERS AND ADDRESSES OF ALL FBI OFFICES LISTED ON BACK.

Identification Order 5172
June 25, 1991

NCIC: PO16131313PI14121607

16 O 5 U OO1 13
I 17 U OOO

CAUTION

SUSPECT CAN SURROUND HIMSELF IN PSYCHOKINETIC "CHAOS FIELD" THAT HURLS OBJECTS AND PEOPLE ABOUT IN POLTERGEIST-LIKE FASHION. SUSPECT *SHOULD BE CONSIDERED* **POWERED AND DANGEROUS.**

William S. Sessions
DIRECTOR
FEDERAL BUREAU OF INVESTIGATION
WASHINGTON, D.C. 20535

Entered NCIC
I.O. 5172
6-25-91

WANTED BY FBI

FBI No.
744 620 S2

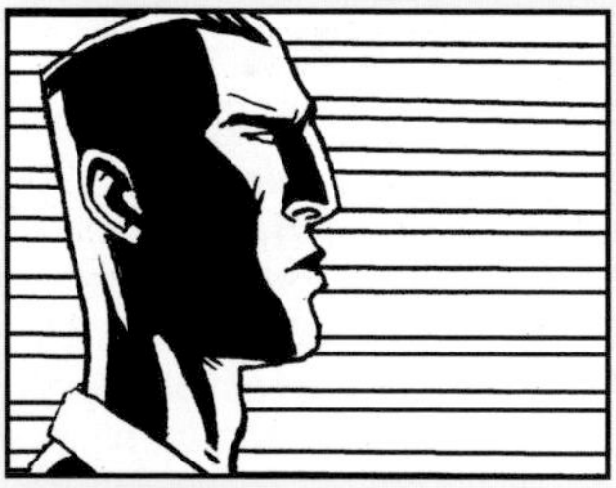

Photograph taken 2002

"JOHNNY PRO"

Real Name:
John-Paul Provenzano
Date of Birth:
Nov. 30, 1972
Place of Birth:
Staten Island, NY

Height: 5' 11"
Weight: 200 pounds
Hair: black
Sex: male
Race: White
Nationality:
American

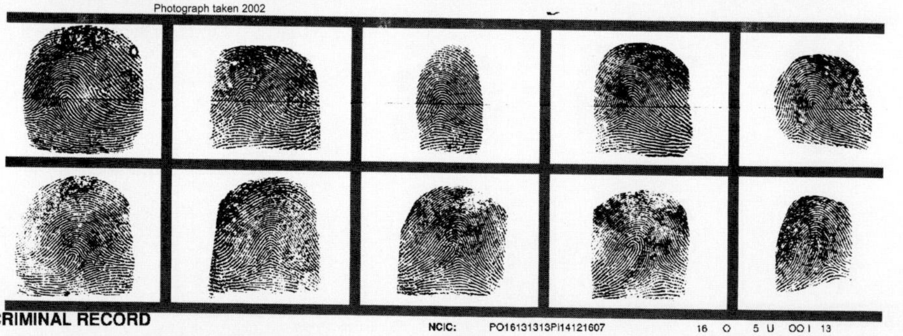

CRIMINAL RECORD

SUSPECT IS **PROVENZANO** CAPO (CAPTAIN) IN CHARGE OF **"THE SILENCERS,"** THE CRIME FAMILY'S SUPERPOWERED ENFORCERS.

IF YOU HAVE ANY INFORMATION CONCERNING THIS PERSON, PLEASE CONTACT YOUR LOCAL FBI OFFICE. TELEPHONE NUMBERS AND ADDRESSES OF ALL FBI OFFICES LISTED ON BACK.

Identification Order 5172
June 25, 1991

NCIC: PO16131313PI14121607

16 O 5 U OO1 13
I 17 U OOO

CAUTION

PROVENZANO HAS BEEN KNOWN TO CARRY A 9mm GLOCK AUTOMATIC PISTOL IN THE PAST AND *SHOULD BE CONSIDERED* **ARMED AND DANGEROUS.**

William S. Sessions
DIRECTOR
FEDERAL BUREAU OF INVESTIGATION
WASHINGTON, D.C. 20535

Entered NCIC
I.O. 5172
6-25-91

WANTED BY FBI

FBI No.
744 620 S2

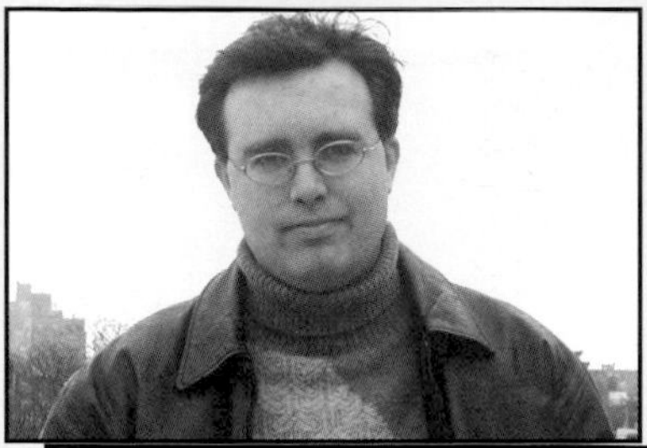

FRED VAN LENTE

M.O.:
Scripter/Letterer/
Layout/Co-creator
Birthday:
Feb. 14
Hometown:
Chagrin Falls, OH

Height: 6' 1"
Weight: 195 pounds
Hair: brown
Sex: male
Race: White
Nationality:
American

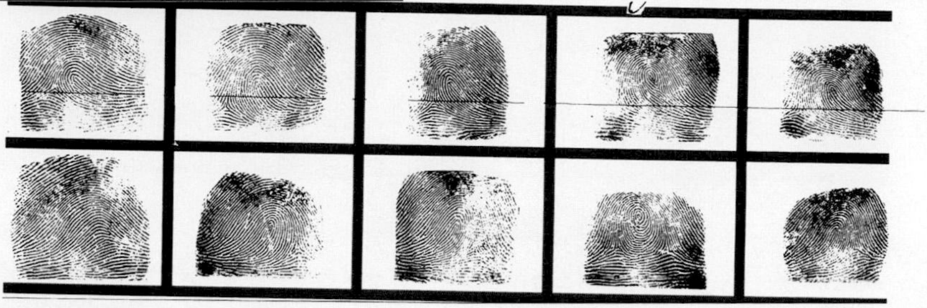

CRIMINAL RECORD

The Xeric Award–winning *ACTION PHILOSOPHERS* (Evil Twin), *AMAZING FANTASY: NEW SCORPION* (Marvel), *TRANQUILITY* (Dreamsmith)

IF YOU HAVE ANY INFORMATION CONCERNING THIS PERSON, PLEASE CONTACT YOUR LOCAL FBI OFFICE. TELEPHONE NUMBERS AND ADDRESSES OF ALL FBI OFFICES LISTED ON BACK.

NCIC: PO16131313PI14121607

16 O 5 U OO I 13
I 17 U OOO

CAUTION
SUSPECT IS CO-CREATOR AND WRITER OF **"THE SILENCERS,"** THE SUPERCRIME COMIC, AND SHOULD BE CONSIDERED **MOSTLY HARMLESS.**

Identification Order 5172
June 25, 1991

DIRECTOR
FEDERAL BUREAU OF INVESTIGATION
WASHINGTON, D.C. 20535

Entered NCIC
I.O. 5172
6-25-91

WANTED BY FBI

FBI No.
744 620 S2

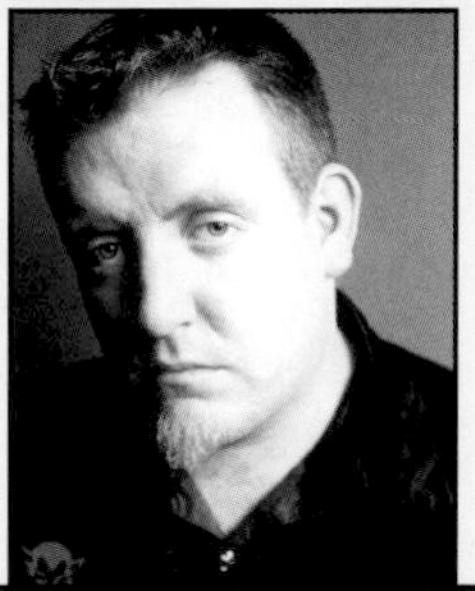

STEVE ELLIS

M.O.:
Penciller/Inker/Cover
Artist/Co-creator
Birthday:
Mar. 14
Hometown:
Sparta, NJ

Height: 6'
Weight: 180 pounds
Hair: varies
Sex: male
Race: White
Nationality:
American

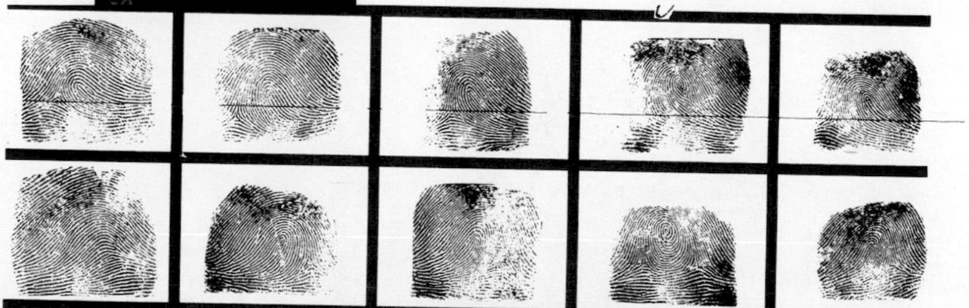

CRIMINAL RECORD

TRANQUILITY (Dreamsmith), *JEZEBEL* (Wildstorm), *LOBO, GEN-13, PROFESSOR X & THE X-MEN, ATOMIK ANGELS* (Crusade), *HAWKMAN, IRON MAN, SPIDER WOMAN*

IF YOU HAVE ANY INFORMATION CONCERNING THIS PERSON, PLEASE CONTACT YOUR LOCAL FBI OFFICE. TELEPHONE NUMBERS AND ADDRESSES OF ALL FBI OFFICES LISTED ON BACK.

NCIC: PO16131313PI14121607

16 O 5 U OO I 13
I 17 U OOO

CAUTION
SUSPECT IS CO-CREATOR AND ARTIST OF **"THE SILENCERS,"** THE SUPERCRIME COMIC, AND SHOULD BE CONSIDERED **MOSTLY HARMLESS.**

Identification Order 5172
June 25, 1991

DIRECTOR
FEDERAL BUREAU OF INVESTIGATION
WASHINGTON, D.C. 20535

THE COMPLETE SILENCERS™ SKETCHES AND EXTRAS

COMMENTARY BY FRED VAN LENTE

ART BY STEVE ELLIS

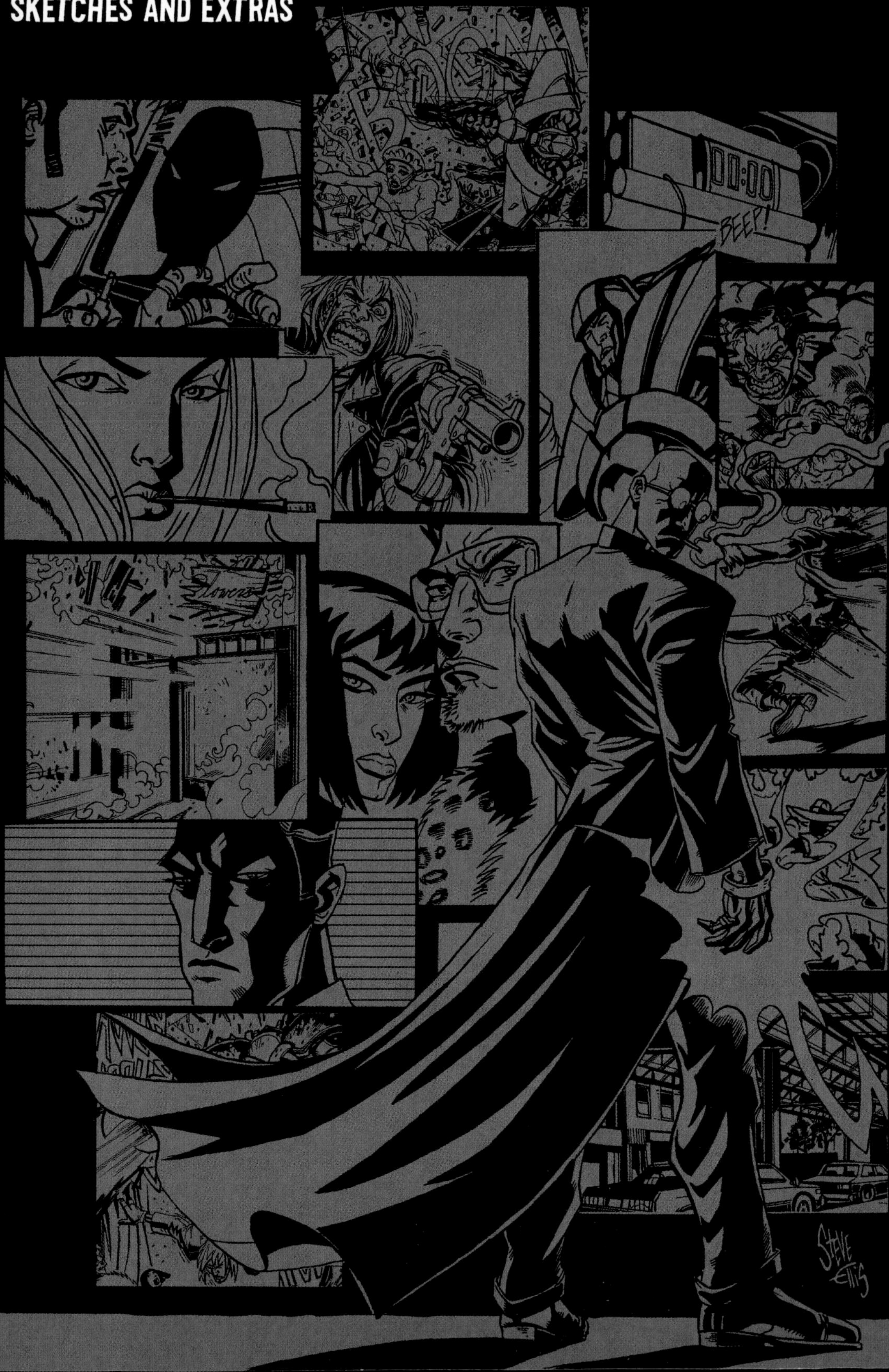

00:00
BEEP!
STEVE ELLIS

These inked pages of the Image Silencers *#2 have never been seen before.*

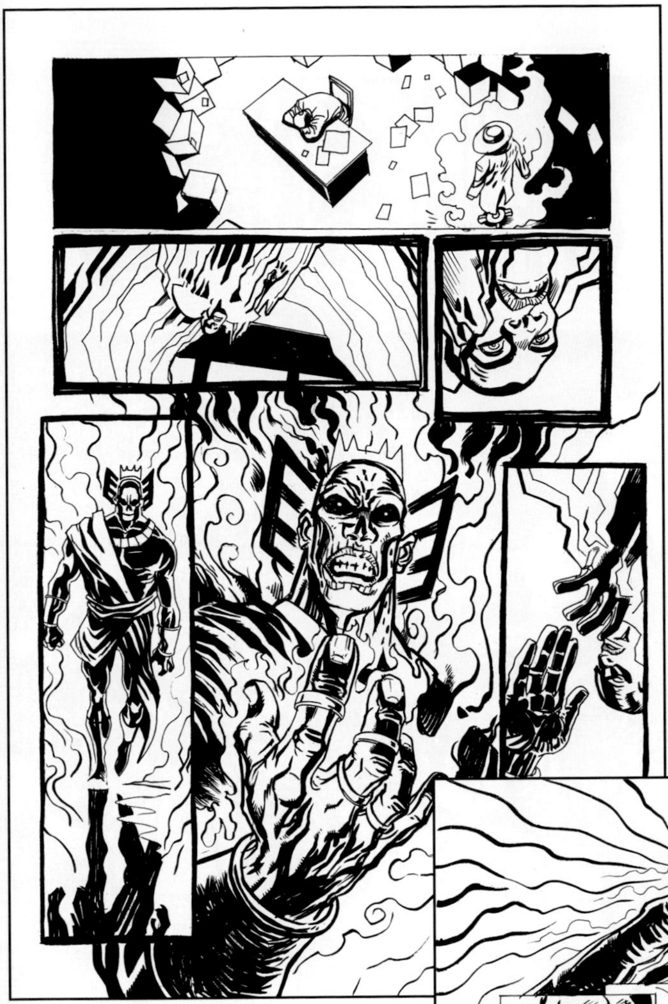

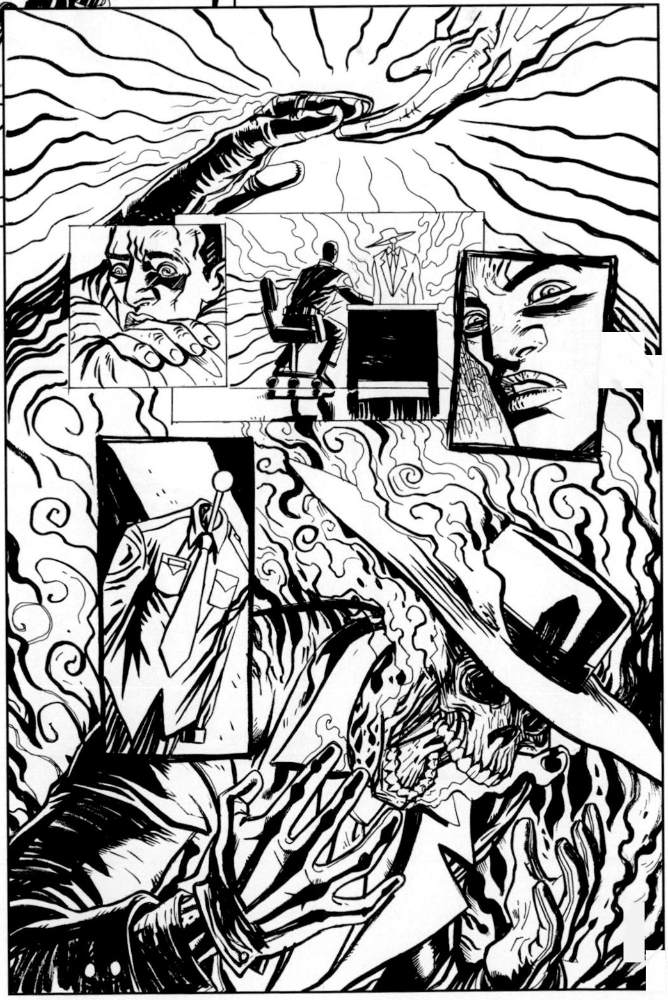

The cursed zoot suit compels Officer Williams to don it, leading to his possession by the orisha, *Chango.*

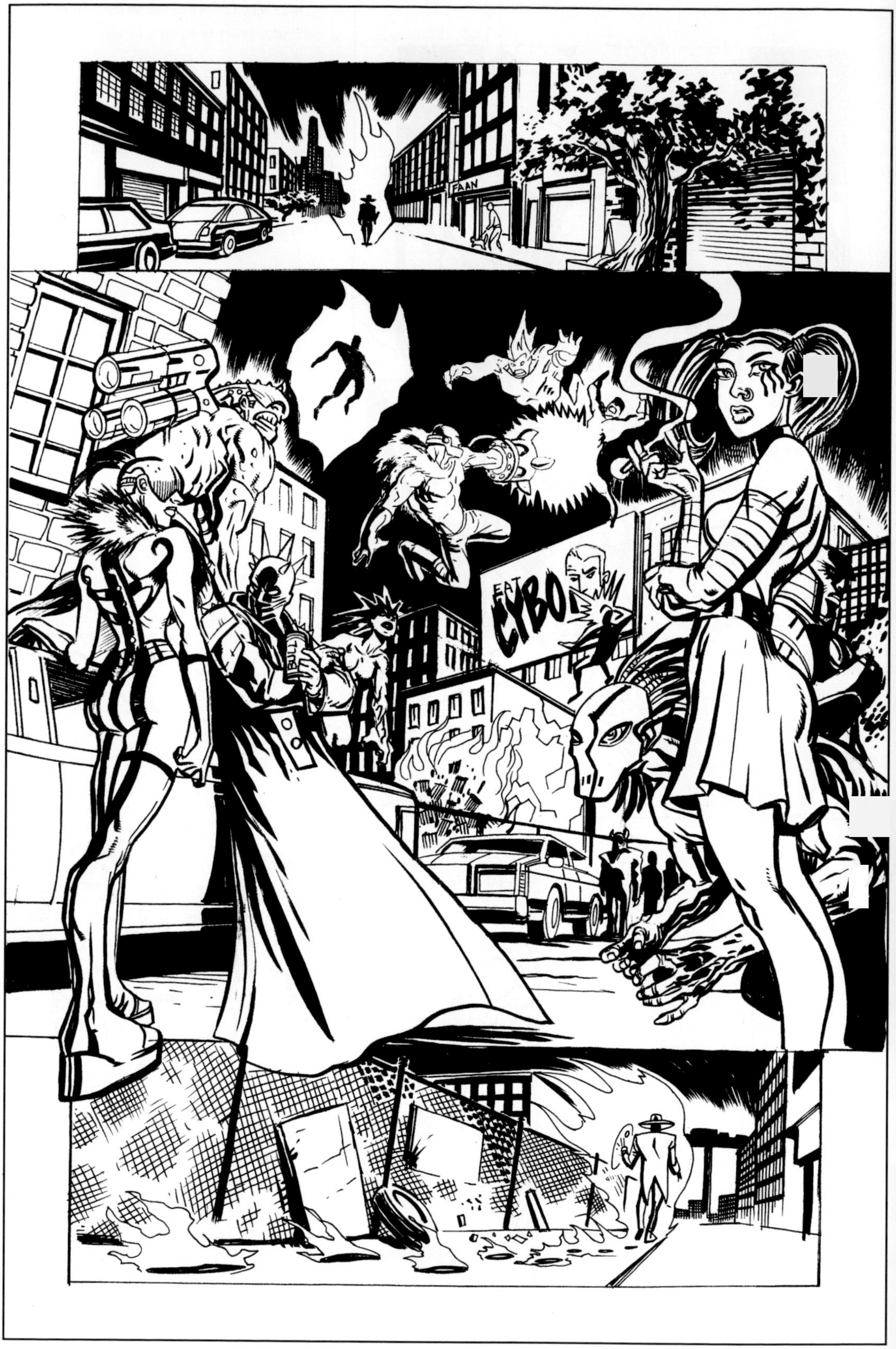
EAT CYBO

Super gangs overrun New York to fill the vacuum left by the Silencers' destruction of the Syndicate.

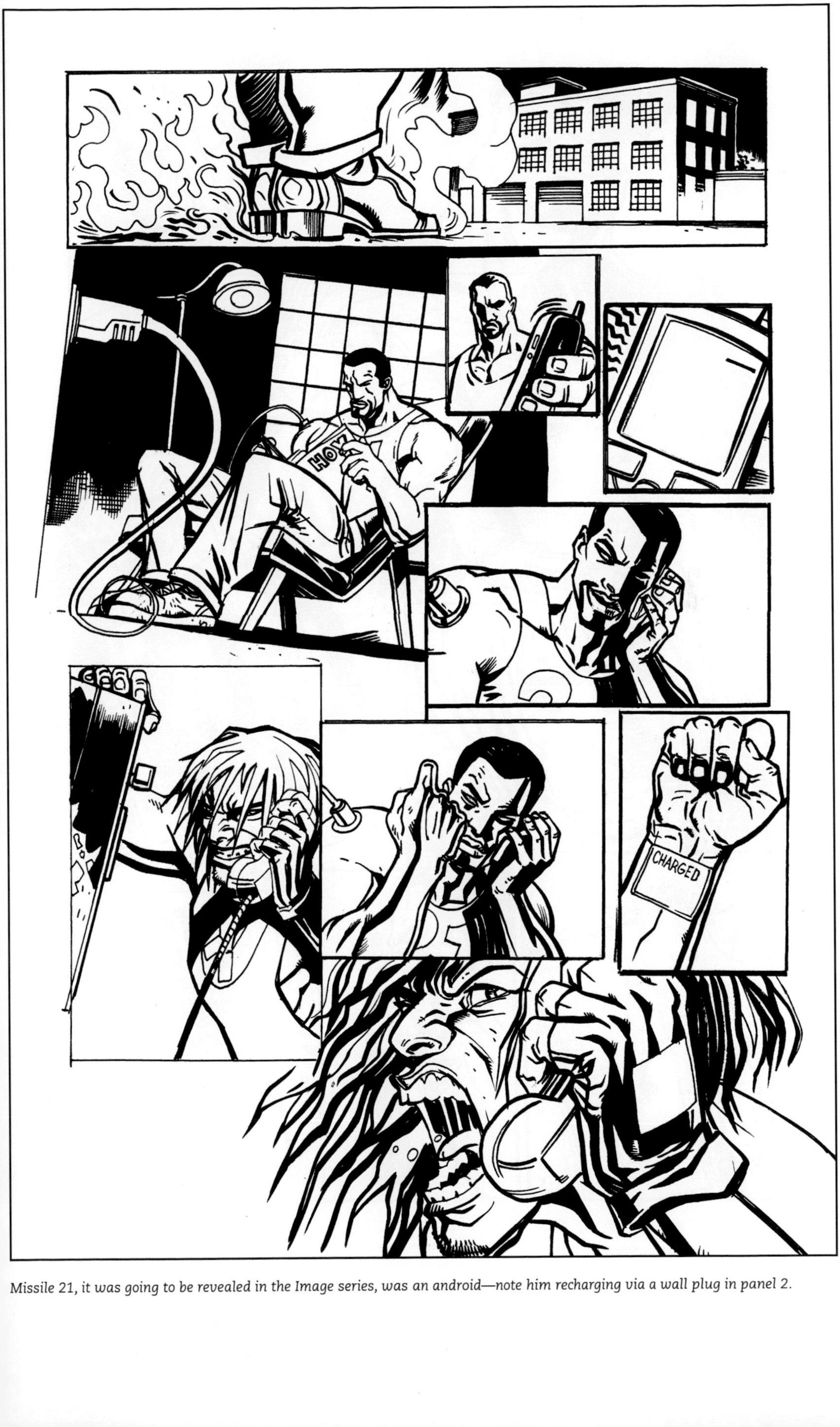
HOY
CHARGED

Missile 21, it was going to be revealed in the Image series, was an android—note him recharging via a wall plug in panel 2.

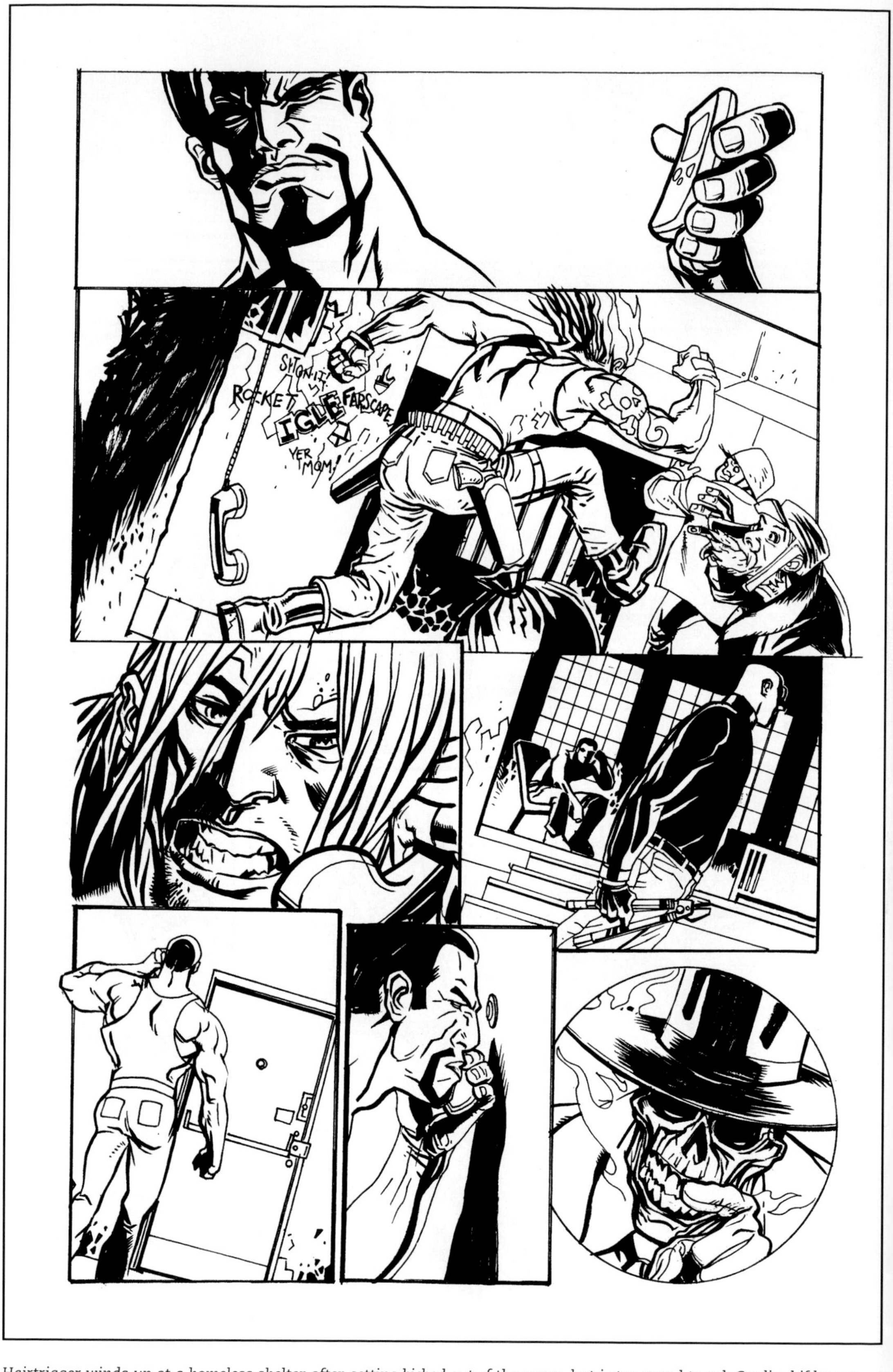
SIT ON IT!
ROCKET
IGLE
FARSCAPE
YER MOM!

Hairtrigger winds up at a homeless shelter after getting kicked out of the group, but is too proud to ask Cardinal if he can come back into the fold.

Steve worked on a couple versions of the fifth page of the Moonstone Silencers #1. The final inked version is below.

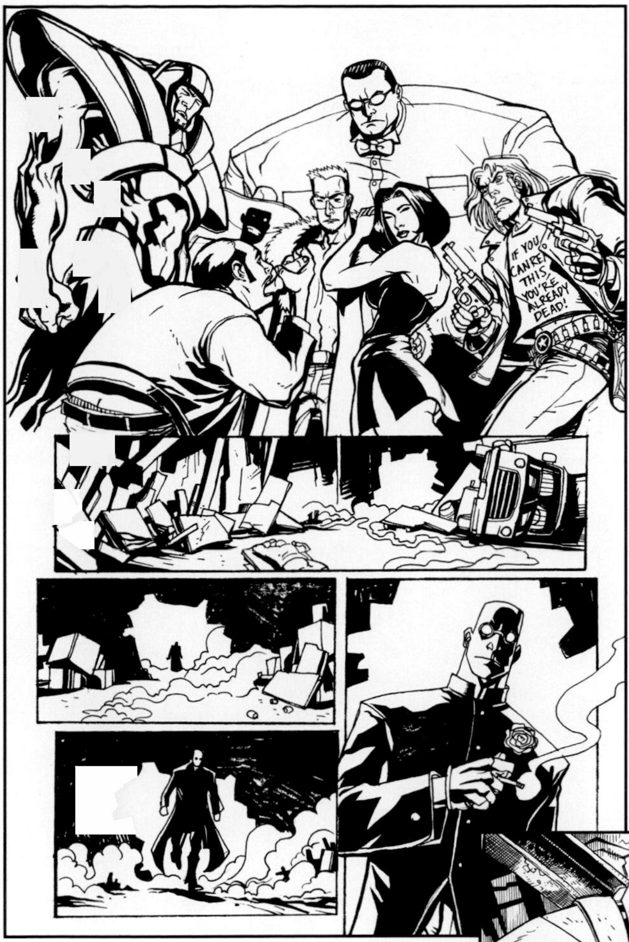
IF YOU CAN RE THIS YOU'RE ALREADY DEAD!

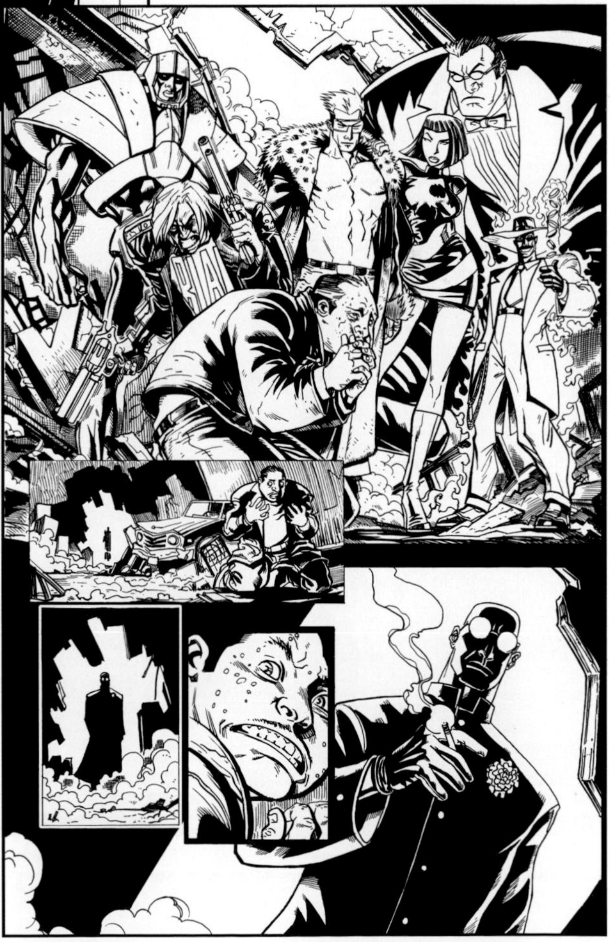

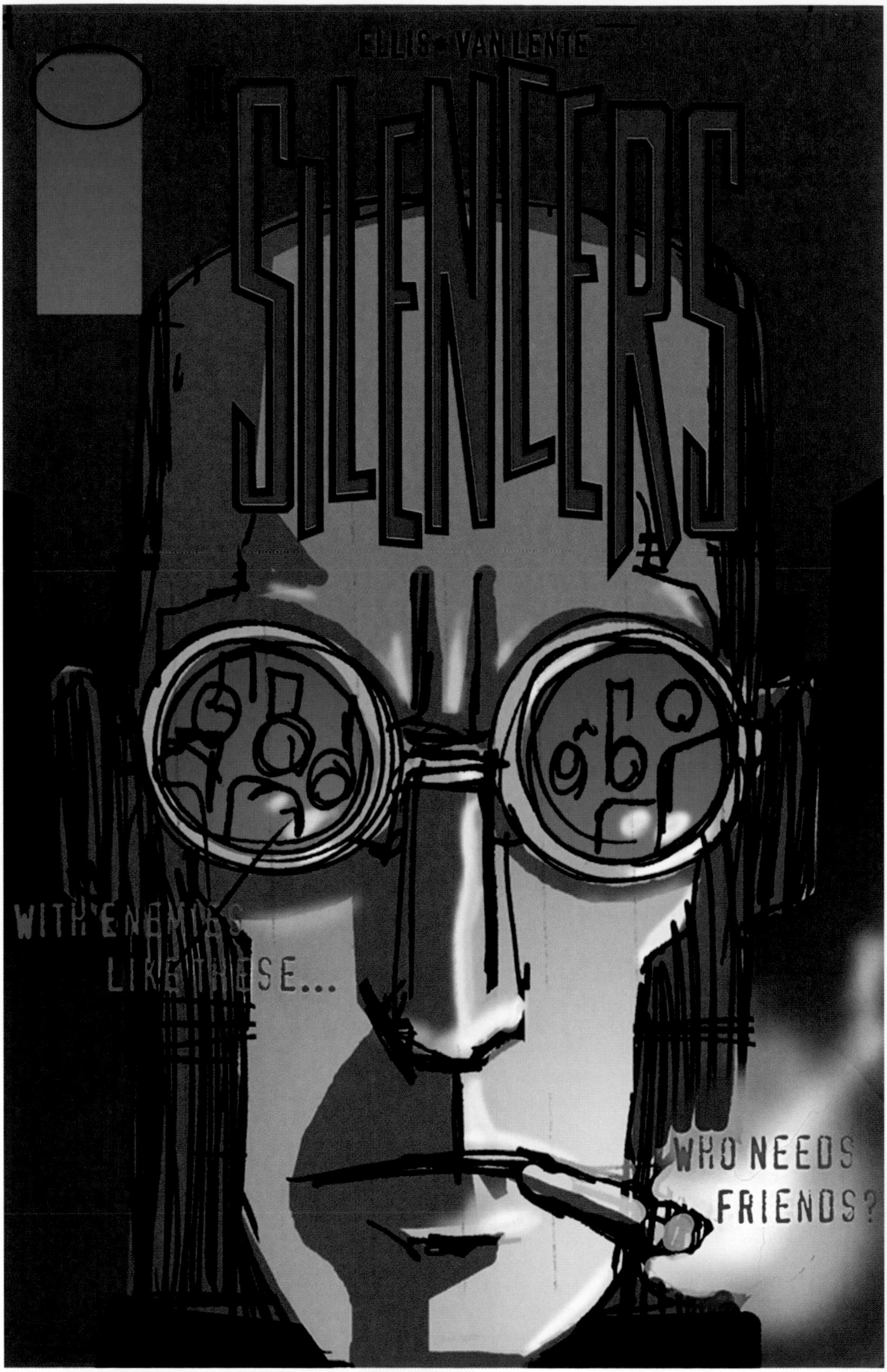
ELLIS • VAN LENTE
SILENCERS
WITH ENEMIES LIKE THESE...
WHO NEEDS FRIENDS?

Rejected roughs of the Image Silencers #1 *cover by Steve Ellis.*

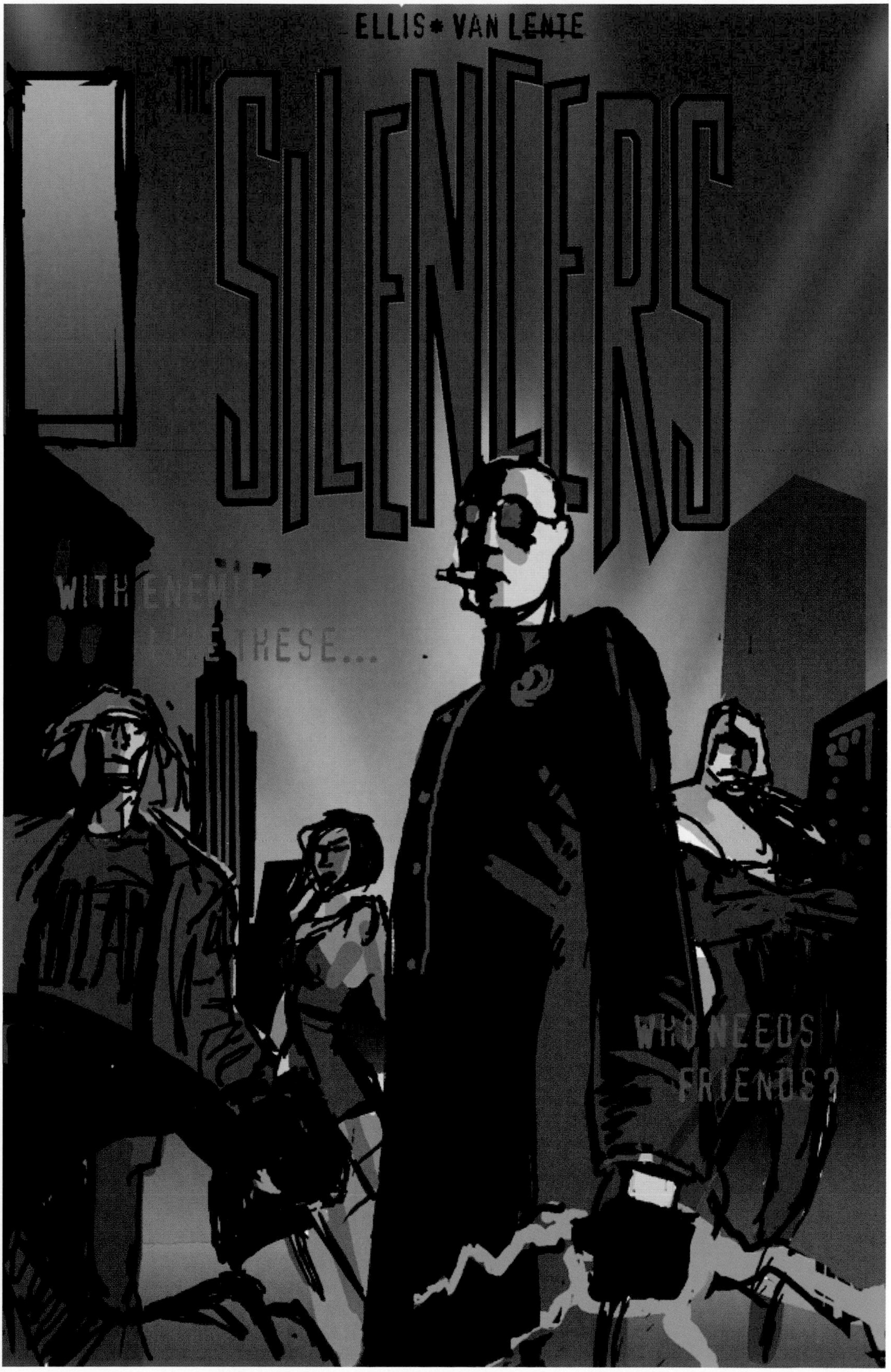
ELLIS * VAN LENTE
THE SILENCERS
WHO NEEDS FRIENDS?

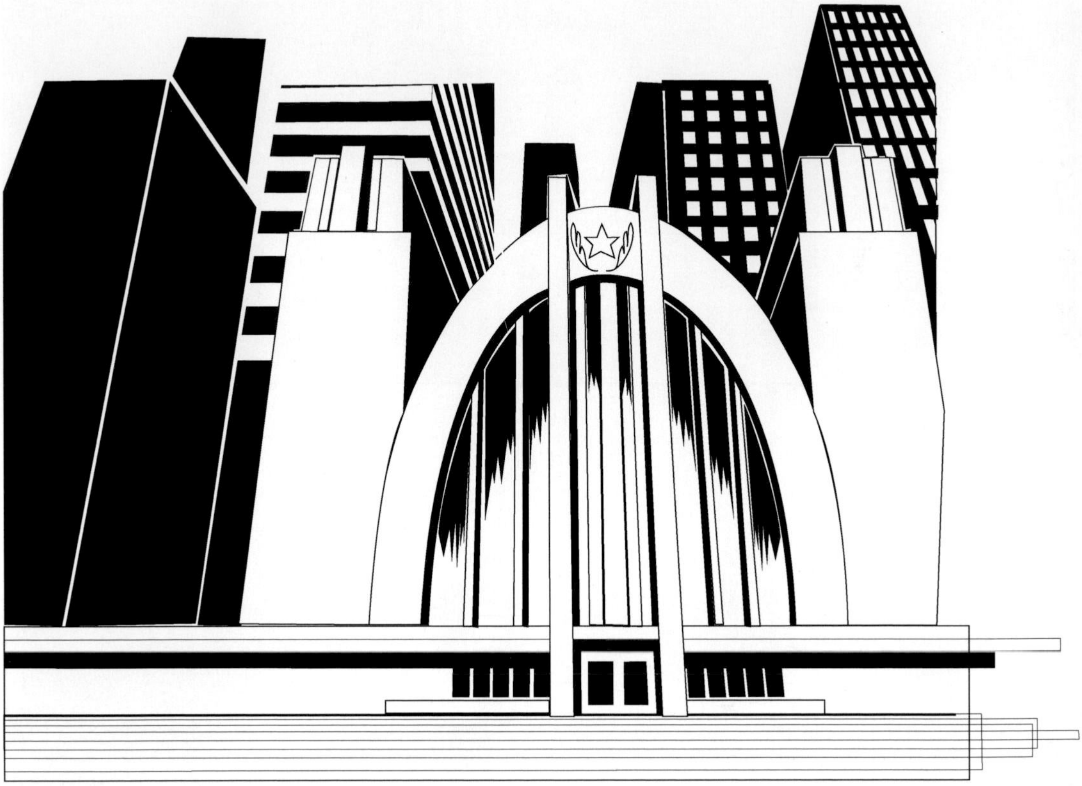

Design of the Justice Hall.

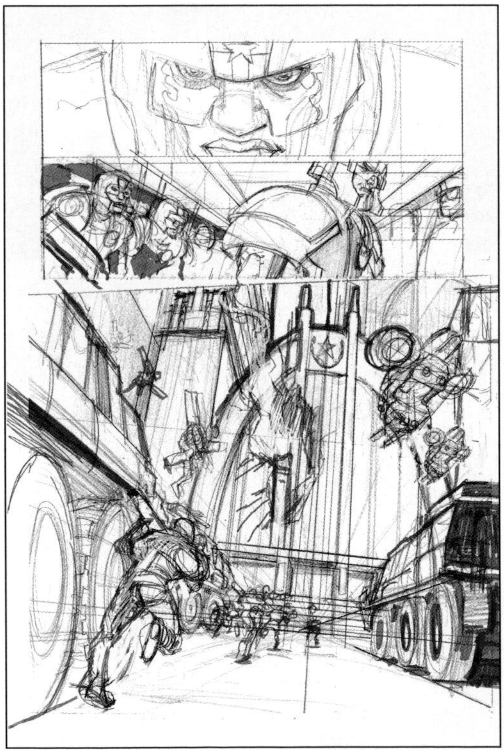

Rough of the first page from the Image issue.

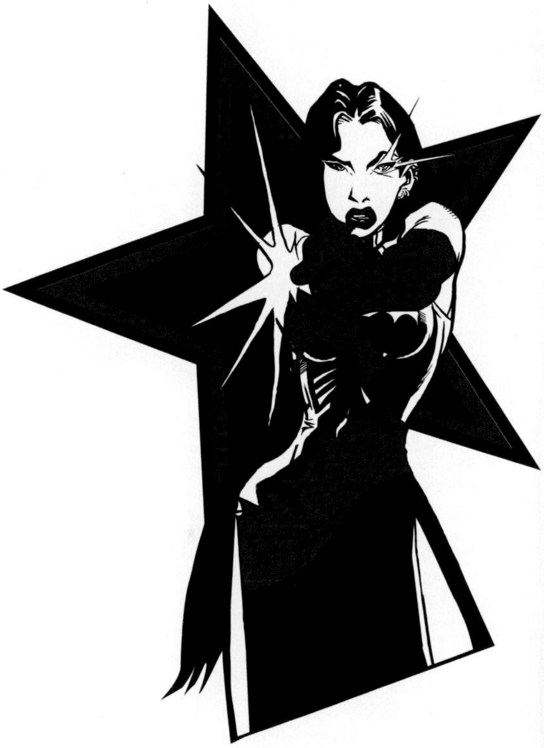

An additional illustration of Stiletto.

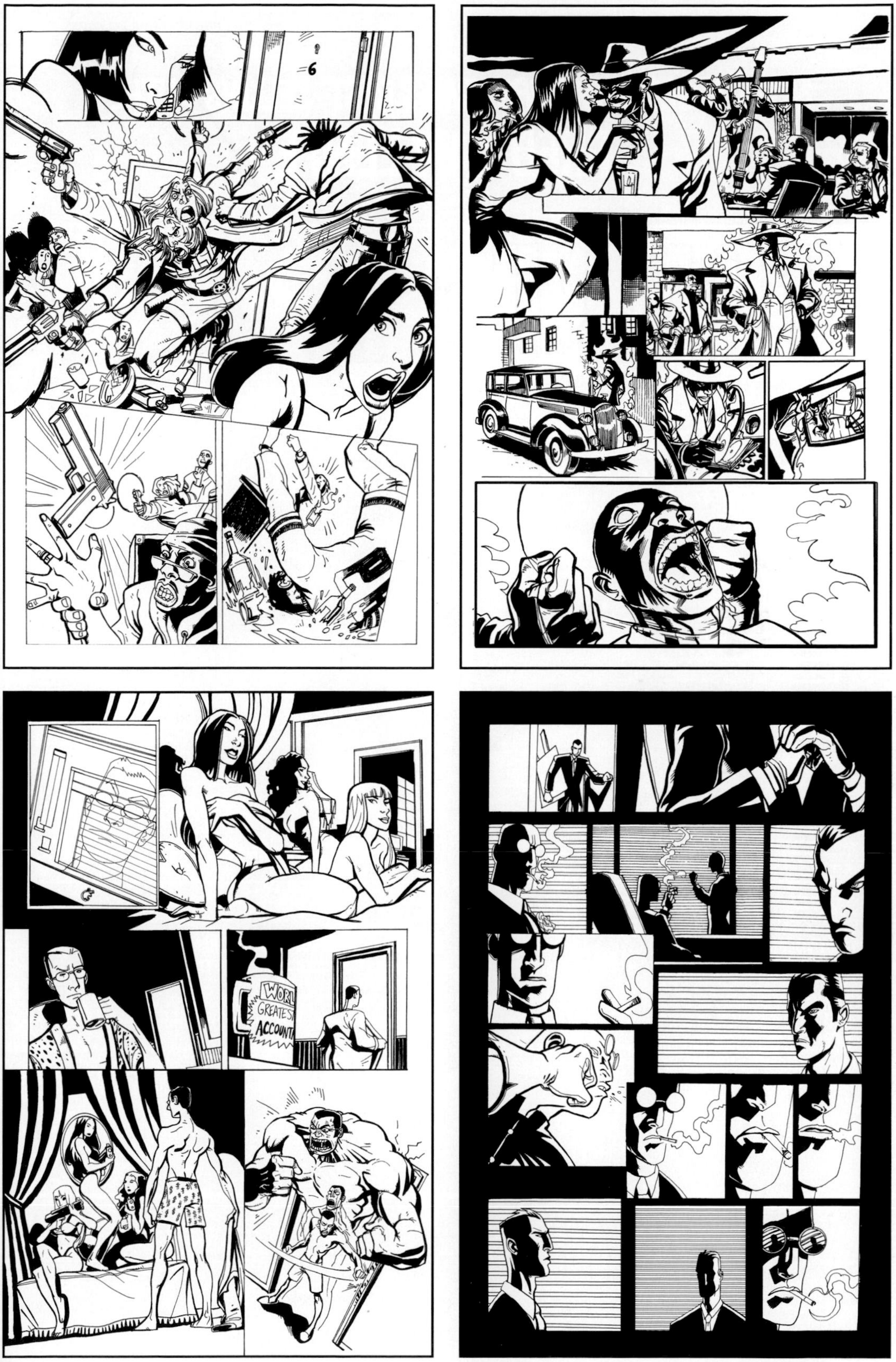
6
WORL
GREATEST
ACCOUNTA

Inks from the original Moonstone Silencers #1.

MORE FROM *NEW YORK TIMES* BEST-SELLING AUTHOR
FRED VAN LENTE

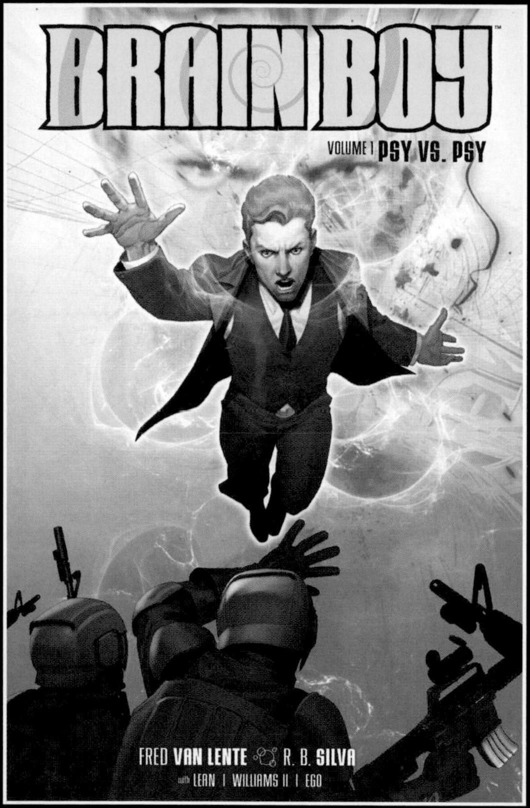
BRAIN BOY™
VOLUME 1 PSY VS. PSY
FRED VAN LENTE R. B. SILVA
with LEAN | WILLIAMS II | EGO

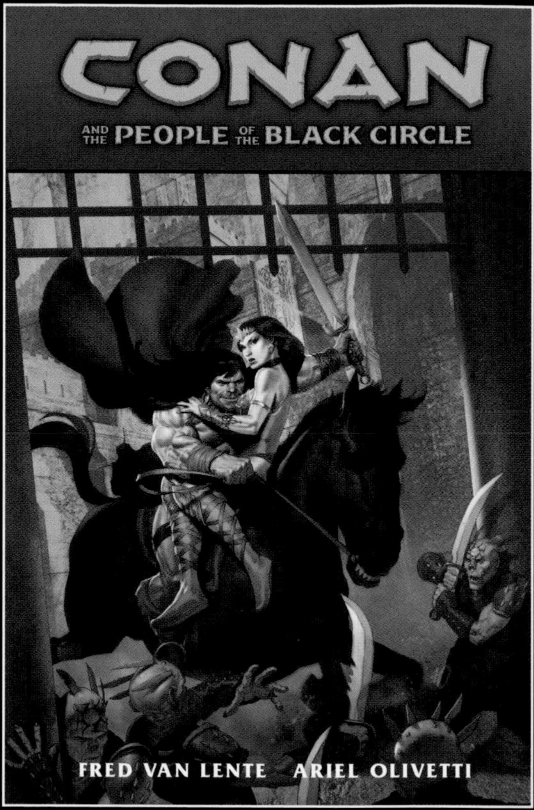
CONAN
AND THE PEOPLE OF THE BLACK CIRCLE
FRED VAN LENTE ARIEL OLIVETTI

BRAIN BOY VOLUME 1: PSY VS. PSY
FRED VAN LENTE, FREDDIE WILLIAMS II, AND R. B. SILVA

Ambushed while protecting an important statesman, Matt Price Jr., a.k.a. Brain Boy, finds himself wrapped up in political intrigue that could derail a key United Nations conference and sets the psychic spy on a collision course with a man whose mental powers rival his own!

978-1-61655-317-3 | $14.99

CONAN AND THE PEOPLE OF THE BLACK CIRCLE HC
FRED VAN LENTE AND ARIEL OLIVETTI

After an agent of the dreaded Black Seers of Yimsha assassinates the king of Vendhya, his sister Yasmina—now a queen—vows revenge! But her plans are derailed when Conan kidnaps her, and soon the Cimmerian has ruthless mercenaries, vengeance-crazed tribesmen, sinister sorcerers, and an entire army hard on his heels! Collects the four-issue miniseries.

978-1-61655-459-0 | $19.99

Available at your local comics shop or bookstore! • To find a comics shop in your area, call 1-888-266-4226.
For more information or to order direct visit DarkHorse.com or call 1-800-862-0052 Mon.–Fri. 9 AM to 5 PM Pacific Time.
Prices and availability subject to change without notice.